P9-APG-906

WHITE CREOLE CULTURE, POLITICS AND IDENTITY DURING THE AGE OF ABOLITION

David Lambert presents a much-needed account of the historical development and expression of white colonial identities, exploring the political and cultural articulation of white creole identity in the British Caribbean colony of Barbados during the age of abolition (c. 1780–1833). This was the period in which the British antislavery movement emerged, to attack first the slave trade and then the institution of chattel slavery itself. Supporters of slavery in Barbados and beyond responded with their own campaigning, which resulted in a series of debates and moments of controversy that were both localised and trans-Atlantic in significance. These debates exposed tensions between Britain and its West Indian colonies, and raised questions about whether white slaveholders could be classed as fully 'English' and whether slavery was compatible with 'English' conceptions of liberty and morality. By exploring these controversies, the book considers what it meant to be a white colonial subject in a place that Barbadians saw as a vital and loyal part of the empire, and yet which was subject to increasing metropolitan attack because of the existence of slavery.

DAVID LAMBERT is Lecturer in Human Geography at Royal Holloway, University of London.

Cambridge Studies in Historical Geography 38

Series editors:
ALAN R. H. BAKER, RICHARD DENNIS, DERYCK HOLDSWORTH

Cambridge Studies in Historical Geography encourages exploration of the philosophies, methodologies and techniques of historical geography and publishes the results of new research within all branches of the subject. It endeavours to secure the marriage of traditional scholarship with innovative approaches to problems and to sources, aiming in this way to provide a focus for the discipline and to contribute towards its development. The series is an international forum for publication in historical geography which also promotes contact with workers in cognate disciplines.

For a full list of titles in the series, please see end of book.

WHITE CREOLE CULTURE, POLITICS AND IDENTITY DURING THE AGE OF ABOLITION

DAVID LAMBERT

CAMBRIDGE
UNIVERSITY PRESS

F
2041
. L3 4
2005

CAMBRIDGE UNIVERSITY PRESS
Cambridge, New York, Melbourne, Madrid, Cape Town, Singapore, São Paulo

Cambridge University Press
The Edinburgh Building, Cambridge CB2 2RU, UK

Published in the United States of America by Cambridge University Press, New York

www.cambridge.org
Information on this title: www.cambridge.org/9780521841313

© David Lambert 2005

This book is in copyright. Subject to statutory exception
and to the provisions of relevant collective licensing agreements,
no reproduction of any part may take place without
the written permission of Cambridge University Press.

First published 2005

Printed in the United Kingdom at the University Press, Cambridge

A catalogue record for this book is available from the British Library

ISBN-13 978-0-521-84131-3 hardback
ISBN-10 0-521-84131-3 hardback

Cambridge University Press has no responsibility for the persistence or accuracy of URLs
for external or third-party internet websites referred to in this book, and does not
guarantee that any content on such websites is, or will remain, accurate or appropriate.

67514589

Contents

Illustrations

Acknowledgements

The research for this book was initially funded by a Domestic Research Scholarship, provided jointly by the University of Cambridge and Sidney Sussex College, and later by the Economic and Social Research Council (Award Number R00429924260). I thank these institutions for enabling me to realise my research. Much of the writing of this book was undertaken when I was a Research Fellow at Emmanuel College, Cambridge, between autumn 2001 and Christmas 2003. I would like to thank the Master and Fellows of the College for welcoming me and providing such a beautiful and stimulating place to work.

As to the people who have provided intellectual guidance and support, I must first thank James Duncan of Emmanuel College, Cambridge, who has acted as my doctoral supervisor. I must also acknowledge the willing assistance and advice given to me by others in the Department of Geography of Cambridge University, especially Phil Howell, as well as James Blake, Stuart Corbridge, Simon Cross, Nic Higgins, Alan Ingram, Niall Johnson, Gerry Kearns, Satish Kumar and Nick Megoran. Simon Hall, a fellow traveller during research, writing and beyond, deserves a special mention. Outside Cambridge, I would like to extend thanks to Mike Heffernan, Alan Lester, Rick Mitcham, Miles Ogborn, Jenny Robinson and Charlie Withers, and to my new colleagues at Royal Holloway, University of London, especially Felix Driver. I also express my gratitude to those experts on the history of the Caribbean who provided me with advice and inspiration. They include Hilary Beckles, Marcia Burrows, Catherine Hall, Jerry Handler, Gad Heuman, Alana Johnson, Cecily Jones, Brigitte Kossek, Melanie Newton, Christer Petley, Mimi Sheller, Mary Turner, Karl Watson and Pedro Welch.

During the course of my research and writing, I have presented papers in Britain, the USA and Canada, and I am grateful for the various opportunities to speak, and for the comments and questions received at these forums. The London Group of Historical Geographers' seminar series, the Caribbean seminar series at the Institute of Commonwealth Studies and the annual conferences of the Society for Caribbean Studies have been sites of particular intellectual inspiration.

This research could not have been undertaken without the aid of many librarians and archivists in Britain, North America and the Caribbean. In particular, I thank Nicola Allen, Terry Barringer, Susan Bennett, Barbara Davis, Chris Denver, Janie Morris and Jane Robinson. In addition, I must express my gratitude to Alastair Bonnett and John Gilmore for providing me with drafts of their unfinished and unpublished work. Thanks also to Owen Tucker at Cambridge for producing the maps, and to Jenny Kynaston and Susan May at Royal Holloway for helping me with the illustrations. I would also like to thank the editorial board of the Cambridge Studies in Historical Geography, especially Alan Baker and Richard Dennis, and the staff at Cambridge University Press, notably Richard Fisher, for their help and encouragement in writing this book.

Finally, I would like to express particular gratitude to my parents, Pat and Alan, for all their financial and emotional support, and to Carolyn, for her advice, patience and encouragement, and for making it all so worthwhile. This book is dedicated to her.

Introduction: white creole culture, politics and identity

This book is concerned with the place of 'whiteness' in the controversy over the enslavement of people of African descent in the British empire during the 'age of abolition'.[1] Focussing on the West Indian plantation colonies, this controversy comprised antislavery campaigning, proslavery lobbying, parliamentary debates, mass petitioning and imperial policy formulation, all in the context of ongoing and intensified resistance from the enslaved populations themselves.[2] As one of the 'great debates of the age', the issue of slavery raised questions about human nature, moral duty, free trade, colonial rights and Britain's imperial future.[3] A recurrent theme was the nature of racial difference and whether enslaved people of African origin were truly 'men' and 'brothers'. The antislavery slogan 'Am I not a man and brother?', accompanied by the kneeling figure of a black enslaved man, evoked the essentially familiar, though culturally and morally inferior, 'other' that was at the heart of antislavery discourse. Grateful, redeemable and silent, the kneeling slave was a passive figure in this discourse – a passivity that was repeatedly contested by enslaved resistance. Against this, those involved in slavery and their supporters portrayed black people as subhuman, un-Christian units of labour who were better off in the colonial plantation societies than they would be in 'barbaric' Africa.

Yet 'blackness' was not the only issue of political and cultural controversy. The figure of the white West Indian master was also a locus of competing pro- and antislavery discourses. For abolitionists, the 'un-English' West Indian was a stock figure of humanitarian rhetoric. Despotic and morally degraded, he – and it was usually he – was symptomatic of a 'bad' white identity that many

---

[1] The 'age of abolition' in the British empire is often dated from 1787, which saw the creation of the Society for Effecting the Abolition of the Slave Trade, to the imperial act of emancipation in 1833. In this book, 1780 provides a useful starting point as this was the year in which Joshua Steele first arrived in Barbados (see chapter 2).

[2] The word 'enslaved' is used in preference to 'slave' to emphasise that enslavement was a practice of subjection, not a state or condition.

[3] G. K. Lewis, *Main currents in Caribbean thought: The historical evolution of Caribbean society in its ideological aspects, 1492–1900* (Baltimore: Johns Hopkins University Press, 1983), p. 100.

metropolitan Britons, especially evangelicals, sought to distance themselves from. The West Indian planters and their metropolitan supporters rejected such assertions, of course, responding with campaigning to defend their rights, especially the right to possess property in people, by emphasising a shared British culture, common political traditions and their essential Englishness. Like black enslaved identities, then, white colonial identities were a site of struggle during the age of abolition.

The focus of this book is this 'war of representation' over the articulation and constitution of white creole culture, politics and identity during the slavery controversy in the British empire.[4] In particular, it explores contested political and cultural discourses of whiteness produced in or about the British West Indian colony of Barbados from the 1780s to the imperial act of emancipation in 1833. Tensions between the British metropole and its West Indian colonies stemmed from questions of whether white slaveholders could be classed as fully 'English' and whether slavery was compatible with 'English' conceptions of liberty and morality. These tensions were particularly acute in the case of Barbados because its white colonists had long seen and portrayed themselves as the empire's most loyal subjects – as evident in the self-description of the island as 'Little England', which gained currency in this period. In this context, what did it mean to be a white colonial subject in a place renowned for its loyalty and allegiance, and yet which was the target of increasing metropolitan attack over the issue of slavery?

In exploring the articulation and counter-articulation of colonising identities in Barbados, this book engages with two major themes. Firstly, there is the increasing attention being given to 'white' identities, which represents, in part, a welcome move beyond the focus on 'white' colonial representations of 'other' identities. To provide a localised account of the articulation of white identities in a broader British imperial context, the book engages with the field of 'whiteness studies', approaches to British imperial history informed by postcolonialism, and work on white identities in the Caribbean region itself. The second major theme addressed by the book is that of Atlantic networks. The rapid growth of 'Atlantic world studies', which addresses the circuits and spaces that connected Europe, Africa and the Americas from the early modern period, has been an important recent historiographical development. Framed by such perspectives, the book attends not only to the material and imaginative networks that bound the British empire together, but also the tensions that afflicted it, tensions that emanated from such issues as colonial slavery. Indeed, events in the single colonial space of Barbados were both linked to, and throw light upon, important cultural and political developments that were occurring in Britain and beyond.

---

[4] C. Hall, *Civilising subjects: Metropole and colony in the English imagination, 1830–1867* (Oxford: Polity, 2002), p. 107.

Historical-geographical context

The geographical focus of the controversy over slavery was the Caribbean region, where Britain's valuable West Indian colonies were located.[5] Forged through settlement, enslavement, clearance and sugar monoculture from the beginning of the seventeenth century, these islands and territories produced large revenues and highly desired consumer products. The planters who resided in the region or returned to the metropole as absentee landowners enjoyed wealth and influence throughout most of the eighteenth century. The West Indian colonies were also the destination for millions of enslaved African men, women and children, most for work on the plantations. Through their labour, sugar cane was cultivated and its products sold on European markets to satisfy a growing 'sweet tooth'.[6] Yet, although they were an integral part of the English, and later British, Atlantic world that developed from the seventeenth century, the West Indian plantation colonies occupied an uncertain place in the metropolitan geographical imagination. Located 'beyond the line' of European geopolitical certainties, with landscapes that were tropically 'other', and the source of wealth for *nouveaux riches* planters, the islands represented a 'different and disturbing culture'.[7] Moreover, when the British Atlantic world was torn apart by the American Revolution, the colonial slaveholding interest was greatly weakened.[8] The emergence of popular abolitionist sentiment in Britain from the 1780s, combined with the intensification of enslaved resistance in the Caribbean,[9] put those involved in slavery on the defensive. The West Indian planters felt themselves to be an increasingly beleaguered colonial interest group and the region seemed ever more marginal to the fortunes of the empire.[10]

---

[5] With a few exceptions, the term 'West Indies' refers to the islands of the Caribbean, including the Greater and Lesser Antilles. Throughout this book, the term will be used to refer to those Caribbean islands under English/British control. Owing to its common social and economic history, the continental territory of British Guiana, which was created in early 1831 from the unification of Demerara, Essequibo and Berbice, is usually also included.

[6] M. Sheller, *Consuming the Caribbean: From Arawaks to zombies* (London: Routledge, 2003), pp. 81–88. See also S. Mintz, *Sweetness and power: The place of sugar in modern history* (New York: Viking, 1985).

[7] D. Arnold, *The problem of nature: Environment, culture and European expansion* (Oxford: Blackwell, 1996); C. Hall, *Civilising subjects*, p. 70.

[8] For a recent discussion of why the West Indian colonies did not also rebel, see A. J. O'Shaughnessy, *An empire divided: The American Revolution and the British Caribbean* (Philadelphia: University of Pennsylvania Press, 2000).

[9] For example, there were revolts by enslaved people in Nevis in 1761, Surinam in 1763 and Jamaica in 1765. See M. Craton, *Testing the chains: Resistance to slavery in the British West Indies* (London: Cornell University Press, 1982).

[10] C. L. Brown, 'The politics of slavery', in D. Armitage and M. J. Braddick (eds.), *The British Atlantic world, 1500–1800* (Basingstoke: Palgrave Macmillan, 2002); J. P. Greene, 'Liberty, slavery, and the transformation of British identity in the eighteenth-century West Indies', *Slavery and Abolition* 21 (2000).

Although during the age of abolition Jamaica was the largest and economically most important of Britain's West Indian possessions, the 'original and quintessential British sugar colony' was Barbados. Colonised by the English from 1627, Barbados was a crucial site for the 'sugar revolution' of the middle of the seventeenth century. This development of a form of economic activity characterised by sugar and enslaved African labour made the island the 'foremost English possession throughout the seventeenth century'.[11] By the second half of the seventeenth century, the wealth produced by this 'fair jewell' in the imperial crown gave its plantocratic elite great political influence.[12] Yet, although the 'quintessential' sugar colony, Barbados was unique in many ways. Its more temperate climate and gently undulating terrain contributed to a widespread perception that Barbados was less 'tropical' than Britain's other Caribbean possessions. Demographically, Barbados was characterised by a relatively stable white population that was proportionally larger than that of other West Indian islands. It was also characterised by a lower rate of planter absenteeism, which in turn contributed to the strength and coherence of the white elite. By the eighteenth century, all these factors were seen as lending Barbados a 'civilised' character.[13] For some present-day scholars, the colony's white culture was the nearest equivalent in the Caribbean to that of the American South.[14] For such reasons, Barbados offers a fascinating opportunity to explore the articulation and constitution of white creole culture, politics and identity during the age of abolition.[15]

---

[11] Craton, *Testing the chains*, p. 105; A. L. Stinchcombe, *Sugar island slavery in the age of Enlightenment: The political economy of the Caribbean world* (Princeton, NJ: Princeton University Press, 1995), pp. 54, 95, 133. See also D. Eltis, 'New estimates of exports from Barbados and Jamaica, 1665–1701', *William and Mary Quarterly* 3rd Series 52 (1995), 631; R. Sheridan, *Sugar and slavery: An economic history of the British West Indies, 1623–1775* (Baltimore: Johns Hopkins University Press, 1973), p. 124.

[12] Cited in L. Gragg, *Englishmen transplanted: The English colonization of Barbados, 1627–1660* (Oxford: Oxford University Press, 2003), p. 1.

[13] K. Watson, *The civilised island, Barbados: A social history, 1750–1816* (Bridgetown: Graphic Printers, 1979).

[14] Craton, *Testing the chains*, p. 254. Andrew O'Shaughnessy argues that one of the main differences between the island and mainland colonies of British America was that former were dominated by 'British sojourners' who continued to see Britain as home. Along with dependence on the protected British sugar market and their vulnerability to enslaved revolts, he argues that 'the strength of the social and cultural ties with Britain restrained the development of a nationalistic Creole consciousness among whites and was a contributory factor in the failure of the British Caribbean to support the American Revolution'. Nevertheless, he acknowledges that, of all the West Indian colonies, it was Barbados that came close 'to developing a creole society of committed settlers'. See O'Shaughnessy, *Empire divided*, pp. 4, 6.

[15] Much of the historiography of the British West Indies is, perhaps understandably, dominated by case studies of Jamaica or regional generalisations that draw heavily on Jamaica. For example, in the recent multi-volume collection, *Slavery, abolition and emancipation: Writings in the British Romantic period*, the work of the Jamaican writers Edward Long and Bryan Edwards are afforded representative status as white West Indian writing. See D. Lee (ed.), *Slavery, abolition and emancipation: Writings in the British Romantic period – the emancipation debate*, 8 vols., vol. III (London: Pickering and Chatto, 1999), p. xxvi. Yet neither Jamaica nor the other colonies were 'typical' of the region as a whole – at least not by every measure. Certainly Barbados offers an interesting contrast with

Summary of the book

The central argument of this book – that the controversy over slavery was fundamentally bound up with the contested articulation of white colonial identities between colony and metropole – is explored in relation to a chronological series of key individuals and episodes. Some are some famous, others are buried deep in the footnotes of history, but all are illuminating because they 'expose important contradictions and tensions' within the contemporary discourses of whiteness, colonialism and slavery.[16] The five episodes addressed here were part of, and shed light upon, broader political and cultural debates. Each was a juncture of textual, causal and thematic density. Within the controversy over slavery, certain texts occupy a prominent position, something reflected in the frequency with which they were referred to in contemporary texts and the attention given to them by modern scholars. These are explored not only in terms of their textual content, but also the web of intertextuality that constituted the political and cultural controversies. The key episodes examined also revolve around events that attracted attention in Barbados and beyond, acting as foci for discussion of slavery, freedom and the colonial order. Some of these events – criminal trials, an enslaved revolt, missionary persecution – were local occurrences with reverberations across the Atlantic world, whilst others – the 1807 Abolition Act, the 1823 ameliorative proposals, the 1833 Emancipation Act – originated in the imperial metropole and impacted upon Barbados. All had causal significance and shaped the development of the slavery controversy. The final enframing feature is a series of key themes, namely contested discourses of whiteness, conflicts between metropolitan and colonial representations of whiteness and the role of non-white subjects in the articulation of white identities.

Chapter 1, 'The geographical "problem of slavery"', situates the five subsequent substantive chapters in relation to the histories and geographies of whiteness, postcolonial theories, Atlantic world studies and the histories of slavery. In particular, it uses David Brion Davis's argument about the 'problem of slavery' as a basis for thinking about the contested articulation of whiteness between colony and metropole, as well as the role of competing notions of place and belonging in this. The historical and geographical focus of the book – colonial Barbados – is then introduced, with particular attention paid to the formation of the settler society, the entrenchment of African slavery, colonial relations with Britain and the emergence of the campaign against slavery. The chapter closes by considering

Jamaica. On the historiography of the region, see B. W. Higman, *Writing West Indian histories* (London: Macmillan Education, 1999).

[16] F. Driver, 'Geography's empire: Histories of geographical knowledge', *Environment and Planning D: Society and Space* 10 (1992), 30. Bonham Richardson has argued that the relationships between ideas, popular thought and policy 'are perhaps clearest in specific places, at particular times, and when set in motion by real people': B. C. Richardson, 'Detrimental determinists: Applied environmentalism as bureaucratic self-interest in the fin-de-siècle British Caribbean', *Annals of the Association of American Geographers* 86 (1996), 214.

how white colonial identities in Barbados can be approached, particularly through theories of 'creolisation'.

Chapter 2, 'Joshua Steele and the "improvement" of slavery', has two main aims: firstly, to trace the initial impact of the emergent British antislavery campaign on Barbados and, secondly, to examine the response of the island's white society. It does both by focussing on the efforts of a metropolitan reformer, Joshua Steele, who came to the island in 1780 to take direct control of a number of sugar estates that he owned. Influenced and feted by leading figures in the British antislavery campaign, Steele sought to promote particular forms of 'improved' and 'enlightened' plantation management, including the gradual ending of slavery. He did so through the creation of the Barbados Society for the Encouragement of Arts, Manufactures and Commerce, which lobbied local political institutions and provided financial rewards for innovation in plantation management practice. He also used his own estates to demonstrate the benefits of his reforms. Despite considerable political, financial and persuasive efforts made by Steele to promote an 'enlightened' vision for Barbados, his actual accomplishments were modest. The chapter describes the emergence of local opposition from Barbados's conservative planters at the end of the eighteenth century and the renewed hostility that accompanied the attempts of the British antislavery movement to revive his ideas in the 1820s. To account for this opposition, two main articulations of white colonial identity are considered. The first, 'white supremacism', was apparent in opposition to Steele's attempts to challenge taken-for-granted racial hierarchies, such as banning the use of the whip on his estates. The second – the 'planter ideal' – comprised notions that slavery was a paternalistic system based on a long history of local expertise. Committed to the amelioration of slavery, white planters already saw and styled themselves as enlightened masters. Steele's new, 'rational' proposals for the reform of slavery were opposed because they ran counter to local notions of how a 'good master' ran 'his' affairs. Both these discourses can be understood as setting limits to the 'improvement' of slavery and the reforms that were conceivable in Barbados. Steele challenged both discourses, but his inability to destabilise them indicates their strength and accounts, in part, for the failure of his 'enlightened' vision. By examining the local response to Joshua Steele's reformist efforts, the chapter considers the most salient articulations of white creole culture in Barbados that were mobilised to defend slavery during the age of abolition.

Turning from differences between colonial and metropolitan visions of reform, chapter 3, 'Making a "well constituted Society": the ambitions and limits of white unity', turns to tensions *within* white Barbadian society in the decades either side of 1800. This period witnessed intensive antislavery campaigning, a reactionary backlash in Britain and the eventual abolition of the British slave trade in 1807. The particular focus of the chapter is John Poyer, author of the *History of Barbados* (1808). Poyer was an important middle-class commentator on local affairs and was at the forefront of efforts to racially re-order the colonial society by marginalising the island's free coloured population and promoting its poor whites. This project was based on notions of an idealised, unified white population in which race – rather than class or status – was the primary marker of identity and privilege. Yet Poyer's efforts received a mixed response from elite white planters and his racialised vision was challenged in a petitioning campaign launched by the free people of colour. Poyer's failure to realise his vision underlines the ambitions and limits of 'whiteness'. Whilst chapter 2 explores the tensions between a metropolitan-originating project of 'improvement' and local ideas of race, slavery and plantation management, chapter 3 examines how the uncertain place of two 'liminal' groups – the poor whites and free people of colour – revealed tensions *within* the local articulation of white colonial identities. These tensions centred on the issue of whether society should be organised around the control of enslaved labour, irrespective of the 'race' of the slaveholders, or whether whiteness should be the basis of social authority, despite socio-economic differences amongst whites. By exploring the representations of, and acts towards, the liminal figures, these competing visions are considered, including the active role played by the poor whites and free people of colour in contemporary debates.

The fourth and fifth chapters move the discussion squarely into the realm of the trans-Atlantic campaign over slavery and form the substantive core of the book. Whilst Barbados's planters had been fairly unperturbed about the abolition of the slave trade, because they had a self-reproducing enslaved population, the antislavery campaign increasingly turned its attention to the internal state of the West Indian societies. It was this 'interference' that planters blamed for inciting the 1816 rebellion, the largest slave revolt in Barbados's colonial history. Although it was suppressed within a matter of days, the uprising became a key moment in the controversy over slavery. In its aftermath, opponents and supporters of slavery tried to establish a dominant account of the rebellion to influence the imperial authorities and British public opinion. Chapter 4, 'Locating blame for the 1816 rebellion', explores the competing accounts and narratives of the rebellion and its origins, as produced by the planter authorities, British abolitionists and the Afro-Caribbean rebels. These competing representations of enslaved resistance were associated with different ways of imagining the connections between Britain, Barbados and other Atlantic sites, such as Haiti. They were also related to differential constructions of white identity. By focussing on the 1816 revolt – sometimes known as 'Bussa's Rebellion' – the chapter provides a theoretically informed re-reading of one of the most significant events in Barbados's history. This is explored as an intense moment of identity-formation, in which different forms of white colonial identity were articulated, enacted, disturbed and challenged. The connections between self-representation and the representation of others are traced and related to acts of enslaved resistance, white violence and pro- and antislavery campaigning. By analysing these, some of the themes addressed in chapters 2 and 3 are revisited. Most importantly, the chapter shows that the enslaved Afro-Caribbean rebels articulated different discourses of whiteness by mocking and provoking colonial notions of sexual propriety, questioning the 'Englishness' of white

Barbadians and marginalising the importance of white people in their struggle for freedom.

The year 1823 saw the resurgence of the British antislavery campaign and a reformist shift in imperial policy. Chapter 5, 'Anti-Methodism and the uncertain place of Barbados', uses local opposition to this metropolitan-originating reformism to explore the status of the colony within a changing British empire and the consequences this had for the articulation of white creole identities. The main focus of the chapter is on the persecution of the local Methodist community by sections of the white population. This included the destruction of a chapel and subsequent flight of the missionary, as well as the circulation of anti-Methodist propaganda and official harassment by the island's authorities. By relating these various forms of anti-Methodism to broader opposition to the antislavery movement and considering the responses in Britain that this colonial opposition engendered, the chapter explores the ambivalent relationship between the articulation of white Barbadian and white British identities. The extremes and limits of white creole identities are evident in chapter 5. Echoing John Poyer's desire for racial re-alignment, anti-Methodism was an expression of a white supremacist identity in opposition to religious Dissent and metropolitan abolitionism. This identity was deeply ambivalent because it combined colonial loyalty with colonial opposition. The latter aspects of the Methodist persecution were seized upon by abolitionists, who challenged white Barbadian claims that they were loyal Britons overseas. This was recognised by upper-class planters in the island, who desperately sought to repair Barbados's reputation by distancing themselves from 'the rabble', whom they blamed for the religious persecution. The ambivalence of anti-Methodism and the elitist response to the metropolitan criticism that it engendered reveal not only class tensions in Barbados, but more general uncertainty about the nature of white West Indian identity in terms of its place within a changing British empire.

The final chapter, '"Days of misery and nights of fear": white ideas of freedom at the end of slavery', has twin aims: firstly, to revisit and connect some of the themes discussed in previous chapters and, secondly, to explore how attempts to shape Barbadian society as the end of slavery approached were framed by earlier articulations of white creole identity. With the emancipation of the enslaved West Indian populations becoming inevitable by the early 1830s, white Barbadians sought to ensure that their socio-economic dominance would be maintained afterwards. To this end, they promulgated favourable representations of slavery to secure financial compensation for the 'loss' of human property. Such efforts involved mobilising the planter ideal discussed in chapter 2 by drawing contrasts between the 'improved' nature of plantation management on the island and the supposedly more brutal forms practised elsewhere in the British West Indies. The chapter goes on to consider the socio-racial implications of 'freedom' for white Barbadians. The importance of a high-profile case in 1832 in which an enslaved black man, Robert James, was tried and convicted for the rape of a poor white woman, Mary Higginbotham, is emphasised. The chapter shows how the James case came to serve as an omen for white supremacist fears about the dangerous, free black person. Ideas of domestic defilement and the loss of home were prevalent in representations of the case, which, in turn, were linked to white concerns that 'freedom' would change Barbadian society for the worse. The chapter then turns to consider the response to the James case by analysing the public demonstrations that greeted the remission of James's death sentence and a stage play performed in this period. Both forms of political and cultural practice are shown to be bound up with the fashioning of a new form of white colonial identity on the threshold of emancipation that was more racially supremacist in outlook. This is a theme that is pursued further in the Epilogue.

Together, the substantive chapters address a series of key episodes during the controversy over slavery in Barbados that throw light upon the articulation and constitution of white creole culture, politics and identity in the age of abolition. Investigating these moments provides a means of writing a grounded, postcolonial account of white colonial identities in the Atlantic world.

1

The geographical 'problem of slavery'

The circuits of capital, commodities and labour that integrated Barbados into the Atlantic world and beyond also formed the basis for 'new habits of causal attribution that set the stage for humanitarianism' in late eighteenth-century Britain.[1] The trade in enslaved people and the chattel slavery that it supplied in plantation societies such as Barbados was the most emotive of all the transactions in which Britons engaged in the eighteenth and early nineteenth centuries. Indeed, David Brion Davis has argued that the mass enslavement of (racialised) others had always been a 'problem' in Western culture.[2] Nevertheless, it was not until the 1760s and 1770s that there emerged a 'widespread conviction that New World slavery symbolized all the forces that threatened the true destiny of man [sic]'.[3] In discussing the shift in attitudes towards slavery, Davis argues that it involved

a profound change in the basic paradigm of social geography – a conceptual differentiation between what can only be termed a 'slave world' aberration and the 'free world' norm.

This 'invidious demarcation', as Davis terms it, was predicated upon a developing consensus in metropolitan Britain that colonial slavery was antithetical to 'human

---

[1] T. L. Haskell, 'Capitalism and the origins of the humanitarian sensibility, part 2', *American Historical Review* 90 (1985), 535. See also C. A. Bayly, 'The British and indigenous peoples, 1760–1860: Power, perception and identity', in M. Daunton and R. Halpern (eds.), *Empire and others: British encounters with indigenous peoples, 1600–1850* (London: UCL Press, 1999); H. V. Bowen, 'British conceptions of global empire, 1756–1783', *Journal of Imperial and Commonwealth History* 26 (1998); T. L. Haskell, 'Capitalism and the origins of the humanitarian sensibility, part 1', *American Historical Review* 90 (1985); M. Ogborn, 'Historical geographies of globalisation, c. 1500–1800', in B. Graham and C. Nash (eds.), *Modern historical geographies* (Harlow: Prentice Hall, 2000); S. Thorne, '"The conversion of Englishmen and the conversion of the world inseparable": Missionary imperialism and the language of class in early industrial Britain', in F. Cooper and A. L. Stoler (eds.), *Tensions of empire: Colonial cultures in a bourgeois world* (Berkeley: University of California Press, 1997).

[2] D. B. Davis, *The problem of slavery in Western culture* (Ithaca: Cornell University Press, 1966).

[3] D. B. Davis, *The problem of slavery in the age of revolution, 1770–1823* (London: Cornell University Press, 1975), p. 41. See also D. Turley, *The culture of English antislavery, 1780–1860* (London: Routledge, 1991); J. Walvin, *Black ivory: A history of British slavery* (London: Harper Collins, 1992).

progress'.[4] Whilst most discussions of the emergence and institutionalisation of the 'problem of slavery' in the antislavery campaigns of the late eighteenth and early nineteenth centuries emphasise religious, economic, philosophical, literary or political dimensions, Davis's comments point to its geographies, both material and imaginary.[5] His comments highlight the deep 'tensions of empire' that were opened up between metropole and slave colonies, between Britain and its West Indian possessions, in the age of abolition.

Davis's description of the spatialisation of the 'problem of slavery' from the late eighteenth century as a 'profound change in the basic paradigm of social geography' can be understood as a shift in the British metropolitan imaginative geographies of the imperial world.[6] Yet, the emergence of a division between a '"slave world" aberration and the "free world" norm' should not be seen as merely another instance of a generalised pattern in the articulation of essentialised differences between metropolitan and colonial space, but as grounded in the more specific cultural politics of the mass enslavement of black people by whites in the Atlantic world. Such a perspective is suggested in the context of American slavery by Joanne Pope Melish who shows how the representation of a 'historically free, white New England' against a 'Jacobin, Africanized South' was central to the articulation of New England identity. Similarly, David Jansson has described the 'othering' of the American South by the North, especially in the context of abolitionism, as a form of 'internal Orientalism'.[7] As these suggest, the 'problem of slavery' in the British empire was framed by antislavery campaigners, in part, as a *geographical problem*, as a problem *of* the West Indies. In this light, emancipation 'may be viewed as one society successfully imposing its view of morality, justice and social relations on another' in that metropolitan, especially evangelical, notions of morality, political organisation and economic activity triumphed over those articulated by the West Indian planters.[8] Moreover, antislavery was an important

---

[4] D. B. Davis, *Slavery and human progress* (Oxford: Oxford University Press, 1984), p. 81.

[5] D. B. Davis, *Problem of slavery in the age of revolution.*

[6] Inspired by the connections between discourse and imperial power, the idea of 'imaginative geographies' has encouraged the exploration of how spaces and places were constructed through, and served to intensify, the subjugating practices of colonialism. The inspiration for much of this has been E. W. Said, *Orientalism: Western conceptions of the Orient* (London: Penguin, 1978). Examples of work that draw on and seek to move beyond the 'colonial discourse' paradigm include D. W. Clayton, *Islands of truth: The imperial fashioning of Vancouver Island* (Vancouver: UBC Press, 2000); F. Driver, *Geography militant: Cultures of exploration and empire* (Oxford: Blackwell, 2000); D. Gregory, 'Between the book and the lamp: Imaginative geographies of Egypt, 1849–1850', *Transactions of the Institute of British Geographers* 20 (1995); A. Lester, *Imperial networks: Creating identities in nineteenth-century South Africa and Britain* (London: Routledge, 2001). For a more general consideration of 'postcolonial geographies', see A. Blunt and C. McEwan (eds.), *Postcolonial geographies* (London: Continuum, 2002).

[7] D. R. Jansson, 'Internal orientalism in America: W. J. Cash's *The Mind of the South* and the spatial construction of American national identity', *Political Geography* 22 (2003); J. Pope Melish, *Disowning slavery: Gradual emancipation and 'race' in New England, 1780–1860* (London: Cornell University Press, 1998), p. 223.

[8] D. Eltis, 'Abolitionist perspectives of society after slavery', in J. Walvin (ed.), *Slavery and British society, 1776–1846* (London: Macmillan Press, 1982), p. 195.

aspect of 'the construction of a new bourgeois subjectivity in Britain and its empire as a whole' and acted as a source of validation for an emergent national identity.[9] Indeed, it can be suggested that central to the hegemonic role of antislavery and to the forging of British metropolitan identity in the late eighteenth and early nineteenth centuries was the representation of West Indian slave societies as 'un-English', *aberrant* spaces that required metropolitan humanitarian intervention. The constitution of the white, British, bourgeois subject could be consolidated, and the 'problem of slavery' resolved, by disowning and repudiating those 'un-British' groups involved in slavery – the West Indian planters – and displacing the spaces of slavery to the margins of Britain's imaginative imperial geographies.[10] As Catherine Hall puts it:

This mapping of difference across nation and empire . . . provided the basis for drawing lines as to who was inside and who was outside the nation or colony, who were subjects and who were citizens, what forms of cultural or political belonging were possible at any given time.[11]

Antislavery campaigners worked hard to represent the West Indian slave colonies as 'un-English', aberrant spaces and to inscribe Davis's Atlantic 'social geography'. Through their representation of a slave world 'other', a British 'free world' norm was articulated.[12] Of course, the emergence of what Gordon Lewis terms an 'anti-Caribbean animus' and its spatialisation in the 'invidious demarcation' drawn between slave world and free world was not merely imaginative. For example, the 1772 court ruling by Lord Mansfield that no slaveowner could deport an enslaved person from England to a slave colony was one of the first instances of the geographical displacement of slavery from metropolitan space. Such legal decisions served to construct the slave world/free world division.[13] On a broader scale, the geographical 'problem of slavery' was also related to what has been termed the 'double switch in imperial focus' from Atlantic to Orient, and protectionism to free

[9] Lester, *Imperial networks*, p. 23. See also L. Colley, *Britons: Forging the nation, 1707–1837* (London: Yale University Press, 1992), pp. 350–360; C. Hall, *Civilising subjects: Metropole and colony in the English imagination, 1830–1867* (Oxford: Polity, 2002); B. Hilton, *The age of atonement: The influence of evangelicalism on social and economic thought, 1785–1865* (Oxford: Clarendon Press, 1988). In a related argument, Davis argues that British antislavery functioned as a source of hegemony by helping 'to ensure stability while also accommodating society to political and economic change'. See D. B. Davis, *Problem of slavery in the age of revolution*, p. 349.

[10] J. P. Greene, 'Changing identity in the British Caribbean: Barbados as a case study', in N. Canny and A. Pagden (eds.), *Colonial identity in the Atlantic world, 1500–1800* (Princeton, NJ: Princeton Press, 1987), p. 264; Pope Melish, *Disowning slavery*.

[11] C. Hall, *Civilising subjects*, p. 20.

[12] As Catherine Hall puts it, 'The gap between metropole and colony was crucial . . . the forms of Englishness which operated in the West Indies had long been anathema to anti-slavery enthusiastics. Jamaican whites did not represent the right kinds of Englishness': C. Hall, *Civilising subjects*, p. 413.

[13] For a discussion of the significance of the James Somerset case, see R. Blackburn, *The overthrow of colonial slavery, 1776–1848* (London: Verso, 1988), p. 100; K. A. Sandiford, *The cultural politics of sugar: Caribbean slavery and narratives of colonialism* (Cambridge: Cambridge University Press, 2000). For more on the role of law in forging space, see N. Blomley, D. Delaney and R. T. Ford (eds.), *Legal geographies reader: Law, power and space* (Oxford: Blackwell, 2001).

tradism.[14] Having profound implications for British imperial culture, this reduced the relative economic, political and cultural significance of the West Indies.[15]

The imaginative geography of the 'problem of slavery' involved more than the assertion of a slave world/free world division by antislavery campaigners and the marginalisation of the West Indies and its colonists. This humanitarian spatial imaginary did not go uncontested, and supporters of slavery in the region and Britain affirmed the centrality of the West Indies to the imperial project by emphasising their economic value, strategic importance, cultural legitimacy and the loyalty they had demonstrated, especially in the light of the American Revolution.[16] Nowhere were such discourses of shared identity and colonial allegiance more powerfully manifest than in the self-description of Barbados as 'Little England'. This term is sometimes used pejoratively to describe the island's supposedly 'quiescent political culture', particularly in contrast with the radical tradition of Jamaica.[17]

In describing a discourse of 'Barbados-as-Little-England' – a Little Englandist discourse – it is not my intention to evoke ideas about a conservative, 'Afro-Saxon' 'Little England mentality', but instead to treat it as an articulation of cultural and political identity that was associated with the response of white Barbadians to the rise of antislavery. Although it is difficult to ascertain when the term was used initially, the first written record is Daniel McKinnen's *A tour through the British West Indies* (1804). Nevertheless, the anonymous author of *Sketches and recollections of the West Indies* (1828) mentions that the term was in use in Barbados in the late 1790s and it may have been in circulation before then.[18] It is no coincidence that such an articulation of colonial identity occurred when the aberrant

[14] M. Craton, *Sinews of empire: A short history of British slavery* (London: Temple Smith, 1974), p. 239; G. K. Lewis, *Main currents in Caribbean thought: The historical evolution of Caribbean society in its ideological aspects, 1492–1900* (Baltimore: Johns Hopkins University Press, 1983), p. 25.

[15] J. Cell, 'The imperial conscience', in P. Marsh (ed.), *The conscience of the Victorian state* (Hassocks: Harvester Press, 1979); P. J. Marshall, 'Britain without America – a second empire?' in P. J. Marshall (ed.), *The Oxford history of the British Empire*, vol. II, *The eighteenth century* (Oxford: Oxford University Press, 1998); A. J. O'Shaughnessy, *An empire divided: The American Revolution and the British Caribbean* (Philadelphia: University of Pennsylvania Press, 2000); A. Porter, 'Trusteeship, anti-slavery, and humanitarianism', in A. Porter (ed.), *The Oxford history of the British Empire*, vol. III, *The nineteenth century* (Oxford: Oxford University Press, 1999).

[16] Sandiford, *Cultural politics of sugar*. For similar observations about British settlers in southern Africa, see Lester, *Imperial networks*, pp. 62–77. On the 'loyalty' of the West Indian colonists during the Revolutionary War, see O'Shaughnessy, *Empire divided*, pp. 202–203.

[17] See R. Segal, *The black diaspora* (London: Faber and Faber, 1995), p. 289; M. Sheller, *Democracy after slavery: Black publics and peasant radicalism in Haiti and Jamaica* (London: Macmillan Education, 2000), p. 39. For discussions of such cultural forms in historiography, see E. K. Brathwaite, *Contradictory omens: Cultural diversity and integration in the Caribbean* (Mona: Savacou, 1974), p. 31; and in literature, see G. Lamming, *In the castle of my skin* (Harlow: Longman, 1953), and A. Clarke, *Growing up stupid under the Union Jack* (Havana: Casa de las Americas, 1980).

[18] See Anonymous, *Sketches and recollections of the West Indies by a resident* (London: Smith, Elder, and Co., 1828); D. McKinnen, *A tour through the British West Indies, in the years 1802 and 1803* (London: J. White, 1804), p. 23. This term has very different connotations to way 'Little England' is used in metropolitan Britain. For example, Richard Gott notes that 'Little Englander'

nature of the West Indies was being asserted. For this perspective, the description of Barbados as Little England not only symbolised the supposed political, social and cultural similarities between metropole and colony – the idea that Barbados was an England 'in miniature'[19] – but also their mutual dependence. Predicated on the loyalty white Barbadians had supposedly shown, especially to the Crown following the regicide in the middle of the seventeenth century and during the American Revolution, such Little Englandist discourse sought to 'construct debts of allegiance and bonds of interests' between colony and centre.[20] Articulated in political discourse and writing, as well local proverbs,[21] this imaginary geography evoked strong familial symbolism, including the positing of a special relationship between mother country and colony, *and* a more equal assertion of a shared whiteness – an avowal of imperial fraternity.

The imaginative geography that the Little England discourse sustained sought to maintain metropolitan support for West Indian institutions and rights. Through such forms of representation, supporters of West Indian interests sought, as Keith Sandiford has it, to *negotiate* a place for the colonies in the changing imaginative and material geographies of the British empire. The term 'negotiation' is used by Sandiford to describe attempts made to 'win a tenuous and elusive legitimacy for an evolving Creole civilization, conflicted by its central relation to slavery and its marginal relation to metropolitan cultures'. This was 'a defensive response to metropolitan attitudes of contempt and calumny' – Lewis's 'anti-Caribbean animus' – and a challenge to the construction of the West Indies as an aberrant and

first appears in print in Britain in the 1890s as a pejorative term to describe those opposed to the Anglo-Boer War. Interestingly, one of the best-known examples that established Barbados's reputation as 'Little England' was the also bound up with an imperial war. This is the oft-repeated story of a communication sent from the colony at the outbreak of hostilities with the encouraging message 'Go ahead England, Barbados is behind you', although the details of which war remain unclear. Thus, whilst Gott traces the genealogy of 'Little Englander' back to anti-colonial and antislavery thought, 'Barbados-as-Little-England' carried diametrically opposite connotations. See R. Gott, 'Little Englanders', in R. Samuel (ed.), *Patriotism: The making and unmaking of British national identity* (London: Routledge, 1989). A similar form of geographical imagination was the contemporary self-description of Barbados as 'Bimshire', as though the island were an English home county in the Caribbean.

[19] D. Coleman, 'Bulama and Sierra Leone: Utopian islands and visionary interiors', in R. Edmond and V. Smith (eds.), *Islands in history and representation* (London: Routledge, 2003), p. 66. For a recent discussion of the efforts made by seventeenth-century colonists to make Barbados 'truly English', see L. Gragg, *Englishmen transplanted: The English colonization of Barbados, 1627–1660* (Oxford: Oxford University Press, 2003).

[20] M. Ellis, '"The cane-land isles": Commerce and empire in late eighteenth-century georgic and pastoral poetry', in Edmond and Smith, *Islands in history and representation*, p. 59.

[21] Famous local sayings at the time include 'Neither Carib, nor Creole, but true Barbadian' and 'What would poor old England do, were Barbadoes to forsake her?' The latter first appears in print in George Pinckard's *Notes on the West Indies*, which recounts a visit by a British medical doctor to the island in 1796. Such phrases recur in similar forms up to and beyond emancipation in the 1830s and are often cited to indicate something about the character of white and, to some extent, black Barbadians. See P. M'Callum, *Travels in Trinidad during the months of February, March and April 1803* (Liverpool, 1805), pp. 11–12; G. Pinckard, *Notes on the West Indies: Written during the expedition under the command of the late General Sir Ralph Abercromby; including observations on the island of Barbadoes, and the settlements captured by the British troops upon the coast of Guiana* (London, 1806), pp. 76, 78, 133, 134.

marginal slave world.[22] As Sandiford's deconstruction of the term suggests, however, negotiation was always beset by anxiety and ambivalence.[23] The increasing influence of the antislavery campaign on metropolitan policy and public opinion, and the greater willingness of the imperial authorities to intervene in West Indian affairs, engendered more hostile reactions from planters and their supporters. Often evoking Lockean notions of sovereign power and appropriating the rhetoric of Revolutionary America, these reactions bordered on an anti-imperial 'embryonic Creole nationalism'.[24] At the same time, however, the threat of imperial intervention was itself portrayed as 'un-English' and West Indian resistance to it as evidence of colonial commitment to English liberties.[25] This is indicative of a white colonial identity that was 'simultaneously assertive, defensive and loudly loyal', particularly over the issue of slavery. This ambivalence, which was evident in many colonial situations,[26] was exacerbated in Barbados because its white population defined itself in terms of loyalty, Anglicanism, royalism, indispensability to empire and adherence to liberty through the discourse of Little Englandism. In consequence, the cultural and political of identity of white Barbadians was conflicted. As Noel Titus puts it:

The intensity of insular pride which they displayed led them on the one hand to see their island as pre-eminent in the region and almost indispensable to England, and on the other hand to resent any challenge to those traditions which they had built up.[27]

The vacillating nature of white Barbadian responses to antislavery and the attempts made to negotiate between loyalty (identity *with* Britain) and opposition (difference *from* Britain) point to the uncertain place of white West Indian identities – of white *creole* identities[28] – in the British empire during the age of abolition.

White identities

Although representations of the enslaved black subject were central to the controversies over slavery – as objects of pity or units of labour[29] – the figure of the white

---

[22] Sandiford, *Cultural politics of sugar*, pp. 3, 6, 14.

[23] Sandiford draws attention to the etymological dichotomy and antagonism rooted in the Latin term *negotium*, which he splits into *neg-* (not) and *otium* (ease, quiet).

[24] G. K. Lewis, *Main currents*, p. 70. Lockean notions about the rights of white subjects to rebel against a despotic crown were an important part of this white creole political consciousness. See C. Hall, *Civilising subjects*, pp. 102–105.

[25] S. H. Carrington, 'West Indian opposition to British policy: Barbadian politics, 1774–1782', *Journal of Caribbean History* 17 (1982); Greene, 'Changing identity in the British Caribbean'.

[26] Lester, *Imperial networks*, p. 65.

[27] N. F. Titus, *The development of Methodism in Barbados, 1823–1883* (Berne: Peter Lang, 1994), p. 2. Similarly Andrew O'Shaughnessy notes that the white West Indian elite 'wanted autonomy and self-government but within the British empire. Their constitutional thought subsequently remained ambivalent. They were never able to reconcile their claims to being both equal and subordinate to Britain.' See O'Shaughnessy, *Empire divided*, p. 248.

[28] See below pp. 35–40.

[29] R. G. Abrahams and J. F. Szwed (eds.), *After Africa* (New York: Yale University Press, 1983); D. A. Lorimer, *Colour, class and the Victorians* (Leicester: Leicester University Press, 1978); M. Wood, *Slavery, empathy, and pornography* (Oxford: Oxford University Press, 2002).

West Indian slaveholder also occupied an important place. Often represented, particularly by abolitionists, as profit-obsessed, degenerate creoles, who brutalised their sable victims, the 'un-English' West Indian was a stock figure of antislavery discourse and a white 'other' against which metropolitan British identity was formulated. Thus, the age of abolition was, in part, a 'war of representation' over 'good' and 'bad' forms of white identity and the imaginative location of these in the British Atlantic world.[30]

Tracing the articulation and counter-articulation of white identities relates to the growing interdisciplinary field of 'white' or 'whiteness studies'.[31] This is based, in part, on recognition that

Racial identities are not only Black, Latino, Asian, Native American and so on; they are also white. To ignore white ethnicity is to redouble its hegemony by naturalizing it.[32]

Within this field, anti-essentialist work on 'white racialisation' – the processes through which certain people became defined as 'white', and the meaning and consequences of this for them and those not so defined – has been of particular importance in disclosing the violent, contested and partial nature of 'white' as identity and positional good.[33] Nevertheless, the overwhelming focus on the American context means that 'a detailed and integrated historical geography of Whiteness is still some way off'.[34] In the context of English and British imperialism, such work would need to explore how, from the early modern period, 'European social

---

[30] For similar observations on metropolitan perceptions of white West Indians, especially in relation to their involvement in slavery, see C. Hall, 'What is a West Indian?', in B. Schwarz (ed.), *West Indian intellectuals in Britain* (Manchester: Manchester University Press, 2003). For comparable comments about Afrikaners in southern Africa, see Lester, *Imperial networks*, pp. 15–16.

[31] See A. Bonnett, *White identities: Historical and international perspectives* (London: Prentice Hall, 2000); R. Dyer, *White* (London: Routledge, 1997); M. Fine et al. (eds.), *Off white: readings on race, power and society* (London: Routledge, 1997); R. Frankenberg, *White women, race matters: the social construction of whiteness* (London: Routledge, 1993). Alastair Bonnett argues that in much Western scholarship there has been 'a perversely intense focus upon the marginal subject-groups constituted within the Western and imperial imagination' whilst the 'White centre of that imagination is not discussed'. He describes such 'collective myopia' as a form of privileging that removes whiteness from 'the realm of debatable "racial" categories, placing it outside history and geography and onto the essentialist terrain of unchangeable nature'. See A. Bonnett, 'Geography, "race" and Whiteness: Invisible traditions and current challenges', *Area* 29 (1997), 194, 195.

[32] C. Fusco cited in D. Roediger, *Towards the abolition of whiteness: Essays on race, politics, and working-class history* (London: Verso, 1994), p. 12. Of course, this is emphatically *not* to say that whiteness is just another form of racial or ethnic identity. Whiteness is, and has been, consistently privileged; part of this privileging is its apparent invisibility to critical inquiry.

[33] See T. Allen, *The invention of the white race*, vol. I, *Racial oppression and social control* (London: Verso, 1994); N. Ignatiev, *How the Irish became white* (London: Routledge, 1995); Roediger, *Towards the abolition of whiteness*; D. Roediger, *The wages of whiteness: Race and the making of the American working class* (London: Verso, 1991).

[34] Bonnett, 'Geography, "race" and Whiteness', 197. There has also been work on white identities in the African and Australian contexts. See W. Anderson, *The cultivation of whiteness: Science, health and racial destiny in Australia* (New York: Basic Books, 2003); D. Kennedy, *Islands of white: Settler society and culture in Kenya and Southern Rhodesia, 1890–1939* (Durham, NC: Duke University Press, 1987); V. Ware, *Beyond the pale: White women, racism and history* (London: Verso, 1992).

and economic paradigms were connoted through the symbols of race, symbols that gave capitalist incursion and modernity a European, and hence white, identity.'[35] Whiteness was a 'dominant element' in the articulation of English and British identity across the empire – which further underlines that Englishness 'cannot be grasped without seeing its intimate and complex connections to the wider imperial world'[36] – and the use of 'white' to refer to Europeans was most fully articulated in colonial slave societies. Indeed, modern racism in its present form 'is a specific product of Atlantic history'.[37] Yet, the relationship between whiteness and Englishness/Britishness was not always self-evident. For abolitionists, the two became disarticulated in the context of slavery and the representation of Barbados as an aberrant space was central to their repudiation of the Englishness of white West Indian planters.[38] Similarly, the articulation of Barbados-as-Little-England was a key aspect of the colonial response. Thus, in the age of abolition, white identities were contested across the space of the British empire and articulated through contested imaginative geographies of the empire.

The 'problematic political semantics of "whiteness"' were not limited to articulations by those involved in various colonising projects. Whiteness must also be interrogated by exploring the production of white subjectivity by non-whites and considering how it has been understood, used, rejected and ignored.[39] Those interested in the 'constitutive role played by colonized groups' on purportedly hegemonic discourses – such as articulations of whiteness – have often drawn on notions of transculturation, métissage, hybridity and creolisation.[40] This

---

[35] Bonnett, *White identities*, p. 48.

[36] C. Bridge and K. Fedorowich, 'Mapping the British world', in C. Bridge and K. Fedorowich (eds.), *The British world: Diaspora, culture and identity* (London: Frank Cass, 2003), p. 3; B. Schwarz, 'Introduction: the expansion and contraction of England', in B. Schwarz (ed.), *The expansion of England: Race, ethnicity and cultural history* (London: Routledge, 1996), p. 1. The relationship between articulations of Englishness and Britishness is a complex and entangled one. In general, I follow Catherine Hall in using 'English' rather than 'British', in that, historically, Englishness has been the hegemonic form of British identity and that central to the construction of Englishness has been a claim to Britishness. See I. Baucom, *Out of place: Englishness, empire, and the locations of identity* (Princeton, NJ: Princeton University Press, 1999), pp. 14–24; C. Hall, *White, male and middle class: Explorations in feminism and history* (New York: Routledge, 1988). Nevertheless, I will often slip between the terms as they were often used loosely in the historical geographical context that this book addresses.

[37] A. Bonnett, 'Who was white? The disappearance of non-European white identities and the formation of European racial whiteness', *Ethnic and Racial Studies* 21 (1998), 1041; J. E. Chaplin, 'Race', in D. Armitage and M. J. Braddick (eds.), *The British Atlantic world, 1500–1800* (Basingstoke: Palgrave Macmillan, 2002), p. 154.

[38] Compare C. Hall, *Civilising subjects*.

[39] A. Bonnett, 'White studies: The problems and projects of a new research agenda', *Theory, Culture and Society* 13 (1996); b. hooks, 'Representations of whiteness in the black imagination', in b. hooks (ed.), *Black looks: Race and representation* (Boston: South End Press, 1992); A. L. Stoler, *Race and the education of desire: Foucault's History of sexuality and the colonial order of things* (London: Duke University Press, 1995), p. 99.

[40] C. Barnett, 'Impure and worldly geography: The Africanist discourse of the Royal Geographical Society', *Transactions of the Institute of British Geographers* 23 (1998), 240; M. L. Pratt, *Imperial eyes: Travel writing and transculturation* (London: Routledge, 1992). On creolisation, see pp. 37–39.

perspective is vital for exploring the contested nature of white identities in the slavery controversy.[41]

The development of white society in Barbados

A Barbadian planter class was fully formed by the 1660s and was dominated by an elite with about 400 estates of between 200 and 1,000 acres of land.[42] Most were descended from the earliest colonists, although their numbers were swelled by Royalist émigrés after the English Civil War (1642–5). The 'sugar revolution' was critical to the consolidation of this plantocracy and the large amounts of land and capital required for profitable sugar production led to the monopolisation of land by the biggest planters. Nevertheless, with smaller holdings than planters elsewhere in the West Indies, fewer could afford to retire to Britain and there was no wholesale absenteeism. Although there was some upward mobility from the middle class, high levels of in-marriage served to retain status and property within the elite.[43]

As well as dominating the island economically, the plantocracy maintained its power through political, military and social institutions, including the Assembly and Council.[44] Other planter-dominated institutions included the Anglican Church, the parish vestries and the militia. The Established Church's presence in Barbados had begun with the arrival of chaplains on the first colonising expeditions. Although the Bishop of London had nominal jurisdiction, it was not until 1824 that the Church of England developed a more formalised presence and for almost two centuries the local Church was '*of* the planters, and *for* the planters'. This reflected the clergy's status as colonists and slaveholders, and the fact that the parish vestries, which

---

[41] This approach is also necessary to avoid recuperative accounts of white identities that serve only to arrogate to white men the historiographic centre stage. Indeed, bell hooks argues that the study of whiteness is not in itself a critical academic project and may be a thoroughly racist pursuit if it serves to recentre and reify white identities. See J. Haggis, 'White women and colonialism: Towards a non-recuperative history', in C. Midgley (ed.), *Gender and imperialism* (Manchester: Manchester University Press, 1998); b. hooks, 'Travelling theories, travelling theorists', *Inscriptions* 5 (1989); Roediger, *Towards the abolition of whiteness*, p. 7.

[42] R. S. Dunn, *Sugar and slaves: The rise of the planter class in the English West Indies, 1624–1713* (Chapel Hill: University of North Carolina Press, 1973), p. 113; J. S. Handler, 'Plantation slave settlements in Barbados, 1650s to 1834', in A. O. Thompson (ed.), *In the shadow of the plantation: Caribbean history and legacy. In honour of Professor Emeritus Woodville K. Marshall* (Kingston, Jamaica: Ian Randle, 2002), p. 141.

[43] H. McD. Beckles, *A history of Barbados: From Amerindian settlement to nation-state* (Cambridge: Cambridge University Press, 1990), p. 23; K. Watson, *The civilised island, Barbados: A social history, 1750–1816* (Bridgetown: Graphic Printers, 1979).

[44] The Council was a twelve-man body, appointed by the Crown from among prominent planters and merchants. Their role was to advise the governor, and all legislation required their support. The real power lay with the Assembly because all bills originated there, including those related to finance. It was an elected body of twenty-two members (two from each parish) drawn from the planter, merchant and professional classes. Elections were held annually and the franchise was limited to white, Christian males who were over twenty-one years old and had ten acres of land, or property with an annual taxable value of £10. Both bodies tended to be dominated by oligarchic, slaveholding interests, though smaller, middle-class proprietors were sometimes able to control the Assembly. See chapter 5, pp. 170–171.

were responsible for local administration, poor relief and church maintenance, were controlled by the plantocracy. This 'clergy–planter nexus' was evident in opposition to the religious instruction of the enslaved because whites feared that Christianisation undermined the racial rationalisation of slavery and that educated enslaved people were a threat to the slave order. The Quakers, for example, faced legislative opposition in the late seventeenth century for allowing enslaved workers to join them in worship.[45] The militia, too, was controlled by the planters and most of its officers were plantocrats. Although imperial forces were occasionally quartered in the island, a permanent military garrison was not established until 1780 and Barbados relied on its own militia for security. Its role was to respond to external attack and guard against enslaved revolt. The latter role was also manifest in the deployment of the militia to police gatherings by enslaved people and recapture runaways.[46]

In the late eighteenth century, Barbados's white upper class consisted of less than a quarter of the total white population of approximately 16,000. The middle class made up a further quarter. Its upper section consisted of cotton planters, plantation managers, professionals and small merchants, whilst the lower section included the 'ten-acre' men who possessed the franchise and were involved in electoral competition with the plantocracy during the early nineteenth century.[47] This was symptomatic of divisions within the white population, because although the white middle class shared much of the planter elite's worldview, there were differences over *how* white domination of society should be maintained.[48] Over half the white population in the late eighteenth century made up a lower class of 'poor whites'. The history of this group had begun with the arrival of white indentured labourers in the colony's formative years.[49] Its numbers were swelled by the transportation of prisoners from Oliver Cromwell's campaigns in Scotland, Ireland and England during the Wars of the Three Kingdoms (1639–52), in addition to convicts and other, particularly Irish, dissidents. Although the number of Irish caused concern amongst Barbados's plantocracy in the seventeenth century, particularly given their involvement in some of the earliest enslaved plots,[50] the population of white

---

[45] K. Davis, *Crown and cross in Barbados: Caribbean political religion in the late nineteenth century* (Frankfurt: Peter Lang, 1983), p. 54; J. Gilmore, 'Church and society in Barbados, 1824–1881', in W. Marshall (ed.), *Emancipation II: A series of lectures to commemorate the 150th anniversary of emancipation* (Bridgetown: Cedar Press, 1987); Titus, *Development of Methodism*, p. 12.

[46] J. S. Handler, 'Freedmen and slaves in the Barbados militia', *Journal of Caribbean History* 19 (1984).

[47] K. Watson, *Civilised island*, p. 137; K. Watson, 'Salmagundis vs Pumpkins: White politics and creole consciousness in Barbadian slave society, 1800–1834', in H. Johnson and K. Watson (eds.), *The white minority in the Caribbean* (Kingston: Ian Randle, 1998).

[48] See chapters 3 and 5.

[49] A. Games, 'Migration', in Armitage and Braddick, *The British Atlantic world*, p. 38; J. Sheppard, *The 'redlegs' of Barbados: Their origins and history* (Millwood, NY: KTO Press, 1977); K. Watson, *Civilised island*, p. 137.

[50] Beckles, *History of Barbados*, pp. 38–39; P. Linebaugh and M. Rediker, *The many-headed hydra: Sailors, slaves, commoners, and the hidden history of the revolutionary Atlantic* (London: Verso, 2000), pp. 123–127.

servants came to be seen as a bulwark against enslaved revolts and external foe alike.

Together, the plantocracy, middle class and poor whites made up a large, and relatively stable, white population. Although enslaved people of African origin were in the majority from the 1670s, the number of whites was proportionally larger than that of any the other true sugar colonies.[51] In addition, there were more whites than free black and coloured people – even after the significant rise in manumissions of the late eighteenth century – again something unique to Barbados. The gender structure in Barbados was also unique and women formed the majority of the black *and* white populations from the early eighteenth century. This tended to produce more stable white family life and lower absenteeism, as well as perhaps tempering the 'brutish frontier mentality of white men'.[52] Dominating Barbados's white population was a conservative, resident plantocratic elite, which, despite tensions with the other sections of the white population, was able to achieve cultural legitimacy. The basis of this was not only a shared racial supremacism, but also common socio-economic interests. The strength of the plantocracy, along with an entrenched middle class and a large number of poor whites, produced a dominant culture that was the nearest equivalent in the West Indies to that of the American South.[53] Unlike whites in Jamaica, for whom England remained home, Barbados's whites came to identify with the island and this encouraged the development of embryonic nationalistic sentiments.[54]

Atlantic world histories and networks

To understand white creole culture, politics and identities in Barbados, we need to situate their articulation in the Atlantic world. The growth of Atlantic world history has been described as 'one of the most important new historiographical developments of recent years', though we should be suspicious about claims regarding its 'inbuilt geography'.[55] Instead, the modern Atlantic world should be viewed as being constituted by 'kaleidoscopic movements of people, goods, and ideas' associated with both the practices and imaginations of the powerful, including West Indian planters, and those of the seemingly powerless, as evident in the submerged

[51] M. Craton, *Testing the chains: Resistance to slavery in the British West Indies* (London: Cornell University Press, 1982), p. 254; Dunn, *Sugar and slaves*, p. 82.

[52] H. McD. Beckles, *Centering woman: Gender discourses in Caribbean slave society* (Oxford: James Currey, 1999), p. 65; C. Jones, 'A darker shade of white? Gender, social class, and the reproduction of white identity in Barbadian plantation society', in H. Brown, M. Gilkes, and A. Kaloski-Naylor (eds.), *White?women: Critical perspectives on race and gender* (York: Raw Nerve Books, 1999).

[53] H. McD. Beckles, 'Rebels and reactionaries: The political responses of white labourers to planter class hegemony in the seventeenth-century Barbados', *Journal of Caribbean History* 15 (1981); Craton, *Testing the chains*, p. 254; C. Jones, 'Mapping racial boundaries: Gender, race, and poor relief in Barbadian plantation society', *Journal of Women's History* 10 (1998).

[54] O'Shaughnessy, *Empire divided*.

[55] Quoted in D. Armitage and M. J. Braddick, 'Introduction', in Armitage and Braddick, *The British Atlantic world*, p. 1.

and subaltern histories of the 'motley Hydra'.[56] Locating Barbados within the Atlantic world during the age of abolition provides a way of addressing the 'multiple, spatially varied, inception of Whiteness' across a broader 'imperial social formation'.[57] Crucial here is a conceptualisation of Atlantic history that David Armitage terms 'cis-Atlantic history'. This approaches

particular places as unique locations within an Atlantic world and seeks to define that uniqueness as the result of the interaction between local particularity and a wider web of connections.[58]

Cis-Atlantic history, then, is the history of any particular place in relation to the wider Atlantic world. This might be the history of a nation, state, region or even a specific institution, though for Armitage the greatest potential lies, perhaps, in integrating the local histories of isthmuses or islands 'into the broader perspective afforded by Atlantic history'.[59] This provides a means of writing Barbados into more general postcolonial perspectives,[60] whilst also demonstrating that 'only localized theories and historically specific accounts can provide much insight into the varied articulations of colonizing and counter-colonial representations and practices'.[61]

Cis-Atlantic perspectives are closely related to the concepts of regionality that have traditionally concerned historical geographers. Although the concept of *pays*, which is of such importance for regional geography, has been criticised for being more suited to pre-industrial, isolated societies than industrial and urban ones, Alan Baker points out that this 'ignored the fact that Vidal de la Blache himself had emphasised the importance not only of the *milieu* and the *genre de vie* of each *pays* but also its *connectivité*, its links with other places through flows of people, commodities, capital and ideas'.[62] Integrating the 'local particularity' of Barbados and the 'wider web of connections' that encompassed the British Atlantic world involves another of Armitage's concepts – 'circum-Atlantic' history. This is a 'mobile and connective' history incorporating everything around the Atlantic basin. Transnational in character, it is concerned with tracing circulations about the Atlantic world.[63]

The approach suggested by combining the cis- and circum-Atlantic perspectives chimes with more recent thinking about regions as 'a series of open, discontinuous

---

[56] Linebaugh and Rediker, *Many-headed hydra*.
[57] Bonnett, 'Geography, "race" and Whiteness', 197; M. Sinha, *Colonial masculinity: The 'manly Englishman' and the 'effeminate Bengali' in the late nineteenth century* (Manchester: Manchester University Press, 1995), p. 9.
[58] Armitage and Braddick, 'Introduction', p. 21.
[59] D. Armitage, 'Three concepts of Atlantic history', in Armitage and Braddick, *The British Atlantic world*, p. 15.
[60] Compare Clayton, *Islands of truth*.
[61] N. Thomas, *Colonialism's culture: Anthropology, travel and government* (Oxford: Polity, 1994), p. xi.
[62] A. R. H. Baker, *Geography and history: Bridging the divide* (Cambridge: Cambridge University Press, 2003), p. 160.
[63] Armitage, 'Three concepts of Atlantic history', p. 16. See also J. Roach, *Cities of the dead: Circum-Atlantic performance* (New York: Columbia University Press, 1996).

spaces constituted by social relationships which stretch across spaces in a variety of ways'.[64] It also relates to increasing interest in imperial (and anti-imperial) networks and in tracing the associated 'geographies of connection' that were both material and imaginative in nature. Anthony Ballantyne, for example, conceives of the British empire as a '"bundle of relationships" that brought disparate regions, communities and individuals into contact through systems of mobility and exchange'.[65] According to Kathleen Wilson, the idea of networks

allows us to treat the metropole and colonies as interconnected analytical fields – which is emphatically *not* to say that the two are 'the same' but that each provides a local translation of a wider imperial circuit that impacted the forms of labor, consumption, servitude, freedom and belonging in specific ways. In these complex historical locations, identity was situational and commodified, bestowed, adopted, marketed or appropriated as an entitlement, an avenue to freedom, or a marker distinguishing who was protected by British 'rights and liberties' and who was not.[66]

The decentring ebbs, flows, currents, eddies and tides of Atlantic approaches to colonial history provide a vital means for exploring competing articulations of whiteness during the age of abolition. A historical geography of white identity framed in these terms would not only pay attention to the reproduction of white metropolitan identities against the non-white colonial or enslaved other, but also consider the articulation of non-metropolitan white identities that sit in an uneasy relationship with metropolitan discourses. In this context, the focus on Barbados is not merely a 'local' study, but one with widespread implications. This is because, in part, 'all empire is local'.[67] From this basis, it is important to locate Barbados within the Atlantic world (figure 1.1) and to highlight some of the most salient features of its society in terms of a 'uniqueness' that was 'the result of the interaction between local particularity and a wider web of connections'.

Barbados and the Atlantic world

The 'expansion of Europe' into the Americas after 1492 involved the seizure of land and people, the establishment of settlements, mines and plantations, the destruction of autochthonous populations, imperial rivalry and the transportation of large numbers of people – voluntarily or forcibly. This 'expansion' brought large

---

[64] Baker, *Geography and history*, p. 162. See J. Allen, D. Massey and A. Cochrane, *Rethinking the region* (London, 1998), pp. 1–5.

[65] T. Ballantyne, *Orientalism and race: Aryanism in the British empire* (New York: Palgrave, 2002), p. 1; Lester, *Imperial networks*, p. 5. See also E. Boehmer, *Empire, the national, and the postcolonial, 1890–1920: Resistance in interaction* (Oxford: Oxford University Press, 2002); E. Wolf, *Europe and the people without history* (Berkeley: University of California Press, 1982), p. 3.

[66] K. Wilson, *The island race: Englishness, empire and gender in the eighteenth century* (London: Routledge, 2003), p. 16. See also Sinha, *Colonial masculinity*; A. L. Stoler and F. Cooper, 'Between metropole and colony: Rethinking a research agenda', in Cooper and Stoler, *Tensions of empire*.

[67] Wilson, *The island race*, p. 213, n. 74. See also K. F. Olwig (ed.), *Small islands, large questions: Society, culture and resistance in the post-emancipation Caribbean* (London: Frank Cass, 1995).

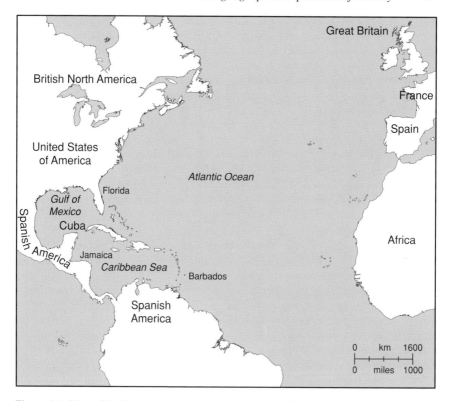

Figure 1.1 Map of the North Atlantic in the early nineteenth century.

parts of Africa, the Americas, Europe and Asia into a developing capitalist world-system and wrought social and environmental change.[68] During the eighteenth century, the Caribbean (figure 1.2) was the 'principal fulcrum' of this emerging world-system as both a microcosm of these transformations and the focus of flows of capital, people, ships, animals, pathogens, trade goods, information and ideas.[69]

---

[68] D. W. Meinig, *Atlantic America, 1492–1800* (New Haven: Yale University Press, 1986); I. Wallerstein, *The modern world-system I: Capitalist agriculture and the origins of the European world-economy in the sixteenth century* (London: Academic Press, 1974), p. 44; I. Wallerstein, *The modern world-system II: Mercantilism and the consolidation of the European world-economy, 1600–1750* (London: Academic Press, 1980); Wolf, *Europe and the people without history*.

[69] F. W. Knight (ed.), *The slave societies of the Caribbean*, vol. III of *General history of the Caribbean* (London: UNESCO Publishing, 1997), p. 3; Ogborn, 'Historical geographies of globalisation, c. 1500–1800'; B. C. Richardson, *The Caribbean in the wider world, 1492–1992: A regional geography* (Cambridge: Cambridge University Press, 1992); D. Watts, *The West Indies: Patterns of development, culture and environmental change since 1492* (Cambridge: Cambridge University Press, 1987).

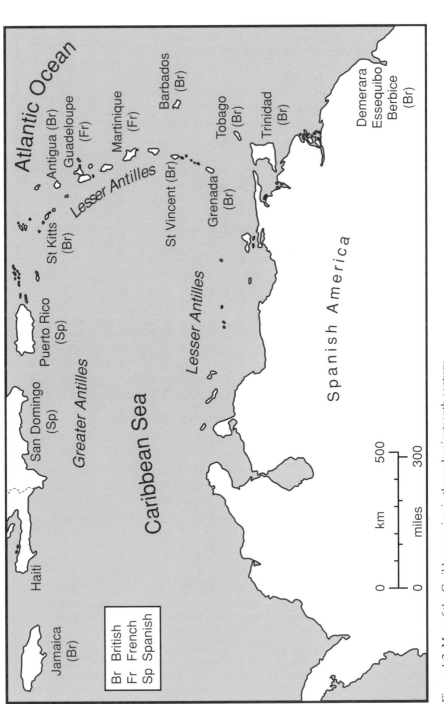

Figure 1.2 Map of the Caribbean region in the early nineteenth century.

The 'discovery' of Barbados by Portuguese navigators in 1536 was part of the 'expansion of Europe'. Low-lying and coralline, it covers only 430 square kilometres and is the most easterly of the West Indian islands. Although the Portuguese found the island uninhabited, as successive Amerindian populations had fled, and allegedly named the island after the bearded fig trees growing there,[70] it was not until the second quarter of the seventeenth century that Barbados was colonised and then by the English. Initial English involvement in the Caribbean was limited to piracy and raids against Spain, but, in 1624, English plantation settlement in the West Indies commenced at St Kitts and in 1627 colonists arrived with the intention of establishing a permanent settlement in Barbados. Far from Spanish attacks, with fertile soil, empty of Amerindian populations and, by virtue of favourable trade winds, well connected to Europe and Africa, the colonisation of Barbados was an important aspect of the creation of an English Atlantic empire.[71]

Between 1629 and 1645, the socio-political pattern of the colony was established, with the foundation of the port capital, Bridgetown, the division of the island into parishes and the creation of a parliament in 1639 (figure 1.3).[72] Initially, the colonists cultivated tobacco utilising white indentured labour on small farms, but as the European markets became glutted, they looked for other opportunities. With the aid of Dutch technical expertise, capital, enslaved labour and trade routes, the commercial production of sugar cane began in the early 1640s.[73] The prosperity that resulted from this 'sugar revolution' transformed Barbados into England's most valuable colony and Bridgetown occupied the premier place in English trade with the colonies.[74] The shift to the growing of labour-intensive sugar cane also led to a dramatic rise in the importation of enslaved Africans. Although Barbados was surpassed by Jamaica in terms of wealth by the end of seventeenth century, its planters remained prosperous and the island became known as a mature sugar colony with a 'settled' character.[75]

---

[70] 'Barbados': the bearded ones. The colony's name was often (mis-)spelt in British metropolitan writing as 'Barbadoes'. To avoid repetition, this has not been indicated with '[sic]'.

[71] Beckles, *History of Barbados*; Dunn, *Sugar and slaves*; Gragg, *Englishmen transplanted*.

[72] For an account of the development of plantation system and the associated landscape in Barbados, see Watts, *West Indies*, pp. 184–211.

[73] G. A. Puckrein, *Little England: Plantation society and Anglo-Barbadian politics, 1627–1700* (New York: New York University Press, 1984); Watts, *West Indies*, pp. 182–184; N. Zahedih, 'Economy', in Armitage and Braddick, *The British Atlantic world*, pp. 56–57. R. Hughes, 'The origin of Barbadian sugar plantations and the role of the white population in sugar plantation society', in A. O. Thompson (ed.), *Emancipation I: A series of lectures to commemorate the 150th anniversary of emancipation* (Bridgetown: Cedar Press, 1984). More recently, Larry Gragg has questioned the relative importance of Dutch finance as against that provided by metropolitan and colonial English sources. See Gragg, *Englishmen transplanted*.

[74] P. L. V. Welch, *Slave society in the city: Bridgetown, Barbados, 1680–1834* (Kingston: Ian Randle, 2003).

[75] J. P. Greene, 'Empire and identity from the Glorious Revolution to the American Revolution', in P. J. Marshall, *The Oxford history of the British Empire*, vol. II; K. Watson, *Civilised island*.

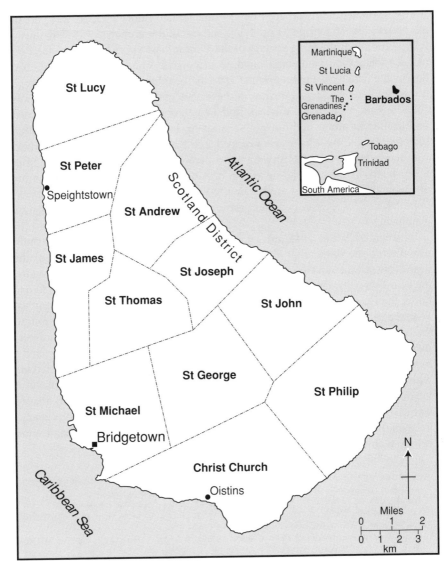

Figure 1.3 Political map of Barbados.

Settlement did not come without problems and the island was afflicted by defor-estation, soil exhaustion, hurricanes, disease, pestilence and drought.[76] In addition,

[76] R. H. Grove, *Green imperialism: Colonial expansion, tropical island Edens and the origins of environmentalism, 1600–1860* (Cambridge: Cambridge University Press, 1995); B. C. Richardson, *Caribbean in the wider world*, pp. 13–37.

the white population lived in fear of French invasion and revolt by the enslaved people. During the eighteenth century, however, Barbados acquired a reputation as relatively free from the revolts that affected other colonies. In contrast, the dread of French invasion intensified, especially during the Anglo-French struggle for continental supremacy of the 'long' eighteenth century, which included the Seven Years War (1756–63), and the Revolutionary and Napoleonic Wars (1792–1815). Nevertheless, Barbados was never captured by imperial rivals and was spared the pillage of other Caribbean islands. Its geographical position made it strategically important and it was used as the base for British military operations in the Eastern Caribbean.[77]

Imperial Atlantic networks

Barbados was a colony within the expanding empire of an emergent English and, from 1707, British state.[78] Throughout its colonial history, the plantocracy sought to secure their property and the right to self-legislate, in the context of centralising and financially extractive impulses emanating from the metropole. During the English Civil War, for instance, Barbados was initially neutral but Royalist sympathisers, including émigrés from England, moved in favour of independence from Oliver Cromwell's Commonwealth. Mythologised as resistance to the 'Usurpation' of the English monarchy, this became an important aspect of white political and cultural identity in Barbados and was frequently evoked as a sign of local commitment to liberty.[79] Parliament responded by dispatching a fleet to subordinate the colony in 1651 and enforce the mercantilist principles enshrined in the Navigation Acts. After a three-month blockade, the colonists agreed to recognise parliamentary rule in exchange for continued self-government as codified in a charter of 1652. For the Barbadian plantocracy, this agreement represented 'imperial constitutional recognition of their right to rule themselves, and a confirmation that propertied Englishmen overseas were also entitled to the same political freedoms that they enjoyed at home'.[80] Yet, after the restoration of Charles II in 1660, the English state continued to impose mercantilist structures. In 1663, for example, a 4.5 per cent duty was established on exports from the island to finance imperial administration and defence. This would remain a source of controversy and trans-Atlantic dispute.

Tensions between metropolitan and colonial authority were most obviously manifest in conflict between the legislature and the various royal governors, who

---

[77] N. A. T. Hall, 'Governors and generals: The relationship of civil and military commands in Barbados, 1783–1815', *Caribbean Studies* 10 (1971).

[78] J. P. Greene, 'Liberty, slavery, and the transformation of British identity in the eighteenth-century West Indies', *Slavery and Abolition* 21 (2000); E. Mancke, 'Empire and state', in Armitage and Braddick, *The British Atlantic world*; I. K. Steele, *The English Atlantic, 1675–1740: An exploration of communication and community* (Oxford: Oxford University Press, 1986).

[79] See chapter 5.

[80] Beckles, *History of Barbados*, p. 26; E. H. Gould, 'Revolution and counter-revolution', in Armitage and Braddick, *The British Atlantic world*, pp. 205, 206; Mancke, 'Empire and state', p. 183.

were appointed by the British Crown to represent imperial interests.[81] Such tensions were exacerbated in the late eighteenth century by the constitutional crisis and eventual war between Britain and its American colonies. Before the American Revolution, there were parallels between the political development of the West Indian and North American colonies, and large numbers of Barbadians were sympathetic to the American cause.[82] Such sentiments were an articulation of what Jack Greene terms an 'imperial constitution' based on the proposition that British colonists in the West Indies and North America were entitled to the same rights as British subjects. In the context of deteriorating trans-Atlantic relations and fearing that its own rights would be curtailed, the Assembly of Barbados challenged the governor's authority and deployed Revolutionary rhetoric, something that would recur in the defence of slavery. Although some imperial officials saw such efforts in proto-revolutionary terms, the colonists based their claims to rights on fundamental English liberties and the British constitution.[83]

France's support for the Americans and its declaration of war on Britain in 1779 curtailed these revolutionary gestures. Fears about French invasion and enslaved unrest, along with economic weakness, meant that the West Indies took a political trajectory different from that of the continental colonies.[84] Although the Assembly aspired to greater administrative autonomy and there were pro-American disturbances, it is unlikely that many Barbadians ever desired separation from Britain. Instead, Barbados's colonists sought to manage their relations with the metropole within the framework of the empire. Of particular importance in this regard were the colonial agents. They were selected and given instructions by the Assembly, and were, in some ways, 'the precursors of modern-day professional lobbyists'. Acting as the main source of intelligence for the colonists and their most active representatives, the colonial agents were chiefly concerned with lobbying against imperial 'interference' in domestic affairs.[85] Barbados's planters were also partly

---

[81] Governors could suggest legislation and all bills required gubernatorial approval. The governor also presided over the local courts of appeal and could recommend individuals to the clemency of the Crown. In the absence of the governor, the most senior Council member took over administration as 'president'. See K. Watson, *Civilised island*; I. K. Steele, *English Atlantic*, chapter 12.

[82] Carrington, 'West Indian opposition'; Greene, 'Liberty, slavery'. For a recent account that downplays the island colonists' political aspirations, see O'Shaughnessy, *Empire divided*.

[83] Gould, 'Revolution and counter-revolution', p. 208; J. P. Greene, *Peripheries and center: Constitutional development in the extended policies of the British Empire and the United States, 1607–1788* (Athens, GA, and London: University of Georgia Press, 1986), p. xi.

[84] Carrington, 'West Indian opposition', 31; Greene, 'Changing identity in the British Caribbean', pp. 259–263. Even Jamaica, perhaps the island best placed for independence, did not go down the revolutionary path. See E. K. Brathwaite, *The development of creole society in Jamaica, 1770–1820* (Oxford: Clarendon Press, 1971).

[85] D. Hall, *A brief history of the West India Committee* (Bridgetown: Caribbean Universities Press, 1971); O'Shaughnessy, *Empire divided*; A. J. O'Shaughnessy, 'The formation of a commercial lobby: The West India Interest, British colonial policy and the American Revolution', *Historical Journal* 40 (1997); L. M. Penson, *The colonial agents of the West Indies: A study in colonial administration, mainly in the eighteenth century* (London: University of London Press, 1924);

represented in Britain by London merchants, absentee planters and members of Parliament with West Indian connections. These came together institutionally, particularly in the London-based West India Committee. Support also came from the royal family, parts of the navy and commercial interests in Bristol, Liverpool and other ports. This 'West India Interest' was not invulnerable, however, and the declining prosperity of the West Indies reduced its size and influence in Parliament. Nor was it a coherent force and there were tensions between merchants and planters, and between the London-based West India Committee and similar bodies in other parts of the country. The actions of the colonists could also create difficulties for the metropolitan West India Interest. Whereas it tended to promote reform to stave off imperial interference, those in the West Indies tended to react more stridently to antislavery campaigning. Moreover, the British-based merchants and absentee planters did not live with slavery every day and were able more easily to assimilate the shift in British public opinion against the institution. For the resident planters who dominated Barbados, on the other hand, race and slavery were determinative facts of everyday life and could not be put aside so easily.[86]

Slavery and race

One of the shortfalls of Atlantic world-historical perspectives is a tendency to portray the ocean as a kind of inland sea of Western civilisation.[87] An alternative model takes inspiration from histories of the black diaspora and its role in the making of the modern world.[88] For Joseph Roach,

[t]he concept of a circum-Atlantic world (as opposed to a transatlantic one) insists on the centrality of the diasporic and genocidal histories of Africa and the Americas, North and South, in the creation of the culture of modernity.[89]

As such a perspective demonstrates, '[n]o longer is Atlantic history available in any color, so long as it is white'.[90] White culture, politics and identity in Barbados must be located in the context of the histories and geographies of slavery and race.

B. M. Taylor, 'Our man in London: John Pollard Mayers, agent for Barbados, and the British Abolition Act, 1832–1834', *Caribbean Studies* 16 (1977). See also I. K. Steele, *English Atlantic*, chapter 12. For an account of North American interest groups, see A. G. Olson, *Making the empire work: London and American interest groups, 1690–1790* (Cambridge, MA: Harvard University Press, 1992).

[86] E. K. Brathwaite, *Creole society*, pp. 178–179; D. B. Davis, *Problem of slavery in the age of revolution*.

[87] Armitage, 'Three concepts of Atlantic history', p. 17.

[88] See C. L. R. James, *The black Jacobins: Toussaint L'Ouverture and the San Domingo revolution* (London: Allison and Busby, 1980); E. Williams, *Capitalism and slavery* (London: André Deutsch, 1964). For examples of more recent interest in the creolisation and hybridisation of culture and identity, rather than commerce or politics, see P. Gilroy, *The black Atlantic: Modernity and double consciousness* (London: Verso, 1993); Roach, *Cities of the dead*.

[89] Roach, *Cities of the dead*, pp. 4–5.

[90] Armitage, 'Three concepts of Atlantic history', p. 15.

The formation of slave society

From the middle of the seventeenth century, the 'sugar revolution' engendered a shift away from indentured white labour, towards the importation of enslaved African labour, and slavery was '*the* determinative institution' in the development of Barbados.[91] Over time, the enslaved population became increasingly dominated by those born locally rather than transported from Africa, particularly as planters sought to promote natural growth during the eighteenth century.[92] Nevertheless, although Barbados was the first island to see natural growth in its enslaved population, rates of death and infant mortality remained high.[93]

Throughout the period of slavery, most Barbadian enslaved people lived on plantations.[94] Spaces of both disciplinary and sovereign power, these estates were characterised by an incarcerating labour regime based on surveillance, punishment and the 'psychology of terror'.[95] Barbados's slaveholders also attempted to control the enslaved population through political, legal and military institutions. The first comprehensive slave code was the 1661 'Act for the better ordering and governing of Negroes', which formed the basis of slave codes in other English colonies. Amended in 1688, the act established provisions that 'covered almost every area of the slave's social existence', including a pass system to limit mobility and punishments for theft, striking a Christian and running away.[96] The 1688 act remained in force throughout the eighteenth century and was buttressed by militia and imperial forces. These laws rendered enslaved people as property: as chattel, to be sold to meet debts or seized in cases of bankruptcy, and as real estate, subject to the laws of inheritance. This status was matrilineal and the children of enslaved women became the property of their mother's owner. Moreover, black people could not give evidence in cases involving whites and a white person could wilfully kill someone they owned and be liable only for a £15 fine. These formal laws, together with acts of coerced servitude in fields, house or town and quotidian practices of subjection, served to define the parameters of everyday race relations.

---

[91] J. Walvin, *Questioning slavery* (London: Routledge, 1996), p. 75. The reasons for this shift to enslaved labour remain a subject of historiographic debate. See F. W. Knight, *The slave societies of the Caribbean*.

[92] See chapter 2.

[93] In 1645, there were 5,680 enslaved people on the island. This number rose to 46,602 in 1683 and to 68,000 in 1748, or four enslaved people per white person. See P. Curtin, *The Atlantic slave trade: A census* (Madison, 1969), pp. 52–64, 89, 119; C. A. Palmer, 'The slave trade, African slavers and the demography of the Caribbean to 1750', in F. W. Knight, *The slave societies of the Caribbean*.

[94] Handler, 'Plantation slave settlements'.

[95] G. K. Lewis, *Main currents*, p. 5. On sovereign and disciplinary forms of power, see M. Foucault, *Discipline and punish: The birth of the prison* (London: Penguin, 1979). For discussions of such ideas in the context of slave and plantation societies, see J. S. Duncan, 'Embodying colonialism? Domination and resistance in nineteenth-century Ceylonese coffee plantations', *Journal of Historical Geography* 28 (2002); T. C. Holt, *The problem of freedom: Race, labor, and politics in Jamaica and Britain, 1832–1938* (London: Johns Hopkins University Press, 1992); L. Stewart, 'Louisiana subjects: Power, space and the slave body', *Ecumene* 2 (1995).

[96] Beckles, *History of Barbados*, pp. 33–34; H. McD. Beckles, 'Social and political control in slave society', in F. W. Knight, *The slave societies of the Caribbean*.

To this extent, Saidiya Hartman talks about white people's 'enjoyment' of black enslavement, a term that links ownership, abuse and the taking of pleasure in enslaved property.[97] This idea expands the understanding of enslavement beyond the immediate property relationship between enslaver and enslaved, into the area of physical, psychic and sexual (dis)possession.[98] It emphasises that whiteness and blackness were positional goods in Barbados because all black people could be subjected to (dis)possessive practices by any white person. One of the most obvious results of the white sexual 'enjoyment' of enslaved people was the emergence of a mixed-race population. Although most continued to labour as enslaved workers, a small *free* coloured population emerged in the eighteenth century as the result of manumission. Yet although they were free, they faced severe social, economic and political disadvantages.[99]

Barbados's slave code represented the codification of English ideas of racial and cultural difference in which black people were a 'brutish', 'heathenish' and 'dangerous kind of people'.[100] Although the exact relationship between slavery and racism remains a subject of controversy, it is clear that the entrenchment of plantation slavery was accompanied by developments in discourses of collective difference. During the seventeenth century, religious concepts of difference were to the fore, and the underlying principle through which enslavement was rationalised was the possession of full Christian knowledge. A racial dimension achieved primacy in the eighteenth century, with blackness no longer seen as the external manifestation of an internal paganism, but itself a source of symbolic degradation and identified with evil bestiality.[101] Naturalised notions of moral, cultural, physical and mental black inferiority served to justify slavery. They were critical to the articulation of a discourse of *white supremacism* that was central to white self-identity. Nevertheless, by the late eighteenth century, a more paternalistic understanding of racial difference had emerged, in which white dominance was linked to duty, benevolence and the mutual dependency of enslaver and enslaved.

---

[97] S. V. Hartman, *Scenes of subjection: Terror, slavery, and self-making in nineteenth-century America* (Oxford: Oxford University Press, 1997), p. 23; M. St Pierre, *Anatomy of resistance: Anti-colonialism in Guyana, 1823–1966* (London: Macmillan Education, 1999), p. 10.

[98] I find '(dis)possession' a useful term with which to refer to slavery because it encapsulates the treatment of enslaved people as property and objects (to be possessed), *and* the quotidian and institutionalised denial of their subjecthood (to be dispossessed).

[99] G. Heuman, 'The social structure of the slave societies in the Caribbean', in F. W. Knight, *The slave societies of the Caribbean*. The terms 'free people of colour' and 'free coloured' are usually used to refer to formerly enslaved people who had been freed or to the children of women of this status. It denotes *both* black and mixed-race people. In late eighteenth- and early nineteenth-century Barbados, the terms 'free coloured', 'free mulatto' and 'free black' were used almost interchangeably and often about the same individual. Members of this group tended to refer to themselves as 'the free coloured people'. Some modern writers use the terms 'freedmen' and 'freed people' to refer to the same group. See chapter 3.

[100] Beckles, *History of Barbados*, pp. 33–34; Chaplin, 'Race', p. 154; T. Allen, *Invention of the white race*, vol. I; W. Jordan, *White over black* (Chapel Hill, 1968).

[101] A. Beahrs, '"Ours alone must need be Christians": The production of enslaved souls on the Codrington estates', *Plantation Society in the Americas* 4 (1997); G. K. Lewis, *Main currents*.

This was an essential component of the *planter ideal* that was expressed and enacted by elite slaveholders. It supplemented but did not replace the dominant white supremacism.[102]

White supremacist ideas and practices did not go unresisted and although enslavement was brutal and destructive, enslaved people did contest and adapt the conditions in which they lived. The largest revolt occurred in 1816 and conspiracies were uncovered in 1649, 1675 and 1692.[103] Unlike Jamaica, the ubiquity of plantations in Barbados and a well-developed security system militated against mass flight and the development of maroon communities,[104] but there were innumerable acts of theft, poisoning, sabotage, foot dragging, temporary flight and mockery. In addition, the growing of food on small plots and involvement in huckstering (the internal marketing system of the island) were forms of 'proto-peasant' activity that challenged enslaved people's constitution as property.[105] Nor was Afro-Caribbean resistance a purely 'local' phenomenon. News and rumours of revolts, uprisings and plots circulated around the Atlantic world and inspired others to seek freedom. Carried in newspapers, reported in the fearful letters of planters and passed by word of mouth, stories surrounding the 1791 revolt in the French colony of St Domingue, later the independent republic of Haiti, were of particular importance. Thus, the actions of black Barbadians were part of a wider 'Revolutionary Atlantic'.[106]

Resistance to slavery could also involve the regeneration and preservation of cultural elements of African origin. The early development of Barbados's plantation system and rapid population turnover produced deculturating conditions and a much less Africanised culture than in Haiti or Jamaica. Nevertheless, enslaved people in Barbados did retain and develop their own cultural forms, as evident in music, dance, magico-religious beliefs and rights of birth, marriage and death.[107] Nor were Afro-Caribbean people only involved in the reproduction of their own cultures; they also contributed to the development of transcultural forms across Barbadian society. In that enslaved people can be said to have interfered with the articulation of discourses of whiteness and the reproduction of 'pure' white

---

[102] Paternalism should not be understood as a 'check' on racism, but another manifestation of enslavement. (Dis)possession occurred *through* paternalism, not despite it.

[103] H. McD. Beckles, *Black rebellion in Barbados: The struggle against slavery, 1627–1838* (Bridgetown: Antilles Publications, 1984); M. Craton, 'Slave culture, resistance and emancipation in the British West Indies', in M. Craton (ed.), *Empire, enslavement and freedom in the Caribbean* (Oxford: James Currey, 1997). See also St Pierre, *Anatomy of resistance*, pp. 12–15.

[104] Maroon communities consisted of enslaved people who had run away and their descendants, often living in the wilderness. See S. W. de Groot, C. A. Christen and F. W. Knight, 'Maroon communities in the circum-Caribbean', in F. W. Knight, *The slave societies of the Caribbean*.

[105] M. Craton, 'The rope and the cutlass: Slave resistance in plantation America', in Craton, *Empire, enslavement and freedom in the Caribbean*, p. 191.

[106] Linebaugh and Rediker, *Many-headed hydra*; Sheller, *Democracy after slavery*, pp. 71–86.

[107] A. Benítez-Rojo, *The repeating island: The Caribbean and the postmodern perspective*, translated by J. Maraniss (London: Duke University Press, 1992), pp. 38–39; M. Craton, 'Forms of resistance to slavery', in F. W. Knight, *The slave societies of the Caribbean*, pp. 233–236.

forms, this transculturation – or rather creolisation – has important implications for approaches to white colonial identities in the age of abolition.[108]

Pro- and antislavery networks

Although enslaved African labour was central to the transformation of Barbados into a prosperous sugar colony, Davis argues that slavery had always been a 'problem' in Western culture. [109] In 1657, George Fox, founder of the Quakers, wrote one of the first pleas on behalf of enslaved Africans, and Quakers also expressed antislavery sentiments in Barbados itself as early as 1671, to which the plantocracy responded with intensified discrimination.[110] Despite such early attacks on slavery, the desire for exotic products and tax revenue ensured metropolitan support and it was not until the 1760s and 1770s that metropolitan attitudes began to shift against slavery. Whilst the question of why slavery was brought to a formal end is one that continues to tax historical scholars,[111] the shift in attitudes has been related to the growth of Christian evangelism in Britain, the loss of the North American colonies that split the slaveholding interest, the increasingly competitive world sugar market, enslaved resistance and the rise of industrial capitalism.[112]

Antislavery became a popular cause in Britain in the 1780s, especially amongst radicals and Nonconformists, and in 1787, the Society for Effecting the Abolition of the Slave Trade was created.[113] Through such organisations, campaigners developed informational networks that brought the brutality of colonial slavery to wider notice. They used information from philanthropic 'fact-finding' missions, sympathetic correspondents – including colonial civil servants and missionaries – and travel accounts as propaganda to lobby government officials and sway public opinion. They circulated it in the mainstream and humanitarian press, in the periodicals of religious and missionary organisations and in published books and pamphlets. Sympathetic MPs, like William Wilberforce, led a parliamentary campaign for the abolition of the trade in enslaved Africans, which, it was believed, would undermine slavery itself. All this fed the popular clamour expressed in petitions, pamphleteering and public meetings. In consequence, antislavery was one of the first examples of extra-parliamentary agitation for reform and attracted

---

[108] See pp. 37–40 below.   [109] D. B. Davis, *Problem of slavery in Western culture.*
[110] D. B. Davis, *Problem of slavery in the age of revolution*, chapter 5; Blackburn, *The overthrow of colonial slavery.*
[111] Walvin, *Black ivory.* For a useful discussion, see Sheller, *Democracy after slavery*, pp. 18–33.
[112] The literature on the causes of the ending of slavery is voluminous. For example, see Blackburn, *The overthrow of colonial slavery*; Craton, *Testing the chains*; D. B. Davis, *Problem of slavery in the age of revolution*; P. J. Kitson (ed.), *Slavery, abolition and emancipation: Writings in the British Romantic period – The slavery debate*, 8 vols., vol. II (London: Pickering and Chatto, 1999); O'Shaughnessy, *Empire divided*; Turley, *The culture of English antislavery*; Walvin, *Questioning slavery*; Williams, *Capitalism and slavery.*
[113] Chaired by Granville Sharp, author of *A representation of the injustice and dangerous tendency of tolerating slavery* (London, 1769), it attracted the support of Thomas Clarkson.

great public support.[114] Its aim was nothing less than to shape imperial policy towards British interests in the West Indies and beyond, and to recast the culture of empire.[115]

The emergence and institutionalisation of antislavery did not go unchallenged and the West Indian planters used their well-developed and formalised webs of support to contest the efforts of antislavery campaigners. At the forefront of this defence was the metropolitan West India Interest, but proslavery lobbying was not the preserve of metropolitan individuals and organisations – colonists in Barbados and elsewhere were also involved in the defence of slavery. Some of these efforts were indirect, occurring through the colonial agents, but West Indian planters and other colonists were also involved in the dissemination of proslavery propaganda and petitions, as well as the production and sponsorship of more diffuse pro-West Indian forms, including landscape paintings, local histories, georgic poems, pro-West Indian plays and novels, and 'guides' to agricultural practice.[116] The aim of these was to penetrate 'the space of metropolitan culture' and saturate Britain with the 'epistemologies of colonization'. These visual and textual artefacts circulated around the Atlantic world, disseminated by supporters of slavery who sought to influence metropolitan opinion and defend colonial rights.[117]

By the 1770s, British opinion had moved sufficiently against slavery that its supporters no longer simply defended it as morally justifiable, but also as a strategic and economic necessity. Key features of proslavery discourse included negative racial stereotypes about people of African origin – including the physical and sexual danger to the white population supposedly posed by emancipation – as well as arguments about the 'English liberties' of West Indian colonists and the sanctity of the planters' property. They also claimed that without enslaved labour and the maintenance of a 'proper' socio-racial order, the West Indies would be ruined to the detriment of the empire as a whole. Antislavery campaigners responded with arguments about the essential unity of humankind, the inefficiency of enslaved

---

[114] Blackburn, *The overthrow of colonial slavery*; Cell, 'The imperial conscience'; S. Drescher, 'Public opinion and the destruction of British colonial slavery', in Walvin, *Slavery and British society, 1776–1846*. British abolitionists were also involved in campaigns in other countries and thus in establishing international humanitarian networks. See L. C. Jennings, *French anti-slavery: The movement for the abolition of slavery in France, 1802–1848* (Cambridge: Cambridge University Press, 2000).

[115] C. L. Brown, 'Empire without slaves: British concepts of emancipation in the age of the American Revolution', *William and Mary Quarterly* 3rd series 56 (1999).

[116] J. Gilmore, *'Creoleana: or, social and domestic scenes and incidents in Barbados in days of yore' and 'The fair Barbadian and faithful black; or, a cure for the gout', by J. W. Orderson: Edited and with a new introduction* (Oxford: Macmillan, 2002); J. Gilmore, *The poetics of empire: A study of James Grainger's* The Sugar Cane (1764) (London: Athlone Press, 2000); G. Quilley, 'Pastoral plantations: the slave trade and the representation of British colonial landscape in the late eighteenth century', in G. Quilley and K. D. Kriz (eds.), *An economy of colour: Visual culture and the Atlantic world, 1660–1830* (Manchester: Manchester University Press, 2003); S. Seymour S. Daniels and C. Watkins, 'Estate and empire: Sir George Cornewall's management of Moccas, Herefordshire and La Taste, Grenada, 1771–1819', *Journal of Historical Geography* 24 (1998).

[117] Sandiford, *Cultural politics of sugar*, p. 16.

labour and the morally corrupting effects of slavery on the white colonists. Barbados was a particular target of the antislavery campaign because its slave laws were seen as harsh and the plantocracy as conservative. Equating 'the defense of colonial liberties with the defense of slavery', Barbadian planters and their agents in Britain reacted 'excitedly' to each attack.[118] What was at stake, they believed, was their cultural status, political rights and white identity.

White creole culture, politics and identity

This book considers white Barbadian identities in terms of their constitution through, and articulation in, contested discourses,[119] practices and projects within the context of the slavery controversy. At the same time, it focusses on those upper- and middle-class colonisers who were the target and authors of such signifying acts. The specific focus is akin to what Gillian Rose terms the 'master subject'. Drawing on the work of Donna Haraway, Rose defines this as 'the subject consti- tuted as white, bourgeois, heterosexual and masculine'.[120] As used here – that is in relation to the place of Barbados in the Atlantic world during the age of abolition – the term has additional purchase as it is suggestive of the link between the artic- ulation of white colonial identity and the (dis)possession of non-white subjects. The master subject in this context, then, is 'white', 'enslaving', 'masculine' and 'creole'.

'White', in its broadest sense, refers to people of European descent; in the Barbadian context, this means mainly people of English, Scottish and Irish origin. 'White' is also used to refer to a shared 'racial' identity that encompasses not only these ethnic nationalisms but also West Indian, including Barbadian, settler identities. In this sense, it is close to the modern usage of 'Anglo-Saxon'. Yet, 'white' is not an essential racial identity, but a political one. In many colonial con- texts, 'the very notion of whiteness was seen not as fixed by birth, but altered by environment and secured by class'.[121] Hence, whiteness was 'an extraordinarily ambitious social project' that judges that 'most whites are unworthy of whiteness'.

---

[118] C. Levy, 'Slavery and the emancipation movement in Barbados, 1650–1833', *Journal of Negro History* 55 (1970); O'Shaughnessy, *Empire divided*, p. 247.

[119] Discourses are understood as 'frameworks that embrace particular combinations of narratives, concepts, ideologies and signifying practices'. More than ensembles of texts, discourses are 'sites of struggle for meaning and also a means of constituting humans as individuals'. See T. J. Barnes and J. S. Duncan (eds.), *Writing worlds: Discourse, text and metaphor in the representation of landscape* (London: Routledge, 1992), p. 8; S. Mills, *Discourse* (London: Routledge, 1997), p. 68; M. Wetherell and J. Potter, *Mapping the language of racism: Discourse and the legitimation of exploitation* (Hemel Hempstead: Harvester Wheatsheaf, 1992).

[120] D. J. Haraway, 'Situated knowledges: The science question in feminism and the privilege of partial perspective', in D. J. Haraway (ed.), *Simians, cyborgs and women: The reinvention of nature* (London: Free Association, 1991); G. Rose, *Feminism and geography: The limits of geographical knowledge* (Cambridge: Polity Press, 1993), p. 6.

[121] T. Allen, *Invention of the white race*, vol. I; T. Allen, *The invention of the white race*, vol. II, *The origin of racial oppression in Anglo-America* (London: Verso, 1997); Bonnett, *White identities*, pp. 21, 22; Stoler, *Race and the education of desire*, p. 105.

Within this project, historically and geographically contingent ideas of racial difference were crucial in defining 'white' as normal. This was particularly the case in slave societies, where the contrast with the 'black' African other was used to forge solidarity across the colonising population. In Barbados, whiteness also came to be defined in terms of Englishness (and, to a lesser extent, Britishness),[122] which became the dominant form of ethnic whiteness by the late eighteenth century, and through links to Anglicanism, liberty, royalism, military sacrifice and colonial loyalty.[123] White identity was codified in law and institutionalised in access to power. It was reproduced through a variety of social, economic and political practices, and expressed in ritualised performances, from sitting in the best seats in church, to striking an enslaved body with a whip. Whiteness rewarded those defined as white with a 'public and psychological wage', which was realised in poor relief and militia tenancies.[124] It was also represented in writing and the spoken word.

The term 'enslaving' draws attention to the critical place of plantation slavery in the formation of West Indian settler culture and constitution of colonial subjecthood. Through the institutionalisation and quotidian performance of racialised identities, white Barbadians were protected from enslavement, whilst non-whites were rendered vulnerable to (dis)possession, acts of psychic and physical abuse, and sexual exploitation. The right and capacity to enslave racialised others was also central to the meaning of 'freedom' in Barbados. Whilst all of white Barbadian society was connected in some way to slavery, it was the upper and middle classes that were most involved in ownership and are the primary focus here. Yet, whilst upper-class planters dominated the society, there were disagreements over, and challenges to, this leadership from smaller proprietors and those involved in the day-to-day management of plantations.

The consideration of white culture, politics and identity in Barbados in terms of 'masculine' articulations reflects, in part, the nature of available historical sources, which are almost entirely those produced by men.[125] This stems, in turn, from male control of judicial and military institutions, and their enfranchisement within the political system. Men were also economically dominant in Barbados and, although some white women were slaveholders, this was primarily within the urban and domestic contexts; most planters were male. Male planters were also the target of the antislavery campaign, whilst white mistresses were generally ignored. Nevertheless, although the main focus is on the political and cultural articulations of Barbados's white, male, upper- and middle-class slaveholders – and

---

[122] On the relationship between Englishness and Britishness, see n. 36 in this chapter.
[123] Greene, 'Liberty, slavery'.
[124] W. Du Bois, cited in Roediger, *The wages of whiteness*, p. 12.
[125] Barbadian material on white women is extremely limited, particularly in comparison with that from the American South. See B. Brereton, 'Text, testimony and gender: An examination of some texts by women on the English-speaking Caribbean from the 1770s to the 1920s', in V. Shepherd, B. Brereton and B. Bailey (eds.), *Engendering history: Caribbean women in historical perspective* (London: James Currey, 1995).

their representation within imperial and humanitarian discourses – the positioning of other groups, including white women, is also of importance.[126]

The final element of how white identities in Barbados are approached is perhaps the most significant. At its simplest, 'creole' is used to refer to non-indigenous people, flora or fauna born in or naturalised to the Americas. It is also used to signify 'processes of cultural change in the Caribbean and elsewhere' that 'contributed to the development of a distinctive society and culture that was neither European nor African, but "Creole"', a process known as 'creolisation'.[127] Most modern uses derive from the Barbadian-born poet and historian, Edward Kamau Brathwaite:

'Creole society' is the result . . . of a complex situation where a colonial polity reacts, as a whole, to external metropolitan pressures and at the same time to internal adjustments made necessary by the juxtaposition of master and labour, white and non-white, Europe and colony, European and African . . . in a culturally heterogeneous relationship.[128]

Crucially, Brathwaite associates creole with those who had 'intimate knowledge of and were in some way committed by experience and attachment to the West Indies' – who had, in short, some commitment to their 'area of living' and 'were possessive of and proud of the space of the Americas'.[129] This definition is important because it highlights the spatiality of creole and the importance of geographical imaginations in the articulation of belonging in the Caribbean.

Creolisation was connected to 'the inescapable consequences of the process of European expansion into the Americas after the sixteenth century'.[130] The associated mass enslavement of Africans by European settlers in the Caribbean served to 'creolize settler identities' in the West Indian societies.[131] In this light, the controversies over slavery in the age of abolition can be seen, in part, as involving a metropolitan assessment of white West Indian creolisation. Here, creolisation is used in relation to whiteness understood 'less as a kind of ontology and more as a kind of cultural identity'.[132] This, then, is a politicised use of creolisation that

---

[126] See chapters 3, 4 and 6.

[127] C. Allen, 'Creole: The problem of definition', in V. A. Shepherd and G. L. Richards (eds.), *Questioning creole: Creolisation discourses in Caribbean culture* (Kingston: Ian Randle, 2002), p. 23.

[128] E. K. Brathwaite, *Contradictory omens*, p. 11. See also K. Balutansky and M. Sourieau (eds.), *Caribbean creolization: Reflections on the cultural dynamics of language, literature, and identity* (Gainesville: University Press of Florida, 1998).

[129] E. K. Brathwaite, *Creole society*, p. xv; E. K. Brathwaite, *Roots* (Ann Arbor: University of Michigan Press, 1993), p. 129; F. Smith, *Creole recitations: John Jacob Thomas and colonial formation in the late nineteenth-century Caribbean* (Charlottesville and London: University of Virginia Press, 2002), p. 3.

[130] F. W. Knight, 'Pluralism, creolization and culture', in F. W. Knight, *The slave societies of the Caribbean*, pp. 272–273.

[131] Greene, 'Liberty, slavery', 28. For example, Michael J. Braddick argues that West Indian planters 'projected an image of gentility that rested on a brutality which came, eventually, to be repugnant to mainland British sensibilities'. See M. J. Braddick, 'Civility and authority', in Armitage and Braddick, *The British Atlantic world*, p. 107.

[132] K. A. Yelvington, 'The anthropology of Afro-Latin America and the Caribbean: Diasporic dimensions', *Annual Review of Anthropology* 30 (2001), 250.

draws attention to the 'tensions of empire' generated by the 'problem of slavery' and to the consequences of the emergence of metropolitan humanitarianism for the colonists of slave societies.

From this basis, creole can be conceptualised in three main ways. Firstly, it is used to refer to a metropolitan discourse through which settler subjects, institutions and cultures were represented as negatively transformed by the colonial encounter. Many British visitors to the West Indies remarked upon the changes in the speech, dress, behaviour, mores and racial purity of the descendants of European colonisers. Like other white West Indians, white Barbadian culture, politics and identity were shaped by slavery and 'it was whiteness which distinguished them from those they held as slaves'. With racial difference such a 'pervasive assumption',[133] many metropolitan commentators and visitors came to view white West Indian culture as not English. It is important to recognise, however, that the purported differences between white West Indians and white Britons was not *solely* a matter of actual cultural change and adaptation in the Caribbean, but also revealed the efforts being made to recast British identity *in the metropole*.[134] Doubts about the 'Englishness' of white West Indians reflected their construction as white 'mimic men' who were not 'English English' because they relied on enslaved labour, lived in tropical climes, engaged in interracial sex and were *nouveaux riches* upstarts. Like many European colonials, white West Indians were often viewed disparagingly from the metropole 'as *parvenus*, cultural incompetents, morally suspect, and indeed "fictive" Europeans, somehow distinct from the real thing'.[135] In this context, the white creole Barbadian subject is understood as a negatively represented figure within a metropolitan discourse that was characterised by an 'anti-Caribbean animus'. 'Creole', then, becomes a marker of asserted white West Indian *difference*.[136]

Secondly, creole is used with respect to the ambivalent signifying practices that metropolitan attacks engendered amongst white Barbadian slaveholders, their supporters, agents and institutions. Here, creole signifies the peripheral manifestation of the 'tensions of empire' as Barbados's whites were 'trapped in a dilemma of discovering themselves to be at once the same, and yet not the same, as the country of their origin'.[137] Again, my interest is not in any *essential* basis for such

---

[133] C. Hall, *Civilising subjects*, p. 75.

[134] A similar point is made by Edward Said in his refusal of the distinction between 'pure' and 'political' knowledge and his argument that 'for a European or American studying the Orient there can be no disclaiming . . . that he comes up against the Orient as a European or an American first, as an individual second' (Said, *Orientalism*, p. 11). Although descriptions of white West Indian culture can be a valuable source of information, it is difficult to afford them an unproblematic ethnographic status, especially at a time when metropolitan attitudes were shifting against slavery.

[135] B. Anderson, *Imagined communities: Reflections on the origin and spread of nationalism* (London: Verso, 1991), p. 92; H. K. Bhabha, 'Of mimicry and man', *The location of culture* (London: Routledge, 1994); Stoler, *Race and the education of desire*, p. 102.

[136] Gragg, *Englishmen transplanted*, p. 191; G. K. Lewis, *Main currents*, p. 25; Smith, *Creole recitations*, p. 3.

[137] John H. Elliott, 'Introduction: Colonial identity in the Atlantic world', in Canny and Pagden, *Colonial identity in the Atlantic world*, p. 9.

conflicted identities but in the cultural and political consequences that stemmed from particular moments of controversy over slavery during the age of abolition. White colonial responses in Barbados were manifested in a vacillation between *loyalty* and *opposition* that was evident in what Sandiford terms 'negotiation'.[138] In the former mode, white Barbadians claimed their rights and identity as freeborn Englishmen, and repudiated their 'creole-ness' through a Little Englandist discourse of allegiance and indispensability to the British empire.[139] Nevertheless, the institutionalisation of the 'problem of slavery' in the British antislavery campaign and the crystallisation of an 'anti-Caribbean animus' also engendered assertions of West Indian difference that paralleled those 'subaltern English nationalisms and countercultural patriotisms . . . generated in a complex pattern of antagonistic relationships with the supra-national and imperial world'. The form this 'creole self-fashioning' took in Barbados is encapsulated by Lewis's term 'Anglo-Saxon and anti-English'.[140] Yet, this creole proto-nationalism did not find overt articulation in pro-independence sentiment, as it did in South America or the United States, partly because of the vulnerability of white slaveholders to enslaved revolt.[141]

Thirdly, creole is used to emphasise the role of subjugated groups in the transculturation, hybridisation and creolisation of purportedly dominant discourses, practices, projects and identities.[142] In the context of the slavery controversy, this emphasises the role of free people of colour, poor whites and the enslaved people themselves in forging, reinforcing, undermining and utilising dominant articulations of whiteness and the proslavery arguments to which they were connected. Thus, rather than an analysis of whiteness that views it as a unified articulation, it is instead treated as a transcultural project in which the acts and representations of non-white and non-elite white subjects were crucial. This perspective is vital for exploring the contested nature of white identities in the slavery controversy. Although the exploration of subaltern acts and representations is a problematic enterprise, strategies that involve reading the colonial archive 'against the grain' can be employed. Such an approach is hindered by the paucity of non-plantocratic texts. Nevertheless, the colonial archive was not shaped by the will of the coloniser alone and 'one may find an "anti-archive" lying *within* the archive itself'.[143]

---

[138] Sandiford, *Cultural politics of sugar*. See p. 14 above.
[139] Gragg, *Englishmen transplanted*, p. 191.
[140] Gilroy, *Black Atlantic*, p. 11; G. K. Lewis, *Main currents*, pp. 25, 75; Pratt, *Imperial eyes*, pp. 5, 172–197.
[141] Greene, 'Liberty, slavery'; O'Shaughnessy, *Empire divided*, pp. 34–57.
[142] Barnett, 'Impure and worldly geography', 240; E. K. Brathwaite, *Contradictory omens*; Pratt, *Imperial eyes*.
[143] J. S. Duncan, 'Complicity and resistance in the colonial archive: Some issues of method and theory in historical geography', *Historical Geography* 27 (1999), 123; C. McEwan, 'Cutting power lines within the palace? Countering paternity and eurocentrism in the "geographical tradition"', *Transactions of the Institute of British Geographers* 23 (1998), 374. For a discussion of the possibilities and limits of counter-histories, see R. Guha and G. C. Spivak (eds.), *Selected subaltern studies* (Oxford: Oxford University Press, 1988); L. Mani, 'Cultural theory, colonial texts: Reading eyewitness accounts of widow burning', in L. Grossberg, C. Nelson and P. Treichler (eds.), *Cultural*

Taking the four elements of the colonial 'master subject' together, white creole culture, politics and identity in Barbados can be understood in a number of ways. The articulation of white identities was an expression of colonial self-identity. This was connected to a project of planter hegemony within Barbados based primarily on a white, ancestrally English, Anglican, proslavery identity, and the values and traditions associated with this. Yet, there was conflict between racialised and propertied visions of the colonial order and, in this sense, different articulations of the whiteness were part of a struggle over legitimacy and power within the colony. White culture, politics and identity were also a focus of the slavery controversy. The Atlantic-wide struggle over discourses of whiteness was part of the effort to influence metropolitan public opinion and the imperial authorities, which were targeted by official campaigning and lobbying and, indirectly, through the rebellious efforts of enslaved people. The antislavery campaign sought to promote intervention in the affairs of Barbados and the other West Indian colonies to bring about verifiable improvements in the social and spiritual condition of enslaved people, and later to grant freedom. Those antislavery attacks that portrayed the brutality of slavery fashioned a 'humanitarian narrative' that sought to encourage such interventionism.[144] Moreover, in the context of the imperial government's reticence about post-American Revolution intervention, and especially given the self-legislating nature of Barbados, the antislavery campaign had to work to undermine the authority and legitimacy of the Barbadian plantocracy as slaveholders *and* legislators. In contrast, positive articulations of white colonial identities formed part of the defence of slavery by emphasising that Barbadian slaveholders were politically responsible, entitled to political autonomy and engaged in the good treatment of the enslaved workforce. These discourses were connected to the contested imaginative geographies of Barbados's location within either a slave or free world, and thus to the necessity for, and legitimacy of, imperial intervention in the colonial society. The articulation of Barbados as Little England was an important part of this and in these ways, the constitution of white identity in Barbados was linked – always – to the (dis)possession of black people.

studies (London: Routledge, 1992); G. C. Spivak, 'Can the subaltern speak?' in C. Nelson and L. Grossberg (eds.), *Marxism and the interpretation of culture* (London: Macmillan, 1988); G. C. Spivak, 'Subaltern studies: Deconstructing historiographies', in D. Landry and G. MacLean (eds.), *The Spivak reader* (London: Routledge, 1996).

[144] T. Laqueur, 'Bodies, details, and the humanitarian narrative', in L. Hunt (ed.), *The new cultural history* (London: University of California Press, 1989).

2

Joshua Steele and the 'improvement' of slavery

In the mid-1810s, the leading British abolitionist, Thomas Clarkson, wrote a short unpublished piece in praise of an obscure figure, Joshua Steele (figure 2.1).[1] Described by Clarkson as 'a Gentleman and a Scholar', Steele had come to Barbados in 1780 to take direct control of a number of sugar plantations. He spent his time on the island up to his death in 1796 seeking to promote a more 'rational' approach to plantation management on the island through the establishment of the Barbados Society for the Encouragement of Arts, Manufactures and Commerce (known simply as the Barbados Society of Arts). This was one of the first learned institutions to be founded in a British colony and was modelled on the London Society for the Encouragement of Arts, Manufactures and Commerce – today the Royal Society of Arts – of which Steele was already a member. He also sought to make more radical changes to the system of slavery on his own estates by banning the use of the whip, paying his enslaved workers and establishing a system of tenancy. Such reforming efforts brought Steele to the attention of the British antislavery campaign, which viewed his approach to plantation management as a 'model for all slave estates'. Indeed, a considerable part of Clarkson's *Thoughts on the necessity of improving the condition of the slaves in the British colonies* (1823), which set out the theoretical agenda of the resurgent British antislavery campaign in the 1820s, was devoted to promoting Steele's ideas.[2] Given his abolitionist plaudits, it is unsurprising that Steele did not enjoy the same distinction amongst his fellow planters in Barbados. The initial enthusiasm that greeted the creation of the Barbados Society of Arts soon waned when it became clear that Steele's reforming vision extended to the institution of slavery. Prior to his death, Steele had become an isolated figure whose theories were dismissed as unrealistic and running contrary to the wisdom and experience of local planters. In the

---

[1] T. Clarkson, 'Encomium', c. 1815, Additional Manuscripts 41267A, fo. 78, British Library.
[2] T. Clarkson, *Thoughts on the necessity of improving the condition of the slaves in the British colonies, with a view to their ultimate emancipation* (London: Richard Taylor, 1823); D. Turley, *The culture of English antislavery, 1780–1860* (London: Routledge, 1991), p. 31. For more on Clarkson and the post-1823 emancipation campaign, see chapter 5, pp. 143–144.

Figure 2.1   Joshua Steele (third from left). Detail from J. Barry, *The distribution of premiums in the Society of Arts*, fifth in the series *The progress of human culture and knowledge* (c. 1777–84), RSA 101464, Royal Society of Arts, London, www.bridgeman.co.uk.

1820s, when Steele's ideas were revived by the antislavery campaign, contemporary supporters of slavery sought to tarnish his reputation by portraying him as a cruel and ignorant master with a dogmatic belief that 'everything [was] wrong in Barbados'.[3]

---

[3] N. Lucas, Miscellaneous Items, Lucas Manuscripts, Vol. 1, Reel 15, p. 64, Bridgetown Public Library (henceforth BPL).

The life and legacy of Joshua Steele embodied many features of the controversy over slavery, particularly as they played out locally in Barbados. Amidst the claims and counter-claims about unsubstantiated theories, local expertise, cruelty and reform, two competing visions of what constituted 'enlightened' plantation management can be discerned. One was local to Barbados. Moves toward the 'amelioration' of slavery were well established amongst Barbados's slaveholders by the late eighteenth century, and they saw and promoted themselves as enlightened masters. Yet, the limits to this amelioration were evident in the opposition to Steele's more far-reaching reforms, which challenged local racial ideologies and extended to the more fundamental alteration of the relationship between slaveholders and enslaved people. For this reason, Steele's ideas were attractive to abolitionists, who were trying to envisage colonial development without slavery.[4] His ideas were similar to the secular abolitionist arguments against slavery, and he provided information for the imperial government on the West Indies and corresponded with abolitionists.

Although Steele spent the final sixteen years of his life as a planter in Barbados, he was part of international networks of scientific exchange and antislavery campaigning. Nevertheless, he is often relegated to the footnotes of history and portrayed as a visionary reformer, an enigma or an eccentric failure.[5] My aim is not to 'rescue' Steele from obscurity, but to use him to exemplify broader issues. By taking Steele, situating him in an intellectual context, sketching his biography and analysing the reception of his ideas, it is possible to consider the relationship between plantation management and white culture in Barbados. The opposition he faced attests to the way in which slavery was naturalised in Barbados, the entrenched nature of white supremacist notions of black inferiority and the extent to which a 'planter ideal' was articulated by the island's elite proprietors.

Amelioration and 'enlightened' plantation management

Before turning to consider Steele's vision for Barbados, a little needs to be said about the model that dominated the practice and theory of plantation management when he came to the island. The 'sugar revolution' of the middle of the seventeenth century had made Barbados reliant on high levels of imports of enslaved African labour and American-grown food. Yet, by the second half of the eighteenth century,

---

[4] Christopher Brown notes that, for the early abolitionists 'the challenge lay not only in the power of vested interests but also in the limited ways they and others troubled by slavery could imagine the future development of the American colonies'. See C. L. Brown, 'Empire without slaves: British concepts of emancipation in the age of the American Revolution', *William and Mary Quarterly* 3rd series 56 (1999), 274.

[5] See M. Martin, 'Joshua Steele', *Journal of the Royal Society of Arts* 117 (1968); J. Newman, 'The enigma of Joshua Steele', *Journal of Barbados Museum and Historical Society* 19 (1951); J. Sheppard, *The 'redlegs' of Barbados: Their origins and history* (Millwood, NY: KTO Press, 1977), pp. 45–46.

the overall aim of most Barbadian planters was to make their estates more self-sufficient and less reliant on expensive inputs.[6] In a sense, they were attempting to produce a more sustainable form of slavery. These efforts were part of a system of thought and practice that can be termed 'amelioration':

> As an economic measure, amelioration can be defined . . . as a system by which money that would otherwise have been spent on hiring and buying . . . [enslaved people] . . . was used to improve the lot of the existing stock of slaves in order to induce them to breed their replacements.[7]

The most obvious consequence of amelioration and its early implementation was that Barbados was the only British sugar colony that experienced a natural increase in its enslaved population before the abolition of the Atlantic slave trade.[8] The positive benefits of amelioration were promoted in writing on plantation management and formed part of the propaganda war with the British antislavery campaign, which attacked plantation slavery as an inhumane, immoral and irrational socio-economic system.

Amongst the most important aspects of amelioration were pro-natalist policies. These evolved as plantation managers reversed their labour supply policy from hostility towards reproduction and a reliance on the slave trade, to an emphasis on natural growth and a reluctance to import. In part, this reflected white fears that African-born people were more resistant to enslavement than those born into slavery. Efforts to encourage the natural reproduction of the enslaved population focussed on the body of the enslaved woman and involved reduced workloads, financial and social incentives for childbirth and rearing, and reductions in physical punishment. Pro-natalist policies were adopted from the middle of the eighteenth century and, as with other innovations in plantation management, this occurred earlier in Barbados than elsewhere in the British West Indies. Indeed, by the 1770s, most plantation managers were committed to 'slave breeding'.[9] Other aspects of

---

[6] H. Cateau, 'Conservatism and change implementation in the British West Indian sugar industry, 1750–1810', *Journal of Caribbean History* 29 (1995); J. H. Galloway, *The sugar cane industry: An historical geography from its origins to 1914* (Cambridge: Cambridge University Press, 1989).

[7] R. Sheridan, *Doctors and slaves: A medical and demographic history of slavery in the British West Indies, 1680–1834* (Cambridge: Cambridge University Press, 1985), p. 140. See also J. R. Ward, 'The British West Indies in the age of abolition, 1748–1815', in P. J. Marshall (ed.), *The Oxford history of the British Empire*, vol. II, *The eighteenth century* (Oxford: Oxford University Press, 1998).

[8] R. B. Sheridan, 'Why the condition of the slaves was "less intolerable in Barbados than in the other sugar colonies"', in H. McD. Beckles (ed.), *Inside slavery: Process and legacy in the Caribbean experience* (Bridgetown: Canoe Press, 1987).

[9] H. McD. Beckles, *Centering woman: Gender discourses in Caribbean slave society* (Oxford: James Currey, 1999), p. 15; H. McD. Beckles, *Natural rebels: A social history of enslaved black women in Barbados* (New Brunswick, NJ: Rutgers University Press, 1989); W. Marshall, 'Amelioration and emancipation (with special reference to Barbados)', in A. O. Thompson (ed.), *Emancipation I: A series of lectures to commemorate the 150th anniversary of emancipation* (Bridgetown: Cedar Press, 1984), p. 73. See also H. McD. Beckles, 'To buy or to breed: The changing nature of labour supply policy in Barbados during the 18th century', unpublished Department of History seminar paper, University of West Indies (1987).

the more general concern with the health of slaves included the growth of short-term hiring, which allowed a manager to conserve their own workforce from arduous labour, improvements in the provision of healthcare and greater self-sufficiency of food provision. In time, the production of locally grown food replaced the purchase of poorer quality imports and led to an improvement in the diet of the enslaved workforce.[10]

The early adoption of ameliorative practices in Barbados is accounted for by J. H. Galloway with a model based on two assumptions about planters as a class: firstly, they 'had access to information about innovations' through personal communications and the burgeoning literature on plantation management that emerged in the second half of the eighteenth century; secondly, they 'adopted innovations only when it made good economic sense to do so'. From this basis, patterns of innovation and conservatism can be related to the net benefits of particular innovations, the available natural resources and the state and size of the markets for sugar products. Consequently, Galloway demonstrates that the early onset of plantation production, limited natural resources and involvement in the competitive international market made Barbados's planters amongst the first to adopt new practices, and the island became a centre of innovation.[11] From the middle of the eighteenth century, economic decline and a steep rise in the price of enslaved labour 'led proprietors to view their slaves as objects of great capital value, and consequently led them to preserve their labour force by any method which seemed expedient'. During the last quarter of the eighteenth century, the American Revolutionary War and the subsequent disruption of trade robbed Barbados of its source of food imports. As a consequence, land was given over to the cultivation of staples. In addition, the emergence of British abolitionism led the promotion of 'improved' plantation management to be viewed as a way of defending slavery. Some far-sighted planters may also have recognised the possibility of a future suspension of the slave trade.[12]

Whilst clearly related to local factors, the adoption of ameliorative policies in Barbados must also be seen in the light of the general culture of 'improvement', which John Gascoigne characterises as the more efficient use of resources based on reason and the elimination of waste. Efforts were made in this direction by British landowners during the eighteenth century and 'improvement' was promoted in domestic agricultural literature. For Gascoigne, 'improvement' is also the accurate description of the commercially orientated, pragmatic, progressive culture that

[10] H. Cateau, 'The new "negro" business: Hiring in the British West Indies 1750–1810', in A. O. Thompson (ed.), *In the shadow of the plantation: Caribbean history and legacy* (Kingston: Ian Randle, 2002); J. S. Handler, 'Plantation slave settlements in Barbados, 1650s to 1834', in Thompson, *In the shadow of the plantation*, p. 131; Sheridan, *Doctors and slaves*, p. 174.

[11] J. H. Galloway, 'Tradition and innovation in the American sugar industry, c. 1500–1800: An explanation', *Annals of the Association of American Geographers* 75 (1985), 335.

[12] Cateau, 'Conservatism and change'; W. Marshall, 'Amelioration and emancipation', 24; A. J. O'Shaughnessy, *An empire divided: The American Revolution and the British Caribbean* (Philadelphia: University of Pennsylvania Press, 2000); R. B. Sheridan, 'The West India sugar crisis and British slave emancipation, 1830–1833', *Journal of Economic History* 21 (1961).

characterised the Enlightenment in England.[13] Thus, the English Enlightenment was 'less oppositional than its continental counterpart, more comprehensive, practical rather than speculative'.[14] Yet, as David Livingstone and Charles Withers have argued, the geography of the Enlightenment was more complex than such *national* differences would suggest:

> Far from simply being understood as a European movement with particular national expression, it becomes possible to conceive of the Enlightenment as being sited, produced, debated in *local spaces and circumstances* as well as being apparent at national levels.[15]

Attention to colonial spaces is crucial here: as is clear from the ameliorative shift in plantation management in eighteenth-century Barbados, efforts at 'improvement' were not confined to Europe and there were clear links with colonisation. Materially and imaginatively, the colonies provided 'a theatre for the Enlightenment project'.[16] Yet, when Enlightenment theories travelled, they were transformed and resisted. For example, when the estate management policies of 'improving' owners were transferred from England to the Caribbean, there was often much greater concern in the slave societies with labour supervision and reproduction, and less with the adoption of technological innovations. As with the ameliorative policies in Barbados, this reflected the dominance of a plantation model predicated on the deployment of a large and relatively disposable labour force. This was a socio-economic practice embedded in particular ideas about race. In the Caribbean, these racialised discourses were not fundamentally altered by the shift towards 'improved' plantation management.[17]

Recognition of the racially embedded character of plantation management strategies in the Caribbean must be added to accounts of amelioration. For example, it is useful to extend Galloway's emphasis on the importance of planters' access to knowledge beyond information about market conditions or new forms of

---

[13] J. Gascoigne, *Joseph Banks and the English Enlightenment: Useful knowledge and polite culture* (Cambridge: Cambridge University Press, 1994).

[14] S. Daniels, S. Seymour, and C. Watkins, 'Enlightenment, improvement, and the geographies of horticulture in later Georgian England', in D. N. Livingstone and C. W. J. Withers (eds.), *Geography and enlightenment* (London: University of Chicago Press, 1999), p. 345. See also D. N. Livingstone and C. W. J. Withers (eds.), *Geography and enlightenment* (London: University of Chicago Press, 1999); R. Porter, *Enlightenment: Britain and the creation of the modern world* (London: Penguin, 2000); S. Wilmot, *'The business of improvement': Agriculture and scientific culture in Britain, c. 1700–c. 1870*, Historical Geography Research Series, vol. 24 (1990).

[15] C. W. J. Withers and D. N. Livingstone, 'Introduction: On geography and enlightenment', in Livingstone and Withers, *Geography and enlightenment*, p. 4.

[16] N. B. Dirks, *Colonialism and culture* (Ann Arbor: University of Michigan Press, 1992), p. 6. See also R. Drayton, *Nature's government: Science, imperial Britain, and the 'improvement' of the world* (London: Yale University Press, 2000); S. Seymour, 'Historical geographies of landscape', in B. Graham and C. Nash (eds.), *Modern historical geographies* (Harlow: Prentice Hall, 2000).

[17] S. Seymour, S. Daniels and C. Watkins, 'Estate and empire: Sir George Cornewall's management of Moccas, Herefordshire and La Taste, Grenada, 1771–1819', *Journal of Historical Geography* 24 (1998). For an account of 'improvement' in another colonial context, see J. Gascoigne, *The Enlightenment and the origins of European Australia* (Cambridge: Cambridge University Press, 2002).

technology, to include 'common-sense' assumptions based on racist stereotypes and prejudices. Planters thought they 'knew' how their enslaved labour forces behaved and how best to treat them. They 'knew' that they were superior to black people. They 'knew' that black people could not be trusted but, if treated moderately, could be worked more easily. An analysis of the practice of plantation management should address these forms of 'knowledge'. Thus, 'knowledge' can be thought of not only as neutral information, but also as discursive understanding. From this perspective, planter rationality must be understood as being embedded within, or framed by, racial ideologies. These provided the discursive context for amelioration, rendering some actions as 'reasonable' and 'rational' responses to the circumstances, whilst others – such Steele's proposals for a gradual shift towards free-wage labour – were 'unrealistic', 'implausible' and 'visionary'. The nature and boundaries of these discourses became evident when the dominant socio-economic system was subject to attack.[18] For this reason, exploring the competing visions of what amounted to 'rational' plantation management policy, as propounded by Steele and local planters, emphasises how Enlightenment ideas of reason and progress could be articulated in different ways in the same space, and how 'improvement' was 'an ideological battleground, a contested terrain'.[19] This, in turn, sheds light on the character of the white slaveholding culture and the constitution of the white identities in Barbados.

Joshua Steele and plantation 'improvement'

The early parts of Joshua Steele's life have been a subject of much conjecture. William Dickson, abolitionist and editor of his work, gives 1700 as the year of Steele's birth and claims that he was Irish, although there is no clear basis for either assertion.[20] Nevertheless, the details of Steele's life from the mid-century are more certain. In 1750, he married Sarah Hopkins Osborn, a wealthy woman whose first husband – Robert Osborn – had been a large landowner in Barbados. Enjoying the life of a leisured gentleman, Steele lived with his wife in Hyde Park Corner, a fashionable part of eighteenth-century London.[21] In 1756, Steele became a member of the Society for the Encouragement of Arts, Manufactures and Commerce. The Society of Arts, as it was commonly known, had been founded in London in

---

[18] For other work that considers cultural aspects of the plantation, see J. S. Duncan, 'Embodying colonialism? Domination and resistance in nineteenth-century Ceylonese coffee plantations', *Journal of Historical Geography* 28 (2002); L. Stewart, 'Louisiana subjects: Power, space and the slave body', *Ecumene* 2 (1995).

[19] Daniels, Seymour and Watkins, 'Enlightenment, improvement, and the geographies of horticulture', p. 347.

[20] W. Dickson, *Mitigation of slavery in two parts. Part 1: letters and papers of the late Hon. Joshua Steele . . . Part 2: letters to Thomas Clarkson* (London, 1814). Dickson's speculations have been reproduced by other writers and form the basis of Steele's entry in the *Dictionary of National Biography*, vol. 54 (1898), p. 129.

[21] Martin, 'Joshua Steele', 41.

1754 by William Shipley. Its general aim was to promote economic, social, cultural and technological 'improvement' through the application of science, reason and endeavour. The society concerned itself with agricultural and arboricultural development in the British colonies, particularly focussing on the promotion of tree planting and plant transfer programmes in the West Indies.[22] Steele's abilities and success within the society were evident from the high-profile posts he held. During his most active period, 1759–63, he chaired five committees – Colonies and Trade, Mechanics, the Polite Arts, Miscellaneous and Correspondence – and in 1779 he was elected vice-president.[23] Beyond the society, he published an influential work on the theory of speech. He was consulted by John Pringle and Joseph Banks, both presidents of the Royal Society, for his views on musical artefacts collected in the South Pacific, and contributed to the *Philosophical Transactions*.[24] He corresponded with Benjamin Franklin, later to be one of the founding fathers of the American state, and wrote a treatise on the relations between Britain and its North American colonies. Steele also corresponded on informal terms with Banks, Pringle and Franklin. In sum, Steele was a respectable, leisured gentleman of the Enlightenment, 'a man very much of the eighteenth century'.[25] Working in both the areas of 'art' and 'science', he was an embodiment of the optimism afforded by 'rationality', 'endeavour' and 'reason'. As he wrote to Banks: 'If any man, according to his abilities, was to endeavour to analise [sic], dissect and thoroughly examine any one subject, much might be done in improving both art and science.'[26]

In 1759, after the deaths of his wife and stepdaughter, Steele came into possession of a series of estates in Barbados, which Sarah had inherited from her first husband. These holdings amounted to over 1,000 acres in extent and included the plantations called Guinea and Kendal's. The latter represented a considerable landholding and both estates were well situated and only twelve miles from Bridgetown. The returns from these estates enabled Steele to continue his life of leisured endeavour in Britain. Although the Society of Arts' interest in the West

---

[22] R. H. Grove, *Green imperialism: Colonial expansion, tropical island Edens and the origins of environmentalism, 1600–1860* (Cambridge: Cambridge University Press, 1995); H. T. Wood, *A history of the Royal Society of Arts* (London: John Murray, 1913). The Society of Arts did not receive its 'Royal' prefix until 1908.

[23] D. G. C. Allan, 'Joshua Steele and the Royal Society of Arts', *Journal of the Barbados Museum and Historical Society* 22 (1954–5).

[24] J. Steele, 'Account of a musical instrument, which was brought by Captain Fourneaux from the Isle of Amsterdam in the South Seas to London in the year 1774, and given to the Royal Society', *Philosophical Transactions* 65 (1775); J. Steele, *An Essay towards establishing the melody and measure of speech to be expressed and perpetuated by certain symbols* (London, 1775); J. Steele, 'Remarks on a larger system of reed pipes from the Isle of Amsterdam, with some observations on the nose flute of Otaheite', *Philosophical Transactions* 65 (1775).

[25] Martin, 'Joshua Steele', 41. Brown argues that the British emancipation schemes of the 1770s and 1780s arose 'in part and indirectly' from the broader tendency of European thinkers to apply 'lessons drawn from the emerging science of human society'. The case of Steele demonstrates that the links between Enlightenment thought and approaches to slavery could be much more direct. See C. L. Brown, 'Empire without slaves', 289.

[26] J. Steele to J. Banks, 28 November 1779, Additional Manuscripts 33977, fo. 111, British Library.

Indies may be attributable to Steele, it was not until the late 1770s that he made any reference to his West Indian holdings.[27] In 1778, however, Steele began to attend meetings of the Society of West India Merchants and Planters, an organisation that had been formed to protect the interests of absentee slaveholders. His interest in plantation management may have flowed from his concern with colonial development or perhaps was a response to financial problems caused by falling returns from his plantations, not an uncommon situation for absentee owners.[28] Whatever his motives, Steele took a direct interest in West Indian affairs by travelling to Barbados in early 1780. Although he only seems to have intended to pay a short visit, he did not leave the island again and died there in 1796.

The Barbados that Steele arrived at in March 1780 seemed to be an island in economic distress. Long-term problems of soil degradation, increased indebtedness and foreign competition had been compounded by the closure of American markets to Barbadian sugar and the cessation of American food and other imports – both occasioned by the Revolutionary War.[29] Planters also complained about drought and crop pests, and six months after Steele's arrival the island was struck by a severe hurricane, which destroyed much of its infrastructure and killed 2,033 enslaved people and over 6,000 cattle, and caused £1,320,000 in damage. Steele also discovered that his own estates had been badly mismanaged, something that lends weight to the idea that it was financial difficulties that had forced him to travel to Barbados in the first place. For Steele, these personal concerns and the general problems facing the island made Barbados an ideal site for the application of his improving zeal.[30] As he wrote later to the Society of Arts:

The novelty of everything here, Plants, Vegetation, seasons, slaves, Brutality of my species, the endeavours of our infant Society to open the Eyes of the people of Capacity & Feeling to amend many things that are amiss, and the attention I give to model the government of my own Estates, so as to add to the happiness of my Slaves, without injury to myself, have so completely amused me, by finding constant occupation for me, that 5 years have passed over, in this eternal Summer Country, like only one.[31]

In response to this self-appointed undertaking, Steele established a body of similar purpose to the London Society of Arts. Although there was a more developed

---

[27] Grove, *Green imperialism*, pp. 268, 275; Martin, 'Joshua Steele'.

[28] West India Committee, *Minutes of the West India Merchants and Planters*, 3 March 1778, fo. 140, 14 April 1778, fo. 150, 29 April 1778, fo. 151, Institute of Commonwealth Studies; D. Hall, 'Absentee-proprietorship in the British West Indies, to about 1850', *Jamaican Historical Review* 4 (1964).

[29] O'Shaughnessy, *Empire divided*, pp. 162–167.

[30] Report of the Lords of the Committee of Council Appointed for the Consideration of All Matters Relating to Trade and Foreign Plantations . . . presented by Hon. William Pitt, 25 April 1789, Part 3, Barbados [facsimile], reproduced in S. Lambert (ed.), *House of Commons Sessional Papers of the Eighteenth Century*, vol. LXIX (Wilmington, 1975), 286–318; J. Steele to W. Dickson, 30 September 1790, in Dickson, *Mitigation of slavery*, p. 3; J. Newman, 'The enigma of Joshua Steele', 13.

[31] J. Steele to London Society of Arts (henceforth LSA), 24 May 1785, A12/34, Royal Society of Arts (henceforth RSA).

tradition of public associations in Barbados than elsewhere in the West Indies,[32] this was one of the first learned societies to be founded in the colonies. On 5 July 1781, the Barbados Society for the Encouragement of Arts, Manufactures and Commerce held its founding meeting:

It is proposed to form a Society of Gentlemen of liberal Education and approved Characters, to have *regular Meetings*, once a month (besides casual Adjournments). For the Purposes of discovering the *useful Qualities* of the *Native Productions*, animal, vegetable, and fossil, *of Barbados*; and to consider of, and to devise the Means of encouraging such *useful Arts*, as may excite *Industry* among the *lower Classes* of the white and free Inhabitants; and in general, to deliberate on, and to promote, as far as they can, whatever they judge will contribute, to the *Advancement* of the *Arts, Manufactures, and Commerce* of this Island.[33]

Standing committees were formed to investigate potential domains for 'encouragement' and 'promotion', including 'Agriculture and Botany', and 'Manufactures and Mechanics'. Initial areas for investigation included the use of native plants to make textiles, the establishment of a workhouse to encourage small-scale manufacturing amongst the island's poor whites and the production of local dyes. The society's initial membership stood at fourteen and included planters, planter-politicians and doctors. Steele was elected president of the nascent body. His first act was to write to the Royal Society and the Societies of Arts in Dublin and London, informing them of the foundation of the Barbados Society and requesting aggregate membership.[34]

For Steele, this was the beginning of a project in which Barbados was to be integrated into a wider network of Enlightenment and 'improvement'. He corresponded with the London Society of Arts and Joseph Banks, and although his request for aggregate membership of the Royal Society came to nothing, he continued to send and receive plant specimens and other organic matter. In 1782, Steele wrote to the imperial authorities, advocating the introduction of new plant varieties to the colony. He was also active in Barbados itself, writing letters to the press in favour of the reform of slavery, publishing a broadsheet on the same subject and using his own estates as models for his improving vision. In 1790, Steele was made a member of the Council at the request of Governor David Parry, who had joined the Barbados Society of Arts and was influenced by Steele's efforts. Steele was later made chief justice and used both posts to promote legal change.[35] Thus, in

---

[32] During the 1780s, Barbados had a Library Society, a Commercial Society and English Society. See K. Watson, *The civilised island, Barbados: A social history, 1750–1816* (Bridgetown: Graphic Printers, 1979); *Barbados Mercury*, 3 May, 7 June, 16 August 1787, Reel 19, BPL.

[33] Society for the Encouragement of Arts, Manufactures and Commerce in Barbados (henceforth BSA), *Institution and First Proceedings* (Barbados, 1784), 5 July 1781, p. 3.

[34] J. Steele to J. Banks, 14 July 1781, Additional Manuscripts 33977, fo. 135, British Library; J. Steele to LSA, 14 July 1781, A11/45, RSA.

[35] J. Steele to J. Banks, 22 June 1783, Additional Manuscripts 33977, fo. 204, British Library; J. Steele to the Lords of Trade and Plantations, 28 February 1782, CO 28/35, fo. 312, The National Archives (henceforth TNA); J. Steele, *To the equity and policy of a great nation* (Bridgetown, 1789); Minutes of Council, 27 July 1790, CO 28/63, fo. 23–24, TNA; 'A judicial charge delivered by the Hon. Joshua Steele, as Chief Justice', in Dickson, *Mitigation of slavery*, pp. 183–192.

his writing, the management of his estates, his official capacities and through the society, Steele set forth his 'enlightened' vision for Barbados until his death in late 1796.

Steele's project must be read in terms of, and as a contribution to, the broader controversies over slavery that had burst into life in the late eighteenth century. He read pro-reform and antislavery texts, such the Reverend James Ramsay's *An essay on the treatment and conversion of African slaves* (1784), and from 1787 his thinking took on a more abolitionist character.[36] At the same time, the antislavery campaign made its presence felt in the British Parliament. In February 1788, a committee of the Lords of the Privy Council was established to gather evidence on the slave trade. Governor Parry asked Steele to contribute and he used the opportunity to set out his particular analysis of the problems facing Barbados and the 'rational' solutions he believed necessary. What was especially significant about Steele's contribution was that he was the only planter actually resident in the West Indies to present evidence and much store would have been set by his views. Steele's involvement in this inquiry also brought him to the attention of the British antislavery campaign.[37] In 1790, the prominent abolitionist, William Dickson, wrote to Steele to request information about his endeavours in Barbados. Dickson had lived on the island and his writing was known to Steele. After Steele's death, Dickson collected together much of his work and produced the *Mitigation of slavery* (1814), an antislavery tract based largely on Steele's efforts in Barbados.[38] It was this book that brought Steele to the attention of Thomas Clarkson. As already noted, Steele was important for the antislavery campaign because after the abolition of the Atlantic slave trade in 1807, attention shifted to *how* emancipation could be achieved. Steele's ideas seemed to provide a means of lessening the worst aspects of slavery and simultaneously preparing enslaved people for their eventual freedom. These arguments were contested by supporters of slavery in the early 1820s and Steele's project continued to be debated over twenty-five years after his death.[39]

In addition to his involvement with the formal politics of antislavery, Steele's personal life in Barbados also became entangled with issues around race and

---

[36] R. J. Ramsay, *An essay on the treatment and conversion of African slaves in the British sugar colonies* (London, 1784); J. Steele to W. Dickson, 30 September 1790, in Dickson, *Mitigation of slavery*. Ramsay was one of the most forceful antislavery pamphleteers of the 1780s. Deeply concerned with the need to curb plantocratic power, he was a staunch advocate of ameliorative measures that would lead to the eventual abolition of slavery. Ramsay, like many others including Steele, was influenced by Adam Smith's writing on the advantages of wage labour in the third book of *An inquiry into the nature and causes of the wealth of nations* (1776). Unlike Ramsay, however, Steele afforded little importance to the role of Christianity in reforming and ending slavery. See C. L. Brown, 'Empire without slaves', 297–303.

[37] 'Queries from His Excellency Governor Parry answered by a planter of 1068 acres', in Dickson, *Mitigation of slavery*, pp. 143–184; Sheridan, 'Why the condition of the slaves was "less intolerable in Barbados than in the other sugar colonies"', p. 39.

[38] W. Dickson, *Letters on slavery, to which are added addresses to the whites and to the free negroes of Barbados; and accounts of some negroes eminent for their virtues and abilities* (London, 1789); Dickson, *Mitigation of slavery*.

[39] Turley, *The culture of English antislavery*, p. 31.

slavery. In the early 1780s, Steele began to co-habit with an enslaved coloured woman called Anna Slatia. She was the human property of Admiral Shirley, the owner of the Byde Mill estate. Both this estate and its enslaved workforce were leased on a long-term basis by Steele. During this time, Steele had two children with Slatia – Catherine Ann and Edward. The keeping of black or coloured mistresses, whether free or enslaved, by white planters was not an uncommon practice, nor were more casual or coerced sexual encounters. What was unusual was that upon his death, Steele left a substantial part of his property to the children – their mother having died earlier – even though they remained enslaved. By co-habiting and having children with an enslaved woman, treating and acknowledging their children as his legal heirs and attempting to leave his property to them, Steele's personal life ran counter to dominant social norms and mores in Barbados.[40]

Steele and the problems of plantation society in Barbados

I now want to turn to a more detailed consideration of Steele's project in Barbados.[41] With experience of both the general areas to which it should apply itself and of bureaucratic procedures, he dominated the Barbados Society of Arts. Nevertheless, he was a newcomer to the island and one of the first tasks he set the society was to identify the problems affecting Barbados. To this end, the period 1781–3 saw the production of a series of reports written by Steele and debated by the society. These sought to identify, analyse and propose solutions for the problems that afflicted Barbados's economy, society and politico-judicial system, and to separate real, underlying difficulties from petty complaints. These reports manifest a gaze of surveillance, which Steele's position as an outsider allowed him to bring to bear. This rhetorical move is critical to the discursive colonisation of territory and the parallels between Steele's vision and that of forms of colonisation will become clear.[42]

The first report submitted to the society was entitled 'Considerations on the present state and interests of Barbados'. It compared the economic structure and performance of Barbados and Britain, relating the cycles of boom and bust in the former to the relatively greater reliance on a single cash crop – sugar cane. This contrasted with Britain's more diversified economy, which included a more

---

[40] S. P. Gibbes, *Letter to John Beckles, Esq., Attorney General at Barbados, and correspondence between them on the subject of the conveyance of the Kendal plantation being unfairly obtained* (London, 1802). On the sexual relationships between white men and enslaved women, see Beckles, *Centering woman*, pp. 22–37; B. Bush, *Slave women in the Caribbean society, 1650–1838* (London: James Currey, 1990). It is unclear why Steele did not manumit his children in his will.

[41] For accounts of other plans for the amelioration and abolition of slavery in the 1770s and 1780s, see C. L. Brown, 'Empire without slaves'. Brown is correct to note that such proposals have received little scholarly attention, although he himself does not consider Steele's ameliorative project. That Steele actually sought to put his enlightened ideas into practice, rather than merely write about them, makes his efforts at producing an 'empire without slaves' particularly important.

[42] D. Spurr, *The rhetoric of empire: Colonial discourse in journalism, travel writing, and imperial administration* (London: Duke University Press, 1993), p. 13.

'reliable' manufacturing sector that brought economic stability. This initial report laid out the framework for those that followed, and committees were established to investigate the specific issues raised. For example, the problem of white poverty and indolence was addressed in a 1782 report. This connected white underemployment to the monopolisation of land by large landholders in the middle of the seventeenth century:

[O]f the able vagrant Poor, many are mechanics, the Descendants of those Families . . . whose industry in former Times by spinning, weaving, &c. supplied many of the *internal* Wants by working up their *native Materials*. Whereas the present Race, thro' Poverty, either not having Materials, or proper Instruments to work with, or wanting a certain Market for such Things as they can make, are thereby discouraged from exercising their trades, and fall into Habits of Indolence.[43]

With the shift toward plantation monoculture, small-scale manufacturing had declined, skills had been lost and the descendants of the indentured white servants had become trapped in poverty. The need to import manufactured goods, especially clothing, also increased Barbados's trade debt to Britain.

The most significant of the early papers, and the one which was to have long-standing implications for Steele's project in Barbados, was submitted on 20 January 1783. Written as part of an inquiry into the island's past and present prosperity, it identified those political and legal issues that retarded economic performance. The report criticised the island's laws as having been framed by seventeenth-century 'adventurers' who sought to make quick profits, an argument with some weight. According to Steele, laws that allowed the dissociation of land, capital and labour in the settling of debts may have favoured short-term speculation when frontier conditions prevailed, but were wholly unsuitable for settlement and long-term prosperity.[44]

The most controversial aspect of the report was its treatment of Barbados's slave laws. Although accepting that a harsh disciplinary regime could be deemed necessary in the formative years of the colony when the enslaved labour force was primarily African-born, the report questioned the morality and wisdom of maintaining such a regime when most slaves were born on the island. In particular, it singled out the law that set a £15 fine for the wanton killing of a slave as indicative of 'the impolitic Oppression of our Black Labourers, under Laws disgraceful to the Character of a civilised Nation'. This law would also be targeted by the antislavery campaign. With the demographic impact of amelioration not yet fully apparent, Steele argued that harsh treatment led to high levels of mortality and low levels of birth, resulting in a declining enslaved population that required replenishment through expensive imports. This 1783 report was Steele's most detailed examination of the problems facing Barbados. The Miscellaneous Committee, on which he

---

[43] BSA, 22 April 1782, 36. See also BSA, 29 October 1781, 17–30.
[44] BSA, 20 January 1783, 76.

sat, was appointed to produce proposals to address these problems. The workings of this committee became the focus of much of the later opposition to Steele.[45]

In Steele's reports for the Barbados Society of Arts, as well as his letters to the London Society of Arts and Joseph Banks, a number of central issues are apparent. Sugar monoculture was a form of cultivation full of uncertainties, which did not support a local manufacturing sector. This exacerbated white poverty and raised the costs of poor relief. The constant need to replenish the enslaved labour force was another unnecessary financial burden and resulted from the brutal practices of plantation overseers. Caring little for the long-term prospects of the plantations they ran, these whites harmed the overall prosperity of the island through corruption and mismanagement. This was enabled and fostered by 'Iniquitous Laws' that seemed to have been 'contrived by a Combination of Fools & Knaves, for the very purpose of covering the Frauds of Stewards and Overseers'. Such laws also encouraged the break-up of estates and allowed the brutal treatment of enslaved workers.[46] This diagnosis reflected the interest of someone concerned both with his own estates and the 'improvement' of the colony. What was being indicted was a range of interconnected problems: sugar monoculture, brutal slavery, white poverty and corrupting laws were understood and portrayed by Steele as features of a flawed plantation system. These features were also metaphorically linked, each acting as signs for and of the others. Finally, each co-signifier pointed to an underlying problem – the ignorance of Barbados's whites of their own self-interest. As he wrote: 'It is a sort of Comfort to the Native Inhabitants, that they are as insensible of their political disorder, as Individuals commonly are, when dying of a consumption of the lungs.'[47] Steele related this self-destructive irrationality to the planters' adherence to orthodox practice:

There is very little enterprise for new undertakings in the genius of the Natives, who being taught by Tradition, from the Experience of the last Century and for about 40 years of the present, that a sugar plantation is a gold mine, they persist in this Orthodox Culture.[48]

Steele represented Barbados as a place in which a historically static native population (i.e. the white population) had failed to make full use of the available resources.[49] David Spurr terms this rhetorical mode 'appropriation' – 'an appeal that may take the form . . . of natural abundance that awaits the creative hand of technology'.[50] Attendant with this trope is a demand for colonisation and Steele's descriptions resonate with the need for an external creative genius. Frequently,

---

[45] BSA, 20 January 1783, 46–77, at 76; BSA, 17 March 1783, 82–83; D. Knight, *Gentlemen of fortune: The men who made their fortunes in Britain's slave colonies* (London: Frederick Muller, 1978).

[46] J. Steele to J. Banks, 20 June 1786, Additional Manuscripts 33978, British Library; J. Steele to LSA, 15 July 1781, A11/45, RSA; J. Steele to LSA, 10 September 1786, A13/29, RSA.

[47] J. Steele to LSA, 24 May 1784, A12/23, RSA.

[48] J. Steele to J. Banks, 20 June 1786, Additional Manuscripts 33978, fo. 70, British Library.

[49] For example, J. Steele to LSA, 5 June 1782, A9/1; 13 June 1783, A10/26, RSA.

[50] Spurr, *Rhetoric of empire*, p. 28.

Steele represented Barbados as a place with a 'delightful and temperate' climate, full of potential:

[W]e have many excellent and durable Materials, well adapted for various Manufactures, which are now neglected, and whether these Materials, by Art and Industry, shall be worked up to the highest Degree in the Island, or only so far as to export them in a Form to be further Manufactured in other Countries, such Operations may furnish profitable Employment for Thousands of our People, who are now, miserable in themselves, and a discouraging load upon the Industry of others.[51]

This notion of developmental potential recurs in colonising discourses. Indeed, something akin to colonisation in the name of 'improvement' was precisely what Steele sought in Barbados. The colonising nature of his project was also evident in the negative representation of the native white population:

It is with great difficulty . . . that we can prevail on the thoroughbred beggars of the 4th & 5th generation, to earn a quarter part of their living by spinning, but they propagate their lazy species to infinity, where Rabbits dwindle.[52]

The poor whites were represented in terms of bestiality, hypersexuality and a lack of self-discipline. The deployment of such tropes of debasement was another aspect of the representation of Barbados as a place of colonial 'unreason' and as an aberrant slave world. Reflecting the influence of Adam Smith, the idea that the planter and the whole West Indian system were the 'absolute enemies of improvement' lay at the heart of Steele's diagnosis of Barbados's problems.[53]

'Improving' solutions

The colonising imperative of Steele's project was also manifest in the transformative role he allotted to external intervention to overcome local traditionalism and indolence. This was embodied in the colonising genius of Steele himself and his relationships with metropolitan Enlightenment figures. It was institutionalised in the Barbados Society of Arts and its links to other improving organisations. It was also physically manifest in the plant specimens that Steele had sent to Barbados so that its tropical environment could be improved. This amounted to a form of symbolic and material colonisation, and a metropolitan intervention that sought to introduce external dynamism. Steele's 'improving' project sought to change the culture of plantation society so its human and natural resources could be developed efficiently. Central to this was the revelation and utilisation of rational self-interest, revolving around notions of reward: planters would see increased

---

[51] BSA, 29 October 1781, 24.
[52] J. Steele to LSA, 24 May 1785, A12/34, RSA; Spurr, *Rhetoric of empire*, p. 76.
[53] C. Philo, 'Edinburgh, enlightenment, and the geographies of unreason', in Livingstone and Withers, *Geography and enlightenment*; M. Wood, *Slavery, empathy, and pornography* (Oxford: Oxford University Press, 2002), p. 302.

profits, poor whites would earn more money and have increased self-esteem and enslaved people would be able to work for themselves. Even those who helped the Barbados Society of Arts would be rewarded with premiums and medallions. The evocation of self-interest through cultural and financial reward signalled a fusion of humanity, morality and profit. Steele sought to reform Barbados's economy and politico-legal system in a way that combined ethical and economic reason, though formal religion was marginalised.

Steele's emphasis on rational self-interest translated into a series of areas for reform. The diversification of the economy was one of the Barbados Society of Arts's primary objectives, an aim that paralleled the emergence of forest conservation efforts elsewhere in the West Indies.[54] To this end, particular importance was attached to the promotion of cotton production. Cotton was the 'pace-setter of industrialization' and its 'meteoric rise' in the 1780s required huge imports of raw cotton to Britain and new sources of supply.[55] Cotton-growing was also envisaged as having synergetic benefits across the Barbadian economy by providing the basis for local industry, employing poor whites and reducing the need for planters to import textile goods. Other resources would also be used in this industry, including dyes derived from native and imported plants. In the politico-legal realm, enslaved workers were to be attached to their plantations to prevent the dissociation of labour, land and capital in the event of planter bankruptcy. Other reforms to the laws on slavery focussed on allowing the testimony of enslaved people against whites, a move designed to militate against the theft of cotton by white people.[56]

The most fundamental solution that Steele propounded involved altering the relationship between slaveholder and slave. The 1783 report had proposed placing the enslaved population 'under milder Conditions, such as were granted to the Slaves of our Saxon Ancestors'.[57] Steele suggested that rather than treating them as '*Villeins in Gross*' – as chattel – enslaved workers should be treated as 'bondsmen', attached to the land in tenements ('*adscripti Glebae*') and paying rent through their work. Failure to do so or indiscipline would see them returned to chattel status. The bonded relationship between labourer and land was termed a 'Manor', and was also seen as a solution to the problems of plantation break-up. All these features were part of the 'copyhold' system, which was most fully elaborated in a series of letters written under the pseudonym 'Philo-Xylon' to the *Barbados Gazette* in 1787 and 1788. These letters were republished in a 1789 pamphlet and again by Dickson in 1814.[58]

---

[54] Grove, *Green imperialism*. See also G. A. Barton, *Empire forestry and the origins of environmentalism* (Cambridge: Cambridge University Press, 2002).

[55] P. J. Marshall, 'Britain without America – a second empire?', in P. J. Marshall, *The Oxford history of the British Empire*, vol. II, p. 586.

[56] See pp. 68–69.   [57] BSA, 20 January 1783, 61.

[58] 'Philo-Xylon' crudely translates as 'friend to cotton'; *Barbados Gazette*, 10 October 1787 to 31 December 1788, *passim*, Reel 19, Bridgetown Public Library; Dickson, *Mitigation of slavery*, pp. 65–142; Philo-Xylon [J. Steele], *Letters of Philo-Xylon, first published in the Barbados Gazettes, during the years 1787 and 1788. Containing the substance of several conversations, at sundry times, for seven years past, on the subject of Negro laws and Negro government on plantations in Barbados* (London, 1789).

Copyhold was the 'tenure of land by bondservice to the lord or superior' and was based on Saxon common law and the practice of *villeinage*, which had originated in England in the fourteenth century.[59] Steele's conception of copyhold was predicated upon a stadial theory of human progress and was presented as a proven model for civilising enslaved Africans because it was 'the same successful Method, by which, all the antient [sic] Slaves in the Mother-Country, were reclaimed, from brutal manners to Civilization'.[60] Part of the potency of the copyhold system for Steele lay with its British origins and, in mobilising such ideas, he was part of the 'widespread reformist nostalgia for supposedly lost Anglo-Saxon liberties'.[61] The institution of copyhold reflected well on ancient Britain and it was only appropriate that Barbados – 'MOTHER OF THE BRITISH WEST-INDIA COLONIES' – should follow this lead.[62] That the original charter to settle Barbados permitted the creation of Manors, together with the fact that *villeinage* had been practised in ancient Britain, confirmed the British character of copyhold. Steele's promotion of this system represented another way in which external ideas and practices were to be implemented to 'improve' and 'anglicise' retarded and aberrant Barbados.

Steele sought to realise his project in three main ways: firstly, through the innovation-promoting programmes of the Barbados Society of Arts; secondly, through political lobbying; thirdly, on his own estates. To encourage economic diversification, the society placed newspaper advertisements offering premiums for the production of dye from native products, suggestions for the use of plantation buildings outside the harvest period and for the successful cultivation of coffee and cocoa. These financial rewards were supplemented by gold and silver ornaments (figure 2.2), a practice that had its origins with the London Society of Arts. In addition, 'occasional Bounties' were granted to the originators of 'any useful Invention or Improvement, tho' not within the particular Scope of the Society's Advertisements'.[63] As well as encouraging innovation by setting the agenda and rewarding success, Steele also used his connections with the London Society of Arts and his friendship with Joseph Banks to import organic specimens for cultivation, including camphor trees, Egyptian wheat and mango seeds. With the help

---

[59] Philo-Xylon, 9 April 1788, in Philo-Xylon [J. Steele], *Letters of Philo-Xylon*, pp. 25–26; *Oxford English Dictionary*, vol. 3 (1989), 637–638. Steele's plan had similarities to the proposals by Granville Sharp, the leading abolitionist, for the political organisation of Sierra Leone on the basis of the ancient English constitution of 'Frankpledge'. See G. Sharp, *A short sketch of temporary regulations (until better shall be proposed) for the intended settlement on the Grain Coast of Africa, near Sierra Leona*, 3rd edn (London: Printed by H. Baldwin, 1788) and D. Coleman, 'Bulama and Sierra Leone: Utopian islands and visionary interiors', in R. Edmond and V. Smith (eds.), *Islands in history and representation* (London: Routledge, 2003), p. 76.

[60] Philo-Xylon, 18 October 1788, in Philo-Xylon [J. Steele], *Letters of Philo-Xylon*, p. 39.

[61] Coleman, 'Bulama and Sierra Leone', p. 76. See also C. Hill, 'The Norman Yoke', in J. Saville (ed.), *Democracy and the labour movement: Essays in honour of Dona Torr* (London: Lawrence & Wishart, 1954). For a very different use of the paradigm of Anglo-Saxon enslavement, see M. Wood, *Slavery, empathy, and pornography*, pp. 358–363.

[62] Philo-Xylon, 12 November 1788, in Philo-Xylon [J. Steele], *Letters of Philo-Xylon*, p. 43.

[63] BSA, 5 July 1781, 4.

Figure 2.2 Sketches of medallions to be awarded by the Barbados Society for the Encouragement of Arts, Manufactures and Science, which appear in a letter from J. Steele to the London Society for the Encouragement of Arts, Manufactures and Science, 5 June 1782, PR.MC/104/10/241. Courtesy of the Royal Society of Arts Archive, London.

of botanists within the Barbados Society of Arts, Steele grew, bred and processed these plants, occasionally sending products for sale in London.[64]

The Barbados Society of Arts was also involved in lobbying the legislature. The 1782 report on the need to encourage poor white industry included a detailed proposal for a bill through which these aims could be realised. This was delivered to the Assembly by Applewhaite Frere, a founding member of the society and representative for St George's parish. On 29 October 1782, 'An Act for encouraging mechanic industry in Barbados by establishing Parochial Magazines or Store Shops' was introduced in the Assembly by Frere. The bill proposed that parishes be enabled to levy up to £100, plus an annual maintenance fee, to establish a storehouse, which would obtain tools and materials for loan to poor whites. The profits arising from the sale of products made would later be used to repay the loans. Receiving no opposition, the bill passed into law in January 1783.[65]

The most radical realisation of Steele's improving vision was undertaken on Kendal's plantation. Towards the end of 1783, he began experimenting with modes of 'Negro Government' by banning the use of the whip – the prime symbol of slavery – and removing the overseers' power to administer arbitrary punishment. Instead, he appointed a magistracy drawn from amongst the enslaved workforce. In 1785, he extended the use of financial self-interest as rational inducement by offering premiums for the performance of task work by enslaved labourers. The system of copyhold was introduced after 1788 when all enslaved adult males were given half an acre of land and a system of rent and wage payments was created.[66] Unsurprisingly, such efforts engendered great hostility from the Barbadian plantocracy. That they were also individual efforts undertaken by Steele outside the auspices of the Barbados Society of Arts reflected his increasing marginalisation.

White racial discourses and the limits of 'improvement'

Steele's scheme amounted to nothing less than the wholesale transformation and 'improvement' of Barbadian society. Compared with such grandiose aims, his actual accomplishments were limited. The Barbados Society of Arts' membership grew at a modest rate, and although it rose from an initial fourteen to thirty-one by the end of 1781, the active membership was limited to half a dozen or so individuals, perhaps prompting the extension of membership to women and non-residents in November 1782. The most significant member was Governor Parry, who joined in

---

[64] BSA, 16 July 1781, 12–13; 29 October 1781, 26–30; J. Steele to LSA, 10 September 1786, A13/29, RSA; BSA, 6 August 1781, 13–14; J. Steele to LSA, 5 June 1782, A9/1, RSA; J. Steele to J. Banks, 7 December 1787, Additional Manuscripts 33978, fo. 159, British Library; D. G. C. Allan, *William Shipley, founder of the Royal Society of Arts: A biography with documents* (London, 1979).

[65] BSA, 22 April 1782, 33–42; Minutes of Assembly, 23 April, 1 October 1782, CO 31/41, fos. 194, 235–239, TNA; Minutes of Assembly, 29 October, 1782, CO 31/41, fo. 243, TNA; Acts: Barbados, No. 141, CO 30/16, fos. 28–32, TNA.

[66] J. Steele to W. Dickson, 30 September 1790, in Cateau, 'Conservatism and change', 28; Clarkson, *Thoughts*, pp. 34–37; Dickson, *Mitigation of slavery*, p. 9.

February 1783, in the aftermath of the society's success with the act to encourage poor white industry. The society also contained a number of Barbadian plantocrats, including the speaker of the Assembly, Sir John Alleyne Gay, and Attorney General John Beckles. Despite such prominent members, the society was unable to repeat its initial success in lobbying the legislature. For example, an address 'on the important Subject of establishing, on proper Principles, an effectual Militia' was presented to the Assembly by John Gay Alleyne in 1783 but with no results.[67]

The presence of plantocrats within the Barbados Society of Arts, most of whom joined in 1783, was not necessarily indicative of Steele's success in promoting his reformist vision. From around 1784–5, he began to face opposition from within:

[S]ome of our members, who were also distinguished and even popular members of the Legislature, began to perceive the advances of this society towards reforming the iniquitous and obnoxious laws concerning Negro government . . . when misled by old habitudes, they began to dislike the further discussion of such topics in the Society of Arts, and some whispering rumours were spread abroad, as if 'gentlemen had been insidiously drawn in, by general expressions in the plan of the institution of the society, which seemed to have had a view to the posterior introduction of these dangerous designs against their established laws and customs, which designs they did not then apprehend'. And after this time it seemed as if, under those impressions, parties were formed to throw cold water on such dangerous designs.[68]

Perhaps expecting to have joined an organisation concerned with technological and biological innovation, the plantocrats became worried about Steele's increasing focus on slavery and claimed that they had joined under a misapprehension. Steele himself attributed this resistance to 'the prejudices of Birth & Education of some very wealthy members', which 'revolted against their cool reason' and was another manifestation of an irrational white creole culture. The opposition was particularly aimed at suppressing the proposals contained in the 1783 report. The discussion of copyhold became locked in the Miscellaneous Committee, with the society in general unwilling to debate such issues. No longer dominating the society's proceedings, perhaps because of the presence of 'distinguished and even popular' plantocrats, Steele became marginalised and focussed his efforts on his own estates. The society itself seems to have dissolved some time in the early 1790s.[69]

The resistance that Steele faced and the failure of many of his schemes can be understood in terms of conflict between his improving vision for Barbados – his diagnosis of its problems and suggestions for solutions – and a set of entrenched racial discourses ('established laws and customs'). Racial discourses framed the thought and practice of amelioration. More broadly, these discourses constituted

---

[67] BSA, 26 November 1782, 31–32; BSA, 18 February 1783, 82; BSA, 29 April 1783, 83–89; Minutes of Assembly, 29 April 1783, CO 31/41, fos. 317–321, TNA; Acts: Barbados, CO 30/16, fos. 266–328, TNA.
[68] J. Steele to W. Dickson, 30 September 1790, in Dickson, *Mitigation of slavery*, p. 7.
[69] J. Steele to LSA, 10 September 1786, A13/29, RSA; J. Steele to W. Dickson, 30 September 1790, in Dickson, *Mitigation of slavery*, p. 7.

the planters' worldview and interests, which, if not hegemonic in white society, were certainly dominant. Thus, whilst amelioration was just one element of the various ideas and practices that sustained the plantation system, the discourses that framed it also framed broader forms of (dis)possession and black subjugation. Yet, the clash between Steele and the dominant culture was not simply one of *ideas* about race, but was also located in the practices of opposition. In reading Steele's failure, I want to focus on two particular fields of conflict between his counter-hegemonic project and the dominant culture, relating opposition to him to the embeddedness of discourses of 'white supremacism' and a 'planter ideal'. By tracing the lines and moments of conflict, the borders and nature of these discourses can be delineated, discourses that were central to the articulation of white identity in the late eighteenth century.

White supremacism

Ideas and acts of white supremacism were central to Barbadian society and served to rationalise slavery. Such ideas also framed the practice of amelioration. For example, the whole notion of 'breeding' enslaved workers was indicative of an embodied and animalistic comprehension of black people. Their socio-sexual lives were viewed as a site for intervention and understood in an instrumentalist manner: better treatment would enable 'naturally' high levels of reproduction to occur. Similarly, the embeddedness of supremacist ideas of black debasement was clear from the fact that amelioration was intended to strengthen slavery by making it more sustainable, not to reform it more fundamentally. Amelioration was further developed in Barbados than elsewhere in the West Indies and 'there is evidence that planters were among the most lenient and humane'. Nevertheless, 'the laws were the most illiberal and harsh' and change to the politico-judicial status of enslaved people was resisted by the planter-dominated Assembly into the nineteenth century. Amelioration's racially enframed nature set limits to reform. It had nothing to do with slaveholders' recognition of black humanity and everything to do with improving productivity through new forms of white supremacist (dis)possession.[70] White supremacism was also central to the controversy over slavery. Assertions of black racial and cultural inferiority, as natural and biblically ordained, recurred in the defence of slavery, and abolitionists would seek to demonstrate that black debasement had its origins in enslavement.[71] Steele's project and the responses it engendered were part of this broader controversy.

Steele's emphasis on the irrationality of Barbadian culture inevitably involved a critique of ideas of natural white superiority. The report on the need to encourage

---

[70] H. McD. Beckles, 'Creolisation in action: The slave labour elite and anti-slavery in Barbados', *Caribbean Quarterly* 44 (1998); Cateau, 'Conservatism and change', 22.

[71] Dickson, *Letters on slavery*; G. Francklyn, *Observations, occasioned by the attempts made in England to effect the abolition of the slave trade; shewing, the manner in which Negroes are treated in the British colonies in the West Indies* (Kingston, 1789 reprint), appendix.

poor white industry included a consideration of the damaging effects of racism on this population, particularly, the 'political Evil' that arose from the existence of 'two legal distinctions of Men, in one of which, Virtue and Industry cannot elevate; and in the other, Profligacy and Sloth cannot degrade'.[72] Steele was fully aware of the obstacles that white supremacism posed to his efforts to encourage poor white industry and he rejected the idea of establishing British-style workhouses because of the association between coerced work and black slavery. Yet, even the voluntary system of self-help codified in the 1783 'Act for encouraging mechanic industry' was resisted. Indicative of little response from the parish vestries, the Barbados Society of Arts decided to advance capital directly to individual poor whites. In those parishes that *did* attempt the scheme there was little success, and most of the money remained unspent or was used for other purposes. The failure of the scheme was explained by Steele as a consequence of an irrational sense of self-worth in a society 'where the poorest free People habitually and legally [look] down upon the best fed slaves'. This led poor whites to shy work in preference for 'the Pleasures of Indolence, although connected with the Discomforts of Beggary'.[73] In a society in which white superiority was legally codified and performed in everyday ways, the most impoverished whites received a 'public and psychological wage'.[74] For Steele, the material benefits and feelings of 'natural' superiority realised through whiteness served to discourage the endeavours of black and white, enslaved and free alike. With his emphasis on the progressive force of reward, such racial supremacism amongst poor whites amounted to a distortion of the rational calculus he sought to utilise. In sum, white supremacist attitudes and whiteness as material privilege were central to plantation society and served to undermine Steele's efforts.

White supremacism also formed the basis for resistance on Steele's own estates. His attempts to ban the use of the whip on Kendal's plantation caused his chief overseer to resign, and soon after Steele had to dismiss his five deputies. A symbol not only of slavery and legally codified white power over enslaved bodies, the whip was also sign of white supremacism.[75] Its use was the enactment of a discourse of black debasement, signifying and reinforcing the notion that black people were thoroughly embodied and that the black body was the appropriate site for the performance of white coercive power. A few months later, Steele appointed a new chief overseer:

But this man, one of the old stamp or school of overseers . . . not only grew careless and indolent, but was so imprudent in conversations among his old acquaintances, as to publish his opinions that my plan of lenity to the Negroes counteracted all his endeavours, and that

---

[72] BSA, 22 April 1782, 37.   [73] BSA, 9 June 1783, 90; BSA, 22 April 1782, 37.

[74] D. Roediger, *The wages of whiteness: Race and the making of the American working class* (London: Verso, 1991), p. 12.

[75] For the antislavery campaign, of course, the whip was the 'emblem of slave-power tyranny'. See M. Wood, *Blind memory: Visual representations of slavery in England and America, 1780–1865* (Manchester: Manchester University Press, 2000), p. 258.

he held himself no way accountable for the ill condition of the estate and its ruinous crops, for that he could obtain no labour from the Negroes; and his insinuations and hints among the Negroes themselves tended to the same malignant purpose.[76]

Unable to perform the usual role of chief overseer – coercing black bodies – and instead forced to serve as superintendent over a magistracy drawn from among the enslaved workforce, the replacement undermined Steele's efforts by sowing discontent on the estate and spreading malicious rumours about Steele. This countered Steele's use of Kendal's as a model for his reforms: he blamed the overseer for the failure of his cotton crops, for example. In consequence, Steele dismissed him and took direct control of the estates himself.[77] Steele's attempts to utilise the enlightened self-interest of his enslaved workforce were resisted by those whites he employed, partly because he sought to remove traditional instruments of white power over black bodies. These efforts challenged the dominant racial discourse in which black people were understood as not being subject to rational behaviour, except in the embodied terms of fear of punishment by the whip.

Ideas of white supremacism and black debasement also found ideological deployment against Steele's idea of copyhold. For Steele, copyhold represented a civilising institution that could raise enslaved blacks to hard-working tenants, just as the *villeins* had become the enlightened, modern Britons of the late eighteenth century. The shared developmental path on which ancient *villeins*, modern whites and Barbados's enslaved people were placed was an explicit assertion of a shared humanity and drew an angry planter response:

How absurd . . . it is, to think of that Species of Creatures, very little above Baboons, in their intellectual Capacity, upon a Level with ourselves, who by our superior Faculties and Penetration, have exceeded all the Race of human Creatures, our Predecessors, in the Invention of Arts and Sciences! And who, has ever, from all Time past, to this Hour, I say, who has ever heard of an African Negro inventing any Thing?[78]

Not only was the rhetoric of bestiality evoked here, but also the stadial underpinnings of copyhold were contested with a polygenic assertion of permanent white racial superiority. Copyhold was part of the debate about 'blackness' and was attacked by many white Barbadians because it undermined notions of racial difference and white superiority.

The embedded supremacist discourse that was manifest in opposition to Steele can be seen in the writing of the Reverend Henry Evans Holder, a Barbadian Anglican minister. Holder had joined the Barbados Society of Arts in 1781 and, as a naturalist, philanthropist, philologist and amateur physiologist, was just the sort of 'Gentleman of liberal Education' whom Steele had sought to attract to his

---

[76] J. Steele to W. Dickson, 30 September 1790, in Dickson, *Mitigation of slavery*, p. 10.
[77] Extract of letter from J. Steele, 20 July 1786, in Dickson, *Mitigation of slavery*, pp. 63–64.
[78] Quoted in Philo-Xylon, 30 April 1788, in Philo-Xylon [J. Steele], *Letters of Philo-Xylon*, p. 28.

society.[79] Yet, his response to the British abolitionist campaign was indicative of a very different attitude towards slavery, for although he was in favour of the religious conversion of enslaved people and the adoption of ameliorative measures, he argued that West Indian slavery was a civilising institution with theological sanction. Deflecting abolitionist attacks, Holder argued that reform was occurring in Barbados and would continue to occur naturally, but only within the existing system. This idea of reform left no place for the radical transformation that copyhold represented. Holder's writing was indicative of the gulf that existed between Steele's ideas and those of 'even the independent and educated gentlemen' of Barbados.[80] It was also symptomatic of the strength of opposition that Steele faced, both within and beyond the society.

The effects of an entrenched white supremacism were also apparent at a personal level following Steele's death. Despite leaving most of his property to his children, his will was ignored, and they were dispossessed of their inheritance. Steele's decision to leave property to enslaved children was the first case of its kind in Barbados and was legally unprecedented:

The opinion that a slave is incapable of holding property has prevailed so universally since the settlement of Barbados, that the laws of that island are entirely silent on the subject.[81]

Steele's actions were so extraordinary that there was no law to prohibit them. Rather, legal opinion in Barbados, which reflected wider cultural norms, simply disqualified his actions on the basis that enslaved people were property and could not own property. Such 'common-sense' assumptions were so ingrained in Barbados that in the legal controversy that followed over the disposal of Steele's property the white supremacist disinheritance of his children was unquestioned. Instead, Francis Bell, Steele's estate manager and the executor of his will, sent Steele's children to Britain, where he had arranged for their manumission. The boy, Edward, went to a school in Norwich with Bell's own son, whilst the older girl, Catherine Ann, went to a finishing school in Camberwell.[82]

In conclusion, ideas and practices of white supremacism were clearly apparent in the opposition that Steele faced. They were evident in the suppression of his copyhold ideas within the Barbados Society of Arts, the failure of his attempts to promote poor white industry, the opposition from white staff on his estates, the sentiments of the Reverend Holder and other planters and the disinheritance of his children. White supremacism was manifested and mobilised by prominent

---

[79] BSA, 6 August, 1781, 14. For examples of Holder's writing, see H. E. Holder, *Fragments of a poem, intended to have been written in consequence of reading Major Majoribank's slavery* (Bath, 1792); H. E. Holder, *A short essay on the subject of Negro slavery, with particular reference to the island of Barbados* (London, 1788). See also J. S. Handler, *A guide to source materials for the study of Barbados history, 1627–1834* (Carbondale: Southern Illinois University Press, 1971), pp. 55, 67.

[80] J. R. Ward, *British West Indian slavery, 1750–1834: The process of amelioration* (Oxford: Clarendon Press, 1988); J. Steele to W. Dickson, 30 September 1790, in Dickson, *Mitigation of slavery*, p. 5.

[81] S. P. Gibbes, *Letter to John Beckles*, p. 58.

[82] S. P. Gibbes, *Letter to John Beckles*, pp. 6–10.

plantocrats, the white poor, plantation overseers and lawyers. Enacted and expressed at various scales, by different groups and in a variety of forms, white supremacism was clearly central to the world the slaveholders had made, to their culture, politics and identity.

The planter ideal

The second broad discourse that can be delineated from the conflict between Steele's project and the dominant culture is a *planter ideal*. This discourse rendered slavery as an 'organic relation' of mutual dependency, in which a paternalistic 'good master' cared for 'his' enslaved workforce and could win their respect and loyalty. The planter ideal was also predicated on claims about the local expertise that Barbadian slaveholders had acquired over the centuries. It was usually larger proprietors and absentees who articulated such sentiments and, to this extent, the planter ideal was an elite discourse. Nevertheless, elite planters also expressed and enacted white supremacism and the two discourses were overlapping rather than distinct. It is also important to stress that this ideal should not be seen as a moderating tendency within slavery or an accurate characterisation of enslaver/enslaved relations.[83] Rather, it was a racial discourse, predicated on ideas of familialism, dependency and duty, which could be just as subjugating as more explicitly supremacist conceptions of enslavement.[84] The planter ideal was predicated on the notion that slaveholders were able to combine the benevolent treatment of their enslaved workforces with self-interest. Following from this, the reform of slavery was a *natural* consequence of self-interested benevolence, but only if metropolitan abolitionists did not interfere in West Indian affairs.[85] The dynamic for reform had its locus in the West Indies, whereas metropolitan abolitionism was a foreign import, which was characterised by misinformed zeal and

---

[83] It is not my claim that planters were 'good masters' in any absolute sense, but that they often viewed themselves as such and that this had consequences. In other words, the planter ideal was an articulation of white creole identity in Barbados that shaped and was shaped by the practices of slaveholding and colonial estate management. A similar claim is made by Eugene Genovese who argues that the private feelings expressed by planters in the American South reveal the existence of a 'paternalist mentality'. My use of 'ideal' signals that even the slaveholders recognised that they fell short of these standards in their treatment of slaves. Furthermore, the extent to which the enslaved population accepted the planter ideal is impossible to determine. Certainly, self-congratulatory rhetoric about a perfect and humane model of plantation management would have been contested by the day-to-day experience of violence, discipline and hardship. See E. D. Genovese, *Roll, Jordan, roll: The world the slaves made* (New York: Pantheon Books, 1972); E. D. Genovese, *The world the slaveholders made: Two essays in interpretation* (New York: Random House, 1969). See also M. Steel, 'A philosophy of fear: The world view of Jamaican plantocracy in comparative perspective', *Journal of Caribbean History* 27 (1993). For a discussion of 'paternalistic explanations' of slavery, see H. McGary, 'Paternalism and slavery', in T. L. Lott (ed.), *Subjugation and bondage: Critical essays on slavery and social philosophy* (Lanham, MD: Rowman & Littlefield, 1998).

[84] S. V. Hartman, *Scenes of subjection: Terror, slavery, and self-making in nineteenth-century America* (Oxford: Oxford University Press, 1997), pp. 5, 52.

[85] Ward, *British West Indian slavery*.

threatened to undermine the mutual bonds of dependency between enslaver and enslaved. This argument was predicated upon an imagined geography of reform that was the inverse of that manifest in Steele's writing: the West Indies was a site of 'natural' improvement and the metropole a source of dangerous destabilisation.

The issue of paternalism was a major site of struggle between supporters and opponents of slavery. For example, the Reverend Holder's defence of the institution was predicated upon a distinction he drew between the laws that had been established when slavery was new and which still remained in force, and the contemporary 'gentleness and humanity' with which enslaved people were treated.[86] This *de jure/de facto* distinction marked the space of paternalism. In contrast, abolitionists and those who favoured the fundamental reform of slavery dismissed claims about paternalistic behaviour or portrayed it as exceptional. Dickson's *Letters on slavery*, for example, was a litany of cruelty, abuse and mistreatment, in which he argued that, though some enslaved domestics and artisans did live well, this was not the general pattern. His shocking descriptions of violence, abandonment and the separation of families contested the discourse of the 'good master'.[87] The body of the enslaved woman was a crucial site in this contest, her treatment an indication of (the lack of) paternalism.[88]

Given the centrality of ideas about the benevolence of slaveholders within the proslavery campaign, it might be tempting to view expressions of the planter ideal as pure propaganda. Yet, such expressions did not only appear in overtly propagandist texts but were also manifest in contemporary plantation management literature. The end of the eighteenth century saw a growth in this corpus, and manuals based on plantation management experience and outlining proper practices were produced and read across the West Indies. Central to this literature was the promotion of amelioration. Of course, it could be argued that plantation management literature also performed a propagandist function, by demonstrating that planters were forward-thinking and reformist. Nevertheless, to dismiss this as mere rhetoric is unsatisfactory, as it ignores the other functions that this literature performed. As well as propaganda, these texts were also descriptions of actual ameliorative practice that had been undertaken, and instructions about best practice. Many were based on written instructions left by owners for their agents and were published as a way of sharing expertise and experience. In this way, they contributed to the diffusion of ameliorative ideas. The planters sought to outmanoeuvre their abolitionist opponents by reforming practice in such a way that would undermine their attacks.[89] Actual changes in management policy, efforts to encourage the more

---

[86] Holder, *A short essay*, pp. 15, 18.

[87] Dickson, *Letters on slavery*, pp. 8, 38–45, 49–59. See also R. R. B. Nicholls, *A letter to the treasurer of the society instituted for the purpose of effecting the abolition of the slave trade* (London, 1787).

[88] H. Altink, '"The agonies of a negress on the loss of her children": Representations of Jamaican slave motherhood in the 1780–1838 discourse on child-death', *Women's History Notebook* 6 (1999).

[89] Cateau, 'Conservatism and change'; T. G. Marshall, 'Post-emancipation adjustments in Barbados, 1838 to 1876', in Thompson, *Emancipation I*.

widespread adoption of such innovations *and* more blatant forms of propaganda were all part of this effort.

Barbadians read and contributed to plantation management literature. For example, the *Instructions for the management of a plantation in Barbados* was based on directives written by the owner of a 250-acre plantation and was one of the most influential texts. It addressed issues of cropping, livestock, the management of white underlings and the treatment of enslaved workers. The tone was one of good husbandry and care:

> If negroes are fed plentifully, worked moderately, and treated kindly, they will encrease [sic] in most places; they will decrease in no place, so much as to require any considerable expence [sic] to repair the loss in number or value. THE INCREASE IS THE ONLY TEST OF CARE WITH WHICH THEY ARE TREATED.[90]

Throughout this literature, references to the 'comfortable establishment' of enslaved women, the subdivision of the enslaved workforce into groups so that 'they may never be employed upon any work, to which their powers are not equal' and assertions that 'self-interest combines with humanity to direct a mild and generous treatment' emphasised the paternalistic underpinnings of amelioration.[91] The contention that management literature was indicative of a planter ideal is augmented by private journals and letters that were not written with the public slavery controversy in mind:

> Upon every well regulated Plantation, they respect their Master as a Father, and are exceedingly vain, in reflecting on the connexion [sic] between them.[92]

Similarly,

> I am very sorry our Negroes have decreased this year. I know not how it has happened, for they have had great care taken of them and have wanted for nothing. The women have been unsuccessful generally in breeding and childbirth.[93]

Of course, the second letter indicates that whilst planters may have seen themselves in paternalistic terms, this did not necessarily, or even ever, translate into good treatment. Nevertheless, the planter *ideal* remained an important aspect of the local constitution of white identity.

The planter ideal was predicated on more than self-interest with benevolent consequences. The relationship between the slaveholder and 'his' enslaved workforce

---

[90] Anonymous, *Instructions for the management of a plantation in Barbados. And for the treatment of Negroes, etc. etc. etc.* (London, 1786), p. 2. See also P. Gibbes, *Instructions for the treatment of Negroes, etc. etc. etc.* (London, 1786, 1797 reprint); J. W. Orderson, *Directions to young planters for their care and management of a sugar plantation in Barbadoes* (London, 1800).

[91] Anonymous, *Instructions for the management of a plantation in Barbados*, p. 24; P. Gibbes, *Instructions for the treatment of Negroes*, pp. 70, 88.

[92] 'Memoirs of J. Senhouse', 1779, Senhouse Papers, Reel 1, Item 18, p. 63, Barbados Department of Archives.

[93] Letter from S. Wood, 26 July 1797, quoted in Beckles, 'To buy or to breed', 30.

was held to be like that between a father and his family. The slaveholder would act *in loco parentis* for the enslaved children, 'communicating instruction to young minds' and seeking to form 'good habits' such as a 'submission to the state, in which it has pleased God to place them'. This mapping of the relationship on to the family served to naturalise the unequal relations of power between the parties and asserted the unquestionable authority of the 'master'. Given a manager's 'fatherly' care, any mortality or morbidity within the enslaved population occurred *in spite* of 'every care and humanity of the owner' and was variously attributable to the enslaved people themselves, less benevolent white underlings or mysterious circumstances.[94]

The importance of a planter ideal to the self-identity of elite slaveholders and to their defence of slavery made Steele's explicit critique all the more threatening. Copyhold was a fundamental reform predicated upon the identification of current failings within the system of slavery. For Steele, the attempt to coerce enslaved workers was inhumane, inefficient, destructive and costly. He challenged the supposedly 'natural' reforms brought about by amelioration and showed that the 'benevolence' of individual planters was thwarted by the system. Opposition to copyhold was manifest in the failure of Steele to persuade other planters to adopt his scheme, which they viewed as implausible. As has already been noted, discussions about copyhold were suppressed and became locked in the Miscellaneous Committee of the Barbados Society of Arts. To avoid this institutional obstruction, Steele adopted the pseudonym 'Philo-Xylon' and wrote a series of letters in the local press. Resistance thus forced Steele to circumvent the structures/strictures of an institution that he had founded and led some six years earlier.

The importance of the planter ideal in the resistance faced by Steele was evident from the particular events that caused him to circumvent the Barbados Society of Arts. In August 1787, John Beckles, attorney general, Assembly representative for St Michael's and member of the society, introduced a bill 'to encourage the planting of cotton'. The bill was designed to prevent 'the pernicious and iniquitous practice of stealing cotton which of late has become so prevalent', particularly that by enslaved workers. To this end, the bill proposed that legal proof of ownership was required for all cotton transactions. Organised by a number of appointed inspectors, registration and inspection were to be legal prerequisites for the sale, transfer and export of cotton. In this way, the bill sought to make stolen cotton as difficult to sell as possible.[95] The promotion of cotton cultivation, to diversify the economy and produce economic synergies, had been one of Steele's primary aims, but the form of legal regulation proposed by the bill – introduced by one member of the Barbados Society of Arts and supported by another, Dottin Maycock – fell far short of the sort of radical solutions propounded by Steele. The first of the

---

[94] P. Gibbes, *Instructions for the treatment of Negroes*, pp. 97, 99–100; Holder, *A short essay*, p. 30; S. Yearwood to A. Frere, March 1796, reproduced in *Journal of Barbados Museum and Historical Society* 16 (1948–9), p. 113.

[95] Minutes of Assembly, 28 August 1787, CO 31/43, fos. 211–217, TNA.

'Philo-Xylon' letters was published in the *Barbados Gazette* when the bill was being debated in a legislative committee. This and subsequent letters argued that the prohibition on the legal testimony of non-whites against whites had the effect of allowing white thieves to steal from or bribe enslaved people with impunity and thus encouraged the widespread theft of cotton. To arguments that the testimony of enslaved people was unacceptable because they were 'uncivilised' and 'untrustworthy', Steele responded that the system of copyhold would be a civilising institution. Representing cotton theft as just another of the problems that afflicted Barbadian society because of its irrational laws and treatment of labour, the seven letters published in 1788 argued strongly in favour of copyhold.[96] He used these letters not only to present arguments in favour of the copyhold system, but also to publish financial and demographic data from his own estates, and the proceedings of the Miscellaneous Committee from the years 1785 and 1786 that would not be published by the society. The gap between Steele's radical proposals and those contained in the cotton bill – which passed into law in August 1788[97] – was symptomatic of the opposition that Steele faced and the conflict between his counter-hegemonic project and the planter ideal. The Cotton Act was a limited form of regulation which did not disturb the supposedly paternalistic relations of slavery, whilst copyhold was a fundamental transformation of a failing system.

The conflict between Steele's counter-hegemonic project and the planter ideal was also apparent in the differences between his writing and that of plantocrats who were members of the society. Plantation management guides were printed on the authority of members, including Philip Gibbes, Francis Ford, William Thorpe Holder and John Brathwaite. All asserted a paternalistic account of Barbadian society and the need for the minor regulation, not fundamental reform, of enslaved/enslaver relations. As Barbados's London agent, Brathwaite was particularly important in promulgating the success of amelioration and the benevolence of the planters. In his evidence before the Committee of the Privy Council in 1788, to which Steele had also contributed,[98] Brathwaite contested the representation of Barbados as an aberrant slave world of irrationality and brutality. He argued that enslaved people were protected by the 'humanity and interest' of their masters and that the mutual bonds of duty were recognised by the enslaved workforce such that 'if freedom was offered to negroes who had good masters, very few would, in my opinion, accept it'.[99] Brathwaite also drew on and referred his questioners to the local expertise represented by the plantation management literature. At these sites and in these texts, the plantocracy sought to establish Barbados as a place managed by 'good masters'.

---

[96] Philo-Xylon, 10 October 1787, in Philo-Xylon [J. Steele], *Letters of Philo-Xylon*, pp. 5–9; Minutes of Assembly, 28 August 1787, CO 31/43, fos. 211–217; Philo-Xylon, 3 January to 31 December 1788, in Philo-Xylon [J. Steele], *Letters of Philo-Xylon*, pp. 14–47.

[97] Acts, no. 178, CO 30/16, fos. 161–164, TNA.   [98] See, p. 51.

[99] Evidence of J. Brathwaite to the Lords of the Privy Council, 21 February 1788, reproduced in *Journal of the Barbados Museum and Historical Society* 18 (1950–1), pp. 24 and 35.

The planter ideal found particular articulation in assessments of Steele's own role as a slaveholder and manager. After his death, when abolitionists were promoting copyhold as a model of how emancipation could be achieved, Barbadian planters and their supporters sought to discredit Steele, and one of their central lines of argument was that copyhold was a foolish form of labour innovation that was not grounded in local knowledge. For example, George Pinckard, a British visitor to Barbados in 1796, described Steele in the following terms:

[Kendal's] is under the direction of a very singular and eccentric character, whose great ambition is to act differently from other men, and who finds a secret pleasure in deviating from all established and common rules. His mill is oddly trimmed, the sales strangely cut, and all the works, by some deviation or other, made peculiar. Among a multitude of other singularities he has planted a patch of pigeon peas in the neighbourhood of a field of canes, in order to allure the borers from sugar, – a piece of policy very like setting a dish of tough beef before an alderman to seduce his appetite from a haunch of venison![100]

Pinckard did not actually meet Steele – perhaps another symptom of Steele's marginalisation, as the visitor socialised with many planters – and his description reflected what he had been told by his plantocratic companions. Steele was portrayed as an eccentric figure of fun, not an embodiment of the Enlightenment. His opponents argued that because he eschewed local methods of plantation management, his plans were 'visionary, without the least Judgment' and an inappropriate model for reform.[101]

In addition to ridiculing Steele, critics attacked him by arguing that his efforts were based on selfish motives. Nathaniel Lucas, a large landholder, member of the Council and social commentator in the 1820s, was asked to draw up an 'Authentic Report' of Steele's achievements. Describing him as a man who came to Barbados 'much involved in debt', Lucas argued that Steele's efforts to change the laws on bankruptcy were motivated by a personal desire to prevent his assets being seized by creditors.[102] His account of copyhold was similar. Lucas described it as 'a complete System of tyranny and oppression' through which Steele sought to acquire 'Cheap Labour . . . and diminish his Plantation Expenses'. According to Lucas 'Self was the Object' and Steele was more concerned with his own finances than the welfare of his workforce.[103] Proslavery claims that opponents of slavery were actually cruel masters were not new. For example, Ramsay, who had argued for the social and moral improvement of the state of enslaved labourers, was painted as 'a Man of worthless morals and a very cruel master over his own Negroes'. Steele himself wrote that because of such attacks, Ramsay's 1784 essay had done 'rather

---

[100] G. Pinckard, *Notes on the West Indies: Written during the expedition under the command of the late General Sir Ralph Abercromby; including observations on the island of Barbadoes, and the settlements captured by the British troops upon the coast of Guiana*, 3 vols. vol. I (London, 1806), p. 363.
[101] N. Lucas, Miscellaneous Items, Lucas Manuscripts, Vol. 1, Reel 15, p. 64, BPL.
[102] Ibid.   [103] N. Lucas, Miscellaneous Items, Lucas Manuscripts, Vol. 1, Reel 15, p. 66.

Hurt, than Service' to his own cause in Barbados.[104] Both Steele and Ramsay were portrayed as hypocrites, whose actions ran contrary to the paternalism of the 'good master'.

According to his proslavery critics, the result of Steele's ill-informed, selfish practices was the total ruin of Kendal's plantation. Lucas produced demographic and financial data to demonstrate the terrible condition in which copyhold had left the estate and James M'Queen – geographer and defender of slavery[105] – wrote a direct refutation of Thomas Clarkson's endorsement of the system:

> Mr. Steele's boasted 'Copyhold System', completely failed; the negroes would not work the lands allotted to them, which Mr. Steele, in consequence resumed. At Mr. Steele's death, the negroes were found to be in a most wretched condition, from the effects of hard labour and disease, brought on by debauchery, and in short, there is not a man in Barbados acquainted with Mr. Steele and his mode of management, but declares that his system was the worst, the most odious and tyrannical that could possibly be devised.[106]

Steele's apparent failure could also be read in the landscape of Kendal's. Far from the pastoral ideal of the well-ordered estate that was the mark of a 'good master', Kendal's contained a diseased enslaved population.[107] M'Queen and others also represented Steele as a thoroughly un-paternalistic master, hated by his enslaved workers – as the manager of an adjoining estate wrote:

> The copyhold system was noxious to the slaves, because the power was placed in the hands of a few ignorant and unfeeling negroes, slaves like themselves, frequently governed by motives of private pique and secret malice. This could not fail to produce jealousies and heart-burnings among them . . . It was very well known that the negroes rejoiced when the change took place, and thanked their God that they were relieved from the copyhold system.[108]

This criticism of copyhold was not only based on the condemnation of Steele's supposed lack of paternalistic benevolence, it was also about his failure to fulfil his responsibilities. Throughout their defence of slavery, planters asserted that emancipation would leave the old, infirm and helpless enslaved people without protection. By reducing the power of the overseers and removing white authority, Steele had failed to act as a guardian to his enslaved workers, leaving them to fall prey to one another's hates and jealousies. He had abdicated his responsibilities and failed to live up to the planter ideal.

A planter ideal characterised much of the resistance Steele faced. Crucial to elite slaveholders' self-identity, paternalistic notions were codified in pro-amelioration

---

[104] J. Steele to LSA, 10 September 1786, A13/29, RSA.

[105] See chapter 5, pp. 145–146.

[106] J. M'Queen, *The West India colonies: The calumnies and misrepresentations circulated against them by the Edinburgh Review, Mr. Clarkson, Mr. Crupper, etc. etc.* (London: Baldwin, Cradock and Joy, 1824), p. 214.

[107] Hartman, *Scenes of subjection*, p. 52; Seymour, Daniels, and Watkins, 'Estate and empire', 316. For more on pastoralism, see chapter 6, pp. 178–181.

[108] Letter from H. Sealy, 26 February 1824, printed in *Gentleman's Magazine* vol. 94 (1824), 420–1.

plantation management texts. The planter ideal represented an assumption about how the plantation system functioned and local proprietors' knowledge of this. Opposition on this basis was most overt in the 1820s when Steele's project was portrayed as a cruel, self-serving disaster, enacted by an ill-informed outsider. Steele's project was seen as running directly counter to the local expertise and paternalistic benevolence evident in how a 'good master' ran 'his' plantation.

Late eighteenth-century Barbados was characterised by a changing socio-economic system in which ameliorative attempts to produce 'sustainable' slavery were widespread. Although partly a rational response to changing economic, environmental and political conditions, these reforms were framed by 'common-sense' cultural assumptions about race and slavery. The discursive basis of amelioration was apparent in responses to the improving endeavours of Joshua Steele in the 1780s and 1790s. His far-reaching, radical and somewhat eccentric analysis of estate management and colonial development policies focussed on the irrationality of Barbadian society. Steele's solutions revolved around the importance of introducing English historical successes, Enlightened British ideas and a metropolitan improving dynamic. Trevor Burnard notes that '[a]n "improved" society was, by definition, an English society'.[109] Thus, to 'improve' a society was, in some ways, to *anglicise* it. By considering Steele's project as an anglocentric 'imperialism of "improvement"', predicated upon his belief that he 'knew better than those on the ground', we can appreciate the conflict between colonial and metropolitan articulations of 'improvement'. That Barbados had acquired a 'recognizably English' reputation by virtue of its cultivated nature in the seventeenth century made Steele's 'colonising' agenda all the more offensive and infuriating, and provoked a local, white, creole resistance that was predicated upon notions of 'natural' white superiority, black embodiment, paternalism and local expertise.[110] Yet, I do not want to overemphasise the internal coherence of the articulation of white identities. In the next chapter, this problem will be addressed by focussing on struggles over the constitution of white identity *within* Barbadian society.

---

[109] T. Burnard, '"The countrie continues sicklie": White mortality in Jamaica, 1655–1780', *Social History of Medicine* 12 (1999), 63.

[110] Drayton, *Nature's government*, pp. xv, 90; J. P. Greene, 'Changing identity in the British Caribbean: Barbados as a case study', in N. Canny and A. Pagden (eds.), *Colonial identity in the Atlantic world, 1500–1800* (Princeton: Princeton Press, 1987), p. 231.

3

Making a 'well constituted Society': the ambitions and limits of white unity

In March 1801, Francis Humberstone Mackenzie, Baron of Seaforth, arrived at Barbados to take up the governorship. Although not opposed to slavery *per se*, Seaforth had been instructed by the Colonial Office to reform the laws covering the enslaved population and, in consequence, spent much of the first decade of the nineteenth century locked in conflict with the conservative, planter-dominated Assembly.[1] Three months after his arrival on the island, Seaforth received an open letter from 'A Barbadian' that sought to persuade him that such reformist concern was misdirected. Promising to provide 'a faithful representation of the moral and political State of the Colony', the letter identified a series of more deserving problems, especially the 'disastrous emigration of the lower classes of [white] People'.[2] The letter contended that the rising wealth, influence and size of the free coloured population threatened the island's racial hierarchy and further marginalised these poor whites. According to the writer, this growing free coloured ascendancy was both encouraged by and reinforced the weakness and immorality of Barbados's white elite. These were all themes to which the author would return in other writing.

If Seaforth's orders reflected the increasing disquiet over colonial slavery in Britain, especially in the early nineteenth century, then the letter can be seen as a white West Indian response to this growing abolitionism.[3] The initial efforts of the British antislavery campaign, which peaked in the early 1790s, focussed on

---

[1] Seaforth was concerned with the legal formalisation of amelioration, and under his pressure the law that set a £15 fine for the wilful killing of an enslaved person by his/her owner was repealed in 1805. See P. L. V. Welch and R. A. Goodridge, *'Red' and black over white: Free coloured women in pre-emancipation Barbados* (Bridgetown: Carib Research and Publications, 2000), and Minutes of Assembly, 9 November 1802, Reel Bs. 7, BDA. He was also interested in the broader socio-racial structure of Barbadian society, and consulted the work of Joshua Steele. See Seaforth Muniments, GD 46/17/81, National Archives of Scotland.

[2] Anonymous [J. Poyer], 'A letter to His Excellency The Right Honourable Francis Lord Seaforth by a Barbadian', 22 June 1801, Seaforth Muniments, GD 46/7/5, NAS; item reprinted as 'John Poyer's letter to Lord Seaforth', *Journal of the Barbados Museum and Historical Society* 8 (1941), 161. All page references are to this reprint.

[3] Welch and Goodridge, *'Red' and black over white*, p. 100.

the abolition of the trade in enslaved Africans. Cutting the supply of labour, it was held, would cause slavery itself to wither.[4] The 1791 enslaved uprising in the French colony of St Domingue was used to discredit the campaign, however, and the French Revolution and declaration of war on Britain in 1793 intensified this opposition. Supporters of slavery sought to link abolitionism to Jacobinism – claims that its extra-parliamentary nature made it vulnerable to – especially after the Revolutionary government had outlawed slavery across the French empire. Yet, Napoleon's reintroduction of slavery in 1802 reduced the potency of this argument and, in the context of war with France, support for abolition became a patriotic British cause.[5] Following a renewed upsurge of campaigning, an abolition bill was introduced in Parliament in 1806. It passed into law on 25 March 1807 and from 1 May 1807 the British trade in enslaved Africans was outlawed.

The letter, then, was a colonial intervention into the controversy over slavery. At the same time, its focus on white elite immorality, lower-class white poverty and free coloured advancement posited concerns that went beyond the future of the Atlantic trade and raised broader, and simultaneously localised, questions about race, class, gender, sex and freedom. This local context is important because Barbados's planters were not particularly concerned about abolition – French invasion was a much greater fear – and their London agent was instructed not to lobby against it.[6] Unlike all the other West Indian colonies, Barbados experienced a natural increase in its enslaved population from 1800 and, with less reliance on imports of enslaved labour and fears that newly enslaved Africans were a destabilising presence within a population that was mainly locally born, abolition did not pose a direct threat. Some local slaveholders even believed that it would give the island a comparative advantage over its British sugar-producing rivals.[7]

Despite this lack of outright hostility to abolition, Barbados was not insulated from the politics of slavery. The revolution in St Domingue, which culminated in the declaration of an independent Haiti in 1804, and the 1795 uprising in Grenada focussed planter attention on the stability of colonial rule, whilst a belief that the British and French antislavery campaigns had encouraged these insurrectionists

[4] J. Walvin, 'The propaganda of anti-slavery', in J. Walvin (ed.), *Slavery and British society, 1776–1846* (London: Macmillan Press, 1982).

[5] L. Colley, *Britons: Forging the nation, 1707–1837* (London: Yale University Press, 1992); D. B. Davis, *The problem of slavery in the age of revolution, 1770–1823* (London: Cornell University Press, 1975); D. Geggus, 'British opinion and the emergence of Haiti, 1791–1805', in J. Walvin (ed.), *Slavery and British society, 1776–1846* (London: Macmillan Press, 1982); J. Jennings, *The business of abolishing the British slave trade, 1783–1807* (London: Frank Cass, 1997).

[6] J. F. Alleyne to W. Fitzherbert, 14 July 1788, Fitzherbert Collection, Reel 1, E20558, Barbados Department of Archives; R. Haynes to T. Lane, 16 September 1806, Newton Manuscripts 523/620, Senate House; G. W. Jordan, *An examination of the principles of the Slave Registry Bill, and of the means of emancipation, proposed by the authors of the Bill* (London: T. Cadell & W. Davies, 1816), pp. 1–2.

[7] See chapter 2, pp. 44–45. By the early nineteenth century, at least 85 per cent of enslaved people were locally born. See K. Watson, *The civilised island, Barbados: A social history, 1750–1816* (Bridgetown: Graphic Printers, 1979), p. 70.

served to link planter anxieties to the broader currents of abolitionism. Of particular concern were the alliances between free people of colour and enslaved people in both Haiti and Grenada,[8] which fuelled local debates about the position of free people of colour[9] and poor whites[10] in Barbadian society and whether these groups strengthened or undermined the planter order in the face of abolitionism and enslaved radicalism. Such debates were given focus by a high-profile murder case in 1796 in which a free man of colour was tried, convicted and controversially pardoned for killing a poor white man.

Whilst the previous chapter emphasised the dilemmas brought about for the local planter order by a metropolitan project of 'improvement', this chapter examines how the uncertain place of two 'liminal' groups in colonial society – poor whites and free people of colour – was revealing of fractures within white society and tensions around the articulation of white identities. These tensions centred on the issue of which social/symbolic hierarchy was central to the planter-dominated colonial order: slavery or race. That is to say, should society be organised around the control of enslaved labour, whatever the racial type of the enslavers, or should whiteness be the basis of social authority, whatever the class or slaveowning status of the whites? Through a consideration of contemporary historical accounts of Barbados at the turn of the eighteenth century, material from the murder trial and legislative debates about white planter authority, these competing visions can be considered. Nor were the two liminal groups passive in all this: both the poor whites

---

[8] For more on the broader impact of the Haitian Revolution on circum-Atlantic slaveholding cultures, see M. Craton, 'Forms of resistance to slavery', in F. W. Knight (ed.), *The slave societies of the Caribbean*, vol. III of *General history of the Caribbean* (London: UNESCO Publishing, 1997), pp. 248–251, and P. Linebaugh and M. Rediker, *The many-headed hydra: Sailors, slaves, commoners, and the hidden history of the revolutionary Atlantic* (London: Verso, 2000), chapters 8 and 9, and Conclusion. See also J. S. Handler, *The unappropriated people: Freedmen in the slave society of Barbados* (Baltimore: Johns Hopkins University Press, 1974), p. 80, n. 48; E. V. Goveia, *Slave society in the British Leeward Islands at the end of the eighteenth century* (London: Yale University Press, 1965), p. 252.

[9] The terms 'free people of colour' and 'free coloured' are used to refer to formerly enslaved people who had been manumitted, or to the children of women of this status – freedom being passed from mother to child. In other words, the terms refer to free males and females who were either black *or* of mixed race. On the entangled nature of the terms 'coloured' and 'black', see M. Newton, '"The Children of Africa in the Colonies": Free people of colour in Barbados during the emancipation era', unpublished DPhil. thesis, Oxford University (2001), pp. 7–11. In late eighteenth- and early nineteenth-century Barbados, the terms 'free coloured', 'free mulatto' and 'free black' were used almost interchangeably. In terms of the self-identification of this group, they tended to refer to themselves as the 'free coloured people'. Some modern writers use the terms 'freedmen' and 'freed people' to refer to the same group, but 'free people of colour' is more common. It is also crucial to emphasise that not all 'free people of colour' were of 'mixed race' – indeed about 45 per cent were 'black' – nevertheless, my focus is mainly on the propertied elite of the free coloured population, a group that tended to be of lighter skin colour. For example, all four of the free coloured plantation owners in the period 1750–1816 were of mixed race, as were the wealthy Montefiore merchant family.

[10] The term 'poor white' denotes Barbados's white lower classes, who constituted around half the total white population. This group was, of course, legally free. Often, I will be referring to the most destitute sections of this group (the poorest half of the lower classes). Contemporary commentators used the term 'poor white' in both senses. See K. Watson, *Civilised island*.

and free people of colour contested and affirmed the parameters of contemporary debates. Focussing on poor whites and free people of colour in Barbados extends the discussion of the slave society beyond the immediate relationship between enslaver and enslaved. Moreover, a consideration of both groups in conjunction throws light upon their interrelation and co-constitution, enriching both materialist accounts of such 'in-between' groups, as well as postcolonial discussions of hybridity.[11]

John Poyer: white settler historian

Although anonymous, the 1801 letter was written by John Poyer, an outspoken contemporary commentator and local historian. Poyer, a member of the island's middle class, was part of that growing body of white Barbadians who saw themselves as 'natives' rather than temporary sojourners.[12] He was the author of *The history of Barbados* (1808), the only general historiographic account produced by a Barbadian during the age of abolition.[13] In addition to this work and his letter to Seaforth, Poyer produced other written pieces in the early nineteenth century, particularly in the *Impartial Expositor* and *Barbados Chronicle* newspapers. These included a series of addenda to the *History* that covered more contemporary periods.[14]

---

[11] For example of a materialist account, see H. McD. Beckles, 'Rebels and reactionaries: The political responses of white labourers to planter class hegemony in the seventeenth-century Barbados', *Journal of Caribbean History* 15 (1981). One of the best theoretical discussions is H. K. Bhabha, 'Of mimicry and man', *The location of culture* (London: Routledge, 1994).

[12] W. Marshall and B. Brereton, 'Historiography of Barbados, the Windward Islands, Trinidad and Tobago, and Guyana', in B. W. Higman (ed.), *Methodology and historiography of the Caribbean* (London: UNESCO Publishing, 1999), p. 549. Evidence for Poyer's socio-economic status includes his concerns for the small creditors of planters, that his family cultivated cotton and the fact that he had not been permitted to consult legislative records whilst writing his *History*. See H. McD. Beckles, 'On the backs of blacks: The Barbados free-coloureds' pursuit of civil rights and the 1816 slave rebellion', *Immigrants and Minorities* 3 (1984), 169; 'Poyer's letter', 155; *Barbados Gazette*, 5 November 1788, Reel 20, Bridgetown Public Library; J. Poyer, *The history of Barbados from the first discovery of the island, 1605, till the accession of Lord Seaforth, 1801* (London: J. Mawman, 1808), p. VII.

[13] Poyer, *History of Barbados.*

[14] Although some of the newspapers remain in existence in the Barbados Public Library, their fragile condition means they cannot be consulted. See M. Chandler, *A guide to records in Barbados* (Oxford, 1965), p. 172; Handler, *The unappropriated people*, pp. 116–117. Poyer's addendum was entitled the *History of the administration of the Rt. Hon. Lord Seaforth late governor etc. etc. etc.* (Bridgetown, 1808). This is reprinted in H. Vaughan, 'Poyer's last work', *Journal of the Barbados Museum and Historical Society* 21 (1954). All page references are to this reprint. In addition, a broadsheet dated 8 January 1797 is likely to have been written by Poyer. Signed 'Brutus' and addressed to Philip Gibbes Jnr, Barbados's chief justice, the broadsheet was sent to the Colonial Office. See Brutus, untitled broadsheet, 8 January 1797, CO 28/65, fo. 387, TNA. There are a number of reasons for thinking that the author was Poyer. Both the broadsheet and Poyer's writing express similar concerns over the influence of free women of colour over white elite men. Identical phrases appear here and in Poyer's other work and the same legal authorities are cited. Of course, it may be that Poyer simply borrowed heavily from this earlier anonymous writer but, even if this is true, it is certain that both Poyer and 'Brutus' wrote from the same perspective.

Poyer's *History of Barbados* formed part of the spate of indigenous West Indian histories that were written in a tone of defensive, righteous indignation at the 'calumnies' spread by abolitionists about slavery. Yet, whilst Edward Long's *History of Jamaica* (1774) and Bryan Edwards's *History, civil and commercial, of the British colonies in the West Indies* (1793) have received much attention – in part because of the representative status often afforded to Jamaica in discussions of the British Caribbean – Poyer's *History* has not.[15] Yet, Poyer's text was one of the five major colonialist histories of Barbados and has been described as 'one of the most informative, and also one of the most revealing, of the West Indian histories of the period'.[16] Although published in Barbados and certainly written for a local audience, Poyer was deeply concerned to promote a positive image of the island society across the British Atlantic world. The *History* covers the period from initial European settlement to the arrival of Governor Seaforth in 1801. Its 692 pages consist of a chronological narrative of political events, interwoven with a personal commentary that often related to contemporary issues such as enslaved resistance, the state of the island's defences and colonial relations with Britain. Poyer said relatively little about slavery itself because he believed that the subject had been 'fully and ably' addressed by Bryan Edwards, an attitude that also points to the institution's unquestioned status for such West Indians.[17] Nevertheless, on those occasions when he did address the controversy over slavery, Poyer was unflinching in his support, portraying the enslaved people as 'an ignorant, superstitious, vindictive race', abolitionists as 'mistaken' and 'misinformed', and slavery itself as civilising servitude. Clearly, Poyer was a 'conservative' writer, concerned with the stability of Barbados's political, economic and social system based on an idealised model for a slave-based order that he termed a 'well constituted Society'.[18] He was vociferously hostile to the free people of colour and believed that white racial unity across the classes was critical to the defence of slavery. Nevertheless, he was far from being an uncritical apologist for the white plantocracy

---

[15] B. Edwards, *History, civil and commercial, of the British colonies in the West Indies* (London, 1793); E. Long, *The history of Jamaica* (London: T. Lowndes, 1774). On West Indian colonial historiography, see E. V. Goveia, *A study of the historiography of the British West Indies to the end of the nineteenth century* (Mexico City: Instituto Panamerico de Geografia e Historia, 1956), pp. 97–165. Poyer is not mentioned in two recent surveys of Caribbean historiography – B. W. Higman, *Writing West Indian histories* (London: Macmillan Education, 1999), and D. Lee (ed.), *Slavery, abolition and emancipation: Writings in the British Romantic period – the emancipation debate*, 8 vols., vol. III (London: Pickering and Chatto, 1999) – though he is discussed in W. Marshall and Brereton, 'Historiography of Barbados', pp. 551–552, and Goveia, *A study of the historiography*, pp. 44–49.

[16] H. Beckles, 'Black people in the colonial historiography of Barbados', in W. Marshall (ed.), *Emancipation II: A series of lectures to commemorate the 150th anniversary of emancipation* (Bridgetown: Cedar Press, 1987); Goveia, *A study of the historiography*, p. 49.

[17] Edwards, *History, civil and commercial*; Poyer, *History of Barbados*, pp. xiv, 144, 577.

[18] This phrase appears in Poyer, *History of Barbados*, p. 162. See also Goveia, *A study of the historiography*, p. 46.

and one of the most striking features of his less-than-conventional attitude was his staunch support for the colony's poor white population.[19]

Poor whites and free people of colour

Given his relative silence on the issue of slavery, the central theme that emerges from the 1801 letter, and from Poyer's writing more generally, were the relationships between Barbados's white elite, poor whites and free people of colour. The poor whites, whose condition so worried its author, totalled around 8,000 or half of the island's total white population in the early nineteenth century. Around half this number belonged to an upper lower class of militia tenants, small holders, shopkeepers, fishermen and skilled craftsmen.[20] The lower lower class of whites, around a quarter of the total white population, lived in destitution, relying on charity and vestry poor relief. They were unable to vote, owing to the property and income requirements, and lived on land unsuitable for sugar cultivation in the remote northern and eastern parishes of the island, especially the parts of St Andrew and St Joseph known locally as 'Scotland' (see figure 1.3). They suffered many tropical diseases and lived in conditions little better than enslaved people[21] – though, of course, they remained free. Their marginalisation and association with criminal, rebellious and Celtic origins – many were descended from Irish and Scottish convicts, prisoners of war and others declared undesirable by the seventeenth-century English state – contributed to the negative opinion of them held by many elite whites and enslaved people. Despite, then, the ideological and material advantages of whiteness, they were marginalised and lived as free but not full citizens.

The free people of colour were also a socially and politically marginalised group.[22] The population had emerged mainly through manumission by the will or

[19] H. McD. Beckles, *A history of Barbados: From Amerindian settlement to nation-state* (Cambridge: Cambridge University Press, 1990).

[20] J. Sheppard, *The 'redlegs' of Barbados: Their origins and history* (Millwood, NY: KTO Press, 1977); K. Watson, *Civilised island*. The militia tenants were created by a 1702 act in response to fears about the large majority enslaved population. The act required planters to provide one militiaman per 30–50 acres of land owned. In return for serving in the militia – which included policing enslaved meetings and capturing runaways – each tenant was given two acres of land.

[21] T. Burnard, '"The countrie continues sicklie": White mortality in Jamaica, 1655–1780', *Social History of Medicine* 12 (1999).

[22] Handler, *The unappropriated people*, pp. 18–19. For other accounts of free people of colour in Caribbean slave societies, see C. Campbell, 'Trinidad's free coloreds in comparative Caribbean perspectives', in H. McD. Beckles and V. Shepherd (eds.), *Caribbean slavery in the Atlantic world* (Kingston: Ian Randle, 2000); E. Cox, *Free coloreds in the slave societies of St Kitts and Grenada* (Knoxville: University of Tennessee Press, 1984); K. S. Hanger, *Bounded lives, bounded places: Free black society in colonial New Orleans, 1769–1803* (Durham, NC: Duke University Press, 1997); G. J. Heuman, *Between black and white: Race, politics, and the free coloreds in Jamaica, 1792–1865* (Westport, CT: Greenwood Press, 1981); Newton, '"The Children of Africa in the Colonies"'; A. Sio, 'Marginality and free coloured identity in Caribbean slave society', *Slavery and Abolition* 8 (1987).

deed of slaveholders, often as a reward for good service, for socio-sexual partners and the children of such relationships, or when an enslaved person's economically useful life was over. Other means of manumission included self-purchase and acts of legislature for those who informed on enslaved conspiracies. The free coloured population also grew naturally as its women had children and passed on their free status. This population remained small and outnumbered by the whites – there were just over 2,000 at the start of the nineteenth century – a unique situation in the British West Indies.[23] The free people of colour were, nonetheless, a highly visible group, partly because of their concentration in Barbados's urban areas. For instance, over half the free coloured population lived in Bridgetown alone by 1800.[24] Although the right to purchase, bequeath and inherit property had allowed a tiny minority of free people of colour to acquire substantial amounts of land and enslaved workers, and become 'propertied gentlemen', racial qualifications to civil rights rendered them vulnerable to physical, verbal and institutional attack, and made a 'mockery' of their freedom. As Melanie Newton puts it:

[N]one, however wealthy and for however long they had been free, enjoyed the legal privileges accorded to even the poorest white or was ever fully safe from the possibility of having their free status challenged.[25]

The connection that the 1801 letter made between the poor whites and free people of colour reflected material and discursive linkages. For example, both groups were involved in intensive economic competition.[26] Most free people of colour shunned plantation labour if possible and worked in huckstering (petty trading) or shop keeping, or sought to acquire trade skills. This put pressure on working-class whites who, in the wake of their displacement from the plantations, had traditionally performed such jobs. There was also competition in the hospitality sector, especially between female tavern owners servicing the maritime trade.[27] Sometimes poor white resentment at the success of some free people of colour was manifested in verbal abuse, theft and assault. The free people of colour complained

---

[23] In 1786, there were only 838 free people of colour (1.1 per cent of the total population), as against 16,167 (20.4 per cent) white people and 62,115 (78.5 per cent) enslaved people. From the beginning of the nineteenth century, the number and proportion of free people of colour rose to 2,209 (2.7 per cent) in 1801 and 2,663 (3.0 per cent) in 1809, as against 15,887 (19.3 per cent) and 15,566 (17.8 per cent) whites respectively. Figures are from Handler, *The unappropriated people*, pp. 18–19.

[24] Welch and Goodridge, *'Red' and black over white*.

[25] Newton, '"The Children of Africa in the Colonies"', p. 63. See also Beckles, 'On the backs of blacks'; Handler, *The unappropriated people*, p. 73; K. Watson, *Civilised island*. A 1721 act had introduced racial qualifications to many civil rights and prevented free people of colour from testifying against whites in court, voting, serving on juries or holding office.

[26] W. A. Green, *British slave emancipation: The sugar colonies and the great experiment, 1830–1865* (Oxford: Clarendon Press, 1976). Relations between free people of colour and poor whites were not simply antagonistic and, as contemporary descriptions make clear, could also involve charity and care. For example, see comments by R. Wyvill, which appear in J. Handler, 'Memoirs of an old army officer', *Journal of the Barbados Museum and Historical Society* 35 (1975).

[27] Handler, *The unappropriated people*, p. 123; Welch and Goodridge, *'Red' and black over white*, pp. 67–68.

that the inadmissibility of their testimony against whites made them vulnerable to such attacks. As a result, they sought to defend and expand their rights through petitioning from 1799.[28] Concurrent with this material competition were 'parallels' between the place of the poor whites and free people of colour in the symbolic colonial order.[29] Such ideas were grounded in local patterns of racial ideas and their articulation to freedom. In Jamaica, a complex system of colour gradations had developed, with 'mixed-race' people described as 'sambo', 'mulatto', 'quadroon', 'mustee', 'mustiphini', 'quintroon' or 'octoroon'.[30] The last two categories were codified as legally white and automatically free, something Mavis Campbell suggests was 'aimed at augmenting the white population'. In contrast, she describes Barbados as having 'no such demographic problem', something that contributed to the more bipolar, exclusionary, American pattern of racial politics.[31] There were also racial and colour categories in Barbados, with 'mixed-race' individuals identified as 'frothy', 'musty', 'yellow', 'light brown' and 'brown'. Yet, whilst such colour gradations *were* socially meaningful, these were neither inscribed with legal meaning nor as taxonomically formalised as those in Jamaica.[32] Their significance lay primarily in the *non-whiteness* they denoted, thus leaving the free people of colour in an uncertain symbolic position – as free but not white. Nevertheless, the partial non-whiteness denoted by the term 'red', which was used to describe poor whites at the same time, suggests that both groups were positioned ambiguously within the dominant bipolar racial taxonomy.

The uncertain, and to some extent parallel, position of the poor whites and free people of colour in the racial hierarchy made their comparison a common feature of eighteenth- and nineteenth-century travel writing. In 1726, Richard Towne, a British physician, was the first to make a formal comparison, declaring that both groups were debased. Griffith Hughes repeated this exercise a quarter of a century later, continuing a long-running debate.[33] The emergence of the controversy over slavery, and the debates about race in the West Indies that accompanied it, further encouraged comparisons by British visitors to Barbados. This was also a feature of the debates about how slavery could be defended through alliances between the white plantocracy and other sections of Barbados's population, debates in which Poyer played an important role.

---

[28] See pp. 93–98.

[29] For a comparative perspective, see C. C. Bolton, *Poor whites of the antebellum South: Tenants and labourers in central North Carolina and northeast Mississippi* (London: Duke University Press, 1994), p. 42; D. Kennedy, *Islands of white: Settler society and culture in Kenya and Southern Rhodesia, 1890–1939* (Durham, NC: Duke University Press, 1987), p. 177.

[30] E. K. Brathwaite, *The development of creole society in Jamaica, 1770–1820* (Oxford: Clarendon Press, 1971), p. 168.

[31] Beckles, *History of Barbados*, p. 66; M. C. Campbell, *The dynamics of change in a slave society: A sociopolitical history of the free coloureds of Jamaica, 1800–1865* (London: Associated University Press, 1976), pp. 40–41.

[32] K. Watson, *Civilised island*, p. 108, n. 7.

[33] G. Hughes, *The natural history of Barbados* (London, 1750); Sheppard, *'Redlegs' of Barbados*, pp. 41–55.

Theorising liminality

A useful concept with which to examine the position of the free people of colour and poor whites in Barbadian society is *liminality*. The word 'liminal' derives from the Latin 'limen', meaning 'threshold'. The term appears in traditional cultural anthropology and amongst postcolonial theorists, where it is associated with cultural hybridity.[34] Liminal groups are those which were neither obviously dominant nor subjugated, occupying a position of 'in-betweenness' in the colonial order. Situated on the border between coloniser and colonised, they were both markers of colonial difference and potentially destabilising loci of transgression.

Liminality is used here in two ways. Firstly, I use it to signify an ambiguity in the symbolic order related to Homi Bhabha's notion of 'ambivalence': a destabilising presence in colonial discourse. As neither white and dominant, nor black and subjugated, the poor whites and free people of colour were unsettling figures in slaveholding culture. They were figures of mimicry – almost the same but not quite – and menace – almost different but not quite. They provoked an 'ambivalence of colonial authority' by threatening the collapse of the symbolic order that revolved around the poles of white/free, black/enslaved.[35] The second approach to liminality is more materialist, with poor whites and free people of colour seen as occupying a social category 'in-between' those of 'master' and 'slave'. They were neither demographically large, nor powerful in economic and political terms. Although neither suffered the (dis)possession of the enslaved majority, their enjoyment of 'freedom' was curtailed by economic, political, cultural and legal constraints. One would not want to exaggerate the problems facing the poor white population nor play down the difficulties faced by many free people of colour. Nevertheless, in a slave society in which access to and exclusion from power, wealth and freedom were starkly polarised, the ambiguous social position of both groups was apparent.

This focus on the ambivalence and in-betweenness of poor whites and free people of colour is not novel. People of 'mixed race' were a liminal group in many colonial societies – the term 'half-breed' itself encapsulates this status. In slave societies, the liminal status of the free people of colour was heightened by the link between race and enslavement: they were 'non-white but free'.[36] Seaforth himself termed them a 'third description of people' apart from the 'whites or slaves'

---

[34] Bhabha, *The location of culture*; P. Werbner, 'The limits of cultural hybridity: On ritual monsters, poetic licence and contested postcolonial purifications', *Journal of the Royal Anthropological Institute* 7 (2001).

[35] Bhabha, *The location of culture*, p. 91; J. Pope Melish, *Disowning slavery: Gradual emancipation and 'race' in New England, 1780–1860* (London: Cornell University Press, 1998), p. 138.

[36] D. W. Cohen and J. P. Greene, *Neither slave nor free* (London: Johns Hopkins University Press, 1972); H. L. Malchow, *Gothic images of race in nineteenth-century Britain* (Stanford: Stanford University Press, 1996). More generally, see A. L. Stoler, 'Sexual affronts and racial frontiers: European identities and the cultural politics of exclusion in colonial southeast Asia', in F. Cooper and A. L. Stoler (eds.), *Tensions of empire: Colonial cultures in a bourgeois world* (Berkeley: University of California Press, 1997).

and called them 'the unappropriated people' of Barbados 'who are not slaves, and yet whom I cannot bring myself to call free'.[37] Yet, it was not only in terms of racial ambiguity that liminal figures were evident in colonial societies. In their work on colonial Kenya and Southern Rhodesia, Carolyn Shaw and Dane Kennedy discuss negative elite attitudes towards impoverished white populations. Similarly, though Barbados's poor whites were free, they remained marginal to the planter order and were often targets of abuse.[38]

One problem with some accounts of 'liminal' groups is that they tend to suggest that they were a disruptive presence within the socio-racial order of colonial societies by their very nature. Thus, liminality is sometimes understood as a stable though interstitial category. Yet, the boundary between coloniser and colonised – and the place of liminal groups in terms of this – was never fixed, but constantly in flux, and whether or not liminal figures were viewed as transgressive cannot be read from some *essential* ambiguity. Rather, it must be explored in relation to the colonial context, as Ann Laura Stoler shows in her work on the regulation of sexuality in European colonial societies in late nineteenth-century Asia.[39] In her examination of changing official attitudes to interracial sexual relationships and whether colonial rule was best maintained through the 'quality' or 'quantity' of white residents, Stoler demonstrates how liminal figures were sometimes seen as threats, and other times not. Thus, as well as viewing liminality as a locus of discursive ambivalence and a material condition of 'in-betweenness', an understanding of the tensions wrought and exposed by liminality requires the consideration of how it became inscribed with meaning – as transgressive of the colonial order, for example – and subject to certain disciplinary practices. Responses towards liminal groups reflected, in part, a series of competing 'models of colonialism'.[40] Questions about how colonial rule was to be maintained and how problems could be dealt with did not produce unchanging answers. Rather, a host of different strategies of control, economic agendas, fears and desires, each associated with different colonial institutions, interests and alliances, produced a multiplicity of readings of the place of liminal groups. In Barbados, these were based on white ideas about race and slavery. Yet, how liminality was understood, represented and subjected to practices cannot only be related to the signifying practices of the

---

[37] Seaforth to Hobart, 6 June 1802, Seaforth Muniments, GD 46/7/7, NAS.

[38] C. Jones, 'A darker shade of white? Gender, social class, and the reproduction of white identity in Barbadian plantation society', in H. Brown, M. Gilkes, and A. Kaloski-Naylor (eds.), *White?women: Critical perspectives on race and gender* (York: Raw Nerve Books, 1999); C. Jones, 'Mapping racial boundaries: Gender, race, and poor relief in Barbadian plantation society', *Journal of Women's History* 10 (1998); Kennedy, *Islands of white*; C. M. Shaw, *Colonial inscriptions: Race, sex, and class in Kenya* (London: University of Minnesota Press, 1995).

[39] A. L. Stoler, 'Carnal knowledge and imperial power: Gender, race, and morality in colonial Asia', in G. Quilley (ed.), *Feminism and history* (Oxford: Oxford University Press, 1996); A. L. Stoler, *Race and the education of desire: Foucault's* History of sexuality *and the colonial order of things* (London: Duke University Press, 1995).

[40] J. L. Comaroff, 'Images of empire, contests of conscience: Models of colonial domination in South Africa', in Cooper and Stoler, *Tensions of empire*; Pope Melish, *Disowning slavery*, p. 77.

white colonial elite. The acts and signifying practices associated with members of these groups must also be considered. Hence, the poor whites and free people of colour are treated here as social, political and economic agents who interacted with prevailing discourses in ways that could involve either identifying with or against dominant articulations of whiteness.[41]

The trial of Joseph Denny and its aftermath

Debates in Barbados about the place of poor whites and free people of colour in society, and how they related to the survival of slavery, were sparked not only by the rise of abolitionism and regional events such as the Haitian Revolution, but also by local incidents. These included attacks and murders carried out by whites on free people of colour and the petitioning campaign for rights this provoked from 1799. For Poyer, the most important commentator on these matters, a particular event that occurred in his home of Speightstown came to encapsulate his concerns. On 6 September 1796, Joseph Denny, a free man of mixed race, was arrested for shooting and killing John Stroud, a poor white neighbour.[42] The bar on non-white testimony against whites prevented Denny or his family from giving evidence to support his claim that he had thought that Stroud was a burglar. Denny was found guilty of Stroud's murder and sentenced to death by the Chief Justice, Philip Gibbes Jnr. Denny's legal counsel then asked Gibbes to sanction a petition from the convicted man to Governor George Poyntz Ricketts, Seaforth's immediate predecessor, hoping that Ricketts would recommend Denny to the clemency of the British Crown. Gibbes agreed and supplemented the petition with a letter in which he argued that the all-white jury had been prejudiced against the accused. With such opinions in mind, Governor Ricketts forwarded Denny's petition to Britain and, as a result, Denny's sentence was altered to one of exile. Knowing that this would be a controversial decision, Ricketts sought to avoid public confrontation by ordering Denny to be taken from the island in secret.[43] He was spotted, however, as he was being taken to a boat and there was uproar amongst the white population of Bridgetown. Captured by a white crowd unaware of the act of royal clemency, Denny was forcibly returned to prison. Yet, even after white Barbadians became aware of the pardon, Denny was still widely believed to have been guilty of murder.

[41] B. Kossek, 'Representing self/otherness and "white women" slaveowners in the English-speaking Caribbean, 1790–1830', paper presented at the Caribbean Studies Seminar Series, Institute of Commonwealth Studies, London, 13 March 2000. Beckles acknowledges this ambivalence when he talks about poor whites being caught up in a radicalism/reaction dilemma. See Beckles, 'Rebels and reactionaries'.

[42] For other accounts of these events, see Goveia, *A study of the historiography*, p. 48; N. Hall, 'Law and society in Barbados at the turn of the nineteenth century', *Journal of Caribbean History* 5 (1972); Handler, *The unappropriated people*, pp. 73–74, n. 32; Newton, '"The Children of Africa in the Colonies"'.

[43] P. Gibbes Jnr to G. Ricketts, 18 December 1796, CO 28/65, fos. 158–159, TNA; 'The humble petition of Joseph Denny', 16 January 1797, CO 28/65, fos. 160–161, TNA; G. Ricketts to Portland, 16 June 1797, CO 28/65, fos. 182–183, TNA.

Although Denny was transported to the prison-island of Ruatan, off what is now Honduras, in June 1797, controversy continued over the role of Chief Justice Gibbes, Governor Ricketts and the solicitor-general and chief prosecutor, John Beckles, in the affair. Gibbes, in particular, was subject to verbal and physical assault by other whites for supporting Denny's petition, and in an effort to clear his name he made accusations about the role of bribes in securing the support of other elite whites for Denny. Called to appear before the Council, he was charged by Governor Ricketts with making malicious and unfounded allegations. Eventually Gibbes was removed as chief justice and suspended from the Council, much to the satisfaction of the white public at large.[44]

The trial of Joseph Denny and its aftermath was an important episode in terms of how the politics of race played out in turn-of-the-century Barbados. This was the only case in which a free person of colour had killed a white during the period of slavery and, unlike elsewhere in the West Indies, there were no specific laws covering the offence.[45] The affair damaged the reputation of the governor and led to the suspension of a councillor and member of one of Barbados's most prominent planter families. There was civil unrest in Bridgetown when Denny's pardon was enacted and a stand-off between white colonists and the imperial forces guarding him. These events also attracted a great deal of written commentary. In addition to Poyer's *History*, other accounts were produced, including one written by Gibbes himself. There was also much traffic of material between the governor and the Colonial Office.[46] Finally, the affair served as a dramatic focus for the debates about the position of subaltern whites and free people of colour in the colony's socio-racial order. To this extent it was part of the broader controversy over race and slavery.

The trial of Denny and its aftermath occupies a central place within Poyer's *History of Barbados*. He devotes more pages to, and goes into much greater detail in, describing these events than any other incident. According to Elsa Goveia, Poyer 'shows considerable restraint, especially in the view of the fact that this was an almost contemporary case, over which tempers had obviously run pretty high'.[47] Nevertheless, he was vociferous in maintaining Denny's guilt and described him as having 'a bold, turbulent and daring temper'. Poyer viewed the events surrounding the trial of Denny as so important 'because the character of the country is deeply

---

[44] G. Ricketts to Portland, 19 May 1797, CO 28/65, fo. 178, TNA; extract from *Barbados Gazette*, 22 July 1797, CO 28/65, fos. 214–215, TNA; Minutes of Council, 1 August 1797, CO 28/85, fo. 205b, TNA. Gibbes later travelled to Britain and won reinstatement to the Council.

[45] N. Hall, 'Law and society'; Handler, *The unappropriated people*, p. 74.

[46] 'A true state of facts upon the case of Joe Denny at the island of Barbados', 10 March 1798, CO 28/65, fos. 248–252, TNA; P. Gibbes Jnr, Untitled, c. 1797, Seaforth Muniments, GD 46/17/81, NAS; Anonymous, *A narrative of facts relative to the tryal of Joe Denny, a free coloured man for the murder of John Stroud, a white-man* (Barbados, 1797). The Colonial Office material can be found in CO 28/65, fos. 154–188, TNA.

[47] Goveia, *A study of the historiography*, p. 48.

involved'. Symbolising the killing of a poor white man by a free man of colour, who was then able to escape justice through the influence of free women of colour over white elite men, the affair served as a synecdoche for his wider concerns about poor whites and free people of colour.[48] Indeed, his account revolves around three rhetorical figures that evoke this broader context: the corrupted elite white man, the free coloured courtesan and the 'legitimate' but silenced white. Tropes of seduction, disease and civil disorder also animate Poyer's account. These were markers of the problems that liminality brought upon the white-dominated colonial order, especially the transgressiveness of the free people of colour.

The first rhetorical figure in Poyer's account is the corrupt elite white man. Poyer portrayed the behaviour of certain elite men, including Denny's legal counsel and Governor Ricketts, not only as an 'unprecedented interposition on behalf of a convicted felon', but as inexplicable.[49] The main target of Poyer's invective was Chief Justice Gibbes. Asking why Gibbes had not expressed his concerns about Denny's guilt during the trial and had only supported the petition for clemency later, Poyer suggested that this was because he had been influenced into subverting Barbados's 'most sacred institutions'. Noting that Gibbes was 'born to affluence, and destined to fill the highest offices in the community', but portraying him as someone who was 'universally disliked' and exposed to 'popular odium', Poyer represented Gibbes as a fallen figure who had failed to live up to the standards expected of someone of his status.[50] Gibbes was also an individual manifestation of the corruption and immorality of the white elite. In Poyer's account 'every individual weakness has its political counterpart – uncivilized society, according to this logic, being little more than the uncivilized mind and body writ large'.[51] Gibbes's moral degeneracy spread to the rest of the Barbadian body politic. He was simultaneously an individual instance of elite failure, a synecdoche of elite failure and, through his actions after Denny's trial, a conduit through which the white order was threatened by corruption. Similar to eighteenth-century English critics of the 'effeminate' Francophile aristocracy, Poyer's account was a critique of white elite leadership that contrasted Gibbes's failings with a folkish 'decent' whiteness.[52]

The source of this corruption was the free coloured courtesan. Much of the controversy surrounding the Denny affair revolved around the question of *why* members of the white elite had acted in support of Denny's petition, and accusations

---

[48] Poyer, *History of Barbados*, pp. 632, 637. The description of the Denny trial and its aftermath appears in the final chapter of Poyer's *History of Barbados*, which covers the appointment of George Poyntz Ricketts as governor in 1794 to that of Seaforth in 1801.

[49] Poyer, *History of Barbados*, pp. 638–639.

[50] Gibbes was the main target of the 1797 'Brutus' broadsheet, which is likely to have been written by Poyer. See n. 14 above.

[51] D. Spurr, *The rhetoric of empire: Colonial discourse in journalism, travel writing, and imperial administration* (London: Duke University Press, 1993), p. 76.

[52] G. Newman, *The rise of English nationalism: A cultural history, 1740–1830* (New York, 1987).

abounded about bribes and the influence of free people of colour more broadly.[53] In Poyer's account, this coloured influence was feminised. He was particularly concerned about the role of the governor's mistress, Betsey Goodwin:

Unfortunately for the governor, unfortunately for Barbados, his excellency had brought with him from Tobago, a mulatto woman, who resided at Pilgrim [the Governor's residence], and enjoyed all the privileges of a wife, except the honour of publicly residing at his table. His excellency's extraordinary attachment to this sly insidious female was the greatest blemish in his character, and cast a baleful shadow over the lustre of his administration. The influence which she was known to possess, produced a visible change in the manners of the free coloured people, who assumed a rank in the graduated scale of colonial society, to which they had been hitherto strangers.[54]

In a language akin to what Howard Malchow describes as the 'Caribbean gothic',[55] Goodwin appears as a witch-like temptress possessing a mysterious 'influence' evident in the governor's 'extraordinary attachment' to her. Her 'baleful shadow' was apparent in the murder trial and Poyer claimed that, whilst in jail, Denny had received assurances that 'she would protect him'. Poyer's conviction was strengthened by Governor Ricketts's previous judicial interventions in favour of other free people of colour, again supposedly at the behest of Goodwin. Poyer also claimed that Goodwin's presence had wider consequences across the colonial society by encouraging the free people of colour to challenge the racial hierarchy. Indeed, his account of 'the illicit intercourse between men in power and the coloured Women of the Country' suggested island-wide free coloured influence over an enfeebled and befuddled white male elite.[56] This was a particular reading of the sexual liaisons between free coloured women and white men that were a common feature of slave societies. Although these relationships usually took the form of concubinage and were often exploitative, this did not prevent free women of colour from using them to their own strategic advantage – to gain manumission for relatives or win patronage for business ventures, for example.[57] For Poyer, these relationships were a menace to the colonial order.

Poyer's portrayal of free coloured influence over the white male elite deployed tropes of hyper-sexualisation and feminisation in a rhetorical gesture that David Spurr describes as *eroticisation*, 'in which an entire people is allegorized by the figure of the female body' (figure 3.1). Within this trope, seduction is represented not only as a locus of desire, but of sexual danger. Eroticisation is linked to white fear and loathing, typically through the figure of the hyper-sexualised

---

[53] Affidavit of Samuel Hinds Jnr, 29 May 1797, CO 28/65, fo. 212, TNA.

[54] Poyer, *History of Barbados*, pp. 639–640.   [55] Malchow, *Gothic images*, p. 201.

[56] 'Poyer's letter', 163–164; Poyer, *History of Barbados*, p. 640. For example, in March 1795, he had sought to have the fines remitted for Samuel Welsh, a free black man charged with assault: Ricketts to Portland, c. March 1795, CO 28/65, fo. 55, TNA.

[57] G. Heuman, 'The social structure of the slave societies in the Caribbean', in F. W. Knight, *The slave societies of the Caribbean*, pp. 149–150; K. Watson, *Civilised island*, p. 108; Welch and Goodridge, *'Red' and black over white*, pp. 100–118.

Figure 3.1 A. Brunias, *The Barbados mulatto girl* (c. 1790). From the collection of the Barbados Museum and Historical Society.

tropical woman, whose dangerous desires correlate to corruption in the social sphere.[58] The figure of the 'mulatta', in particular, came to embody discourses of 'cupidity, immorality, sexual corruption, and tropicalization'. In slave societies,

[58] Spurr, *Rhetoric of empire*, pp. 173, 180.

the menacing presence of *free* women of colour was heightened because she was 'no longer constrained by the bonds of slavery' and therefore 'constituted an uncontrollable site of potential racial mixing'.[59] Poyer's description of 'certain coloured courtezans, who were known to be favourites with some men in power', was given particular resonance by free women of colour's domination of the commercial sex work sector.[60] Free coloured hotel owners were important figures in Bridgetown's economy and wielded considerable influence. These hotels were sites of sexual and racial transgression, and illicit mixing.[61] In portraying free women of colour in terms of erotic desire and danger, Poyer was evoking a heady mix of interracial sex, disease, miscegenation and immorality.

The portrayal of free coloured/white relations in terms of dangerous desires was most evident in Poyer's representation of Gibbes:

In those soft unguarded moments when, trying to forget the scorn and contempt which you daily encounter, you fondly recline on the saffron bosom of your favourite *Squaw*, your amorous soul, softened by the *chaste embraces*, the tender endearments of *virtuous affection*, is artfully prepared for the reception of the poison which she infuses into your mind. Then is the time when your fond heart is capable of receiving and consenting to the most nefarious proposals which her treachery or her ambition can suggest.[62]

Portraying the relationship between Gibbes and his 'yellow' mistress in savagely sarcastic and unromantic terms, the latter appears as an 'artful' agent for the free people of colour, amongst whom 'one general sympathy pervades the whole'.[63] Thus seduced, Gibbes betrayed the interest of his own race. This scene of seduction was a scene of infection. It brought together two meanings of 'corruption' – as inappropriate sexual and political relations, *and* degeneracy. This link was also made through the evocation of racial mixing and metaphors of venereal disease, especially syphilis. Historically, syphilis has been understood as 'pollution' and throughout his description of Barbados's ills, Poyer uses terms such as 'filth', 'impurities', 'errors', 'defects' and 'decay'. Syphilis has also been understood as 'punishment for an individual's transgression', especially sexual activity with 'dangerous others'.[64] This was apparent in Gibbes's 'degeneracy' and in how he was shunned by white society.[65] Owing to their sexually transmitted nature, venereal diseases have also traditionally been used to identify 'transgressing' populations,

---

[59] Pope Melish, *Disowning slavery*, p. 125; M. Sheller, *Consuming the Caribbean: From Arawaks to zombies* (London: Routledge, 2003), p. 116. See also P. Mohammed, '"But most of all mi love me browning": The emergence in eighteenth- and nineteenth-century Jamaica of the mulatto woman as the desired', *Feminist Review* 65 (2000).

[60] Poyer, *History of Barbados*, p. 639.

[61] H. McD. Beckles, *Centering woman: Gender discourses in Caribbean slave society* (Oxford: James Currey, 1999), p. 25; Linebaugh and Rediker, *Many-headed hydra*, p. 259.

[62] Brutus, untitled broadsheet.   [63] 'Poyer's letter', 164.

[64] J. M. Coetzee, *White writing: On the culture of letters in South Africa* (New Haven: Yale University Press, 1988), p. 142; S. Sontag, *Illness as metaphor/AIDS and its metaphors* (London: Allen Lane, 1991), pp. 17, 27, 46.

[65] 'Poyer's letter', 164.

including feared and despised minority groups, as the free people of colour were for Poyer. In this way, expressions of anxiety about racial purity and pollution – disease, infection, miscegenation and the threat posed by 'the half-breed' – were brought together in the 'gothic' figure of the free coloured courtesan.[66]

If she was a baleful figure in Poyer's narrative and the corrupt white elite the conduit and sign of her dangerous desires, then the ultimate victim was the 'legitimate' white Barbadian.[67] These included poor whites, members of the white middle classes – such as Poyer himself – and those elite whites who had not been corrupted. They were the decent majority of Barbados's white community and the heart of its society. They do not figure prominently in Poyer's account of the Denny affair. Yet, when they do, they appear as silenced and outraged figures. Firstly, there was John Stroud himself. He represented the poor whites that Poyer sought to champion, yet only appears in Poyer's account as Denny's victim, silenced by his death.[68] During the trial, Stroud was further silenced because although he had named Denny as his assailant before he died, his sworn deposition was not produced in court. For Poyer, this was another aspect of the suspicious circumstances surrounding the trial. The jurors who had found Denny guilty were also silenced when Gibbes denounced and set aside their decision.[69] Poyer was incensed by Gibbes's dismissal of the voices of ordinary white men and it was this action that provoked the initial calls for his removal from office. Poyer noted that the transmission of Denny's petition to Britain had 'excited a considerable ferment in the country' and, after the governor's abortive attempt to remove Denny from the island in secret, a committee was formed amongst Bridgetown's population to demand that justice be done. This agitation was a manifestation of the desire of 'legitimate' whites 'to maintain their civil rights' and challenge their marginalisation.[70] The most vociferous calls for justice came from the author himself and through his role as 'native' historian and social commentator, Poyer presented himself as the one able to give the ordinary whites voice and expose guilty men such as Gibbes:

I have long been an attentive, tho' a silent, observer of your conduct: I have privately laughed at your vanity, and secretly despised your follies, and detested your vices: And should in all probability, have continued to remark the unfoldings of your degenerate principles with the same contemptuous taciturnity had not your vicious propensities lately become dangerous.[71]

For Poyer, the 'legitimate' whites were portrayed as silenced and marginalised figures, who required a spokesperson if their call for justice were to be heeded and Barbados's descent into disorder averted.

---

[66] Sontag, *Illness as metaphor*, p. 54. These are also elements that Malchow associates with the 'Caribbean gothic'. See Malchow, *Gothic images*, p. 201.
[67] 'Poyer's letter', 163.
[68] Stroud was a fisherman. See Beckles to Ricketts, 15 January 1797, CO 28/85, fo. 162, TNA.
[69] Minutes of Council, 11 July 1797, CO 28/85, fos. 200–201, TNA; P. Gibbes Jnr to Ricketts, 18 December 1796, CO 28/85, fo. 158b, TNA.
[70] Poyer, *History of Barbados*, pp. 639, 642.   [71] Brutus, untitled broadsheet.

Poyer's account of the Denny affair brings together white elite corruption, coloured seduction and the silencing of 'legitimate' whites. Though manifested in individual figures such as Gibbes, Ricketts, Stroud, Denny and Goodwin, the consequences were not limited to the individual. Rather 'synecdoche and metaphor combine marking the individual as both cause and emblem of a more general degradation'.[72] Linking free coloured demographic growth, illicit sex, racial mixing and seduction, Poyer saw the Denny affair as a sign of the potentially terminal weakness in white society. He portrays a society on the verge of self-destruction. For instance, the discovery of Rickett's plan to remove Denny from the island in secret was portrayed as presaging civil warfare:

The effect of this intelligence could not have been greater if the capital had been invaded. The whole town was a scene of uproar and confusion . . . Knowing of no authority for transporting the cause of this disturbance, several of the most eminent merchants ran to Rickett's battery and fired upon the brig [in which Denny was being transported].[73]

After Denny was taken back to prison, there was also a stand-off between local whites – including members of the colonial militia – and the imperial forces guarding him. In both instances, Barbados appears as a society at war with itself, subverted from within:

[T]he Metropolis exhibited a Scene of confusion and dismay; when the peace and tranquillity of the community was disturbed, its safety endangered and the Public mind completely convulsed.[74]

The trial and its eventful aftermath occurred at a time of conflict with France across the Caribbean when there was a fear of invasion. Yet, for Poyer, there was also a terrible threat from within. The shadow of civil disorder was a symptom of rising free coloured influence and wealth. The outcome could be apocalyptic, causing white society to turn against itself and threatening to bring about its self-destruction. Corruption and disorder were a 'cause and emblem' of white weakness.

A 'well constituted Society'

The Denny affair was a synecdoche for Poyer's concerns about Barbadian society. Seduction, disease, prostitution, concubinage, interracial sex, miscegenation, bribery and murder all appeared in his account. Signalling that there was 'something rotten in the State', they were signs of the transgression of 'proper' boundaries between white and black, rich and poor, powerful and servile. For Poyer, the existence of non-whites who subsisted at a higher level than some whites was 'a

---

[72] Spurr, *Rhetoric of empire*, p. 76.   [73] Poyer, *History of Barbados*, p. 641.
[74] 'A true state of facts upon the case of Joe Denny', 10 March 1798, CO 28/85, fo. 250, TNA; 'Poyer's letter', 163–164.

fundamental ideological contradiction which, if not resolved, could erode the very conceptual apparati which held it together'.[75] Poyer's fears about such erosion, as apparent in the Denny affair, were predicated upon a particular set of ideas about how a West Indian society should be ideally organised:

[I]n every well constituted Society, a state of subordination necessarily arises from the nature of civil Government. Without this no political Union could long subsist. To maintain this fundamental principle, it becomes absolutely necessary to preserve the distinctions which naturally exist or are accidentally introduced into the Community. With us, two grand distinctions result from the state of Society: First between the White Inhabitants and free people of Colour, and Secondly between Masters and Slaves. Nature has strongly defined the difference not only in complexion, but in the mental, intellectual and corporeal faculties of the different Species, and our Colonial code has acknowledged and adopted the distinction.[76]

A 'well constituted Society' was one in which the practices through which the necessary 'state of subordination' was maintained, and served to reflect and reinforce 'natural' divisions. This combination of racial and legal divisions amounted to an understanding of slave society in which power, influence and wealth were ideally organised along racial lines: those powerless and enslaved should be non-white, those free and powerful should be white. White unity was critical to the strength of Barbadian society and how well it would withstand non-white radicalism and metropolitan humanitarianism. This was an inclusionary view of white Barbadian society in which subaltern whites had to be brought back into the fold. At the same time, the free people of colour – despite the social and legal limitations they faced – posed a threat to this 'well constituted Society'. For Poyer, there was a direct link between the increasing size and wealth of this population and the impoverishment of the poor whites, particularly as the free people of colour came to dominate occupations that had been the preserve of the white lower classes. Furthermore, the influence of free women of colour led to the 'immorality of some men in the higher walks of life', and the 'contagious example' these elite men set further led the free people of colour to assume 'an insolent and provoking deportment towards the legitimate inhabitants of the Island'.[77] This was to the detriment of the poor whites and white society as a whole. Thus, both the state of the poor whites and free people of colour indicated a slippage from an idealised, racialised conception of Barbadian society: poor whites were not free enough, and free people of colour were too free. Both groups were transgressive in their liminality.

Poyer's vision of a 'well constituted Society' also framed his responses to, and portrayal of, these liminal groups. For instance, the rhetoric of debasement, centred on the production of images of fear and loathing, was clearly deployed

---

[75] H. McD. Beckles, 'Black over white: The "poor-white" problem in Barbados slave society', *Immigrants and Minorities* 7 (1988), 9; 'Poyer's letter', 160.
[76] 'Poyer's letter', 162.   [77] 'Poyer's letter', 163.

in descriptions of free coloured women. Related to what Julia Kristeva terms the abject – 'the crisis of the subject'[78] – debasement involves the obsessive exclusion of the other because of the threat it poses to the colonial order. One might argue that debasement is a vital strategy in the constitution of liminal figures as the ambivalence of their mimicry/menace makes them less obviously 'other', but all the more dangerous for it. In this sense, debasement is an attempt to shift the liminal to the space of marginality. Such rhetorical debasement was mirrored by the material practices that Poyer propounded, which sought to push the free people of colour to the margins of the colonial order by increasing the costs of manumission, and limiting their accumulation and intergenerational transference of property. Such attempts at restricting the biological and economic reproduction of the free coloured population sought to realise the sterility of the 'half-breed' that was often confidently asserted within white circum-Caribbean slaveholding cultures.[79] In these ways, Poyer sought to remove the 'contradiction' posed by the free people of colour and marginalise them into a fully subaltern position:

[The free people of colour] should not be suffered to exceed the boundaries of that subordinate State in which Divine Providence has placed them and to which the welfare of the Colony requires that they should be restricted.[80]

In contrast, the poor whites were to be rescued from liminality. Whilst often viewed as 'a source of amusement' by planters, Poyer represented them through tropes of idealisation and a rhetoric of romanticism.[81] For him, they were a people of 'strength and courage' and 'a hardy peasantry' that formed the 'physical strength of the country'. Yet, the decline in the size and wealth of the poor white population had reduced the militia to 'an undisciplined rabble' and represented a 'growing evil'.[82] Although Poyer believed that white interests as a whole lay with a strong white labouring class, he argued that a short-sighted search for profit amongst planters, who employed enslaved workers in skilled jobs – in addition to free coloured influence – had marginalised poor whites. As a result, its members were squeezed out of their traditional occupations and left landless.

Poyer's obsessive debasement of the free people of colour and idealisation of the poor whites signalled a concern with the breakdown of a 'well constituted Society' and the importance he attached to preventing this. The poor whites were to be made fully white again by providing them with land and employment; the free people of colour were to be made less free by reducing their demographic growth and curtailing their acquisition of property. Taken together, such solutions

---

[78] J. Kristeva, 1983, cited in Spurr, *Rhetoric of empire*, p. 78. For Kristeva, the abject is 'that which must be expelled if psychic and social order is to be established and maintained. These expelled elements, however, continue to haunt the subject and its world with disruption or dissolution.' See R. Edmond, 'Abject bodies/abject sites: Leper islands in the high imperial era', in R. Edmond and V. Smith (eds.), *Islands in history and representation* (London: Routledge, 2003), p. 135.

[79] Malchow, *Gothic images*, p. 179.   [80] 'Poyer's letter', 163.

[81] Beckles, 'Rebels and reactionaries', 19.   [82] Poyer, *History of Barbados*, pp. 60 n. 61, 131.

represented the racial realignment of Barbadian society, re-establishing the link between race and status/wealth. The attempts to achieve this involved the expression and enactment of particular articulations of white colonial identity. At the same time, the liminal groups that Poyer sought to include and exclude from his 'well constituted Society' contested and affirmed this project of realignment, thus helping to reveal the ambitions and limits of white unity.

The struggle for free coloured rights

Poyer was not the first to voice concerns about the free people of colour. As well as the 1721 act, which had first established a link between full rights and whiteness, the freeing of enslaved people had been brought under legislative control in 1739 with the setting of manumission fees at £50. In an 1801 act, the manumission fees were further raised to £300 for enslaved females and £200 for males.[83] This was a clear attempt to prevent the natural increase of the free coloured population by controlling the reproductive power of free women of colour. For Poyer and others this was a necessary device to protect white interests. As John Foster Alleyne, a wealthy planter and Council member, wrote: '[t]his law I hope will operate to our preservation'. Nevertheless, he did not believe it went far enough:

I am very sorry to hear of the large purchases made by the coloured people in our country of land and Slaves: if it is permitted to go on without some check, We shall perhaps in no great distance of Time find ourselves in the same situation that the neighbouring island of Grenada was in not long since. I am astonished that we are so blind to our own Interest and safety.[84]

A campaign was started for immediate measures to curtail the free people of colour's ability to accumulate wealth, an effort articulated most clearly in Poyer's 1801 letter to Seaforth.

These sorts of anti-free coloured moves did not go uncontested. Throughout the early nineteenth century, free people of colour attempted to negotiate their position with the planter elite through strategies aimed at stabilising their liminal status. Their adoption of Christianity – Methodism, in particular, became dominated by free people of colour – was one, as was participation in the militia, especially during the 1816 revolt.[85] Moreover, between 1799 and 1814, seven petitions were submitted by free people of colour to the governor, Assembly or Council, marking 'the beginning of a civil rights struggle which, despite many vicissitudes, frustrations, and the intransigence of a basically reactionary plantocracy, was to continue

---

[83] Acts: Barbados, No. 225, CO 30/17, fos. 48–50, TNA.

[84] J. F. Alleyne to S. Hinds, 10 September 1801; J. F. Alleyne to J. Thorne, 20 November 1801, Alleyne Letters, fo. 66, Alleyne Letters, fos. 108–109, West India Committee collection, Institute of Commonwealth Studies.

[85] For more on Methodism, see chapter 5, p. 161, and Newton, '"The Children of Africa in the Colonies"'. For a comparison, see Hanger, *Bounded lives, bounded places*, chapters 4 and 5.

to the end of the slave period'. Although mainly an expression of the interests of elite free men of colour, they were an important intervention in the public debate about Barbados's socio-racial order and connected rhetorical self-representation to the political struggle for rights.[86]

The first petition had been submitted in October 1799. Signed by fifty-eight people and addressed to Governor Ricketts and the Council, this memorial was a response to assaults upon, and murders of, free people of colour by whites, which, owing to the bar on free coloured testimony, went unpunished. The memorial contained features that were to recur in later petitions. Firstly, it was couched in language that combined loyalty with submissiveness. On the one hand, the memorialists asserted their 'inviolable attachment . . . to our King and Constitution'. One the other, they acknowledged their 'subordinate state' and duty 'to use our constant endeavours by every act of gratitude, obedience, and loyalty, to endear ourselves to all in authority'.[87] Secondly, the memorial called for free people of colour to be granted the right to give legal testimony against whites. It was this prohibition that had contributed greatly to Denny's conviction in 1796 and most limited their 'free status'.[88] The 1799 memorial came at a time of general white reaction against free people of colour – much related to the aftermath of the Denny trial – and did not succeed in winning an expansion of their civil rights. In contrast, the petitions that came later were a direct engagement with efforts to *curtail* their rights. For example, one produced in October 1801 came only months after Poyer had called for limits to the free coloured acquisition of property.[89]

Despite these petitions, Poyer and those who shared his views continued in their efforts to marginalise the free people of colour. In autumn 1802, Robert Haynes, a prominent plantocrat, brought a bill before the Assembly 'to prevent the accumulation of real property by free Negroes and free persons descended from Negroes'. The bill passed through the Assembly with almost total support and was sent to the Council for approval. Its provisions sought to restrict free coloured slaveowners to a maximum of five enslaved persons and to prevent non-holders

---

[86] Handler notes that '[t]here are no known books or pamphlets written by freedmen, no freedmen newspapers existed during the slave period, and there are very few known letters by freedmen'. See Handler, *The unappropriated people*, pp. 4, 75. The group petitions and addresses are important sources, therefore, though there are clearly problems. As well as being relatively few in number, the petitions reflect elite male free coloured interests, in which freedom was linked to slave ownership rather than understood in terms of full racial equality. Nevertheless, they do bring together rhetorical (self-)representation and political struggle, and were clearly part of the public debate about the racial order in Barbados. Campaigns for rights were also waged by different populations of free people of colour across the Caribbean. See Heuman, 'The social structure of the slave societies in the Caribbean', pp. 159–160.

[87] 'The humble memorial . . . of the free coloured people', Minutes of Council, 15 October 1799, Lucas Manuscripts, Vol. 32, Reel 14, BPL.

[88] Newton, '"The Children of Africa in the Colonies"', p. 74; Welch and Goodridge, *'Red' and black over white*, p. 102.

[89] There is no trace of this petition. Evidence of its contents comes from Alleyne to Thorne, 1 February 1802, Alleyne Letters, fo. 138, WIC, ICS.

from purchasing any at all. Free coloured ownership of land was to be set at a maximum of ten acres. In addition, the inheritance of property was to be limited to legal heirs, a deliberately discriminatory move given that patterns of non-marital relations were common in the free coloured community. The Council returned the bill to the Assembly with modifications and the Assembly passed a new version in mid-1803.[90]

The new version of the Poyer-inspired bill roused members of the free coloured population to produce another petition directed towards the Council. Signed 'by upwards of three hundred' persons, this focussed on the sanctity of private property and the loyalty of the free people of colour to the planter-dominated order:

We are aware that in a country like this it is necessary to make distinctions and lay restraints. To such restrictions as have been already laid we have always submitted . . . with cheerfulness . . . But should we not only be prevented from acquiring property, but even be bereaved of that which we have honestly and lawfully acquired, what must be our state of wretchedness and despondency, as well might we be reduced to a state of slavery.[91]

The petitioners accepted Barbados's hierarchically structured society and demonstrated their support for it by evoking a trope common in proslavery accounts of the West Indies – that of the contented subaltern.[92] Yet, this 'cheerfulness' was predicated upon the retention of existing economic rights, for without them, they would be degraded to a 'state of slavery'. The connection made between freedom and slave ownership was a significant feature of the 1803 petition:

Many of our children who are now grown almost to the years of maturity have from their earliest infancy been accustomed to be attended by slaves; if this bill should pass into law, when we are no more, these children cannot posses a single slave. What will then be the meaning of their condition? Surely death would be preferable to such a situation![93]

Here, the petitioners evoked their long-standing support for slavery as the central institution in Barbadian society through reference to free children of colour, who had been socialised into the system. Moreover, the right to possess enslaved people was linked to freedom and life, whereas the removal of this right was figured as 'death'. This relates to the fact that 'many coloureds regarded slaves as a legitimate and *desirable* form of property and had a significant ideological commitment to the principle of slave ownership'. Given the importance of the right to (dis)possess enslaved subjects as a marker of freedom in Barbados, the wealthy petitioners were at pains to assert their support of, and involvement in, slavery. Yet, this was also a

---

[90] Handler, *The unappropriated people*, p. 78; Minutes of Assembly, 9 November 1802, Reel Bs. 7, BDA.

[91] 'The humble petition of the free coloured people, inhabitants of the island', Minutes of Council, 1 November 1803, Lucas Manuscripts, Vol. 32, Reel 14, BPL.

[92] A. O. Thompson, '"Happy – happy slaves!": Slavery as a superior state to freedom', *Journal of Caribbean History* 29 (1995).

[93] 'The humble petition', 1 November 1803, BPL.

way in which dominant white racial norms could be challenged.[94] For the free coloured elite, slave ownership was a marker of their not-white-but-free status and their expressions of support for slavery were an attempt to contest efforts to marginalise them. The petitioners concluded their address with a stark warning for the white elite:

Such a law would not only be oppressive in the highest degree, but totally ruinous to us, and that it must utterly destroy that spirit of industry which we have always thought to be the wise policy of the governing power to encourage, as congenial to the good of the country and beneficial to every civilized society, and that to deprive us of our property will remove the best security for our loyalty and fidelity.[95]

This warning was based on two elements. Firstly, the petitioners approved of the division of the non-white population by class, based on the inculcation of an elite view of property.[96] Secondly, the petitioners evoked white fears of a free coloured/enslaved coalition, fears that were strong after revolution in St Domingue and revolt in Grenada.[97] In this way, the petitioners sought to demonstrate the foolishness of abandoning the strategy of divide-and-rule and the dangers inherent in such a policy.

The petition had the desired effect. John Alleyne Beckles, an influential member of the Council and the chief opponent of the 'cruel' bill, was particularly critical of the clauses that sought to prevent free people of colour from purchasing enslaved people. Echoing the 1803 petition, he emphasised the socialising function of slave ownership:

These [free coloured] children have had good educations, and have been brought up with all the tenderness of white children, and have been accustomed to be attended by slaves from their earliest infancy.[98]

Beckles believed that free people of colour should be able to share the 'tenderness' that came with the enjoyment of racial servitude. More generally, the maintenance of slavery required the fashioning of a racially inclusive slaveholding fold. He concluded the Council debate with an explicit reassertion of the importance of a divide-and-rule strategy for planter dominance:

I am inclined to think that it will be politic to allow them to possess property; it will keep them at a greater distance from the slaves, and will keep up that jealousy which seems naturally to exist between the free coloured people and the slaves; it will tend to our security, for should the slaves at any time attempt to revolt, the free coloured persons for their own safety and the security of their own property, must join the whites and resist them. But if we reduce

---

[94] K. Watson, *Civilised island*, p. 106; Welch and Goodridge, *'Red' and black over white*, p. 76. See also R. B. Allen, *Slaves, freedmen, and indentured laborers in colonial Mauritius* (Cambridge: Cambridge University Press, 1999); Hanger, *Bounded lives, bounded places*, pp. 1, 70–80.

[95] 'The humble petition', 1 November 1803, BPL.

[96] See Ricketts to Portland, 20 March 1795, CO 28/65, fos. 51–52, TNA.

[97] Handler, *The unappropriated people*.

[98] Minutes of Council, 1 November 1803, Lucas Manuscripts, Vol. 32, Reel 14, BPL.

the free coloured people to a level with the slaves, they must unite with them, and will take every occasion of promoting and encouraging a revolt.[99]

Decreasing the freedom of the free people of colour by curtailing their right to (dis)possess others articulated a dangerous 'race first' strategy in a society in which less than a fifth were white. Instead, promoting the linkage between freedom and slaveholding could act as a source of planter hegemony.

At its second reading, the Council voted against the bill and it was returned to the Assembly. Despite an attempt to revive it in 1804 it was eventually dropped. Of course, it was not simply the petitioning that caused the bill to be abandoned. It had threatening implications for the rights of *all* proprietors. John Ince, who also spoke against the bill, argued that the central characteristic of freedom was the right to hold property. This was a defining feature of freedom in a social order that revolved around the (dis)possession of the majority of its population by a minority. There were concerns amongst some plantocrats that any act might have been disallowed by the metropolitan authorities, perhaps under the guidance of the reform-minded Governor Seaforth. Fears about French invasion may have further militated against the adoption of measures that could create internal disquiet.[100] Nevertheless, whilst the petitions were not the sole reason for the failure of attempts to marginalise the free people of colour, they did coincide with, and draw strength from, plantocratic concerns about property and the broader regional and trans-Atlantic context, including the slavery controversy. Poyer's failure did not mean that the petitioners achieved the extension of their civil rights, however. Although no further efforts were made to curtail them, it was only after they had demonstrated their 'loyalty' to the white-dominated order during the 1816 rebellion that limited rights were granted to some free people of colour.[101]

The failure of Poyer's vision has been attributed to the 'triumph of political pragmatism over ideological dogmatism'.[102] Yet, this fails to recognise the culturally embedded nature of both pragmatism *and* Poyer's racist idealism. White elite opponents of the 1803 bill articulated a vision of Barbadian society that did not revolve around the trope of race, which was so central to Poyer's vision, but of slavery. It was not whiteness that was critical to the defence of the Barbadian order, but slaveholding. Furthermore, this was not simply an instance of white plantocratic manipulation of free coloured ambitions but, in part, represented the influence of elite free people of colour on the white plantocracy. Their support of slave ownership was linked to a conception of Barbadian society that contrasted with, and contested, Poyer's 'well constituted Society'. Whereas he identified

[99] Ibid.

[100] Ibid.; Handler, *The unappropriated people*, p. 81, n. 51; Welch and Goodridge, *'Red' and black over white*, p. 102.

[101] Beckles, 'On the backs of blacks'. For more on the civil rights struggle of the free people of colour, see Newton, '"The Children of Africa in the Colonies"'.

[102] Beckles, 'Black over white', 11.

'grand distinctions' between white and non-white, free and enslaved, the petition-ers focussed on the distinction between enslaver and enslaved. Those whites (and people of colour) who were not slaveowners were banished into a liminal state of little importance. In other words, the petitioners asserted a division based on enslaved property-owning status and economic criteria, rather than the legal or racial divisions central to Poyer's theory. The acts of representation of the elite free coloured petitioners served to resist Poyer's agenda, challenging the centrality he afforded to whiteness within Barbadian society. They evoked and drew upon the contested place of whiteness in the articulation of colonial identity.

'Redlegs' and 'true Barbadians'

The centrality of white unity to Poyer's vision meant that the liminal status of poor whites had to be erased and their idealised status realised. This translated into a series of policy plans. Non-whites, free and enslaved, should be confined to agricultural occupations:

> Were this done, Barbadoes would furnish employment and subsistence for her numerous sons at home; the security of the country would be strengthened by the aggregation of faithful and loyal subjects; the community would enjoy the advantages of a general circulation of the wages of industry; and our planters would no longer require fresh importations of Africans for the cultivation of the land.[103]

Like Joshua Steele, Poyer saw the elevation of the poor whites as a means of curing a series of ills within Barbadian society,[104] as well as reducing reliance on the increasingly questioned trade in enslaved African people. Furthermore, the 'superfluous wealth of the opulent' whites was to be used to provide 'homes for the poor, and employment for the industrious'. Yet, it was not just material resources that had to be redistributed, but also social power. Thus, Poyer argued for the extension of the franchise 'to every Christian freeman, possessed of the smallest real estate', with 'Christian' denoting 'white'.[105] By diffusing the wealth and influence of the corrupt white elite, white society as a whole could be strengthened.

Poyer's solution for the problem of poor white liminality was a project of white racial unity. Yet, he did not succeed in having any of his ideas enacted. In part, this relates to the ambivalence of elite whites towards subaltern white populations, common in many colonial situations. As Stoler asks: 'were those legally classified as Europeans who fell short of the economic and cultural standards to be pulled back into these communities or banished from them?'[106] In other words, were subaltern whites 'poor but white' and worthy of inclusionary efforts as Poyer asserted, or 'white but poor' and to be excluded? Such contradictory projects of

---

[103] Poyer, *History of Barbados*, p. 61 n.   [104] See chapter 2, p. 53.
[105] Poyer, *History of Barbados*, pp. 242, 286.   [106] Stoler, *Race and the education of desire*, p. 107.

inclusion and exclusion are evident in Cecily Jones's discussion of vestry poor relief in Barbados, which was used in an attempt to 'incorporate disenfranchised poor whites in general, and poor white women in particular, into a white ruling-class cultural sphere that rested on an ideology of white supremacism'. This disciplinary strategy relied upon the threat that women who did not meet certain standards of conduct could be struck from the poor roll. Socio-sexual relationships with non-white men were a basis for exclusion. When one considers the use of such sanctions along side the well-established debasement of poor white women as socially and sexually degenerate – they were often described as 'sluts', 'loose wenches' and 'white niggers'[107] – it is apparent that poor white women were subject to strategies of inclusion *and* exclusion.

White elite ambivalence was also manifested towards the poor whites as a whole and Hilary Beckles asserts that the ideology of 'race first' was only really articulated when the social order was under threat.[108] The indifference of elite whites to poor whites reflected their overwhelming focus on acquiring cheap, black labour through slavery. Thus, although Poyer's efforts to curtail free people of colour's rights attracted the support of many within the white elite, the same cannot be said of his attitude towards poor whites. In this area, there was no policy failure, because there was no policy formulation. Indeed, Sheppard claims that white elite attitudes 'revealed themselves . . . in a mainly negative sense – through activities that were not undertaken, essential measures that were not introduced, or obstacles that were put in the way of reforms'.[109] In other words, the dominant discourse about poor whites was apparent in a *lack* of action. This reflected a general reluctance to provide support, other than that provided through the parish vestries, for a poor white population that was seen to be undeserving.

Accompanying the lack of elite white action were negative representations of the poor whites. Whilst Poyer idealised them, for many whites they were an indolent, venal and tainted group of outcasts, deserving little sympathy or help. For example, William Dickson was scathing about the 'rum-drinking and venery' of the poor whites, Daniel McKinnen bemoaned their 'mean and disingenuous behaviour' and even the more sympathetic Joshua Steele described them as 'a Race of idle Beggars'.[110] Although many of the descriptions of the poor whites were produced by British visitors or residents in Barbados, these sentiments were informed by local opinions. For instance, the description by George Pinckard of 'obscure individuals . . . descended from European settlers, but . . . little superior to the condition of free negroes' was a reflection of the views of those plantocrats with whom he

---

[107] H. McD. Beckles, *Afro-Caribbean women and resistance* (London: Karnak House, 1988), p. 134; C. Jones, 'Mapping racial boundaries', 10.

[108] Beckles, *History of Barbados*, p. 48.   [109] Sheppard, *'Redlegs' of Barbados*, pp. 45, 118.

[110] W. Dickson, *Mitigation of slavery in two parts. Part 1: letters and papers of the late Hon. Joshua Steele . . . Part 2: letters to Thomas Clarkson* (London, 1814), p. 155; D. McKinnen, *A tour through the British West Indies, in the years 1802 and 1803* (London: J. White, 1804), pp. 30–31; J. Steele to London Society of Arts, 24 May 1785, A12/34, Royal Society of Arts Archives.

socialised.[111] That most visitors to Barbados were taken to see the poor whites living in the Scotland district of the island suggests an almost compulsive need for elite whites to continually display and abject their poorest compatriots. As Bhabha has argued, colonial discourse is 'a form of knowledge and identification that vacillates between what is always "in place", already known, and something that must be anxiously repeated'.[112] This repeated debasement was an attempt to reinforce and secure their own superior whiteness.

The discursive debasement of poor whites was evident in their description as 'redlegs'. This term had its origins in seventeenth-century Scotland, where 'red-shanks' was used to refer to Highlanders whose limbs had been exposed to the elements. Many Highlanders were forcibly transported to Barbados in the 1640s and 1650s in the context of Oliver Cromwell's wars. In time, the term 'redshanks' was extended to other nationalities,[113] and by the 1780s, the term 'redleg' was used to describe the poor whites in general. An early instance of this appeared in the writings of J. W. Williamson, a medical doctor who visited Barbados in 1798. He provides a typical representation of the poor whites:

A ridge of hills, in the adjacent country, about the middle of the island, is called Scotland, where a few descendants of a race of people, transported in the time of Cromwell, still live, called Redlegs. I saw some of them; tall, awkward made, and ill-looking fellows, much of a quadroon colour, unmeaning, yet vain of ancestry, as degenerate and useless a race as can be imagined.[114]

In the early nineteenth century, 'redleg' had negative connotations and become an abusive term (figure 3.2). Barbados's poor whites were described as idle, wretched, proud of their Caucasian origins, yet often inferior to blacks and coloureds, blood-less yet burnt red. Although the notion of degeneration would not become fully developed within a racialised scientific discourse until the middle of the nineteenth century, Barbados's poor whites were certainly understood within a taxonomy of decline and tropicality.[115] Furthermore, the emphasis placed on their Celtic origins

---

[111] G. Pinckard, *Notes on the West Indies: Written during the expedition under the command of the late General Sir Ralph Abercromby; including observations on the island of Barbadoes, and the settlements captured by the British troops upon the coast of Guiana*, 3 vols., vol. II (London, 1806), p. 132.

[112] Bhabha, 'The other question', *The location of culture*, p. 66.

[113] Sheppard, *'Redlegs' of Barbados*.

[114] J. W. Williamson, *Medical and miscellaneous observations relative to the West India islands* (Edinburgh, 1817), p. 27.

[115] [Mrs Flannigan], *Antigua and the Antiguan: A full account of the colony and its inhabitants*, vol. II (London, 1844), p. 144; R. W. Jeffery (ed.), *Dyott's diary, 1781–1845, a selection from the journal of William Dyott, sometime general in the British Army and Aide-de-Camp to his Majesty King George III*, vol. I (London: Archibald Constable and Co., 1907), p. 91; McKinnen, *Tour through the British West Indies*, pp. 30–31. On discourses of tropicality and degeneration, see J. S. Duncan, 'The struggle to be temperate: climate and "moral masculinity" in mid-nineteenth century Ceylon', *Singapore Journal of Tropical Geography* 21 (2000); D. N. Livingstone, 'The moral discourse of climate: historical considerations on race, place and virtue', *Journal of Historical Geography* 17 (1991).

Figure 3.2   J. B. Colthurst, *Sergeant Redshanks moving to muster* (c. 1838), Ms.U.1.2. Courtesy of the Boston Public Library Rare Book Department.

can be related to anglocentric claims that Englishness represented 'normal' whiteness. Also significant in the descriptions of poor whites is that they were represented as 'red' – not white – and as pale, 'sickly white', or 'albino' – as *too* white.[116] Any form of deviance from an idealised whiteness was figured as debasement.

The negative representation of Barbados's poor whites shows that, whilst Poyer's project of racial realignment was contested with regard to the free people of colour, its commitment to a unified, white population was *utterly rejected* by most members of the white elite. Representations and practices that reproduced the poor whites as marginal were dominant and enslaved people evoked this in their mocking descriptions of poor whites as 'poor backras' and 'ecky-beckies'.[117] In his rhetorical idealisation and calls for socio-economic support for poor whites, Poyer sought – but failed – to contest this 'redleg' discourse. Nevertheless, Poyer's project was not the only attempt to contest dominant ideas and practices, and just as the free people of colour petitioned against Poyer's attempts to realise a 'well constituted Society', so the poor whites were not passive figures. In her work on poor relief,

---

[116] J. Davy, *The West Indies, before and since slave emancipation* (London, 1854), pp. 65–66; J. Kelly, *Jamaica in 1831: Being a narrative of seventeen years' residence in that island* (Belfast, 1838), p. 1. For a discussion of complexion in the Caribbean and the problems of being 'too white,' see D. Coleman, 'Janet Schaw and the complexions of empire', *Eighteenth-Century Studies* 36 (2003).

[117] Sheppard, *'Redlegs' of Barbados*.

for example, Jones has demonstrated that relations between poor white women and the vestry boards were sites of resistance, as well as regulation. Some women challenged attempts to discipline their social and sexual beings by forming intimate relations with the (free) black community. Jones goes on to speculate that given the large number of women of non-English, especially Irish, origin in the poor white population, such 'poor white female–black male sexual relationships may be interpreted as a measure of defiance against prevailing and dominant English mores'.[118]

Poor whites also contested their representation as 'redlegs'. The most striking example of this revolved around the geographical meanings associated with white identity. A recurrent feature of the 'redleg' discourse was the idea that the poor whites exhibited a tainted whiteness. For example, Pinckard's comment that they might be 'mistaken for children born in England' was an implicit reference to the idea that the poor whites were not really English, but merely false whites. Such 'de-anglicisation' of Barbados's poor whites was associated with a 'de-whitening'. Yet, this was more than an act of external imposition. Pinckard went on to discuss the pride of the poor whites, a motif that recurs in accounts. Twice he cited their self-description as '*neither Carib, nor Creole, but true Barbadian*', an assertion linked to Barbados's position within the British empire as a whole – and the poor whites' importance to this – by the rhetorical question which the poor whites ask: '*What would poor old England do, were Barbadoes to forsake her?*' which Pinckard also cites twice.[119] This proverbial assertion of Barbadian loyalty and pre-eminence within the British empire was associated with that well-worn phrase 'Little England', which appeared in print around the same time that Pinckard was in Barbados.[120] Such assertions of 'true Barbadian' pride were used by the critics of the poor whites to demonstrate a misplaced sense of self-importance that contrasted sharply with the realities of their impoverished condition. For example, Henry Nelson Coleridge stated that the poor whites were 'proud as Lucifer himself, and in virtue of their freckled ditchwater faces consider themselves on a level with every gentleman in the island'.[121] An alternative reading, which recognises the role of subaltern groups in contesting and transforming dominant narratives, might view this 'de-anglicisation' as a claim to cultural distinctiveness founded upon a re-spatialisation of the locus of true white identity. The construction of the poor whites as false English was not simply an unmediated form of othering, but also a claim to a separate white West Indian identity predicated upon a self-belief in the poor whites' importance to the British imperial project, particularly through their participation in the militia. Similar arguments about Barbados's position on the front line of empire and its inhabitants' patriotism abound in Poyer's writing, and

---

[118] C. Jones, 'Mapping racial boundaries', 25–26, n. 61.
[119] Pinckard, *Notes on the West Indies*, pp. 76, 78, 133, 134.
[120] For more on the discourse of Barbados-as-Little-England, see chapter 1, pp. 13–15.
[121] H. N. Coleridge, *Six months in the West Indies in 1825* (London, 1826), p. 99.

he repeatedly stressed the 'distinguished part borne by the Barbadians' in wars with France.[122]

The evocation of this *'true Barbadian'* identity is suggestive of a sense of Barbadian embryonic nationalism. To be West Indian in the age of abolition was increasingly to be marginal and peripheral, particularly in the context of the slavery controversy. The assertion of *'neither Carib, nor Creole'* posits a cultural exceptionalism that places Barbados beyond the British West Indies and perhaps evokes a non-English white identity. Yet, its linkage to the notion of Little England suggests a more complex cartography of identity, as also apparent in Pierre M'Callum's comment that Barbadians *'will not allow the island to be in the West Indies*, much less that he is either a Crab (Caribbee) or Creole, but a true Barbadian'.[123] The linkage of *'true Barbadian'* to *'poor old England'* asserts a loyalty and centrality to empire. In sum, we have a colonial identity that is not 'part' of the empire yet central to it; a peripheral white identity that rejects its marginality; an imperial white identity that denies its colonial origins (*'nor Creole'*). This ambivalence about the 'location' of white Barbadian identity – as manifest in the vacillation and overlap between discourses of loyalty and opposition to empire – was not limited to Barbados's poor whites.[124] Nevertheless, this sort of white creole spatial imaginary was particularly important for subaltern whites because it challenged their marginalisation in the dominant 'redleg' discourse, which linked authentic white identity to an ideal of upper-/middle-class Englishness. Against this, such self-representations located poor whiteness at the centre of empire.

Although Barbados's slaveholders were somewhat insulated from abolitionism in the early nineteenth century, there were local debates about the position of liminal groups – poor whites and free people of colour – in the socio-racial order and how the plantocracy should relate to them in its defence of slavery. Liminality was a locus of disturbance and a focus for governance. In the American context, Joanne Pope Melish argues that before the scientific codification of a discourse of race, the terms 'black', 'white', 'free' and 'slave' were floating metaphors.[125] Although less true of the West Indian context until emancipation loomed, liminal groups were a troubling presence in the Barbadian socio-racial order. Liminality raised questions in and about Barbadian society. By considering the answers that were produced, this chapter has explored competing models of social organisation and varied articulations of white Barbadian identities.

Poyer occupied a central place in these debates. His account of the Denny affair was a particular reading of liminality. For him, the liminal groups transgressed the structure of a 'well constituted Society' in which wealth, power and influence

[122] Poyer, *History of Barbados*, pp. 323, 392, 501, 576.
[123] P. M'Callum, *Travels in Trinidad during the months of February, March and April 1803* (Liverpool, 1805), pp. 11–12, emphasis added.
[124] See chapter 5.   [125] Pope Melish, *Disowning slavery*, p. 138.

were organised along racial lines and in which white unity was critical to the defence of slavery. Seeking to have his vision enacted in policy, Poyer's ideas were variously affirmed and rejected by members of the white elite and the liminal groups themselves. Poyer's vision and its reception raise broader questions about the articulation of white identities during the slavery controversy. The debate about poor whites and free people of colour revolved around different conceptions of the relationship between race, class and slavery. For Poyer and some planters, as well as the poor whites themselves, racial distinctions between white and non-white were central to the slave society's order and crucial to the defence of slavery against internal and external threats. Race was conceived as the organising principle and whiteness as a source of unity. Poyer sought to manage liminality by re-establishing the linkage between slavery and race. In contrast, some plantocrats and elite free people of colour saw class and slaveholding status as axiomatic. By forging interracial alliances between white and non-white slaveholders, slavery could be defended. Non-slaveholding poor whites were marginalised as an elite white identity was forged, supported by loyal non-white slaveholders.

The models for social organisation based on race or slaveholding status and class relate to the two discourses outlined in chapter 2. Whereas opposition to Joshua Steele was manifested in the mobilisation and enactment of discourses of white supremacism *and* a planter ideal, the slightly different emphasis each placed on the importance of racial difference became apparent in debates about liminality. The *herrenvolk*-ish supremacism exhibited by Poyer contrasted with the propertied vision of elite slaveholders and the upper echelons of the free people of colour whom they sought to co-opt.[126] These divergent articulations of white Barbadian identity will reappear in chapters 4 and 5.

A central concern in this chapter has been to demonstrate how liminal groups interfered in the processes of their subjectification. In particular, the free people of colour's petitions have shown how non-whites engaged with, contested and affirmed dominant articulations of white colonial identity. In the next chapter, I will explore a much more fundamental symbolic and material challenge: the 1816 rebellion.

---

[126] P. Parish, *Slavery: History and historians* (New York, 1989), p. 126.

4

Locating blame for the 1816 rebellion

Around 8 o'clock on the evening of Easter Sunday, 14 April 1816, cane fields in the parish of St Philip were set alight, marking Barbados's largest revolt by its enslaved population. The revolt was led by the enslaved elite – rangers, drivers, skilled mechanics and favoured domestics – in alliance with some free people of colour. Focussed initially on Bayleys plantation, the revolt spread throughout most of the southern and central parishes, eventually affecting around half the island (see figure 4.1). The rebels used arson tactics to signal the outbreak of the revolt and damage the economic base of the planters by destroying a fifth of the island's sugar cane crop. Martial law was declared at 2 o'clock on Monday morning, and militia and imperial forces were mobilised. The first major engagement was around midday, between the Christ Church battalion of the militia and rebel forces at Lowthers estate. A second clash occurred at Bayleys on the morning of Tuesday, 16 April, involving the black imperial troops of the First West India Regiment. It is likely that Bussa (or Bussoe), the African enslaved man popularly identified as the revolt's leader, was killed here. These two major engagements 'more or less broke armed resistance' and by midday on Wednesday the uprising was effectively over. Nevertheless, martial law remained in force until 12 July – for eighty-nine days in total. The death toll amongst the rebels was high: according to the conservative official figures, more than fifty were killed in combat, seventy summarily executed and another 144 executed later. Other accounts claim that between 400 and 1,000 enslaved people were killed. In contrast, only one white militiaman and two black imperial soldiers were killed, though some elderly and infirm white civilians may have had their deaths hastened by the shock and distress that resulted from the uprising.[1]

[1] H. McD. Beckles, *Bussa: The 1816 revolution in Barbados* (Barbados: Department of History, UWI, and Barbados Museum and Historical Society, 1998); M. Craton, *Testing the chains: Resistance to slavery in the British West Indies* (London: Cornell University Press, 1982), pp. 254–266; M. Mullin, *Africa in America: Slave acculturation and resistance in the American South and the British Caribbean, 1736–1831* (Urbana and Chicago: University of Illinois Press, 1992).

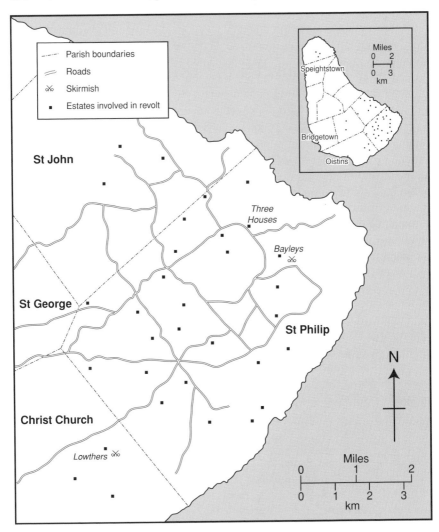

Figure 4.1 Map showing the parts of Barbados affected by the 1816 revolt. Adapted from M. Craton, *Testing the chains: Resistance to slavery in the British West Indies* (London: Cornell University Press, 1982), p. 255.

Whilst modern historians have related the rebellion to the frustrated expectations of the enslaved elite in the face of planter intransigence over reform, the development of black consciousness and long-running Afro-Caribbean opposition to slavery, early nineteenth-century commentators argued about the role of abolitionist campaigning and planter brutality in inciting the revolt. This contemporary struggle to locate the blame for the revolt was central to the controversy over slavery in the late 1810s. Making Barbados the centre of official and public attention, it was imperative for both the pro- and antislavery campaigns to establish an account of the revolt that tallied with its overall representation of the West Indies. Of particular importance was the question of whether the revolt signalled that Barbados was part of an aberrant slave world that required imperial intervention to end slavery. In this 'war of representation' over the revolt,[2] two representations of Barbados were rendered: for the abolitionists, Barbados was a land of un-British despotism and slavery in its purest form; for the planters and their supporters, Barbados was beleaguered Little England, besieged by the ignorant forces of humanitarianism. Central to the latter was the claim that external interference threatened to upset the improving relationship between paternalistic 'masters' and their contented 'slaves'. Yet, even in proslavery accounts of the revolt, other articulations of white identity were manifest, with reform itself seen as dangerous, vengeance as necessary and white rule to be ensured through terror. Thus, in the context of the revolt, the constitution of white creole identity was characterised by accommodation *and* retrenchment, conciliation *and* vengeance, paternalism *and* supremacism. By exploring these tensions, some of the themes addressed in chapters 2 and 3 are revisited.

The revolt, then, was a moment of pro- and antislavery struggle over the representation of Barbados and its imagined position within a slave world or free world. Yet, Afro-Caribbean people played an important role in focussing metropolitan attention on the 'problem of slavery' – in *problematising* slavery. Indeed, what is required is 'an interpretation of the relationship between anti-slavery thought and the sociopolitical aspirations of the Afro-Caribbean masses, as expressed through rebellion, day-to-day resistance, and, sometimes, in word'.[3] In the case of the 1816 revolt, it was the rebellious actions of enslaved people that precipitated the subsequent 'war of representation' to locate its origins. Moreover, in plotting, rumours, confessions and other acts and representations, the rebels articulated other discourses of white identity. In particular, the enslaved rebels interfered in this moment of identity formation by mocking and provoking notions of white purity, contesting Barbados's status as Little England and marginalising the importance of white people in their struggle for freedom. In this way, the rebellion was a traumatic moment in the creolisation of white colonial identity.[4]

Interpreting the 1816 rebellion

In a 1986 lecture, the historian Hilary Beckles called for 'historiographic decolonisation' in Barbados, replacing the '"rightest" "whitest"' myths of colonialist

---

[2] C. Hall, *Civilising subjects: Metropole and colony in the English imagination, 1830–1867* (Oxford: Polity, 2002), p. 107.

[3] R. K. Richardson, *Moral imperium: Afro-Caribbeans and the transformation of British rule, 1776–1838* (London: Greenwood Press, 1987), p. 15.

[4] See chapter 1, pp. 37–39.

writing with 'an unbiased approach and conception, based upon close investigation of the evidence'. Such sentiments are part of a post-Second World War tradition of anti-colonial Caribbean historiography. Connected to post-independence projects of nation-building, this has involved the search for a 'usable and epic past by identifying forms of resistance to the institution of slavery and to colonial rule'.[5] An important focus of this has been the investigation of enslaved revolts. Following C. L. R. James's account of the St Domingue revolution, scholars have demonstrated that enslaved people were not passive objects of labour, waiting to be rescued by abolitionists, but active agents in their own histories and societies. Although most revolts did not result in the immediate ending of slavery, they did belie planter myths of a contented enslaved population.[6] In the British West Indian context, scholars have sought to establish links between the revolts in Barbados (1816), Demerara (1823) and Jamaica (1831–2), and other aspects of the slavery controversy, such as abolitionist campaigning, imperial policy and planter responses. Investigations of the 1816 revolt have been an important feature of Barbadian historiography since the late 1970s.[7]

Although attention to enslaved revolts has been a paradigmatic feature of anti-colonial West Indian historiography, it may entail problems. For instance, a focus on overtly physical forms of resistance serves to make black women 'invisible'. Although women were clearly involved in physical resistance, it is important to examine other less 'masculine' forms of resistance, such as African cultural reproduction. Certainly, revolts are no longer the sole focus of work on enslaved resistance and there has been recognition of the spectrum of forms of agency – from revolt, to running away, to internal rejection, to (apparent) accommodation.[8] To this I would add that the role of enslaved people in the articulation of discourses of *whiteness* must also be considered. Such ideas lie behind David Roediger's recent collection of material by black writers on the meaning of whiteness. Although Roediger focusses on prominent black Americans, his argument about the role

[5] H. McD. Beckles, 'Black people in the colonial historiography of Barbados', in W. Marshall (ed.), *Emancipation II: A series of lectures to commemorate the 150th anniversary of emancipation* (Bridgetown: Cedar Press, 1987), pp. 142, 143. See also B. W. Higman, *Writing West Indian histories* (London: Macmillan Education, 1999); H. Johnson and K. Watson (eds.), *The white minority in the Caribbean* (Kingston: Ian Randle, 1998), p. ix.

[6] M. Craton, 'Slave culture, resistance and emancipation in the British West Indies', in M. Craton (ed.), *Empire, enslavement and freedom in the Caribbean* (Oxford: James Currey, 1997); C. L. R. James, *The black Jacobins: Toussaint L'Ouverture and the San Domingo revolution*, revised edn (London: Allison and Busby, 1980); M. St Pierre, *Anatomy of resistance: Anti-colonialism in Guyana, 1823–1966* (London: Macmillan Education, 1999).

[7] K. Watson, *The civilised island, Barbados: A social history, 1750–1816* (Bridgetown: Graphic Printers, 1979), chapter 7; R. Morris, '"The 1816 uprising – a hell-broth"', *Journal of the Barbados Museum and Historical Society* 46 (2000); E. O'Callaghan, *The earliest patriots* (London: Karia Press, 1986).

[8] H. McD. Beckles, *Centering woman: Gender discourses in Caribbean slave society* (Oxford: James Currey, 1999); B. Bush, *Slave women in the Caribbean society, 1650–1838* (London: James Currey, 1990); M. Craton, 'The rope and the cutlass: Slave resistance in plantation America', in Craton, *Empire, enslavement and freedom in the Caribbean*; M. Sheller, *Democracy after slavery: Black publics and peasant radicalism in Haiti and Jamaica* (London: Macmillan Education, 2000), p. 27.

of black people's actions and representations in producing white identity can be extended. When one recognises that enslaved subjects were not only rendered by the discourses and practices of slavery, but were also able to intervene in, and interfere with, these systems of power and signification, the link between resistance and the enslaved production of whiteness becomes apparent.[9] Enslaved people did not simply reproduce their own cultures, but were also involved in broader transcultural processes. In other words, enslaved people played a crucial role in the creolisation of white colonial identities.

The 1816 Barbados revolt was the largest enslaved uprising in two centuries of slavery on the island. Although there were localised plots in 1649 and 1701, and island-wide conspiracies in 1675 and 1692, these were all discovered or abandoned. For over a century, no plot had been detected and in the words of the speaker of the Assembly the events of 1816 were the 'most momentous crisis in the annals of the country'. On a regional scale, Michael Mullin describes the revolt as 'the most violently destructive – and improbable – of all nineteenth-century Anglo-America [sic] revolts'.[10] It was also the first of three across the British West Indies in the final two decades of slavery that shook the confidence of West Indian slaveholders. Although the 1816 revolt did not have the same impact in Britain as those in Demerara and Jamaica, it did result in an imperial declaration that emancipation was not the immediate object of government policy.[11] The revolt was also an intense focus for practices of representation. Many pro- and antislavery accounts were produced, reflecting the importance of securing a particular version of the revolt for both campaigns. Representations of the revolt also include the testimonies of enslaved people who were witnesses in the post-rebellion investigation and a series of images from flags carried by the rebels into battle. These sources enable some access to enslaved 'voices' and provide evidence of enslaved interference in the constitution of white identities.

A consideration of the 1816 revolt raises issues about historiography, nation, postcolonialism and positionality. The uprising, popularly known as 'Bussa's Rebellion' after the African-born man believed to have been the leader, has become an important aspect of contemporary Barbadian culture. It has been celebrated in calypso, researched and popularised by local scholars and, in 1998, 'Bussa' was named as one of Barbados's National Heroes. Indeed, so great has been the impact of 'Bussa's Rebellion' that the Emancipation Statue outside Bridgetown, Barbados, is often referred to as 'Bussa' (see figure 4.2).[12] Symbolising the struggle against slavery, colonialism and white domination, and a sign of Barbados's link to

---

[9] B. Kossek, 'Representing self/otherness and "white women" slaveowners in the English-speaking Caribbean, 1790–1830', paper presented at the Caribbean Studies Seminar, Institute of Commonwealth Studies, London, 13 March 2000; D. R. Roediger (ed.), *Black on white: Black writers on what it means to be white* (New York: Shocken Books, 1998).

[10] Beckles, *Bussa*, p. 1; John Beckles quoted in Morris, '"The 1816 uprising – a hell-broth"'. See also Mullin, *Africa in America*, p. 260.

[11] Craton, 'The rope and the cutlass'.

[12] The statue is actually a memorial to the formal ending of slavery. For information on Barbados's National Heroes and Heroines, see http://www.bgis.gov.bb/.

Figure 4.2 The Emancipation Statue, outside Bridgetown, Barbados. Original photograph by Jerome Handler and reproduced with his kind permission.

Africa, 'Bussa's Rebellion' has been important to the construction of post-colonial national identity in Barbados. Yet, the revolt has also been a field of controversy, with heated academic exchanges over the composition of the leadership and how the revolt should be known.[13]

In approaching the revolt, I am not seeking to uncover the 'truth' about the chain of events, leadership, ideological underpinnings or causes. Rather, I am adopting a similar perspective to Joan Dayan, who argues that attempts to establish particular readings of the Haitian Revolution should be abandoned for an acknowledgement of its uncontrollable hybridity. For this reason, I do not intend to give a definitive narrative account of the revolt (other than that briefly recounted at the start of this chapter). Relating to Richard Clarke's insistence that the past is constituted as it is described and that investigating this process is crucial,[14] my treatment of the revolt approaches it as a moment of intense cultural articulations related to specific political projects. In particular, I treat the revolt as a site of contested expressions of white colonial identity. I trace the connections between self-representation and the representation of others, relating this to acts of enslaved resistance, white violence and pro- and antislavery campaigning. The proslavery campaign used the revolt to resist registration, discredit abolitionism, win imperial compensation and protect Barbados's reputation as a stable slave society. The abolitionist campaign attempted to reveal the brutality of slavery, undermine claims about paternalistic 'masters' and contented 'slaves', and disavow any blame for the loss of life and property. For the rebels, certain ways of imagining and telling the revolt were important in garnering support, in the tactics that were used, in the overall strategic vision and in contesting planter dominance. These representations circulated before the revolt, in proslavery warnings about the dangers of interfering in domestic affairs and in enslaved conspiracies; they were present during the revolt, in rumours and panics, and on rebel battle-standards; and they were produced afterwards, in official reports, confessions and speeches. By emphasising the thoroughly *narrated* character of the revolt and treating it as an intensely discursive moment, I want to question too easy a distinction between the 'reality' of the events and their representation.

A particularly interesting aspect of early nineteenth-century accounts is how they sought to *locate* the origins of the revolt in different sites – be it Barbados,

---

[13] The term used to refer to the revolt is controversial. Like Michael Craton, Hilary Beckles refers to it as 'Bussa's Rebellion', after the enslaved African man whom he identifies as its leader. Jerome Handler has challenged Beckles's arguments about leadership, however, and claimed that it should not be named after Bussa. Karl Watson has suggested that it be known as the 'Endeavour Revolt' – a reference to the wording contained on battle-standards carried by the rebels (see pp. 130–131). See Beckles, *Bussa;* Craton, *Testing the chains;* K. Watson, 'The iconography of the 1816 slave revolt: Some brief comments', *Journal of the Barbados Museum and Historical Society* 46 (2000). See also the exchanges between Jerome Handler and Hilary Beckles in the Barbadian press: *Sunday Advocate,* 26 March, 9, 16, 30 April 2001; *Daily Nation,* 5, 15 April 2001.

[14] R. L. W. Clarke, 'The literary nature of the historical text: Some implications of the postmodernist critique of "realism" for Caribbean historiography', *Journal of Caribbean History* 32 (1998); J. Dayan, *Haiti, history, and the gods* (Berkeley: University of California Press, 1995).

specific parts of the island, Haiti or the imperial metropole. In this way, the accounts were spatial imaginaries and the revolt was a field of struggle between projects to establish different 'geographies of blame'.[15] The importance of representing the revolt and locating its origins was clear from the writing of John Rycroft Best, a white Barbadian plantocrat and militia commander. Only days after the revolt had been suppressed, Best expressed concerns that the events would be seized upon by metropolitan abolitionists:

> Such has been the abuse that the party in England has tried to vilify the white inhabitants with here, that we should not be surprised to hear this rebellion justified by the Puritans, and we (the Barbadians) accus'd as being monsters for putting to death those whom we found with arms in their hands, those caught in the act of plundering and destroying, and those tried since and convicted of being Ring Leaders.[16]

Best's sentiments were indicative of the centrality of representations of the revolt to the slavery controversy and capture the defensive tone of the proslavery interest. Moreover, they allude to the divisive imaginary geographies articulated by the antislavery lobby, which Barbadian slaveholders sought to challenge. The struggle to locate blame for the revolt was a conflict over Barbados's alleged status as an aberrant slave world. The spatial imaginaries revolved around the deployment and contestation of particular discourses of whiteness: were the slaveholders victims or sadists? Were the abolitionists agitators or humanitarians? Was white agency important in causing the revolt or did the rebellion express long-standing black opposition? Linking representations to spatial imaginaries to discourses of whiteness, the revolt was a moment of intense struggle over the nature and location of white colonial identities.

In the next three sections, different sets of representations of the rebellion are examined: firstly, how Barbados's planters imagined a revolt before it actually occurred; secondly, British abolitionist accounts of the revolt after the events; and, thirdly, the proslavery representations designed to counter this abolitionist vision. In each case, I explore the rhetorical practices through which particular spatial imaginaries of white identity and geographies of blame were charted.

A pre-imagined revolt

Even before the events of 1816, some Barbadians were already suggesting that a revolt might be incited by abolitionist campaigning. Later proslavery representations drew on this pre-imagined spatial causality. The 1807 Abolition Act had

---

[15] This phrase is borrowed from P. Farmer, *AIDS and accusation: Haiti and the geography of blame* (Berkeley: University of California Press, 1992).

[16] J. R. Best to A. Dottin, 27 April 1816, Barbados Manuscripts, New York Public Library (henceforth NYPL). These manuscripts are bound into the library's copy of J. Poyer, *The history of Barbados from the first discovery of the island, 1605, till the accession of Lord Seaforth, 1801* (London: J. Mawman, 1808).

been intended by the antislavery lobby to produce automatic improvements in the treatment of enslaved labour by denying slaveholders imports of labour to replenish their losses. Yet, evidence of continuing ill-treatment and an illegal trade undermined these hopes. In response, the abolitionist campaign sought the registration of the West Indian enslaved populations to acquire information with which to assess claims about improving treatment and detect smuggling. In 1813, the enslaved populations of Trinidad, Demerara, Essequibo and Berbice were registered. As these were possessions that had been acquired from European rivals, the imperial government was able to take direct legislative control. The introduction of registration to self-legislating colonies such as Barbados and Jamaica was much more problematic. In 1815, William Wilberforce, parliamentary leader of the British antislavery campaign, introduced a Slave Registry Bill for the self-legislating colonies. It was met with great anger in Barbados, where slaveholders viewed it as a step towards emancipation. The furore over the Slave Registry Bill was significant because it represented the arrival of the controversy over slavery in the slave societies themselves, whereas abolitionism had been more about conditions on slaving ships.[17] This second phase of abolitionist campaigning was doubly significant in the Barbados's case because, given the relatively relaxed attitude towards abolition,[18] this was the first time that abolitionism seemed to pose a direct threat to the planter order.

After the 1816 revolt, supporters of slavery argued that it had been caused by the rebels' misunderstanding of the Slave Registry Bill. They claimed that the rebels had believed it was an act for their emancipation that was being withheld by local whites. The proslavery lobby blamed this misunderstanding on reports of the antislavery campaign's activities, which had been maliciously promulgated by literate rebel leaders. Although, as will be discussed, the 1818 Assembly report was the prime codification of these sentiments, such an understanding had already been posited *before* the revolt in anti-registration texts that condemned metropolitan interference in local affairs and alluded to the possible dangers of an uprising. Indeed, it is possible to talk about a 'pre-imagined' revolt for which the spatial-causal framework had already been assembled. Although a major enslaved conspiracy had not been discovered in Barbados for over a century and there was complacency amongst the island's whites, enslaved unrest had become increasingly evident after the Abolition Act.[19] Whilst allusions to this in anti-registration texts were part of a proslavery propaganda campaign, they also suggested heightened

---

[17] J. Stephen, *Reasons for establishing a registry of slaves in the British colonies* (London: Ellerton & Henderson, 1815); J. Walvin, 'The public campaign in England against slavery, 1787–1834', in D. Eltis and J. Walvin (eds.), *The abolition of the Atlantic slave trade: Origins and effects in Europe, Africa, and the Americas* (London: University of Wisconsin Press, 1981).

[18] See chapter 3.

[19] Beckles, *Bussa;* Craton, *Testing the chains*, pp. 254–255. See, for example, Minutes of Assembly, 10 December 1810, CO 31/45, The National Archive (henceforth TNA); R. Haynes to T. Lane, 23 September 1816, Newton Manuscripts, 523/781, Senate House.

fears about revolt. Most whites did not expect one, but they did contemplate the possibility of rebellion.

Before the revolt, the Slave Registry Bill was roundly attacked in Barbados. The *Barbados Mercury and Bridgetown Gazette* denounced it as 'an interference by the British Parliament' that would have the effect of 'impairing the confidence and weakening the attachment of the Colonists to the mother country'. A report of the Joint Committee of the Council and Assembly argued that the bill cast aspersions on the West Indian character as it was based on the belief that slaveholders were cruel and engaged in smuggling. This, it was argued, was a manifestation of the fact that the legislation had been drafted at such a distance (in the British Parliament) that information on the 'true' condition of slavery was ignored.[20] Notions of occluded local knowledge, legislative distance and metropolitan misrepresentation recurred in anti-registration texts. The link to the possibilities of revolt was made by John Beckles, Speaker of the Assembly, who described the Slave Registry Bill as 'most dangerous in its tendency, to the peace, the prosperity, and the existence of the Colonies'.[21] This connection was most explicit in the writing of Barbados's London agent, Gibbes Walker Jordan. He dismissed arguments in favour of registration and claimed that its real aim was to induce the British government to intervene in the internal affairs of the West Indian colonies, so as to bring about the end of slavery.[22] According to the petition to the regent that accompanied Jordan's text, the outcome of interference would be both terrible and counterproductive:

[A]ll legislative interference between Master and Slave, is leading to consequences directly opposite to the professed object of those deluded philanthropists, who would thus increase instead of diminish the sum of human misery, by exciting ill-defined expectations that cannot be gratified, and encouraging insubordination necessarily (if not of still more horrid evils) of that very severity which they seem most anxious to restrain.[23]

By upsetting the paternalistic relation between enslaver and enslaved, the anti-slavery campaign generated discontent and mutual suspicion, if not the 'still more horrid evils' of a revolt.

In anti-registration texts, the Slave Registry Bill was also represented as a violation of the rights of the colonial legislature. Jack Greene has shown how colonial claims to enjoy the English system of law and liberty were predicated on West

---

[20] *Barbados Mercury and Bridgetown Gazette*, 24 February, 16 March 1816, Reel 24; Minutes of Assembly, 28 November 1815, printed in *Barbados Mercury and Bridgetown Gazette*, 6 April 1816, Reel 24: all in Bridgetown Public Library (henceforth BPL).

[21] Quoted in Minutes of Assembly, 14 November 1815, in *Barbados Mercury and Bridgetown Gazette*, 30 March 1816, Reel 24, BPL. See also E. M. W. Cracknell (ed.), *The Barbadian diary of Gen. Robert Haynes, 1787–1836* (Medstead, Hampshire, 1934), pp. 22–23; J. W. Orderson, *Cursory remarks and plain facts connected with the question produced by the proposed Slave Registry Bill. By J. W. Orderson, late of Barbadoes* (London, 1816).

[22] See G. W. Jordan, *An examination of the principles of the Slave Registry Bill, and of the means of emancipation, proposed by the authors of the Bill* (London: T. Cadell & W. Davies, 1816), pp. 88–117.

[23] G. W. Jordan, *Examination of the principles of the Slave Registry Bill*, pp. 145–147.

Indian assertions of their cultural 'Englishness'. The importance of establishing this connection was heightened during times of tension with the imperial government. This link between cultural identity and political liberty was apparent in Jordan's account of his response on first viewing the registration proposals: 'I seemed to cease, at that moment, to be a freeman of a free country.' A system of registration had already been introduced in 1813 to British possessions captured from European rivals and, according to Jordan, the new bill threatened to replicate this and treat Barbados as a 'conquered Foreign Colony'.[24] Seeking not only to challenge the legal basis of such moves but also their cultural logic, the status of the colonists as 'His Majesty's most faithful Subjects' of this 'antient [sic] and loyal colony' was emphasised:

> Yielding to none of our European fellow-citizens in zeal and affection to your Royal Highness's illustrious house, and attachment to the glory and interests of the United Kingdom and its Dependencies, we beg leave, with all due deference, to claim, in a spirit strictly accordant with these professions, for ourselves, our constituents, and our posterity, all the acknowledged and well-known rights and privileges of British subjects.[25]

In this way, white Barbadian opponents of registration sought to assert the rights *of* Englishmen by virtue of their status *as* Englishmen.[26]

In these pre-revolt texts, a causal groundwork for post-revolt writing was laid. Registration was portrayed as metropolitan interference, based on false representations of Barbadian slaveholders and framed without attention to local knowledge. It impinged upon the 'Englishness' of white Barbadians and threatened social stability. Although a revolt was certainly not expected, the possibility was conceived. This spatial-casual logic would be activated after the revolt.

'This unhappy state of society': abolitionist discourse

Whenever enslaved revolts occurred in the British West Indies, attacks on abolitionism intensified. Part of the antislavery response was to distance itself from revolutionary actions. For example, in a parliamentary debate two months after the Barbados uprising, Wilberforce argued that '[w]hatever had happened had no reference to himself or his friends; he had no share in creating the explosion that had been felt: he washed his hands clear of the blood that was spilt'. As a 'middle-class, religious, liberal segment' of British society, antislavery campaigners neither supported, nor could be seen to condone, the actions of enslaved rebels. Yet, they

---

[24] G. W. Jordan, *Examination of the principles of the Slave Registry Bill*, pp. 19, 42, 44–48. See also J. P. Greene, 'Liberty, slavery, and the transformation of British identity in the eighteenth-century West Indies', *Slavery and Abolition* 21 (2000).

[25] 'The humble address and petition of the Council and Assembly of Barbados to the Regent', 17 January 1816, reproduced in G. W. Jordan, *Examination of the principles of the Slave Registry Bill*.

[26] According to Jordan, the interference represented by the Slave Registry Bill disregarded Barbados's cultural identity to the metropole, as had been exemplified by local resistance to the 'Usurpation' of the English monarchy. See chapter 5.

did not simply distance themselves from revolts and, to some extent, 'British anti-slavery was forced to come to terms with the rebels' perspective of a slave revolt'. Symptomatic of this was Wilberforce's ascription of blame for the rebellion to 'the intemperance of the colonists themselves'.[27]

The role of antislavery campaigners in establishing a geography of blame for the events in Barbados, rather than simply distancing themselves from them, was best exemplified by the anonymous *Remarks on the insurrection in Barbados* (1816).[28] Attributed by supporters of slavery to the antislavery African Institution, this was the most important abolitionist textual representation of the revolt and was published both in the *Christian Observer* and as a pamphlet. It sought to challenge the belief that the uprising had been caused by rumours over the Slave Registry Bill and argued that such ideas had been promulgated by the West India Interest to discredit Wilberforce's attempts to ameliorate slavery. Against this, it insisted that 'a concise view of the nature and bearings of that unhappy occurrence' would locate the origins of the revolt in local circumstances, not external stimuli. As in Wilberforce's speech, the *Remarks* argued that if the enslaved people's misunderstanding of registration had precipitated the revolt then it was the speeches and petitions of the Barbadian legislature, as well as local press coverage, that had propagated this confusion.[29] In their eagerness to attack Wilberforce's proposals by arguing that emancipation was the ultimate aim, Barbadian slaveholders had succeeded only in inciting unrest. This point was reiterated through the image of fire that was used throughout the *Remarks* to symbolise the self-destructive character of the system of slavery and the self-inflicted nature of the revolt:

Wishing to keep the light of a Registry Bill from their plantations, they would persuade us that those plantations are inflammable magazines. Yet they themselves at the same moment, as we have seen, are shaking torches and firebrands within them.[30]

In its discussion of white Barbadian responses to the Slave Registry Bill, the *Remarks* sketched a geography of blame in which the revolt's causes were located in Barbados itself:

[The planters demand that] . . . [w]e must speak in a whisper, even when we speak at the distance of 6000 miles, of slavery in the West Indies. But in the islands we find, instead of this extreme caution, a most wanton publicity and noise on the subject.[31]

---

[27] Speech of W. Wilberforce, House of Commons, *Hansard parliamentary Debates*, 19 June 1816, 1st Series, vol. XXXIV, 1151–1168, ref. on 1159; D. Turley, *The culture of English anti-slavery, 1780–1860* (London: Routledge, 1991), p. 6; G. Matthews, 'The other side of slave revolts', *The Society for Caribbean Studies Annual Conference Papers*, 1 (2000), available from http://www.scsonline.freeserve.co.uk/olvol1.html.

[28] Anonymous, *Remarks on the insurrection in Barbados, and the bill for the registration of slaves* (London, 1816).

[29] Anonymous, *Remarks on the insurrection*, pp. 1, 4.

[30] Anonymous, *Remarks on the insurrection*, p. 6.

[31] Anonymous, *Remarks on the insurrection*, p. 5.

Crucial in establishing this argument was the pamphlet's account of the geography of the uprising itself. It insisted that although the revolt was a calamity, its scope had been exaggerated by supporters of slavery and it was 'far from exhibiting any distinct marks of an extensive insurrection'. According to the *Remarks*, the spatial contiguity of the four main parishes affected by the revolt – St John, St George, Christ Church and St Philip – suggested 'some local and peculiar cause', such as disaffection with a manager over food shortages, rather than the existence of a general, 'preconceived plot'.[32] In another geographical move, the factors against a successful revolt being carried out, including the presence of large military forces and the open terrain, were used to suggest that general revolt could not have been conceived. This was manifested in the rebels' failure to seize any arms and in the fact that 'only two White men were killed'. The 'inherent follies' with the uprising further indicated that it was a localised disturbance that got out of hand. Such reactions were likely in a society with such an unreformed system of slavery. As the *Remarks* put it: 'In no part of the British dominions does this unhappy state of society, exist in a more unmitigated form than in the island of Barbadoes.'[33] The fundamental point is that local causes were stressed.

Whilst the *Remarks* argued that the revolt was not a large-scale conspiracy, this did not mean that it was not a tragedy. The widespread damage and death toll were attributed not to the rebels but to the white creole militia, whose indiscriminate use of violence resulted in many deaths and caused the rebels to flee across the island:

A thousand human lives it seems – some accounts say two thousand – have been lost by this calamity, in the field, or by summary military execution; how justly, may perhaps hereafter appear; how mercifully, the Barbadian militia can best tell. It is not so that insurrections are suppressed in England; and yet these are our fellow-subjects.[34]

The asserted death toll and the tone of disbelief in the final line ('yet these are our fellow-subjects') served to emphasise the alterity of the Barbadian militia, their violence serving as a marker of their 'un-Englishness'. It was also a sign of the self-destructiveness of slavery:

It is highly probable . . . that no small proportion of the twenty-five or thirty estates, which suffered from the conflagration of their canes, owed their loss, either to the firing of the militia on the fugitives, or to the burning of the adjoining huts.[35]

In suppressing the revolt, white Barbadians damaged their island's estates, just as the local misrepresentation of the Slave Registry Bill may have incited the revolt. Similar descriptions of militia violence appear in accounts by British military

---

[32] Anonymous, *Remarks on the insurrection*, pp. 6, 7. Similar arguments were made by Wilberforce. See Speech of Wilberforce, House of Commons, *Hansard Parliamentary Debates*, 19 June 1816, 1st Series, vol. XXXIV, p. 1160.
[33] Anonymous, *Remarks on the insurrection*, pp. 3, 6. In fact, only one white man was killed.
[34] Anonymous, *Remarks on the insurrection*, p. 8.
[35] Anonymous, *Remarks on the insurrection*, p. 7.

commanders. For example, in his reports, Colonel Edward Codd, commander of the imperial garrison, maintained a distance between his forces on the one hand, and the colonists and the militia on the other, by emphasising the emotional response of white creoles to the revolt – both in terms of the 'zeal' of the militia and the 'dismay and alarm which had seized the Colonists'. Enthusiasm and fear combined to produce vengeance:

[U]nder the irritation of the moment and exasperated at the atrocity of the insurgents some of the Militia of the Parishes in Insurrection were induced to use their arms rather too indiscriminately in pursuit of the fugitives.[36]

As with the antislavery *Remarks*, such portrayals of militia violence posited a distinction between a white creole militia and a more disciplined imperial force.

The *Remarks* presented the revolt and its violent suppression as symptomatic of slavery-as-usual. Portraying an unplanned and geographically limited riot, born of localised grievances amongst an enslaved population subjected to the most brutal form of slavery in the West Indies, it rejected assertions that the abolitionist campaign was to blame. Such representations of the revolt mapped a spatial imaginary in which Barbados's aberrant status was emphasised and members of its white population were portrayed as violent, sadistic creoles. They exhibited an 'un-Englishness' that was very different from evangelical humanitarianism central to abolitionist identity. Such representations were key to the articulation of Barbados as a slave world and to the fashioning of a 'humanitarian narrative' that insisted upon metropolitan intervention.[37] The difference in the behaviour of imperial and colonial troops posited in the accounts of British military commanders suggests that such a portrayal went beyond the formal texts of abolitionism and into the broader metropolitan imagination.

'A hell-broth': proslavery discourse

In the articles, letters, reports and tracts written after the revolt, the link between enslaved unrest and the Slave Registry Bill was asserted by opponents of abolitionism:

They have pierced the inmost recesses of our island, inflicted deep and deadly wounds in the minds of the black population, and engendered the Hydra, Rebellion which had well nigh deluged our fields with blood.[38]

---

[36] E. Codd to J. Leith, 25 April 1816, CO 28/85, fos. 12a, 14a, TNA. See also J. Harvey to J. Croker, 30 April 1816, CO 28/85, fo. 124a, TNA.

[37] T. Laqueur, 'Bodies, details, and the humanitarian narrative', in L. Hunt (ed.), *The new cultural history* (London: University of California Press, 1989).

[38] Letter from 'A Planter', *Barbados Mercury and Bridgetown Gazette*, 7 September 1816, Reel 24, BPL.

Whilst enslaved revolts posed a challenge to the abolitionist campaign, it was also imperative for supporters of slavery to establish their own account of these events. It was vital that the metropolitan origins of the revolt – in terms of abolitionist propaganda or the actions of their agents – were asserted. As Michael Craton puts it: 'By stressing the effect of rumours of change the planters hoped to forestall actual changes. They also hoped that by attributing slave unrest to actual or imagined changes imposed from outside they might draw attention away from local circumstances.' A failure to locate blame in this way would undermine paternalistic proslavery claims, would add weight to assertions about the inherent brutality of slavery and might even persuade the imperial authorities that it was too costly a system to maintain. Failure would also detract from Barbados's reputation as a stable society that had been able to avoid the maroon wars and revolts that characterised other colonies.[39] Another imperative behind placing the locus of blame in Britain was to win compensation for proprietors' losses. Indeed, it was Jordan, Barbados's London agent, who suggested that the revolt's causes be recorded to support his lobbying efforts in this regard.[40]

The prime codification of the proslavery representation of the revolt was an 1818 select committee report from the House of Assembly.[41] Soon after martial law was lifted, this committee was appointed to 'enquire into the more immediate and proximate, as well as the more remote, causes which may have led the slaves into the commission of these enormities'. The unanimous report (after Colonel Best was no longer on the committee) was published on 7 January 1818 and 250 copies were printed, some being sent to the governor and the colonial agent. Careful editing and selective circulation indicate the importance attached to establishing an appropriate representation of the revolt.[42] The report itself was in two parts: the official findings of the committee, which provided a background, narrative and account of the revolt's origins; and a series of appendices, which included testimonies and confessions of captured rebels, plantation managers, military commanders and others, on whose testimony the report purportedly drew. Given the importance of the report in efforts to win compensation, the economic costs of the revolt were emphasised:

---

[39] M. Craton, 'Slave culture, resistance and the advancement of emancipation in the British West Indies, 1783–1838', in J. Walvin (ed.), *Slavery and British society, 1776–1846* (London: Macmillan Press, 1982), p. 268. See also A. O. Thompson, '"Happy – happy slaves!": Slavery as a superior state to freedom', *Journal of Caribbean History* 29 (1995).

[40] G. W. Jordan, *Papers on subjects relating to the British colonies in the West Indies, by the late G. W. Jordan, Esq., . . . Colonial Agent for Barbados* (London, c. 1820), pp. 46–71; Morris, '"The 1816 uprising – a hell-broth"'.

[41] Barbados House of Assembly, *The report from a select committee of the House of Assembly, appointed to inquire into the origin, causes, and progresses, of the late insurrection* (Barbados, 1818). See also Minutes of Assembly, 6 August 1816, CO 31/47, fos. 16a–20b, TNA.

[42] Barbados House of Assembly, *The report from a select committee*, p. 4; Minutes of Assembly, 6 August 1816, CO 31/47, fos. 138b–140b, TNA. See Craton, *Testing the chains*, p. 265.

[D]uring the period of anarchy and confusion, nearly the whole of the four largest and most valuable Parishes [were] exposed to the ravages of the Insurgents – the canes upon one-fifth of the Estates of the Island burnt.[43]

Central to arguments for compensation and to the defence of slavery was the substantiation of the spatial causality of the revolt. This involved reiterating the framework laid out in the anti-registration texts by blaming misunderstanding and rumours over the Slave Registry Bill. Additional 'evidence' was provided by the confessions of captured rebels and other testimonies. The report also identified the particular institutions and media responsible for the diffusion of the confused ideas over registration: the *Christian Observer*, the African Institution and 'English newspapers'.[44] In this way, the report sought to add empirical and theoretical weight to the pre-revolt causal framework and emphasise the importance of external forces in causing the insurrection.

The Assembly report also refuted abolitionist accounts, particularly the geographically localised and causally local arguments of the *Remarks*, which it described as full of 'various mis-statements and misrepresentations'. The report denied that there were food shortages in Barbados and emphasised the ameliorative steps that had been taken to improve the diet of enslaved workers. The *Remarks'* claim that the revolt was limited in extent was also dismissed as exhibiting 'a wilful desire of deceiving the uninformed or unwary reader' and a deliberate geographical misrepresentation. The report further noted that the actions of the imperial troops in the revolt's suppression were 'carefully omitted' in the *Remarks*, whilst the colonial militia was portrayed as bloodthirsty. This points to recognition that the abolitionist *Remarks* was seeking to draw an imagined geographical demarcation between white Britons and white creoles.[45] In these ways, the report challenged the abolitionist argument that the revolt and its suppression were characteristic of an aberrant slave world.

In attempting to externalise the origins of the revolt, the proslavery lobby was faced with the stark fact that a large number of enslaved people *had* rebelled. To resolve this, the Assembly report emphasised the role of the small number of free people of colour who had 'directed and encouraged' the enslaved rebel leaders by disseminating newspaper reports. Yet, only four free people of colour were convicted and the report had to acknowledge that the conduct of most had been 'highly meritorious'.[46] How could the fact that most of the rebels were enslaved people be squared with paternalistic claims about a contented population? To do

---

[43] Barbados House of Assembly, *The report from a select committee*, pp. 3–4. The report estimated the financial cost of the revolt at £170,000, and noted that many buildings had been destroyed and nearly 400 enslaved workers killed.

[44] Barbados House of Assembly, *The report from a select committee*, pp. 6, 13.

[45] Barbados House of Assembly, *The report from a select committee*, pp. 13–15, 17.

[46] Craton, *Testing the chains*, p. 260; Barbados House of Assembly, *The report from a select committee*, pp. 8, 11. The 'loyalty' shown by most free people of colour to the whites resulted in the extension of their civil rights, and a bill allowing free coloured testimony against whites was passed on 5 February 1817. See H. McD. Beckles, 'On the backs of blacks: The Barbados free-coloureds' pursuit

so, proslavery accounts of the revolt drew a distinction between the category of the 'insurgent' and the rest of the enslaved population – usually characterised as the 'slave'. The insurgent was a figure 'charged with Rebellion, breaking open Buildings, and committing Depredations', engaged in a 'mad career' of 'ravages' and 'pursuing a system of devastation which has seldom been equalled'.[47] The insurgent was portrayed by one militia commander in striking terms:

> Evidence is everywhere apparent of most wanton destruction by fire and pillage; to an extent at present incalculable, but without question irreparable of many weeks. Truly, the vengeance of this horde, inflamed with every vile passion, which committed every imaginable and filthy outrage in its path, has afforded but a fore-taste of what would have been the fate of us all had these miscreants succeeded in wreaking their savage will.[48]

In contrast, the passivity of the 'slaves' – the insistence that they were not, and could not possibly be, rebellious – was apparent even in descriptions of death tolls: the revolt 'deprived the Colony of nearly four hundred of its finest Slaves'.[49] Not only did this represent the enslaved people as lost property rather than dead rebels, but also insisted upon the external origins of their decision to revolt. The distinction between 'insurgent' and 'slave' was not simply based on the fact that not all enslaved people had revolted. It was also a discursive move that sought to externalise the rebellious elements beyond an idealised, paternalistic system, thus simultaneously accounting for the revolt in the figure of the externally incited 'insurgent' *and* reiterating the passivity of the 'slaves' as a whole. This portrayal of 'slaves' as 'unwilling participants or misled children' was a common move in (discursively) re-establishing slavery-as-usual.[50]

Proslavery accounts emphasised the external causes of the revolt through a variety of moves – arguing that it was not localised, nor due to food shortages and that metropolitan newspapers were a source of rumours – and figures (Wilberforce, the African Institution, free people of colour and the 'insurgent'). In so doing, a spatial imaginary was articulated in which the vulnerability of Barbados to outside forces was emphasised; even the executed rebels were victims. The revolt was explained in terms of the agitator myth: 'demonic, subversive forces ready to risk even slave rebellion for the purpose of destroying a social order they hated too much to understand'. This was a common trope beyond the West Indies, and conservative

---

of civil rights and the 1816 slave rebellion', *Immigrants and Minorities* 3 (1984); M. Newton, '"The Children of Africa in the Colonies": Free people of colour in Barbados during the emancipation era', unpublished DPhil. thesis, Oxford University (2001), pp. 109–113.

[47] Barbados House of Assembly, *The report from a select committee*, p. 3; Proclamation by President, 16 April 1816, CO 28/85, fo. 16a; *Barbados Mercury and Bridgetown Gazette*, 30 April 1816, CO 28/85, fos. 24a–25a, TNA.

[48] Cracknell, *Diary of Gen. Robert Haynes*, p. 35.

[49] Barbados House of Assembly, *The report from a select committee*, p. 4.

[50] S. Seymour, S. Daniels, and C. Watkins, 'Estate and empire: Sir George Cornewall's management of Moccas, Herefordshire and La Taste, Grenada, 1771–1819', *Journal of Historical Geography* 24 (1998), 337.

elites in many, particularly rural, contexts vilified the 'outside agitator . . . for creating discontent among the otherwise happy masses'.[51]

The proslavery representation of the revolt parallels Alan Lester's account of early nineteenth-century settler responses in South Africa to humanitarian attacks, which emphasised their vulnerability to the 'savage' African enemy, the ignorance of humanitarian claims and their fundamental Britishness. It was around such 'legitimations and external representations that a broad, emotive and defensive sense of settler affinity first coalesced'.[52] Similarly, the white Barbadian account of the revolt portrayed a happy, peaceable colony of loyal, white, reforming slave-owners. Traduced by the abolitionist campaign as smugglers, brutal masters and bloodthirsty militiamen, proslavery writing sought to establish the true location of responsibility for the revolt, the sameness of Barbados and Britain, and the duties of protection and compensation that the latter owed to the former. As one militia commander put it: 'From England all these evils come, to England we look for the measures which are to quiet the ideas novel and rebellious.'[53]

Tensions in proslavery discourse

In their respective spatial imaginaries of the revolt's causality, the pro- and anti-slavery campaigns provided contrasting representations of Barbados: as a place of brutal masters, discontented enslaved people and a bloodthirsty militia; or as belea-guered Little England, its paternalistic system shattered by outside interference, its loyal subjects calling for protection from the imperial mother. The situation was not as straightforward as this pro/anti dichotomy would suggest, however, and there were also tensions *within* white Barbadian discourses around the upris-ing. Although the Assembly report was the prime codification of the proslavery spatial imagination of the revolt, it was not a manifestation of a monolithic white society. The most obvious indication that the report was not an untroubled tex-tual product was that it took seventeen months after its commission before it was finally published. Although much of this delay can be attributed to the dif-ficulties in undertaking an investigation in the aftermath of a major revolt, there was also internal dissent within the committee. The six-man committee appointed was reduced to five with the exclusion of Colonel Best.[54] As well as a militia

[51] G. K. Lewis, *Main currents in Caribbean thought: The historical evolution of Caribbean society in its ideological aspects, 1492–1900* (Baltimore: Johns Hopkins University Press, 1983), p. 19; H. Southall, 'Agitate! Agitate! Organize! Political travellers and the construction of a national politics, 1839–1880', *Transactions of the Institute of British Geographers* 21 (1996), 189.

[52] A. Lester, *Imperial networks: Creating identities in nineteenth-century South Africa and Britain* (London: Routledge, 2001), p. 67.

[53] Best to Dottin, 27 April 1816, Barbados Manuscripts, NYPL.

[54] H. McD. Beckles, 'Inside Bussa's rebellion: Letters of Colonel John Rycroft Best', *Journal of the Barbados Museum and Historical Society* 37 (1984). Robert Morris has suggested that Best may have removed himself from the committee because of a 'serious conflict of interest' as he was the attorney for the plantations at the epicentre of the revolt: Morris, '"The 1816 uprising – a hell-broth"', 9.

commander, Best was an Assembly member for Christ Church and a plantation attorney. He had led a detachment of the Christ Church battalion against rebels near Lowthers plantation, achieving a victory that was said to have broken their morale. Although initially sharing the widely held belief that the rebels had been deluded into revolt by misrepresentations of the Slave Registry Bill, he later changed his opinion:

It is no longer delusion amongst the slaves ... [as] I once thought before, I am now convinced that they were not entirely, if at all, led away in the last business by Delusion. They conceiv'd themselves to be sufficiently numerous to become the masters, instead of the slaves of the island, and that opinion influenc'd them to Acts of Rebellion.[55]

The discovery of a minor plot in September 1816 seemed to have convinced Best that the enslaved people continued to cherish beliefs in the possibility of revolutionary success. It was this confidence, combined with opposition to slavery *per se*, that was behind the revolt and not a local reaction to metropolitan politics. Best's opinion was clearly at odds with the official planter line that the 1818 report came to codify and posited an actively insurgent enslaved population, not the passive but deluded body of the report. Best's unconventional views were indicative of the variance within the plantocracy and raised questions about the restoration of a paternalistic order.

The text of the report was also indicative of tensions, with inconsistencies between the committee's official findings, and the confessions and examinations on which they were supposedly based. This pointed to concerns about how the report would be received in Britain and emphasises the importance attached in Barbados to establishing an appropriate proslavery account of the revolt. A striking example of divergence between official and unofficial opinion was evident in the testimonies of managers of estates at the heart of the revolt. Whilst the committee emphasised the amelioration that had occurred – both to place greater blame on the British anti-slavery lobby and to portray Barbados in a favourable light – the managers argued that better treatment had had negative effects on the character of enslaved people by resulting in 'more exalted ideas of their own value and consequence'. Indulgence and the self-worth it engendered was manifest in their deportment, dress and increased leisure time. References to 'constant parties and dances on Saturday and Sunday evenings' were significant as they symbolised increased freedom and cultural resistance *and* were potential sites of conspiracy. The managers placed particular emphasis on the fact that the elite enslaved people, who had benefited most from amelioration, had led the revolt.[56] The managers also drew a distinction between themselves and the 'indulgent' owners, seeking to demonstrate that those involved in the day-to-day running of plantations had foreseen the dangers

---

[55] Best to Dottin, 28 September 1816, Barbados Manuscripts, NYPL.
[56] Barbados House of Assembly, *The report from a select committee*, pp. 41–52. See also H. McD. Beckles, 'Creolisation in action: The slave labour elite and anti-slavery in Barbados', *Caribbean Quarterly* 44 (1998); Craton, *Testing the chains*, p. 258.

of leniency. This was perhaps indicative of a hope that future policy would be less accommodating and that the managers would be allowed to run the plantations in ways that they held to be appropriate and safe.

The sentiments expressed by the managers portrayed the reform of slavery as dangerous, with indulgence forming the backdrop against which the misrepresentation of the Slave Registry Bill had had such explosive effects. These anti-ameliorative implications contrasted with the committee's more accommodationist line, which held that slavery was being reformed and that it was metropolitan interference that was dangerous. The managers' statements also hint at a more conservative outlook amongst the wider white community which saw reform itself as dangerous. Suggestive of such attitudes was the perception that 'the most indulgent masters have suffered most' during the revolt. Similarly, before the uprising, Elizabeth Fenwick, a British resident in Barbados, recounted the commonly held view amongst whites that the island's enslaved people were the worst behaved in the West Indies because they were less severely treated than elsewhere.[57] The attitudes apparent in the managers' statements suggest a distinction between an official, accommodationist line and a more popular, conservative position. This can be understood in terms of tensions between an elite planter ideal and the broader culture of white supremacism, and can also be related to the conflict between propertied and racialised principles of social organisation that were discussed in the previous chapter.[58]

Tensions were also apparent in the immediate white response to the revolt. John Spooner, who was acting as president during the revolt in the governor's absence, made two proclamations in this capacity, the first on the third day of the revolt, and the second two days later. The first spoke of the 'Depredations' carried out by the rebels, which 'demanded the most summary and exemplary punishment'. Spooner called for field commanders to carry out the 'immediate execution' of any prisoners charged with pillaging, looting, resistance or arson. In contrast, the second proclamation was more conciliatory in tone and policy, something perhaps attributable to the violent excesses engendered, or at least excused, by the first. Seeking to temper the militia's response, Spooner called for the 'utmost humanity' in the treatment of all enslaved people, especially women and children, and for particular lenience to be shown to those who might have been coerced into rebellion. The second proclamation also extended 'His Majesty's FREE PARDON to all and every such Slave or Slaves, not being a principal Instigator or Adviser in such Insurrection, who, within five days from the proclamation hereof, shall deliver themselves up, or return to their respective Owners and Occupations.' On the

---

[57] Haynes to Lane, 23 September 1816, Newton Manuscripts, Senate House; E. Fenwick to M. Hays, 11 December 1814, 21 March, 12 April 1815, all in A. F. Wedd (ed.), *The fate of the Fenwicks: Letters to Mary Hays (1796–1828)* (London, 1927), pp. 161–170.

[58] See chapters 2 and 3.

same day, Spooner placed Colonel Edward Codd, the British commander of the imperial garrison, in overall charge of military operations on the island, including the militia.[59]

These two proclamations suggest a switch in the white authorities' response. The first called for a swift and vengeful deployment of the white population's virtual monopoly of the means of violence, whilst the second proclamation can be seen as part of an attempt to re-establish the paternalistic order, which many planters had (wrongly) believed would protect them from revolt in the first place. Through conciliation, it sought to restore the relation between a 'good master' and dutiful 'slaves'. Other attempts to 'normalise' Barbadian society were evident in the externalisation of blame on to the 'insurgent' and in the attempt to 'forget' the revolt. As Karl Watson notes: 'White Barbadian society at the end of the 1816 was still in a state of shock, an attitude mirrored by absentee owners. They seem to evince a desire to wipe the month of April out of their memories and certainly the *Barbados Mercury* stopped reporting on the revolt at a surprisingly early period.'[60]

Nevertheless, the violent excesses of the first proclamation and the militia's actions (which, significantly, were to be curtailed by placing a non-Barbadian in command) not only belie paternalism, but were also indicative of tensions across white society. The militia's rank and file was made up of small landholders and landless freemen, for whom the suppression of the revolt was an opportunity to enact a subaltern white supremacism. Moreover, the strength of such tensions had been apparent before the revolt in the parish at the heart of the uprising – St Philip – which Robert Morris describes in terms of a 'virtual civil war as the poor whites were locked in a power struggle with the plantation owners over who should control the political organs of the assembly and vestry'.[61] Much of this struggle was over whether slavery should be defended through ameliorative concessions or total opposition to all reforms. St Philip was also the site of many attacks by poor whites on free people of colour.

The switch from vengeance to conciliation in the two proclamations and the occlusion of anti-ameliorative views from the Assembly report's official findings cannot simply be explained as the plantocracy's attempt to re-establish a paternalistic hegemony over subaltern white classes, however. Rather, the mixture of vengeance and conciliation was indicative of a more general white ambivalence. This can be glimpsed in an account written by Colonel Best of his militia battalion's role in suppressing the revolt:

---

[59] Proclamation by President, 16 April 1816, CO 28/85, fo. 16a; Proclamation by President, 18 April 1816, CO 28/85, fo. 20a, TNA; Circular from General [sic] Codd to Militia Commanders, 18 April 1816, Lucas Manuscripts, Miscellaneous Items, Vol. 6, Reel 17, p. 318, BPL.

[60] K. Watson, *Civilised island*, p. 132.

[61] J. S. Handler, 'Freedmen and slaves in the Barbados militia', *Journal of Caribbean History* 19 (1984); Morris, '"The 1816 uprising – a hell-broth"', 20.

We endeavour to be just and where we can be merciful too, but the numbers not only implicated, but actively employed is great. And as Colonel Codd observes, 'they are all ring leaders'.[62]

Captured by the ambivalence of 'but', Best's self-proclaimed efforts to be humane contrasted with the 'zeal' of his counter-insurgency efforts. Moreover, his belief in the widespread nature of the revolt threw into question the possibilities of distinguishing between 'insurgents' and contented 'slaves'. If 'they are all ring leaders', how could a paternalistic order be re-established? Similar evidence of an uneasy mixing of a desire for vengeance with the attempt to restore paternalism was apparent in the first debate of the House of Assembly after the revolt. Reports of the actions of the white creole militia commander, Colonel Mayer, commended the 'spirited manner' in which he sought out the rebels, whilst also applauding his desire to 'spare unnecessary effusions of blood'.[63]

The somewhat contradictory character of white responses to the revolt suggests that not all the blame could be externalised. The 'insurgent' was not as easily separable from the 'slave' as the official report tried to suggest. In militia acts of counter-insurgency, anti-ameliorative sentiments and white 'common sense', a discourse of justified vengeance was articulated and enacted. This was associated with a form of white identity based on terror. Roediger argues that white people find and reproduce unity by committing, and more often by witnessing, acts of violence. Certainly the violence perpetrated during and after the revolt was overwhelmingly the work of whites. From the official figures alone, nearly 300 enslaved people were killed, as against one white militiaman. In the deployment of superior firepower, summary executions, brutal rituals of capital punishment and the display of executed rebels across the island, white Barbadians enacted a terrifying white identity. As in other colonial contexts, fears about rebellion and cathartic moments of violence were important in the forging of settler identity and solidarity.[64]

Whilst terror was a crucial component in the constitution of white identity that occurred in the context of the revolt,[65] this was not the whole story. Rather, the articulation of white identities was characterised by paternalism *and* terror, conciliation *and* vengeance. White Barbadian planters were keen to shift the origins of the revolt to external forces, disaffected free people of colour and the discursive category of the 'insurgent', in part because of the importance of a planter ideal to the articulation of white identity. Nevertheless, the mixture of vengeance and

---

[62] Best to Dottin, 27 April 1816, Barbados Manuscripts, NYPL.
[63] Minutes of Assembly, 6 August 1816, CO 31/47, fos. 18a–19a, TNA.
[64] b. hooks, 'Representations of whiteness in the black imagination', in b. hooks (ed.), *Black looks: Race and representation* (Boston: South End Press, 1992); D. Kennedy, *Islands of white: Settler society and culture in Kenya and Southern Rhodesia, 1890–1939* (Durham, NC: Duke University Press, 1987); Roediger, *Black on white*. For an account of the forms of violence enacted against the rebels, see General Colonial Order, 26 April 1816, Lucas Manuscripts, Miscellaneous Items, Vol. 6, Reel 17, p. 339, BPL.
[65] Beckles, *Bussa*, pp. 37–38.

conciliation in the acts and texts of counter-insurgency points to the tensions within the white community and the difficulties of re-establishing a symbolic paternalistic order given that many enslaved people had revolted. There was an 'unresolved tension' in many accounts of colonial insurgency,[66] and this troubled the articulation of white creole culture, politics and identity. It also undermined the idea that a beleaguered and vulnerable white identity could be unproblematically asserted in imagining the revolt.

Afro-Caribbean representations of the rebellion

The previous section demonstrated the fractured nature of proslavery spatial imaginaries and thus the constitution of the white colonial identity itself. Yet, to leave this account here would be incomplete, as it would suggest that Barbados's enslaved people were passive figures in the discourses surrounding the revolt. This would reiterate features of both pro- and antislavery accounts of enslaved people: that they were inactive until disturbed by external forces, or that they reacted automatically to local problems, having no real understanding of the wider controversies over slavery. Although clearly different in sympathy and political intent, both accounts tend to treat enslaved people as property – either the physical property of the slaveholders or the ideological property of the antislavery campaign.[67] In order to avoid reproducing enslaved people as the objects in white spatial imaginaries of the revolt, Afro-Caribbean rebel representations must be explored.

As often with moments of colonial insurgency, there are no direct subaltern accounts of the Barbados revolt; rather there are fragments of rumours, culturally significant acts and white reportage. The sources most commonly used by historical scholars are the confessions made by rebels, often prior to their execution. The chillingly detached, third-person form in which the confessions are rendered ('This Examinant saith, That . . .', 'And Examinant further saith . . .') was indicative of the epistemic violence that was concomitant with the physical violence of interrogation, corporeal punishment or execution. Although the confessions are the closest source to the direct quotations of oppressed people prized in counter-readings of colonial texts, given the circumstances in which they were gathered, it should not be surprising that they tend to support the official line: the revolt had its origins in the misunderstanding of the Slave Registry Bill. Nevertheless, there is evidence that the coercion was not unresisted. One rebel, Jack Groom, 'attempted to deny all knowledge of the causes of the Insurrection, or his being concerned in it', whilst another, James Bowland, refused to speak any more – 'And further Deponent saith not'. Although only superficial moments of resistance, they are

---

[66] C. Hall, *Civilising subjects*, p. 62.
[67] A. J. Barker, *Slavery and antislavery in Mauritius, 1810–1833: The conflict between economic expansion and humanitarian reform under British rule* (London: Macmillan, 1996); S. V. Hartman, *Scenes of subjection: Terror, slavery, and self-making in nineteenth-century America* (Oxford: Oxford University Press, 1997).

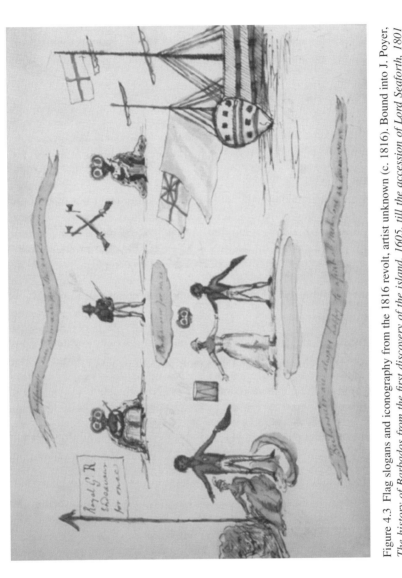

Figure 4.3 Flag slogans and iconography from the 1816 revolt, artist unknown (c. 1816). Bound into J. Poyer, *The history of Barbados from the first discovery of the island, 1605, till the accession of Lord Seaforth, 1801* (London: J. Mawman, 1808), General Research Division, New York Public Library, Astor, Lenox and Tilden Foundations.

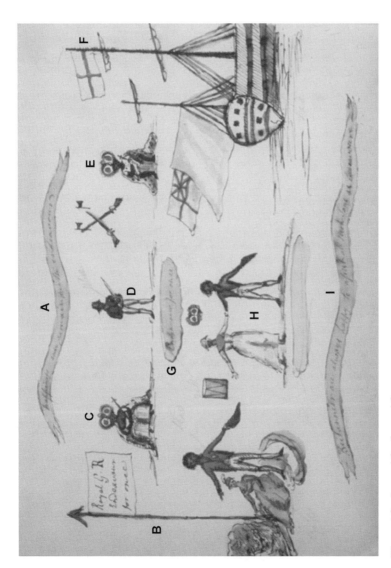

Figure 4.3a Legend for figure 4.3.

manifestations of the more widely observed phenomenon of the subaltern's refusal to speak.[68]

A source that has been remarkably underused in the historiography of the revolt are the flags 'of White Cotton, with the figures crudely drawn' that are described by a number of whites. These standards were captured from the rebels who had carried them into battle.[69] The most detailed description of their iconography combines racial mixing, a reworking of abolitionist symbolism and the evocation of Wilberforce:

> One of their flags [represented] . . . a white woman kneeling to a black man, in the act of raising her from her suppliant attitude, with the motto of 'Wilberforce for ever'.[70]

None of the standards survive and there have even been suggestions that they might have been figments of the white imagination. Yet, a rebel confession about a flag that 'belonged to Cooper' but was carried by 'Johnny, the standard-bearer' belies this.[71] Moreover, there exists a page of crude watercolour sketches of images from these flags, most likely drawn by a white Barbadian (figure 4.3).[72] Whereas visual representations of slavery are receiving increasing critical attention,[73] visual images produced *by* enslaved people have received very little, in part because they are rare. Nevertheless, these are important sources because they demonstrate that the visual culture of Atlantic slavery was not the preserve of white supremacist power and psychosis. More than this, these flags, with their representation of the British monarch and white women in the company of black men, demonstrate how white subjects were objects of display, spectacle and representation by people of African descent.[74] As well as the images, the sketches also record the slogans used on the flags:

---

[68] Barbados House of Assembly, *The report from a select committee*, pp. 34, 37. For a discussion of subaltern silence as resistance, see K. M. Morin, 'British women travellers and constructions of racial difference across the nineteenth-century American West', *Transactions of the Institute of British Geographers* 23 (1998).

[69] Harvey to Croker, 30 April 1816, TNA.

[70] J. Marryat, *More thoughts still on the state of the West India colonies, and the proceedings of the African institution* (London, 1818), p. 19.

[71] Barbados House of Assembly, *The report from a select committee*, p. 34. Michael Craton, for instance, questions the existence of the flags. See Craton, *Testing the chains*, pp. 372, n. 33.

[72] To help with identification, the individual parts of figure 4.3 are labelled with letters A to I; see legend, figure 4.3a.

[73] See, for example, B. E. Lacey, 'Visual images of blacks in early American prints', *William and Mary Quarterly* 3rd series 53 (1996); P. Mohammed, 'The emergence of a Caribbean iconography in the evolution of identity', in B. Meeks and F. Lindahl (eds.), *New Caribbean thought: A reader* (Kingston: University of the West Indies Press, 2001); G. Quilley and K. D. Kriz (eds.), *An economy of colour: Visual culture and the Atlantic world, 1660–1830* (Manchester: Manchester University Press, 2003); M. Wood, *Blind memory: Visual representations of slavery in England and America, 1780–1865* (Manchester: Manchester University Press, 2000). An attempt to collect images of 'The Atlantic slave trade and slave life in the Americas' can be found at http://hitchcock.itc.virginia.edu/Slavery/.

[74] See D. Lambert, 'Deadening, voyeuristic and reiterative? Problems of representation in Caribbean research', in S. Courtman (ed.), *Beyond the beach, the blood and the banana: New directions in Caribbean research* (Kingston: Ian Randle, 2004).

Happiness ever remains the endeavour. (Image A)
Royal G. R. Endeavour for once. (Image B)
Endeavour for once. (Image G)
Britannier are always happy to assist all such sons as endeavour. (Image I)

These banners were a call for Barbados's enslaved population to strive for freedom.[75] This iconography – recorded in text and image – is important because it brings together acts of resistance, rebel self-identity and the enslaved representation of others.

A third source that can be probed are white accounts of the revolt. By reading white texts 'against the grain', enslaved rebel spatial imaginaries and representations can be sought out. Whilst there is always a danger of 'fetishising' archival fragments, such strategies are useful for exploring the white creole identities articulated in representations of the revolt.[76] Partly due to the structure of the colonial archive, the rebel representations are fragmentary, lacking in coherency and often taking the form of rumours. Nevertheless, such rumours – whether recorded in confessions, described by whites or inspired by flags – had actual effects. They were circulating before the outbreak of the revolt and were critical to its plotting and planning. Rumours were used by the rebel leaders to encourage support for the revolt, force the whites into entrenched positions and rob the slaveholders of their psychologically sustaining belief in enslaved contentment.[77]

In the following sections, three aspects of rebel representations and their associated spatial imaginaries are discussed. The first two challenged the constitution of white colonial identity – by raising the spectre of 'black peril' and emphasising the metropole/colony tensions caused by the slavery controversy – whilst the third representation marginalised white agency in the struggle for freedom by evoking a black diasporic identity.

Provoking white fears

A recurrent theme in white descriptions of the revolt was fear about black male sexual attacks. References were made to the intentions of the rebels, who believed that 'the island belonged to them, and not to white men, whom they proposed to

---

[75] Thus far, Karl Watson is the only scholar to have discussed the flags, and many thanks to him for bringing my attention to the existence of these sketches. See K. Watson, 'Iconography of the 1816 slave revolt', 45. The page of sketches precedes a collection of manuscripts referred to as 'Barbados Manuscripts' in n. 16 above.

[76] J. S. Duncan, 'Complicity and resistance in the colonial archive: Some issues of method and theory in historical geography', *Historical Geography* 27 (1999), 127.

[77] G. Matthews, 'The rumour syndrome, sectarian missionaries and nineteenth-century slave rebels of the British West Indies', *The Society for Caribbean Studies Annual Conference Papers*, 2 (2001), available from http://www.scsonline.freeserve.co.uk/olvol2.html; Craton, 'Slave culture, resistance and emancipation in the British West Indies', p. 268. For more on rumours and resistance, see J. Scott, *Domination and the arts of resistance* (New Haven: Yale University Press, 1991); St Pierre, *Anatomy of resistance*, pp. 19–21.

destroy, reserving the females, whose lot in case of success, it is easy to conceive'. Similarly, the rebels' plan was described as one to 'murder all the White Men, and reserve the White Women for the gratification of the Negroes'.[78] Such fears of 'black peril' – about the black rape of white women – were common to many colonial situations and given 'the connections between white male power and sexual authority, it was not surprising that white fantasies of black revenge included the rape of their wives, daughters and mothers'. Whilst (coerced) interracial sex between white men and black women was one of the ways in which enslaved property was 'enjoyed' in Barbados, sexual relations between white women and black men were strongly prohibited by cultural taboos and institutional practices.[79] This was related to the idealised inviolate status of white women as a marker of racial purity and to concerns with controlling access to freedom. The strength of such prohibitions was evident from the extremely brutal punishment meted out to black men convicted of raping white women.[80]

White expressions of fear about black sexual assault can be read in terms of racially supremacist discourse. Nevertheless, we can also detect some insurgent intent here. This is not because there is *any* evidence that sexual attacks *were* carried out, but because the rebels deliberately made play of the danger that white people believed they posed. For example, descriptions abounded of 'a rude drawing [that] served to inflame the passions, by representing the Union of a Black Man with a White Female'.[81] Image H depicts a black man and a woman of lighter colour holding hands, though whether she was intended to be white (by the original artist or recorder) is unclear. Image B shows a white woman seated at the feet of a black man. In the context of Barbadian strictures on interracial sex, these flags represented a 'deliberately calculated insult' by the rebels, striking at the core of masculine, heterosexual, white identity and contesting discourses of white purity.[82] They were a figurative displacement of white masculinity in which power was signified as access to white women's bodies. Moreover, these signifying practices were terrorising, and, whilst there is no direct evidence of white women's responses, white men described panic and anxiety:

---

[78] Codd to Leith, 25 April 1816, CO 28/85, fo. 15a, TNA; Harvey to Croker, 30 April 1816, TNA. See also Barbados House of Assembly, *The report from a select committee*, p. 57.

[79] C. Hall, *Civilising subjects*, p. 258; Hartman, *Scenes of subjection*, p. 23; C. Jones, 'Mapping racial boundaries: Gender, race, and poor relief in Barbadian plantation society', *Journal of Women's History* 10 (1998). For discussions of 'black peril' in other colonial contexts, see Kennedy, *Islands of white;* J. McCulloch, *Black peril, white virtue: Sexual crime in Southern Rhodesia, 1902–1935* (Bloomington: Indiana University Press, 1999).

[80] K. Watson, 'Iconography of the 1816 slave revolt'. See also chapter 6.

[81] Codd to Leith, 25 April 1816; private letter, 27 April 1816, CO 28/85, fo. 23a; Harvey to Croker, 30 April 1816, all TNA. Metropolitan periodicals reported and elaborated on such accounts. One, for example, described a flag portraying 'a black chief, with a white woman, with clasped hands, imploring mercy'. See *Annual Register . . . for the Year 1816*, 77, cited in H. L. Malchow, *Gothic images of race in nineteenth-century Britain* (Stanford: Stanford University Press, 1996), p. 264, n. 59.

[82] K. Watson, 'Iconography of the 1816 slave revolt', 45.

It is distressing to see the women hurrying with their children to the fort for protection. My sister was safe and I was comparatively happy as I had no wife or daughter to take care of.[83]

A strategic purpose for these terror tactics might even be suggested. When troops moved to engage the rebels, part of the force was left behind to defend Bridgetown against 'black peril'. Moreover, during the battle at Bayleys – at which the standard showing interracial sex was flown – Colonel Codd received a 'most alarming report' that 'a body of insurgents had threatened Bridgetown and thrown it into the greatest confusion'.[84] In response, he ordered some of his troops to fall back to defend the capital, again splitting the white military forces. Even after the revolt was suppressed, white confidence remained shattered:

The alarm however, among the white females chiefly, is considerable, though there is no reason whatever to believe that the mass of the slave population are forming designs to revolt.[85]

These standards played *up* and played *on* white terror. Fears about 'black peril' struck at the heart of the proper reproduction of the white race. This terror shaped a militant and paranoid society and would recur in the 1830s, when 'black peril' became a metaphor for emancipation. One of the consequences in 1816 was the terrible white vengeance meted out against the rebels: '[t]he fear that blood will be mixed . . . intensifies the ritual expectation that blood must be spilt'.[86] Whilst dread of 'black peril' contributed to white solidarity, and terror was central to the articulation of white colonial identity, it must be recognised that black people may have deliberately provoked this. This was more than a self-defeating rebel action for, in provoking white violence, the rebels made it difficult to disentangle the 'insurgent' from the 'slave' – an important move in the proslavery account of the revolt – and undermined paternalistic claims. In this way, the rebels were contesting discourses of white purity through their mocking portrayal of interracial sex *and* affirming whiteness by confirming white peoples' deepest fears. In both ways, the rebels played an active role in the constitution of white identities.

Troubling Little England

The coerced confessions of enslaved rebels were used to support the official proslavery line. Yet, these were more than a parrot-like repetition of anti-registration arguments and were embellished with a host of metropolitan figures who had supposedly granted the enslaved people their freedom: 'The Queen and

[83]   Best to Dottin, 27 April 1816, Barbados Manuscripts, NYPL.
[84]   Codd to Leith, 25 April 1816, TNA.
[85]   T. Moody to Bathurst, 20 October 1816, CO 28/85, fos. 43a–44a, TNA. See also Haynes to Lane, 23 September 1816, Newton Manuscripts, Senate House.
[86]   Malchow, *Gothic images*, p. 26; J. Roach, *Cities of the dead: Circum-Atlantic performance* (New York: Columbia University Press, 1996), p. 122. On the metaphorical role of 'black peril', see chapter 6.

Mr. Wilberforce', 'a black woman who was a Queen', 'people in England', 'the King of England', 'the Governor' and 'the Prince Regent'.[87] Two of the banners also evoked 'Royal G. R.' and 'Britannier' (images B and I), calling for, and insisting upon, metropolitan support for the rebels' 'endeavour'. Such embellishment points to a sophisticated, albeit confused, awareness of the wider Atlantic politics of the age of abolition as gleaned from newspapers, rumours and overheard conversations. These images relate to the 'wish-fulfilling rumors, that the slaves had external allies and had only to act in concert to receive their support, defeat the local whites, and obtain freedom'. Akin to the phenomenon that Eric Hobsbawm has described as 'populist legitism', the distant ruler came to represent justice and embodied the aspirations of the rebels.[88] Such rumours were spread by rebel leaders to increase support for the revolt.[89]

As well as being central to plotting and planning, the representation of metropolitan figures as supporters of freedom was indicative of a rebel representation in which the plight of Barbados's enslaved population was placed within a trans-Atlantic framework of abolitionist campaigning and imperial humanitarianism. For example, whilst George III was actually a supporter of slavery, he was evoked as a sympathetic metropolitan force with the power to overturn local opposition to emancipation.[90] Many of the figures on the flags stand with arms open, appealing for imperial justice and aid (images B and H). The black man in image B is accompanied by a white woman sitting next to the British imperial lion. Metropolitan policies on slavery – such as making the murder of enslaved people a capital offence and the abolition of the trade in enslaved people – showed that there was willingness in Britain to enact reforms. This was evoked in the rebels' bid for freedom. Moreover, references to British aid served to challenge white Barbadian claims that they had a special relationship with the metropole and that they were culturally and political identical to metropolitan Britons. Thus, whilst it has been argued that the evocation of the monarchy suggests that the rebels exhibited a conservative, rather than a revolutionary democratic, ideology, this might be seen as troubling the discourse of Little England.[91]

This challenge to white Barbadian identity was focussed on the figure of the British governor, James Leith. His absence from island when the revolt broke out was worked into a rebel geopolitical imagination, in that he was believed to be either bringing the manumission papers or waiting off-shore to help the 'endeavour' for freedom. One enslaved man said that before the revolt, a rumour circulated that 'the Governor was on the seas, waiting until they could make a stand, to be

[87] Barbados House of Assembly, *The report from a select committee*, pp. 27, 34, 35, 36.
[88] Craton, *Testing the chains*, p. 262; E. J. Hobsbawm, *Primitive rebels: Studies in archaic forms of social movement in the nineteenth and twentieth centuries* (New York: Norton, 1965), pp. 119–120.
[89] Barbados House of Assembly, *The report from a select committee*, p. 27.
[90] K. Watson, 'Iconography of the 1816 slave revolt'.
[91] D. B. Gaspar and D. P. Geggus, *A turbulent time: The French Revolution and the Greater Caribbean* (Bloomington and Indianapolis: Indiana University Press, 1997).

their friend'. With the revolt as the catalyst, striking at the plantocracy, the imperial forces would help the rebels: 'the King's troops would join them' and 'the
men of war would fire upon the Town'.[92] In this way, the presence of large numbers of imperial troops in or near Barbados was not indicative of a foolhardy
lack of planning as the abolitionist *Remarks* suggested, but an ideal moment for
revolt when allies were at hand. Such sentiments are suggested by the image of
a British vessel of war in the standards, which symbolised a source of external
aid (image F). The strength of the rumours about Leith was evident in his decision to travel around the island after the revolt had been suppressed and have an
address promulgated in which he sought to dismiss the notion that 'I was in possession of your Manumissions, and that my return to Barbados would have put
you in possession of your Freedom.' The prominence of Leith within rebel imaginations indicated an awareness of his place at the cusp of metropolitan/colonial
relations and perhaps something of his reformist sympathies.[93] The notion of
imperial aid for the rebels was not simply a wish. It also points to recognition
of the tensions between colony and metropole that had developed during the age of
abolition.

The evocation of imperial aid sketched an imagined geography that located
Barbados as an aberrant space requiring humanitarian intervention. In this way, it
can be read as a challenge to the notion that Barbados was Little England. Images
C and E show a black woman and a black man dressed as queen and king. These
figures represent the ultimate aim of the 'endeavour' – the right of self-possession,
portrayed here as sovereignty. When placed alongside the description of 'a black
woman who was a Queen' and the appeals to the King to help the rebel cause, this
'blackening' of the royal family also contested white Barbadian claims to a shared
racial and cultural identity with Britain. This was also evident from a detailed
description of one rebel banner:

bearing the figure of a general officer (supposed to be intended for the King), placing a
crown in the hands of a negro who had a white woman on his arm. Beneath these figures
was the following motto: 'Brittanie are happy to assist all such friends as endeavourance
[sic].'[94]

The concern of local whites to give their own account of the revolt was indicative
of a recognition that Barbados's place as stable, civilised Little England was at
stake in the slavery controversy. By evoking imperial aid and metropolitan support
for their cause, the rebels contested such colonial discourses.

---

[92] Barbados House of Assembly, *The report from a select committee*, pp. 35, 45.
[93] J. Leith, 'An address to the slave population of the island of Barbados', 1816, in S. A. L. Hay,
*Memoirs of the late Lieutenant General Sir James Leith, GCB, with a precis of some of the most
remarkable events of the peninsular war, by a British officer* (Bridgetown, 1817), pp. 16–20; J. Leith
to Bathurst, 30 April 1816, CO 28/85, fos. 8a–10a, TNA.
[94] A. Ellis, *The history of the First West India Regiment* (London, 1885), p. 168.

Hopes for Haitian intervention

Reports indicate that the rebels at Bayleys plantation gave 'three cheers' when they saw the First West Indian Regiment because they believed 'that the Black Troops would not fight against them'. There were also worries amongst white Barbadians about the conduct of the black troops during the revolt and those left in Bridgetown were viewed with great apprehension. One anonymous writer noted that 'a report has been circulated, that the Bourbon Regiment had joined the Rebel Party'. The rebels' confidence that they would not be attacked by black troops – and the palpable relief of the whites who saw them proved wrong[95] – was not simply part of a belief in imperial aid or racial solidarity. The rebel cheers were also connected to their imagination of Haiti and to rumours that its ruler, King Christophe, would send troops to their aid. The black troops of the First West India Regiment were from the Bourbon Regiment, which had been raised in the French Indian Ocean islands of Bourbon (Réunion) and Mauritius in 1810, after they had been captured by Britain. The regiment was ordered to disband in late 1814 and members of its rank and file were shipped to the Caribbean, arriving in Barbados in October 1815.[96] The ex-Bourbons of the First West India Regiment were not only black, but were almost certainly wearing their green uniforms and would speak French. In the context of 'rumours in the slave lines that a Haitian revolutionary army would be landing at Barbados to assist them in their struggle for freedom', the rebels' reaction to the black troops was unsurprising.[97] It is bitterly ironic that these troops, so invested with hope, had already been involved in the suppression of an enslaved uprising on Bourbon in November 1811.

Given that the revolt in St Domingue had only occurred two decades before and was the only successful enslaved revolt that had ever been carried out, it is little wonder that Haiti occupied a vague but important place in the imaginations of the rebels, not to mention that of the whites. News of the revolt, war and the eventual independence of Haiti had circulated around the Caribbean and beyond since the 1790s.[98] Opponents of the republic, particularly amongst the slaveholding classes, promulgated negative representations of Haiti:

---

[95] Codd to Leith, 25 April 1816, CO 28/85, fo. 12b, TNA; anonymous letter, 17 April 1816, Lucas Manuscripts, Miscellaneous Items, Vol. 6, Reel 17, pp. 327–328, BPL. See also Bathurst to Leith, 12 June 1816, CO 82/85, fo. 26a, TNA; private letter, 27 April 1816, CO 28/85, fo. 23a, TNA. Fears of a coalition between black soldiers and enslaved people were common amongst white colonists. See R. N. Buckley, *Slaves in red coats: The British West India Regiments, 1795–1815* (New Haven: Yale University Press, 1979), p. 38.

[96] R. Jones, 'The Bourbon Regiment and the Barbados slave revolt of 1816', *Journal of the Society for Army Historical Research* 78 (2000), 7. Many of the West Indian regiments were being disbanded in the context of the end of the Napoleonic Wars. See Buckley, *Slaves in red coats*.

[97] H. McD. Beckles, *Black rebellion in Barbados: The struggle against slavery, 1627–1838* (Bridgetown: Antilles Publications, 1984), p. 103.

[98] Beckles, *Bussa*, p. 10. For more on the Haitian Revolution, including its wider effects, see Dayan, *Haiti, history, and the gods;* C. E. Fick, *The making of Haiti: The Saint Domingue revolution from below* (Knoxville: University of Tennessee Press, 1990); D. P. Geggus, *Haitian revolutionary studies* (Bloomington: Indiana University Press, 2002).

Gripped by fears of contagious slave uprising, Europeans articulated their claims to 'whiteness' and 'civility' in contradistinction to Haitian 'barbarism' through a set of stories that can be collectively referred to as the 'Haytian Fear'.[99]

Yet, for many enslaved and free coloured people elsewhere in the Caribbean, the former French colony came to symbolise liberation and they 'built their own racial projects around a symbolic alliance with Haiti'.[100] It provided long-standing inspiration to enslaved rebels and references to the republic recur in representations of the Barbados revolt:

[Cuffee Ned, an enslaved man at Three Houses] was told that the negroes had been freed in some of the Islands, and that they were to be freed in all the West Indies, and that in one they had fought for it and got it. And, upon being asked if he should [sic] recollect the name of the Island if he heard it? and having answered in the affirmative, several Islands were named, but when Saint Domingo was named, he said 'that was the Island – he knew it by the name of *Mingo*'.[101]

Before the revolt, one of the rebel leaders, a woman called Nanny Grig, was reported to have used Haiti to show what the rebels could achieve if they revolted and also how they should go about it: burning cane to damage the planters economically. In this way, just as other leaders promulgated notions about the granting of freedom and metropolitan support, Grig invested in the representation of Haiti and it had real effects. During the revolt, one-fifth of the cane fields were burnt and the rebels in Barbados were the only Anglo-American insurrectionists to use a tactic that was so deeply feared by whites – perhaps only less than mass murder – something which partly explains the militia's violent response.[102]

It was not just the rebels for whom Haiti was a significant space in representations of the revolt. For instance, the author of the abolitionist *Remarks* felt it necessary to deny the presence of a Haitian fleet off the coast of Barbados.[103] Another report conjectured that one of the flags, by virtue of its spelling, was 'the composition of a Frenchman'.[104] The most striking white example of the strength of the idea of Haitian intervention was from Joseph Marryat, the London agent for Grenada who shared the same concerns as Barbados's planters. He made great

---

[99] P. Linebaugh and M. Rediker, *The many-headed hydra: Sailors, slaves, commoners, and the hidden history of the revolutionary Atlantic* (London: Verso, 2000), p. 302; Sheller, *Democracy after slavery*, p. 71.

[100] M. Craton, 'Forms of resistance to slavery', in F. W. Knight (ed.), *The slave societies of the Caribbean*, vol. III of *General history of the Caribbean* (London: UNESCO Publishing, 1997), pp. 248–251; D. Geggus, 'The enigma of Jamaica in the 1790s: New light on the causes of slave rebellions', *William and Mary Quarterly* 3rd series 44 (1987); Sheller, *Democracy after slavery*, p. 85.

[101] Barbados House of Assembly, *The report from a select committee*, pp. 28, 29, 34.

[102] Beckles, *Bussa*, p. 26; Mullin, *Africa in America*; Barbados House of Assembly, *The report from a select committee*, p. 29.

[103] Anonymous, *Remarks on the insurrection*, p. 13.

[104] Harvey to Croker, 30 April 1816, TNA. This observation may have been in reference to such words as 'Brittanie' and 'Britannier'.

play of the 'circumstantial evidence' that pointed to the presence of Haitian agents who had aided the Barbadian rebels. Marryat drew parallels between events in Barbados and an account of a Haitian-backed conspiracy in Cuba in 1812. In the latter, John François, a free coloured man described as a 'confidential friend and emissary of Christophe', was to be crowned king after the Cuban whites had been overthrown. In Barbados, Marryat emphasised the 'conspicuous part as ringleaders' played by free coloureds, especially 'George Pitt Washington Franklin'.[105] As well as suggesting that Franklin was a Haitian agent, Marryat claimed that the same outcome was intended in both conspiracies: the murder of white men and the distribution of white women amongst the victorious rebel leaders. He concluded with an attack on British antislavery:

The St Domingo chiefs are joined in their views respecting the West Indies, by certain fanatical enthusiasts in this country; but what the former avow openly, and attempt by force of arms, or insurrection, the latter, while they disavow, promote insidiously by their speeches and their writings.[106]

Marryat's writing was indicative of the strength of the Haitian motif within white accounts of the revolt and of fears that rebellion could spread across the Caribbean.

Even after the revolt, Haiti would continue to loom large in the imaginations of both the enslaved people and colonists. This is evident from the experience of Loveless Overton, a free man of colour who served in the band of the British King's Dragoon Guards.[107] Whilst on leave, he returned to his native Barbados for the first time in twenty-four years. Landing in February 1817, he was arrested by magistrates within days 'on a charge of having landed from the Island of St Domingo'. Forced to prove his free status and that he was not carrying papers of a conspiratorial nature, Overton was kept in prison until an imperial officer interceded on his behalf. His lengthy imprisonment and the charges of sedition that were put to him 'caused a great sensation among the Slaves' who thought his arrival 'was in some measure connected with them'. He was arrested again for attempting to stir up insurrection and was eventually placed back on board the ship on which he had arrived.[108] Free non-whites were a troubling, 'liminal' presence in slave societies, as is evident from attempts to blame certain free people of colour for inciting the revolt. This was doubly so when they were suspected of being foreign agents and Overton's treatment was indicative of continuing white fears and black hopes about Haitian intervention.

Whereas the first two rebel representations were primarily anti-white Barbadian in their focus, the hopes and imaginings of Haitian intervention articulated an

---

[105] Marryat, *More thoughts still*, pp. 16, 18. Presumably Marryat was referring to Joseph Pitt Washington Franklyn, who was mentioned in the rebel confessions as the free coloured man who was to be governor if the uprising had succeeded.

[106] Marryat, *More thoughts still*, p. 19. For a discussion of the role of Haitians in 'conspiracies' elsewhere in the British West Indies, see Sheller, *Democracy after slavery*, pp. 227–246.

[107] Beckles, *Black rebellion*, p. 104.

[108] L. Overton to Teesdale, 30 June 1817, CO 28/86, fo. 153a–b, TNA.

imagined geography that located Barbados within a pan-Caribbean and black diasporic framework. The figure of Haiti was part of an enslaved representation that
marginalised *all* white people, even those opposed to slavery. Whiteness, as a
significant factor in achieving freedom, was dismissed. Through the evocation of
Haiti, the struggle in Barbados was linked to a broader history of resistance across
the 'black Atlantic'.[109]

The 1816 rebellion was an intense moment of competing and fractured narrations, spatial imaginaries, rumours and culturally significant acts, many of which
involved articulations of white colonial identity. Firstly, in the context of the shift
in focus of the slavery controversy to conditions in colonies such as Barbados,
there was a pro-/antislavery struggle over the slave world/free world division. This
centred on whether the uprising, and the colonists' subsequent response, allowed
white Barbadians to be considered as truly 'English'. Secondly, proslavery attempts
to portray themselves as beleaguered and vulnerable in the face of metropolitan
humanitarian meddling were ridden by tensions and manifested ambivalence over
the need for vengeance or conciliation. Finally, white colonial identity was mocked,
provoked, dislocated and marginalised in the signifying practices of the enslaved
rebels themselves. These three aspects of subjectification were linked: it was an
enslaved rebellion, in the context of metropolitan antislavery attack, which neces-
sitated a proslavery defence and made visible the tensions across white Barbadian
society.

This chapter has shown that enslaved black people were actively involved in contesting articulations of colonial whiteness. Yet, whilst the rebels in Barbados may
have been inspired by events in Haiti, they were unable to replicate this success.
The 1816 revolt was brutally suppressed and Afro-Caribbean hopes for freedom
were set back. Moreover, British abolitionism's hopes of forcing further reforms
on the West Indian plantocracies were dashed. The British government was so
worried by the revolt that it persuaded Wilberforce to withdraw his Slave Registry
Bill and settle for a compromise that merely encouraged the colonial legislatures to
establish local registration schemes.[110] In response, Barbados introduced its own
measures in 1817 and a militia commander who had presided at the courts-martial
was appointed as first registrar. This was little more than a gesture towards reform
designed to appease the imperial government, however. More characteristic of
white responses to the revolt were the repair and extension of the island's military
infrastructure. Meanwhile, abolitionist disillusionment over the fate of the Slave
Registry Bill was to lead to a re-doubling of their efforts in the early 1820s. As
will be seen, this would be met with further opposition from Barbados's whites.

---

[109] The term comes from P. Gilroy, *The black Atlantic: Modernity and double consciousness* (London:
Verso, 1993). See also Linebaugh and Rediker, *Many-headed hydra*, p. 302; Sheller, *Democracy
after slavery*, p. 71.

[110] D. B. Davis, *Slavery and human progress* (Oxford: Oxford University Press, 1984).

5

Anti-Methodism and the uncertain place of Barbados

Henry Nelson Coleridge was a British visitor to Barbados in 1825. He witnessed the much-welcomed arrival of Bishop William Hart Coleridge – no relation – to take charge of the newly created Anglican Diocese of Barbados and the Leeward Islands. He was also present when the Reverend Moses Rayner, a Methodist missionary, decided against landing at the island after public threats from an anonymous '*Exterminator*'.[1] Rayner had been sent to re-establish the Methodist missionary presence after the flight of the Reverend William Shrewsbury from Barbados in 1823 and the destruction of his chapel. In the starkly different responses to Bishop Coleridge and the Reverend Rayner, a particular form of white Barbadian identity found articulation: loyal to the Established Church and State, but opposed to Dissenting 'fanatics'. Yet, each cleric's journey to Barbados – although markedly different in outcome – occurred within the same framework established by the adoption of slavery amelioration as official imperial policy in 1823.[2] Both the welcome offered to the Anglican bishop and the threat to the Methodist missionary were Barbadian responses to this reformist shift and the resurgent antislavery campaign in the early to mid-1820s. Each was also symptomatic of competing local visions of whether

---

[1] H. N. Coleridge, *Six months in the West Indies in 1825* (London, 1826).

[2] The term 'amelioration' needs clarification. In chapter 2, it was used to denote the attempts made by slaveholders to produce a more sustainable form of slavery, which Woodville Marshall refers to as the 'West Indians' Amelioration'. The period after abolition but before 1823 was characterised by 'West Indians' and Abolitionists' Amelioration' in which slaveholders sought to cope with the loss of labour supplies whilst the antislavery campaign pressed for verifiable reforms through registration. The concern of this chapter is from 1823, when preparing enslaved people for freedom, at an unspecified date, became the policy of the British government. This 'official amelioration' – or imperial amelioration – was essentially the policy of the antislavery campaign, though the absentee West India Interest supported it in order to delay emancipation. In contrast, slaveholders in the West Indies were unaccommodating and continued to assert the need for 'spontaneous' local reform, rather than imperial regulation. Some white West Indians went even further and rejected all reform. See D. B. Davis, *Slavery and human progress* (Oxford: Oxford University Press, 1984), p. 193; W. Marshall, 'Amelioration and emancipation (with special reference to Barbados)', in A. O. Thompson (ed.), *Emancipation I: A series of lectures to commemorate the 150th anniversary of emancipation* (Bridgetown: Cedar Press, 1984).

140

it was best to respond to metropolitan humanitarianism by partial concessions or outright opposition.

As well as witnessing the different treatment of the two clerics, the general opposition in Barbados to antislavery also afforded Henry Nelson Coleridge the opportunity to ruminate on the relationship between Britain and its West Indian possessions. He noted that white West Indian colonists sought to 'carry their freedom with them and claim a right to the same or similar privileges' as those living in Britain, something that was institutionalised in the self-legislating assemblies.[3] Yet, the imperatives of imperial rule meant that it was 'absolutely necessary' for even a 'free state' such as Britain to have dominion over its colonies. In practice, this meant that the West Indian legislatures had to be subordinate to the British Parliament, even though this provoked anger in the colonies and exacerbated tensions between centre and periphery.

Coleridge's account of the 'eternal difficulties and apparent contradictions' within a 'Transatlantic Empire' is suggestive of the uncertain place of Barbados that arose from a disjuncture between the white colonists' self-identity as 'free-born Englishmen overseas' and their constitutional status as inhabitants of a colonial territory.[4] The tensions that stemmed from this became acute in the age of abolition. They were further exacerbated because Barbados's white population defined itself in terms of loyalty, Anglicanism, indispensability to empire and adherence to liberty – the pillars of Little Englandism. Indeed, Coleridge commented repeatedly on white Barbadian pride that the island was the 'most ancient, most loyal, and most windward colony in the West Indies'. Yet, when such insular pride was manifested as colonial resistance – in opposition to the reform of slavery and the persecution of religious Dissenters, for instance – this only served to confirm antislavery claims about the aberrant nature of white West Indians. As Coleridge put it: 'the well meaning but inconsiderate enthusiasts of this country' threatened to bring about exactly the opposite of what they sought – imperial intervention to reform slavery.[5]

This chapter considers the early to mid-1820s, a period characterised by antislavery campaigning and intense white opposition that saw Barbados at the centre of the slavery controversy. In its condemnation of slavery, attacks on the colonial legislatures and the unfavourable comparisons made between West and East Indies, the antislavery campaign mapped a moral geography of humanitarian duty towards enslaved people and inscribed a demarcation between slave and free worlds. As part of the former, Barbados was represented as an aberrant colonial space requiring metropolitan intervention. This imaginative geography found realisation, to some extent, in the imperial government's adoption of amelioration as official policy in 1823. West Indian responses to this reformist turn and the spatial imaginary

---

[3] Coleridge, *Six months*, pp. 292–293. For a discussion, see J. P. Greene, 'Liberty, slavery, and the transformation of British identity in the eighteenth-century West Indies', *Slavery and Abolition* 21 (2000).
[4] Coleridge, *Six months*, p. 297.   [5] Coleridge, *Six months*, pp. 46, 291, 298.

on which it was predicated were varied. The importance of not upsetting 'natural' reform was stressed, and the cultural similarities between West Indians and Britons were evoked to stave off intervention. Nevertheless, strident West Indian attacks upon the religious basis of humanitarianism served to posit differences between metropole and periphery. Such attacks were seized upon by their antislavery opponents, for whom they were confirmation of the slave world/free world division. In Barbados, the opposition to antislavery occasionally bordered on anti-imperial opposition, though even this was portrayed as a sign of the colonists' essential Englishness. This blurring of loyalty and opposition, which Gordon Lewis captures with the term 'Anglo-Saxon and anti-English',[6] pointed to an uncertainty about the place of white Barbadian society within the imaginative geographies of the British empire.

To explore the uncertainties revealed by white Barbadian opposition to antislavery, the focus of this chapter is the persecution of Methodists. In Barbados, Methodist missionaries and their congregations were harassed, partly because the white colonists believed they were connected to antislavery and partly because Methodism was a Dissenting offshoot of the Established Anglican Church. The 1823 enslaved revolt in Demerara intensified such feelings and, in October of that year, a white crowd destroyed Barbados's Methodist chapel and forced the resident missionary, William Shrewsbury, to flee to St Vincent. The next two years of persecution were characterised by anonymous threats and harassment by the civil authorities. This anti-Methodism also had a racial dimension, because free people of colour were prominent in the missionary church. As a locus of reactionary Anglicanism, racial supremacism and embryonic settler nationalism, the complex nature of white resistance to antislavery can be read in anti-Methodism.[7]

Mapping the post-1823 slavery controversy

The year 1823 'brought a fundamental shift in British antislavery strategy and expectations', marking the start of the phase of campaigning that would eventually culminate with the imperial act of emancipation in 1833.[8] Crucial to this was the publication of William Wilberforce's *Appeal . . . on behalf of the Negro slaves.* A product of the 'disillusioning experience' of registration and a recognition that abolition had not led to the automatic decline of slavery, Wilberforce condemned

---

[6] G. K. Lewis, *Main currents in Caribbean thought: The historical evolution of Caribbean society in its ideological aspects, 1492–1900* (Baltimore: Johns Hopkins University Press, 1983), p. 75.

[7] For other accounts of colonial missionary projects, see J. Comaroff and J. Comaroff, *Of revelation and revolution: Christianity, colonialism and consciousness in South Africa*, 2 vols., vol. I (London: University of Chicago Press, 1991); C. Hall, *Civilising subjects: Metropole and colony in the English imagination, 1830–1867* (Oxford: Polity, 2002); A. Lester, *Imperial networks: Creating identities in nineteenth-century South Africa and Britain* (London: Routledge, 2001); N. Thomas, *Colonialism's culture: Anthropology, travel and government* (Oxford: Polity, 1994).

[8] D. B. Davis, *The problem of slavery in the age of revolution, 1770–1823* (London: Cornell University Press, 1975), p. 23.

the entire *system* of slavery, rather than the actions of particular proprietors.[9] He also set forth emancipation as antislavery's new objective. The direct consequence of the appeal was the formation of the Society for the Mitigation and Gradual Abolition of Slavery Throughout the British Dominions – or Antislavery Society – with Thomas Fowell Buxton as president. In May 1823, Buxton proposed the gradual ending of slavery by pressing the imperial government to introduce a series of ameliorative measures. These included the promotion of Christianity and monogamous marriage amongst enslaved people, and limitations on physical punishment.[10]

Thomas Clarkson and the marginalisation of the West Indies

The year 1823 also saw Thomas Clarkson, vice-president of the Antislavery Society, produce *Thoughts on the necessity of improving the condition of the slaves in the British colonies* – a major emancipationist tract that encapsulated the campaign's new aims.[11] Whilst Clarkson admitted that there was evidence of improving treatment by slaveholders, emancipation itself seemed a distant prospect. Like fellow campaigner, James Stephen, Clarkson believed that faith in the goodwill of the planter-dominated West Indian legislatures was misplaced and that direct imperial intervention was required to bring about amelioration.[12] For Clarkson, reforms that altered the relationship between enslaver and enslaved – such as Joshua Steele's plan of copyhold – were crucial for preparing the way to emancipation.[13]

In addition to exemplifying a new resolve, Clarkson's tract mapped the imaginative geography that characterised the resurgent antislavery campaign. Although Clarkson insisted that 'It is against the *system* . . . and not against the West Indians as a body, that I am warm', his condemnation of the colonial legislatures as despotic and the unfavourable comparisons he drew between British and West Indian labour practices served to constitute the region as an aberrant slavedom.[14] Clarkson also represented the West Indies as an un-Christian place: 'the whole system of our planters appears to be one so directly in opposition to the whole system of our religion'.[15] The West Indies was not only geographically contrasted with the metropole, however. Indicative of the influence on antislavery of free

---

[9] W. Wilberforce, '*An appeal to the religion, justice and humanity of the inhabitants of the British Empire, on behalf of the Negro Slaves in the West Indies*', in D. Lee (ed.), *Slavery, abolition and emancipation: Writings in the British Romantic period – the emancipation debate*, 8 vols., vol. III (London: Pickering and Chatto, 1999), pp. 3–79. See also D. B. Davis, *Slavery and human progress*, p. 179.

[10] House of Commons, *Hansard parliamentary Debates*, 15 May 1823, 2nd Series, vol. IX, 255–360.

[11] T. Clarkson, *Thoughts on the necessity of improving the condition of the slaves in the British colonies, with a view to their ultimate emancipation* (London: Richard Taylor, 1823).

[12] D. B. Davis, *Slavery and human progress*, p. 179.

[13] House of Commons, *Hansard parliamentary Debates*, 15 May 1823, 2nd Series, vol. IX, 336–337. For Clarkson's view of Steele, see chapter 2, p. 41.

[14] Clarkson, *Thoughts*, preface.   [15] Clarkson, *Thoughts*, pp. 6, 11, 54.

tradism and an evangelical conception of imperialism were the unfavourable comparisons made with the 'East Indies' (India). For Clarkson, this was both a source of cheaper sugar that was 'not stained with blood', because it was produced by free labour, *and* a less costly imperial project because a large military presence was not needed to protect the colonists from revolt.[16] Moreover, the activities of the East India Company demonstrated the benefits to Briton and 'Native' alike if colonialism was separated from slavery:

> They distribute an equal system of law and justice to all without respect of persons. They dispell [sic] the clouds of ignorance, superstition, and idolatry, and carry with them civilization and liberty wherever they go . . . You [West Indian planters] *hinder liberty* by your cruel restrictions on manumission; and dreading the inlet of light, *you study to perpetuate ignorance and barbarism.*[17]

Owing to the planters' lack of civilising influence, the West Indies had no 'Superior claims . . . upon Parliament or upon us'. In this vein, other emancipationists, such as James Cropper, sought the equalisation of East and West Indian sugar duties, believing that such fiscal policies would undercut slavery.[18]

Clarkson's tract mapped a moral geography of colonial immorality and metropolitan duty in which the West Indies was represented as an aberrant space. After publishing his 1823 *Thoughts*, Clarkson embarked on a national tour in which he sought to re-establish the antislavery network that had campaigned for abolition. In such efforts, as well as Wilberforce's attacks on the whole system of slavery, Stephen's animosity towards the colonial legislatures and Cropper's promotion of East Indian sugar, antislavery campaigners inscribed a slave world/free world division. Although this demarcation had been present in antislavery narrations of the 1816 revolt and before, it would be more heavily drawn from 1823. Eventually such a humanitarian spatial imaginary would become a vital part of early Victorian imperial culture.[19] Yet, the 1820s was a transitional moment in this re-mapping of empire, and the marginalisation of the West Indies was not uncontested.

---

[16] Clarkson, *Thoughts*, pp. 48–50. For more on the anti-saccharite movement, see C. Midgley, 'Slave sugar boycotts, female activism and the domestic base of British anti-slavery culture', *Slavery and Abolition* 17 (1996); M. Sheller, *Consuming the Caribbean: From Arawaks to zombies* (London: Routledge, 2003); C. Sussman, *Consuming anxieties: Consumer protest, gender and British slavery, 1713–1833* (Stanford: Stanford University Press, 2000).

[17] Clarkson, *Thoughts*, p. 60.   [18] D. B. Davis, *Slavery and human progress*, p. 181.

[19] J. Cell, 'The imperial conscience', in P. Marsh (ed.), *The conscience of the Victorian state* (Hassocks: Harvester Press, 1979); P. J. Marshall, 'Britain without America – a second empire?', in P. J. Marshall (ed.), *The Oxford history of the British Empire*, vol. II, *The eighteenth century* (Oxford: Oxford University Press, 1998); A. Porter, 'Trusteeship, anti-slavery, and humanitarianism', in A. Porter (ed.), *The Oxford history of the British Empire*, vol. III, *The nineteenth century* (Oxford: Oxford University Press, 1999). See chapter 1, pp. 11–13.

James M'Queen: geographer of slavery

The British-based Society of West India Planters and Merchants sought to undercut the emancipationists' moral authority by drafting its own ameliorative proposals. The West India Interest also produced propagandist texts that combined arguments about race, the sanctity of private property, the civilising influence of slavery and the geopolitical importance of the West Indies.[20] Exemplary of such efforts was James M'Queen's *The West India colonies* (1824), which was a direct refutation of Clarkson's *Thoughts*. M'Queen was a geographer, who had lived in Grenada and came to edit the pro-West Indian *Glasgow Courier*. His 'unremitting and disinterested . . . defence of the West Indies' won him £500 from the Barbadian legislature.[21]

Whereas Clarkson inscribed a slave world/free world demarcation within a changing imperial map, key to M'Queen's defence was his emphasis on the centrality of the West Indies to the British empire. He stressed their 'vast importance' on the 'agricultural, commercial, and political scale', and argued that there was no distinction between white West Indians and their British 'brethren' – they are 'our sons and our brothers'.[22] M'Queen also refuted claims that East Indian sugar could be produced more cheaply or in more humane circumstances than in the West Indies. Challenging Clarkson's endorsement of the East India Company and his unfavourable comparison of West Indian planting with 'East Indian' colonialism, M'Queen gleefully drew on a barrage of Orientalist tropes – Indian superstition, idolatry, ignorance and 'Mohammedan' white female slavery – whilst portraying the West Indies as a place of civilisation.[23] He also contrasted the planters' paternalistic treatment of their enslaved workforce with the supposed political tyranny of the East Indian Company. Despite such attacks, M'Queen was at pains to state that he was not opposed to Britain's eastern empire *per se* but merely sought to refute antislavery arguments. Indeed, he argued that the professed supporters of 'East Indian sugar' were, in reality, 'actuated by principles alike hostile to ALL our Colonial possessions' and that the forces of antislavery threatened to destroy the fabric of the empire.[24] Nevertheless, he did argue that, whereas the loss of India

---

[20] W. Marshall, 'Amelioration and emancipation'. For other examples of such propaganda, see F. Clarke, 'Plan of treatment of the negroes on the estates in Barbados, 1823', reproduced in *Journal of the Barbados Museum and Historical Society* 2 (1934–5); R. J. Hampden, 'A commentary on Mr. Clarkson's pamphlet, entitled "Thoughts on the necessity of improving the condition of the slaves in the British colonies, with a view to their ultimate emancipation"', in Lee, *Slavery, abolition and emancipation.*

[21] J. M'Queen, *The West India colonies: The calumnies and misrepresentations circulated against them by the Edinburgh Review, Mr. Clarkson, Mr. Crupper, etc. etc.* (London: Baldwin, Cradock and Joy, 1824); Barbados: Acts, No. 469, CO 30/21, The National Archives.

[22] M'Queen, *The West India colonies*, pp. vii, 379.

[23] M'Queen, *The West India colonies*, pp. 92–118. The classic account of such discourse is E. W. Said, *Orientalism: Western conceptions of the Orient* (London: Penguin, 1978).

[24] M'Queen, *The West India colonies*, p. xx.

might be a short-term setback, that of the West Indies would wipe out centuries of political, social, cultural and economic investment. For M'Queen, the 'unnatural' ending of slavery – that is to say intervention before it faded away – would lead to the loss of the West Indian colonies and bring about a chain of events culminating in the end of empire and British sovereignty. In contrast, the maintenance of slavery and the retention of the West Indian colonies was the basis for utopian imperial projects such as the civilisation of Africa.[25]

M'Queen provided a determined defence of slavery, which linked its retention to imperial strength. His portrayal of the treacherous motives of the 'anti-colonists' contrasted their un-British activity with the shared culture of white West Indians and Britons. By challenging the geographical marginalisation of the West Indies and attempting to relocate the region at the centre of the British imperial project, M'Queen sought to contest the slave world/free world division. Yet, the defence of West Indian colonial interests did not rest on claims about a shared white culture across the British Atlantic world alone. By evoking the inalienable rights of the colonists, the unknowability of the region to outsiders and decrying the dangers of metropolitan intervention, the *difference* of the West Indies was posited. Such sentiments went in tandem with an emphasis on the threat posed by antislavery – as in M'Queen's description of 'anti-colonists' – and the West Indian legislatures 'warned repeatedly of the dangers of being "enslaved" by Parliament, echoing the rhetoric used half a century earlier by their North American brethren'.[26] Indeed, the spectre of the American Revolution was used by West Indians to argue that humanitarian intervention imperilled the loyalty of colonies and to suggest that they might have to resort to similarly 'disloyal' acts to defend their 'English liberties'. A vacillation between loyalty (sameness) and opposition (difference) characterised white Barbadian opposition to antislavery in many realms.

West Indian responses to amelioration

In the midst of campaigning and lobbying, the imperial government tried to mediate between the metropolitan pro- and antislavery interests. The foreign secretary, George Canning, seized the ameliorative proposals of the West India Committee as the basis for the government's own ameliorative resolutions.[27] His strategy was to appease the emancipationists whilst giving the metropolitan West India Interest the impression that the government was keeping the humanitarians at bay. Henry Bathurst, secretary of state for the colonies, sought to realise the new

---

[25] M'Queen, *The West India colonies*, pp. 263, 348–349.

[26] D. B. Davis, *Slavery and human progress*, p. 127.

[27] G. Canning, 'The speech of the Rt. Hon. George Canning, in the House of Commons, on the 16th day of March, 1824, on laying before the House the Papers in explanation of the measures adopted by His Majesty's Government, for the amelioration of the condition of the Slave Population in His Majesty's Dominions in the West Indies', in Lee, *Slavery, abolition and emancipation*. See D. J. Murray, *The West Indies and the development of colonial government, 1801–1834* (Oxford, 1965); H. Temperley, *British antislavery, 1833–1870* (London, 1972).

imperial policy by sending circulars to the West Indian governors in May 1823.[28] These contained instructions about the measures that were to be introduced by the colonial legislatures, including outlawing the whip, the recording of punishments and reductions in manumission fees. Bathurst also made it clear that delay would lead the imperial parliament to intervene directly to bring about amelioration.

Bathurst's instructions were angrily received in the West Indies, especially in the self-legislating colonies. Although based on the proposals of the West India Committee and part of its strategy to undercut calls for immediate emancipation, this accommodationist approach was unpopular amongst resident whites, and reformism was met with local defiance. The underlying cause of this was that 'the absentee owners were not only separated by vast geographic distance from their agents, employees, and the less successful planters; the two groups were also divided by class, culture, and political circumstance'.[29] With its high levels of planter residence, the differences between the metropolitan West India Interest and white opinion in Barbados were attenuated and Bathurst's proposals were universally condemned. In a debate in Barbados's Assembly, the speaker, Cheesman Moe, described the arrival of the instructions as the most important event since the establishment of the colony. He argued that the reformist turn in imperial policy reflected the 'diabolical falsehoods and infamous aspersions' cast by 'a few interested and designing hypocrits [sic]'. Like M'Queen, he claimed that the humanitarian-inspired instructions threatened to cast the West Indies 'headlong into the gulph [sic] of destruction'. Yet despite this strident tone, Moe called for a moderate response, so as to prevent their antislavery opponents from undermining the familial link between West Indians and their 'transatlantic brethren' in Britain.[30] Such comments were aimed at those Assembly members who advocated an uncompromising response to amelioration.

Moe's speech contained many of the features that would characterise white West Indian responses to the resurgent antislavery campaign. Firstly, the contemporary ameliorative turn in imperial policy was placed in the context of two centuries of Barbados's colonial history. This prefigured the importance attached in Barbados to a foundational episode for white creole culture, politics and identity – the island's opposition to the Cromwellian state in the middle of the seventeenth century.[31] Secondly, there was the notion that the forces of antislavery and their realisation in imperial policy threatened to displace and dislocate Barbados from the material and ideological heartlands of the British empire. Thirdly, Moe's call for caution

---

[28] D. B. Davis, *Slavery and human progress*, pp. 192–193; Circulars, 28 May, 9 July 1823, CO 29/30, fos. 246–264, 265–291, TNA.

[29] D. B. Davis, *Slavery and human progress*, p. 194; G. Heuman, 'The British West Indies', in A. Porter, *The Oxford history of the British Empire*, vol. III.

[30] Barbados Council, *Report of a debate in Council on a despatch from Lord Bathurst to His Excellency Sir Henry Warde, Governor of Barbados*, (Bridgetown, 1823); Minutes of Assembly, 23 September 1823, CO 31/49, fos. 128–129, TNA; *Barbadian*, 4 and 29 October 1823, Reel UF12, Bridgetown Public Library (henceforth BPL).

[31] See pp. 162–165.

signalled the ever-present concern that the adoption of an oppositional position would play into the hands of Barbados's enemies. Moe's speech was characteristic of white West Indian responses to the controversy over slavery in the early nineteenth century. It encapsulated the anxious attempts to 'negotiate' a place for slave colonies in a changing late Georgian empire.[32] Responses were not limited to official politics, however.

Anti-Methodism in Barbados

Beyond the legislative realm, an illuminating manifestation of white responses to metropolitan-originating reformist impulses was the treatment of Barbados's Methodists in the period 1823–5. The Methodists were one of two missionary bodies active on the island at the time, the other being the Moravians.[33] Yet, whilst the Moravians, who had arrived in 1765, won the plaudits of the plantocracy for the spirit of obedience they attempted to instil in enslaved people, the Methodists were treated with great hostility. Methodism, which was part of the English evangelical revival that began in the seventeenth century, traced its origins to John Wesley's conversion in 1738. At first, Methodists operated within the Church of England, but their break in 1784 attracted the ire of some Anglicans. Furthermore, its association with the working class and charges of links to Jacobinism meant that Methodism's loyalty to the British establishment was constantly questioned. All this contributed to anti-Methodist feeling in Britain and beyond.[34]

The Methodist Society's work in the West Indies began in Antigua in 1760 and a mission was established in Barbados in 1788. Although a chapel was opened in Bridgetown in 1789, the society's membership remained under fifty, and it represented Methodism's only failure in the West Indies.[35] What little growth in membership there was occurred amongst the free coloured population, and it remained unpopular among the island's white population. The 1816 revolt worsened the situation and, even though there were no missionaries in the island at the time, the general secretary of the Methodist Missionary Society still felt the need to respond to accusations of involvement.[36]

---

[32] The term 'negotiation' is used in K. A. Sandiford, *The cultural politics of sugar: Caribbean slavery and narratives of colonialism* (Cambridge: Cambridge University Press, 2000). See chapter 1, pp. 14–15, and this chapter, pp. 160–165.

[33] K. Lewis, *The Moravian mission in Barbados, 1816–1886* (Frankfurt: Peter Lang, 1985); N. F. Titus, *The development of Methodism in Barbados, 1823–1883* (Berne: Peter Lang, 1994).

[34] F. W. Blackman, *Methodism: 200 years in Barbados* (Bridgetown: Caribbean Contact, 1988); D. Hempton, *Methodism and politics in British society, 1750–1850* (London: Hutchinson, 1984); M. F. Snape, 'Anti-Methodism in eighteenth-century England: The Pendle Forest riots of 1748', *Journal of Ecclesiastical History* 49 (1998).

[35] Titus, *Development of Methodism*, p. 16.

[36] G. Matthews, 'The rumour syndrome, sectarian missionaries and nineteenth-century slave rebels of the British West Indies', *The Society for Caribbean Studies Annual Conference Papers*, 2 (2001), available from http://www.scsonline.freeserve.co.uk/olvol2.html, pp. 10, 11.

Much of the hostility towards Barbados's Methodists reflected perceived links between missionary activity and antislavery, especially after Wesley's attack on slavery in 1774.[37] Although missionary bodies warned their agents 'against meddling with political parties, or secular disputes', the attack on slavery and the appearance of the missionaries in the West Indies were 'inextricably connected'.[38] Leading proponents of antislavery were also key figures within the missionary organisations and both groups shared evangelical concerns about the lack of religious instruction for enslaved people. Indeed, missionaries were often asked to report on the state of slavery by their parent organisations.[39] Moreover, Bathurst's circulars contained specific references to the role of missionaries in serving the spiritual needs of enslaved people.[40] Yet, religious instruction remained controversial because many slaveholders believed it would undermine the socio-racial order. Thus, everything that threatened the planters 'became condensed into the hated figure of the missionary'.[41]

The strength of anti-Methodist feeling in Barbados and the relative failure of the mission were also related to the character of the local Anglican Church. Although the bishop of London had nominal jurisdiction over Barbados, the Church of England did not develop a more formalised presence until 1824.[42] As a result, the local church was more responsive to slaveholding interests than evangelical imperatives to Christianise enslaved people. Even the activities of some more moderate Anglicans were resisted.[43] Such opposition to most forms of reformist religious activity – Established and Dissenting, of local and metropolitan origin – reflected the socio-cultural, institutional and familial links between the plantocracy and the local church:

---

[37] J. Wesley, *Thoughts on slavery* (London, 1774).

[38] J. A. Brathwaite, *Methodism in the Caribbean* (Bridgetown, 1998); W. Peirce, *The ecclesiastical principles and polity of the Wesleyan Methodists*, 3rd edn (London: Wesleyan Conference Office, 1873), pp. 747, 794; M. Turner, *Slaves and missionaries: The disintegration of Jamaican slave society, 1787–1834* (London: University of Illinois Press, 1982), p. 10. See also Matthews, 'The rumour syndrome'.

[39] For example, W. J. Shrewsbury to Wesleyan Methodist Missionary Society (henceforth WMMS), 25 August 1823, Methodist Missionary Society Archives (henceforth MMS), Box 4, No. 195. All MMS references are to microfiche in the Special Reading Collection at the School of Oriental and African Studies, London.

[40] Bathurst to H. Warde, CO 29/30, fos. 265–291, TNA. See also O. M. Blouet, 'Education and emancipation in Barbados, 1833–1846: A study of cultural transference', *Ethnic and Racial Studies* 4 (1981).

[41] D. B. Davis, *Slavery and human progress*, p. 195; C. Hall, *Civilising subjects*, p. 106.

[42] J. Gilmore, 'Church and society in Barbados, 1824–1881', in W. Marshall (ed.), *Emancipation II: A series of lectures to commemorate the 150th anniversary of emancipation* (Bridgetown: Cedar Press, 1987); M. Turner, 'Religious beliefs', in F. W. Knight (ed.), *The slave societies of the Caribbean*, vol. III of *General history of the Caribbean* (London: UNESCO Publishing, 1997), p. 314. See also C. G. Pestana, 'Religion', in D. Armitage and M. J. Braddick (eds.), *The British Atlantic world, 1500–1800* (Basingstoke: Palgrave Macmillan, 2002).

[43] See A. Beahrs, '"Ours alone must need be Christians": The production of enslaved souls on the Codrington estates', *Plantation Society in the Americas* 4 (1997); J. H. Bennett, *Bondsmen and bishops: Slavery and apprenticeship on the Codrington plantations of Barbados, 1710–1838* (Berkeley: University of California Press, 1958); Gilmore, 'Church and society'.

The Anglican Church in Barbados was historically, and traditionally, the Church *of* the planters, and *for* the planters. The Church of England had been established in the Island primarily for the religious purposes of the white settlers and planters. Most of the churches had been erected on lands donated by the planters, and most of the money spent in building them had come from the planters. There could be little doubt therefore, that the planters regarded the Anglican Church as *their* Church.[44]

The main targets of this 'clergy–planter nexus' were the Methodist missionaries.[45] They were harassed and attacked by its organs, including the *Barbadian* newspaper – a conservative mouthpiece for the Established Church – as well as the magistracy and the legislature.

The Reverend William Shrewsbury

At the same time as the Barbadian legislature was debating its response to Bathurst's instructions, news reached the island of a major enslaved revolt in the British colony of Demerara on the South American mainland.[46] Just as white West Indians attributed the 1816 Barbados rebellion to enslaved peoples' misunderstanding of the Slave Registry Bill, so Bathurst's ameliorative instructions and the upsurge in antislavery campaigning were held responsible for this revolt. In addition, missionary activity was believed to have been a contributory factor. The Reverend John Smith of the London Missionary Society was arrested in Demerara after it was claimed that he had encouraged the revolt through his teaching. Convicted of treason and sentenced to death, Smith died in prison in February 1824.

The Demerara revolt focussed suspicions in Barbados on the resident Methodist missionary, William Shrewsbury (figure 5.1). Shrewsbury had arrived at Barbados in March 1820 and his four-year stint was even more difficult than that of his predecessor, Moses Rayner.[47] Often the sole missionary in Barbados, Shrewsbury was critical to the fortunes of the Methodist mission. He was a forceful character, who was very energetic in his missionary duties and inclined to be forthright in his criticisms of sinful behaviour. Indeed, within weeks of arriving in Barbados, Shrewsbury and a colleague had written a letter about the moral condition of the island's population, which was published in the *Methodist Magazine* of October 1820. Written with what Noel Titus terms a 'haughty attitude', the letter

---

[44] K. Davis, *Crown and cross in Barbados: Caribbean political religion in the late nineteenth century* (Frankfurt: Peter Lang, 1983), p. 54.

[45] Titus, *Development of Methodism*. A personification of this 'nexus' is the Reverend Henry Evans Holder. See chapter 2, pp. 63–64. For a comparative perspective in Jamaica, see C. Hall, *Civilising subjects*, pp. 98–106.

[46] Governor Warde received word of the revolt on 26 August 1823. See CO 28/92, fos. 159–179, TNA. For a discussion of the revolt itself, see M. Craton, *Testing the chains: Resistance to slavery in the British West Indies* (London: Cornell University Press, 1982), pp. 267–290; M. St Pierre, *Anatomy of resistance: Anti-colonialism in Guyana, 1823–1966* (London: Macmillan Education, 1999).

[47] Shrewsbury had previously served in Tortola (now part of the British Virgin Islands) and Grenada. See Titus, *Development of Methodism*, pp. 29–30.

Figure 5.1 The Reverend William Shrewsbury, from J. V. B. Shrewsbury, *Memorials of the Rev. William J. Shrewsbury* (London, 1868), 4454.h.12. By permission of the British Library.

portrayed Barbados as a place in which 'the fear of God is hardly to be seen'.[48] In the context of rising anti-Methodism engendered by Bathurst's 1823 ameliorative instructions, parts of this letter were reprinted in the local press as 'evidence' of Shrewsbury's anti-West Indian sentiments. Attempting to silence his critics and demonstrate that he had not attacked the white Barbadian character, Shrewsbury made a complete copy of his letter available in the Bridgetown commercial rooms, but this only served to inflame his white opponents. Some accused him of arrogant

[48] Titus, *Development of Methodism*, p. 30; W. Shrewsbury and W. Larcom to WMMS, 28 March 1820, MMS, Box 3.

incitement, whilst others argued that the letter he had produced was '*a sham*' to 'blind our eyes', whereas 'in reality, he has written dreadful things against us'. Rumours that Shrewsbury used red ink to underline words not meant for publication in the *Methodist Magazine*, and that this enabled him to vilify Barbados, posited secretive links with metropolitan antislavery organisations.[49] Shrewsbury had written little about the white population, nor attacked slavery directly during his time in Barbados, although he *was* critical of the lack of religious instruction. Nevertheless, he was reviled. White Barbadians were more concerned with how they thought they had been represented by Shrewsbury than with what he had to say about slavery *per se*.

Attitudes became more hostile in the aftermath of the Demerara revolt, and pamphlets were circulated that alleged Methodist involvement. In early October 1823, Methodist religious services were disrupted. Shrewsbury tried and failed to have his enemies prosecuted and he was actually ordered by constables to appear before a magistrate for his failure to join the island's militia. Anglican ministers were not expected to serve in the militia and Shrewsbury maintained that, under the terms of the 1689 Toleration Act, this also covered non-Anglican clergy. Yet, as will become clear, Barbados's authorities argued that the Toleration Act did not extend to the West Indies and, hence, Shrewsbury was liable for militia service. In this way, the actions of the constables and magistrates paralleled the broader view that Methodism was a 'mock' religion, and official harassment accompanied popular persecution.[50] Shrewsbury also sought protection from Governor Henry Warde, only to be told that he would have to rely on the very authorities that were harassing him.[51] Whilst Shrewsbury trying to secure Warde's help, an anonymous handbill was circulated that called for the destruction of the Bridgetown Methodist chapel on Sunday, 19 October.[52] Shrewsbury received warning of the plot and fled to the neighbouring island of St Vincent.[53] Meanwhile, a crowd of up to two hundred white Barbadians began the demolition of the chapel.

[49] Shrewsbury to WMMS, 3 July 1823, MMS, Box 4, No. 192; J. V. B. Shrewsbury, *Memorials of the Rev. William J. Shrewsbury* (London, 1868), p. 135.
[50] Shrewsbury to WMMS, 20 June 1820, MMS, Box 3, No. 121.
[51] Warde to Barbados Council, 21 October 1823, CO 28/92, fo. 244, TNA. One of the reasons why Shrewsbury's appeal elicited little help was that Warde was unpopular and at odds with the Assembly. The immediate cause for this opprobrium was the governor's attempt to bring several whites to justice for the assault and murder of enslaved people. In pursuing these prosecutions, he was seeking to enact aspects of Bathurst's ameliorative instructions. Thus, both Shrewsbury and Warde were experiencing local white reaction to the reformist turn in imperial policy: Warde to W. H. Clinton, c. mid-1823, Warde Papers, Y9/1/17, Barbados Department of Archives (henceforth BDA).
[52] Anonymous, 'Spirit of West Indian society – outrage at Barbadoes', *Edinburgh Review* (August 1825), Foreign and Commonwealth Office Library, London.
[53] Shrewsbury eventually resettled in Africa on the Cape Colony's eastern frontier, where he became the first missionary to the Gcaleka Xhosa. Whilst there, he encountered resistance to his efforts at proselytisation and the selective adoption of Christianity by the indigenous population. This contributed to a marked shift in his political attitudes, and during the Frontier War of 1834–5 he agitated for more severe punishment and regulation of the Xhosa than either his Mission Society or the Colonial Office were prepared to contemplate. Indeed, Shrewsbury came to be known as the 'Kaffir-hating Methodist'. See Lester, *Imperial networks*, pp. 100–101.

In the aftermath of the chapel's destruction, Governor Warde attempted to investigate the civil authorities' failure to prevent it. It was not until February 1825 that a Council report was produced and, although it indicated that Bridgetown's magistrates could have acted, it advised Warde to take no action other than express displeasure at the 'very culpable dereliction of duty'.[54] The failure of the magistrates to act, the Council's limited censure and the fact that no one was convicted for the demolition point to the broader anti-Methodist culture in which physical and epistemic violence occurred. This left the Methodists themselves in a precarious position. Despite a public declaration that they were not connected to British anti-slavery campaigning, further acts of persecution occurred over the next two years, especially around the anniversary of the chapel's destruction or when the missionary society attempted to re-establish its presence. Effigies of Shrewsbury and leading opponents of slavery were burnt – underlining the connection between anti-Methodism and broader white West Indian opposition to reformism – and Methodist houses were attacked. Two missionaries appointed to replace Shrewsbury did not come to Barbados because they feared they would be assaulted.[55] Meanwhile, Barbados's Methodists were forced to maintain a low profile.

Anti-Methodist discourse

Following the complete destruction of the chapel on 20 October, the anti-Methodists were at pains to put their actions in a favourable light. Such attempts at self-justification can be seen in the anonymous proclamations that were disseminated over next two years, the first appearing in a handbill that was delivered to the Assembly and Council on the day after the chapel's demolition.[56] This broadsheet celebrated a 'Great and signal triumph' over Methodism:

The Inhabitants of this island are respectfully informed, that in consequence of the unmerited and unprovoked attacks which have repeatedly been made upon the Community by the Methodist Missionaries, (otherwise known as agents to the villainous African Society,) a party of respectable Gentlemen formed the resolution of closing the Methodist Concern altogether: with this view they commenced their labours on Sunday Evening; and they have the greatest satisfaction in announcing that by 12 o'clock last night they effected the TOTAL DESTRUCTION OF THE CHAPEL. It is hoped that as this Information will be circulated throughout the different Islands and Colonies; all persons who consider themselves true Lovers of Religion will follow the laudable example of the BARBADIANS, in putting an end to Methodism and Methodist Chapels throughout the West Indies.[57]

---

[54] Minutes of Council, 12 April 1825, Lucas Manuscripts, Vol. 34, Reel 15, p. 511, BPL.

[55] J. Nelson, 'An appeal of the Wesleyan Methodists of this island to the public', reproduced in J. V. B. Shrewsbury, *Memorials*, pp. 169–170. See also J. V. B. Shrewsbury, *Memorials*, p. 164; Titus, *Development of Methodism*.

[56] CO 28/92, fo. 244, TNA. The handbill and other materials relating to the destruction of the chapel were reproduced by the Methodist Missionary Society as *The late insurrection in Demerara, and riot in Barbados* (London, 1823).

[57] Reproduced in Methodist Missionary Society, *Late insurrection*.

This was the first of four anti-Methodist broadsheets printed in the aftermath of Shrewsbury's flight. The proclamations were linked to particular acts of persecution in that they sought to mobilise popular support, planned violent acts, challenged the authority of the British governor and terrorised the Methodists themselves. These decrees were also the textual codification of the political and cultural project of anti-Methodism: to unify the white population against 'subversives', to protect the Established order against Dissenters, to purify Barbados of Methodism and to defend the colonial (and imperial) state against the forces of antislavery.[58] Encompassing popular and official forms, this anti-Methodism was part of a broader white West Indian reaction to antislavery and therefore connected to legislative obstruction to amelioration. Yet, anti-Methodism was not a coherent political and cultural project, but rather a locus of West Indian anxieties. For this reason, the modes of representation that accompanied, and were directed toward, anti-Methodism can be read as part of a strategy of negotiation on the part of the white colonists that aimed at stabilising their place *vis-à-vis* metropolitan opinion. At the same time, this anti-Methodism was a target for countervailing *anti*-West Indian efforts by British forces opposed to slavery.[59]

The anti-Methodist proclamations were anonymous.[60] Despite this secrecy, the proclamations were implicated in the articulation of a particular form of white colonial identity. Throughout the controversy that followed the chapel's demolition, the presumed social status of the perpetrators was of great importance because it determined how seriously the events were taken in Britain and whether the island's plantocracy were held responsible. Sections of Barbados's elite, particularly that associated with Council, claimed that the poor white 'rabble' of the island's population had been to blame and that their actions should not be used to condemn white society as a whole. Their fear was that such condemnation would engender a more interventionist approach to slavery. In contrast, the perpetrators, though remaining anonymous, claimed respectability and refused to be dismissed as 'the Mob'. These anti-Methodists portrayed themselves as a 'party of respectable Gentlemen', 'true Lovers of Religion' and, most emphatically, as 'BARBADIANS'. Many antislavery campaigners in Britain accepted the claim of the perpetrators to represent the interests of the entire white population and used this to condemn white society as a whole. In so doing, they rejected Barbadian claims about their essential Englishness and articulated the division between slave world and free world.

---

[58] For more on the character of anti-Methodism in England, see Snape, 'Anti-Methodism in eighteenth-century England'.

[59] Sandiford, *Cultural politics of sugar*.

[60] From the evidence available, it is difficult to be certain about the social status of the anti-Methodists. There are various references to the involvement of lawyers, magistrates and even members of the legislature – which suggests that some were drawn from Barbados's white middle and upper classes – but this is far from conclusive. Only one free man of colour was said to have been involved. See Anonymous, 'Spirit of West Indian society'.

During the legislative session to which the first proclamation was brought, Governor Warde was advised by the Council to restore order by evoking the Riot Act. The Assembly blocked this course of action, however, which was another sign of Warde's politically weak position and of the strength of white opposition to the imperial authority he embodied.[61] Consequently, the only response available to the governor was to issue a proclamation on the 22 October condemning the 'outrageous violation of all Law and Order' and offering a reward for information leading to the conviction of those involved. A day later, Warde's authority was defied when another anti-Methodist broadsheet was published.[62] This took the form of a counter-proclamation that mimicked the governor's. It warned that anyone who was inclined 'from pecuniary temptation or vindictive feeling' to respond to the governor's call would '*RECEIVE THAT PUNISHMENT* which their Crimes will justly deserve'. This direct challenge to Warde was combined with the evocation of an idealised white, Barbadian community, which could survive the governor's ire – and, by implication, metropolitan condemnation – if 'the People are firm to themselves'. The counter-proclamation concluded with a threat that, if Methodist missionaries were to attempt to return to Barbados, '*it will be at their own peril*'. Again, a striking feature of this text was a concern with the identity of the perpetrators. In his proclamation, Warde had condemned the demolition as the actions of 'the Mob'. In contrast, the authors of the counter-proclamation sought to represent themselves as much more respectable:

[W]hereas it may appear to those persons who are unacquainted with the circumstances which occasioned the said Proclamation, that the demolition of the Chapel was effected by the Rabble of this Community, in order to create Anarchy, Riot, and Insubordination, to trample upon the Laws of the Country, and to subvert good order: – It is considered an imperative duty to repel the charge, and to state, – *Firstly*, That the majority of the Persons assembled were of the first Respectability, and were supported by the concurrence of nine-tenths of the Community: – *Secondly*, That their motives were patriotic and Loyal, – namely, to eradicate from this soil the germ of Methodism, which was spreading its baneful influence over a certain class, and which ultimately would have injured both Church and State.[63]

References to the 'patriotic and Loyal' motives of the anti-Methodists and their concern for the 'Church and State' evoked the discourse of Barbados-as-Little-England, defender of the Established Church, Great Britain and its empire. As will become apparent, such rhetoric was related to the Barbadian settler myth of Royalist, Anglican resistance to Cromwell's Puritanical 'Usurpation'.[64] Some of the anti-Methodists sought to realise this self-proclaimed leading role in 'putting an end to Methodism and Methodist Chapels throughout the West Indies' by travelling

---

[61] Warde to Council, 25 October 1823, CO 28/92, fo. 251, TNA; Warde to Clinton, 30 October 1823, Warde Papers, Y9/1/17, BDA.
[62] Both Warde's proclamation and the counter-proclamation are reproduced in Methodist Missionary Society, *Late insurrection*.
[63] Reproduced ibid.   [64] See pp. 162–165.

to Tobago, Trinidad and Grenada to incite anti-Methodist sentiments, though they met with no success.[65] The proclamation's final flourish – '*GOD SAVE THE KING, AND THE PEOPLE*' – echoed Warde's '*GOD SAVE THE KING*', but combined loyalty and populism to articulate a local patriotism to an imperial institution. This evocation of Barbados as most loyal colony and repository of true Englishness was a pre-emptive response to those metropolitan critics who would condemn the destruction of the chapel as an act of anti-imperial rebellion.

Later articulations of anti-Methodism were equally strident. For example, in 1825, the Methodist Missionary Society sought to re-establish its presence by re-appointing Moses Rayner, who had been Shrewsbury's predecessor, as his successor. Despite imperial support for this move – Warde was ordered to take all necessary measures to protect missionaries, for example[66] – white animosity towards the Methodists had not abated. The editor of the *Barbadian* described Rayner's impending arrival as an 'insulting attempt' to foist Methodism upon the population.[67] The paper also published an open letter written under the pseudonym 'Philo Ecclesiae' addressed to William Hart Coleridge who, in another sign of the ameliorative shift in imperial policy, had just arrived in Barbados as the new Anglican bishop.[68] Philo Ecclesiae sought to incite hostility towards Methodism by claiming that the Toleration Act did not extend to Barbados and that Methodism's threat to the Established Church should be removed immediately. Echoing the statements of Assembly members, Philo Ecclesiae argued that allowing the 'obnoxious' Rayner to land was an unnecessary 'Evil' given the increasingly active role played by the Anglican Church on the island.[69] Having been left in no doubt about the opposition he would face, and with the governor unwilling or unable to protect him, Rayner returned to St Vincent without setting foot on Barbados – a decision that was celebrated in the local press.[70] Highlighting the deeply embedded nature of anti-Methodist feeling, Philo Ecclesiae's appeals to the Established Church portrayed anti-Methodism not as an act associated with an aberrant slave world but with a normal, Anglican society.

The period July 1823 to April 1825 was the high point of opposition to antislavery in Barbados. Beginning with the unfavourable responses to Bathurst's proposals and ending with Rayner's decision not to land, this period was characterised by a combination of anti-ameliorative obstruction and anti-Methodist persecution.

[65] Shrewsbury to WMMS, 1 December 1823, MMS, Box 5, No. 200.
[66] Bathurst to Warde, 11 April 1825, CO 28/95, fos. 103–104, TNA.
[67] *Barbadian*, 5 April 1825, Reel UF12, BPL.
[68] The Bishopric of Barbados and the Leeward Islands was one of two Anglican dioceses created by the British government in the Caribbean. It encompassed all the West Indian colonies except Jamaica. See A. Porter, 'Religion, missionary enthusiasm, and empire', in A. Porter, *The Oxford history of the British Empire*, vol. III. See also Pestana, 'Religion', pp. 70–74.
[69] Letter from Philo Ecclesiae (loosely translatable as 'Lover of the Church'), *Barbadian*, 8 April 1825, Reel UF12, BPL; Address of the Assembly to Warde, 5 April 1825, CO 28/95, fos. 105–106, TNA.
[70] Warde to Rayner, 9 April, CO 28/85, fo. 109, TNA; Rayner to Shrewsbury and the Committee of the MMS, no date, MMS, Box 5, no. 236; *Barbadian*, 17 May 1825, Reel UF12, BDA.

Both were facets of broader opposition to metropolitan antislavery and the defence of the white order. Although legislative resistance to antislavery was not limited to Barbados, it was here and in Jamaica that opposition was strongest. Only in January 1824 had a bill to adopt some ameliorative measures been introduced in the Barbadian Assembly – half a year after Bathurst's original circular – and, eventually, the Consolidated Slave Act was passed in March 1825.[71] Although proclaimed by Barbadians as evidence of their willingness to respond positively to the imperial instructions, this act fell far short of the reforms envisioned by the Colonial Office. In consequence, it was viewed in the metropole as yet another demonstration of West Indian resistance to British public opinion and to the imperial will.

Anti-Methodist anxieties

At first sight, anti-Methodism would seem to be a locus for confident colonial articulations of a British 'Imperial identity'.[72] Yet, there were anxieties. For example, letters sent by planters at the time expressed concern that the events would damage Barbados's reputation and be used to attack white society as a whole.[73] Evidence of these anxieties can also be seen within the discourse of anti-Methodism itself. Nowhere is this clearer than in the proclamation produced in 1824 on the first anniversary of the chapel's destruction. The ostensible purpose of this proclamation was to call for renewed attacks on the Methodist community. The way in which the original destruction was commemorated is significant:

[I]t is hereby made known to all whom it may concern, that for the avowed purpose of rooting *eternally* from their shores the damned doctrine, and public exhibition of Methodistical hypocrisy now again rearing its baleful head, and spreading its blasted and pestilential principles amongst us, we have decreed that from and after the said memorable, the blessed 21st October, more dear to firm and true Barbadians than Trafalgar to Britons, that we will, with fire and sword, root and out and destroy, all and every abettors of Methodism and Methodists.[74]

The 'blessed 21st October', the date on which the chapel's destruction was first celebrated, was also the anniversary of the Battle of Trafalgar (1805). Trafalgar was an important victory for British West Indians because it marked a check to the French naval threat in the Caribbean.[75] After news of the battle reached Barbados, white society engaged in celebrations and mourned the death of Admiral Horatio Nelson. An appeal was also launched to commemorate the events 'WITH a view of testifying the high regard and veneration which the people of this ancient

[71] CO 31/49, fo. 136, TNA.
[72] J. P. Greene, 'Empire and identity from the Glorious Revolution to the American Revolution', in P. J. Marshall, *The Oxford history of the British Empire*, vol. II, p. 208.
[73] See, for example, Methodist Missionary Society, *Late insurrection*, p. 2.
[74] This 1824 decree is reproduced in J. V. B. Shrewsbury, *Memorials*, p. 174.
[75] J. R. Ward, 'The British West Indies in the age of abolition, 1748–1815', in P. J. Marshall, *The Oxford history of the British Empire*, vol. II, p. 421.

and loyal Colony entertain of the transcendent services rendered to the BRITISH EMPIRE by the late heroic LORD NELSON'.[76] A statue was unveiled to much pomp on 23 March 1813 in a central part of Bridgetown named 'Trafalgar Square' (see figure 5.2).[77] For white West Indians, the commemoration of Nelson and Trafalgar was not only about thanksgiving. It marked the importance of the colony within the empire, especially as Barbados had been the base of military operations in the eastern Caribbean during the Revolutionary and Napoleonic Wars. It was also crucial to the articulation of a loyal, white Barbadian identity. The significance of Nelson to white settler culture was remarked upon by British visitors to Barbados, with one acknowledging that Nelson was 'a great favourite', whilst another noted that 'Barbadians pride themselves not a little' on the statue of Nelson.[78]

Despite the importance of Nelson and Trafalgar in white Barbadian settler culture, the evocation of the battle in the 1824 anti-Methodist proclamation was ambiguous. It equated domestic controversy with international conflict by elevating the chapel's destruction to the status of a glorious triumph over a foreign foe. Yet by downgrading the commemoration of Trafalgar against the 'Great and signal triumph' over Methodism ('the blessed 21st October, more dear to firm and true Barbadians than Trafalgar to Britons') a difference between the public mythologies of Barbados and Britain was posited. What was important to white Barbadians was not the grand imperial conflict with France, but a local struggle against 'Methodistical hypocrisy'. By suggesting that white Britons and white Barbadians did not have the same commemorative priorities, the decree implied that there were differences between West Indians and their 'trans-Atlantic brethren'. When it is also noted that the 1824 decree was circulated by the 'committee of public safety' but signed by the enigmatic 'ROCK', this ambivalence becomes more evident. The former title alluded to the reactionary organisations that had emerged in Britain in the 1790s in the context of fears about revolution and Jacobinism.[79] It is significant, in terms of how the Barbadian opponents of Methodism styled themselves, that 'radical' abolitionists had been amongst the targets of such vigilante organisations. In contrast, the appellation 'ROCK' evoked 'Captain Rock', a semi-mythical figure who was the supposed leader of the agrarian insurgency that swept Munster, in southern Ireland, in the early 1820s. Captain Rock headed 'the most notorious insurgent movement in nineteenth-century Ireland' and the use of 'ROCK' to identify anti-Methodism – which led Buxton, the British leading abolitionist, to describe the religious persecution as of an 'Irish model' – served to represent

---

[76] *Barbados Mercury and Bridgetown Gazette*, 21 and 24 December 1805, 4, 7 and 14 January 1806, Reel 20, BPL.

[77] Anonymous, 'Some Nelson statues', *Journal of the Barbados Museum and Historical Society Library* 18 (1950–1).

[78] F. Bayley, *Four years' residence in the West Indies, during the years 1826, 7, 8 and 9* (London: William Kidd, 1830), p. 30; Coleridge, *Six months*, p. 44.

[79] In J. V. B. Shrewsbury, *Memorials*, p. 174.

Figure 5.2 Statue of Admiral Horatio Nelson, Trafalgar Square, Bridgetown, Barbados. Reproduction from an engraving 'drawn from Nature and on Stone' by Lieutenant J. Carter, from R. Schomburgk, *The history of Barbados* (London, 1848), 1303.l.5. By permission of the British Library.

opposition to imperial reformism as an *anti-colonial* struggle by a marginalised white population.[80] Along with the uncertain place of Nelson and Trafalgar in

---

[80] L. Gibbons, 'Between Captain Rock and a hard place: Art and agrarian insurgency', in T. Foley and S. Ryder (eds.), *Ideology and Ireland in the nineteenth century* (Dublin: Four Courts Press, 1998), p. 24. Of course, 'ROCK' could also be an allusion to Gibraltar or perhaps St Peter, but 'Captain Rock' was certainly the contemporary interpretation. See Methodist Missionary Society, *An Authentic Report of the Debate in the House of Commons, June the 23rd, 1825, on Mr. Buxton's motion relative to the demolition of the Methodist Chapel and Mission House in Barbadoes, and the expulsion of Mr. Shrewsbury, a Wesleyan Missionary, from that Island* (London: J. Hatchard and Son, 1825), p. 42.

anti-Methodism's collective memory, the two very different designations of the 'committee of public safety' and Captain Rock encapsulate the ambivalence of white West Indian responses to antislavery as they oscillated anxiously between loyalty and opposition.[81]

Other anti-Methodist texts betray similar anxieties. In April 1825, when Rayner, the replacement Methodist missionary, was anchored offshore, another anti-Methodist broadsheet was published. Addressed 'TO ALL TRUE LOVERS OF THEIR COUNTRY' and signed by the '*Exterminator of Methodism, and sworn Delegate*', the circular called on the island's whites to 'hurl the thunder of their excited fury at the daring miscreant's head' and for popular resistance to Rayner's arrival. The decree represented the persecution of Methodism as a critical opportunity for Barbadians to 'prove that the proud blood of Englishmen yet flows uncontaminated in the remains of their West India progeny'.[82] That anti-Methodism was a *proving* ground suggested an anxiety about metropolitan perceptions of the religious persecution and West Indian culture more broadly. Indeed, the strenuous need to assert the 'English' nature of anti-Methodism throughout the period 1823–5 betrayed a lack of white colonial self-assurance and seemed to point to awareness that a backlash was inevitable, particularly in the context of the increasing influence of evangelical and antislavery politics in Britain.

Negotiating the place of anti-Methodism

Much of the uncertainty in the articulation of white West Indian identity during the controversies over slavery stemmed from fears that West Indian complaints would invite greater anti-creole hostility. In Barbados in the early 1820s, this uncertainty centred on white colonial concerns about how anti-Methodism would be interpreted in the metropole, particularly the destruction of the chapel and the opposition to the attempts made by the colonial governor – the embodiment of imperial authority – to protect religious freedom. Something of the response to this, or more properly an attempt to pre-empt it, can be seen in the efforts involving the colonial agent, George Carrington, to attribute the destruction of the chapel to explicable factors such as the revolt in Demerara, Shrewsbury's 'perverse adherence to falsehood' and the broader context of antislavery campaigning. Such efforts to explain, if not excuse, anti-Methodism turned on the normalisation of white Barbadian responses within the British Atlantic world. 'Human feelings' were, according to Carrington, the 'same in all countries and in all ages' and therefore there was nothing aberrant about white Barbadian behaviour.[83]

---

[81] For similar observations about white eastern Cape settlers in the same period, see Lester, *Imperial networks*, pp. 65–67.

[82] The 1825 decree is reproduced in J. V. B. Shrewsbury, *Memorials*, pp. 178–179.

[83] Committee of Correspondence of House of Assembly (henceforth CCHA) to G. Carrington, 28 June 1824, Carrington to Bathurst, 3 May 1824, Agents' Letter Books (henceforth ALB), Reel Bs. 9, BDA. See also *Barbados Mercury and Bridgetown Gazette*, 4 November 1823, Reel 26, BPL.

The efforts made through the colonial agent were part of an attempt to negotiate a place for white West Indian politics and culture – as articulated in anti-Methodism – in the metropolitan imagination. This negotiation involved attempts at winning legitimacy for white creole culture, politics and identity in the face of an emergent 'anti-Caribbean animus' fed by the rise of antislavery.[84] A prime example of this can be seen in the official harassment of a relatively wealthy free coloured Methodist, Sarah Ann Gill. As has been noted, it was amongst the free people of colour that Methodist missionary activity had achieved most success in Barbados, as many planters preferred the Moravians to instruct their enslaved workforces.[85] It was this population that one anti-Methodist proclamation referred to as 'a certain class' over which Methodism was 'spreading its baneful influence'. Free people of colour remained a liminal group in Barbados and, even after most had demonstrated their 'loyalty' to the white order during the 1816 revolt, they continued to be viewed suspiciously by many whites.[86] The adoption of Methodism was a strategy through which some free people of colour attempted to 'stabilise' their liminal status,[87] but it also led whites to view them as anti-Anglican – especially when the Methodist Church came to be led by free people of colour. Indeed, Governor Warde feared that in the climate of unrest accompanying Methodist persecution 'a conflict may take place between the white inhabitants and the Free People of Colour', which might lead to 'the total destruction of the whole'.[88] In these ways, the persecution of Barbados's Methodists, and particularly of Gill, was related not only to opposition to antislavery, but also to a broader white supremacist defence of the social order. Indeed, anti-Methodism was an articulation of a particular form of white identity.[89]

After the chapel's destruction, Gill became the effective leader of the Methodist community in the absence of a missionary and the Methodists were soon holding meetings at her house.[90] In consequence, both it and its owner, became targets for attack. She was also harassed by the island's authorities, with visits from magistrates and summons to appear before the legislature.[91] The actions of the

---

[84] G. K. Lewis, *Main currents*, p. 25; Sandiford, *Cultural politics of sugar*, p. 3.
[85] K. Lewis, *Moravian mission;* Turner, 'Religious beliefs', p. 315.
[86] Titus, *Development of Methodism.*
[87] The free people of colour were not a homogeneous population, and the 1820s saw increasing tensions between the elite and non-elite sections. On tensions within the free coloured population, as well as with whites, see M. Newton, '"The Children of Africa in the Colonies": Free people of colour in Barbados during the emancipation era', unpublished DPhil. thesis, Oxford University (2001), pp. 127–132.
[88] Warde to Bathurst, 25 October 1823, CO 28/92, fo. 249, TNA. See also S. A. Gill to Shrewsbury, 30 October 1824, in Shrewsbury to WMMS, 14 December 1824, MMS, Box 5, No. 254; 'Native of Barbadoes' to Shrewsbury, 22 December 1823, MMS, Box 5, No. 200.
[89] For instances of free coloured persecution, see Gill to Shrewsbury, 30 October, 1824, MMS, Box 5, No. 254.
[90] Sarah Ann Gill was the only woman designated amongst the ten National Heroes and Heroines in April 1998. See http://www.bgis.gov.bb. See also F. W. Blackman, *National heroine of Barbados: Sarah Ann Gill* (Barbados: Methodist Church in Barbados, 1998).
[91] For details of Gill's harassment, see Notification from Magistrates to Gill, 21 October 1824, MMS, Box 5, No. 254; Gill to Shrewsbury, 30 October 1824, in Shrewsbury to WMMS, 14 December 1824,

civil authorities were symptomatic of the entrenched nature of anti-Methodism: the forms taken by official harassment mirrored the anonymous threats made to her. The politico-judicial logic evoked to justify the official harassment of Gill and the settler mythology on which this logic was based is extremely significant.

The formal reason for much of the official persecution was that Gill was guilty of holding a 'conventicle'. The Conventicles Act, which had been passed in 1664 during the reign of Charles II, had forbade gatherings – 'conventicles' – of more than five people for divine worship unless in a licensed meeting place and led by a licensed preacher.[92] Although it had been made obsolete in England by the 1689 Toleration Act, legal opinion in early nineteenth-century Barbados declared that the Toleration Act did not extend to the island and that the Conventicles Act remained in force.[93] The significance of its enforcement in early nineteenth-century Barbados relates to use in the suppression of Dissenting religion after the restoration of the monarchy in 1660. During the English Civil War, many of the island's planters were keen to remain out of the conflict.[94] Nevertheless, after the victory of parliamentary forces and the 'Usurpation' of the monarchy – the execution of Charles I and Oliver Cromwell's later ascendance to the status of lord protector of the Commonwealth – Royalist sympathisers in Barbados moved in favour of independence from the Commonwealth. Although the colony was later subordinated by a parliamentary fleet, the colonists won the right to self-government as codified in the 1652 charter.[95] For the plantocracy, this charter represented confirmation of 'the inherited and customary rights' of Englishmen overseas. As well as guaranteeing certain political rights as enshrined in the charter, opposition to the Cromwellian state and the 'Usurpation' of the monarchy became mythologised as a symbol of white Barbadians' commitment to 'liberty' and was, as such, crucial in the articulation of colonial identity.[96] The notion that white

MMS, Box 5, No. 254; Gill to WMMS, 16 May 1825, MMS, Box 5, No. 228; Gill to Shrewsbury, 2 July 1825, Barbados, MMS, Box 5, No. 230.

[92] Blackman, *National heroine*, p. 26.

[93] See letter from Attorney General and Solicitor General to Governor Henry Warde, dated March 1825, reproduced in *Journal of the Barbados Museum and Historical Society*, 21 (1953–4), p. 13. See also E. H. Gould, 'Revolution and counter-revolution', in Armitage and Braddick, *The British Atlantic world*, p. 202.

[94] L. Gragg, *Englishmen transplanted: The English colonization of Barbados, 1627–1660* (Oxford: Oxford University Press, 2003), pp. 42–57; G. A. Puckrein, *Little England: Plantation society and Anglo-Barbadian politics, 1627–1700* (New York: New York University Press, 1984). For more on the ramifications of the Civil War on the wider Atlantic world, see M. J. Braddick, 'The English government, war, trade, settlement, 1625–1688', in N. Canny (ed.), *The Oxford history of the British Empire*, vol. I, *The origins of empire* (Oxford: Oxford University Press, 1998); Gould, 'Revolution and counter-revolution', pp. 199–201.

[95] H. McD. Beckles, *A history of Barbados: From Amerindian settlement to nation-state* (Cambridge: Cambridge University Press, 1990), p. 26; H. McD. Beckles, 'The "hub of empire": The Caribbean and Britain in the seventeenth century', in Canny, *The Oxford history of the British Empire*, vol. I, pp. 236–239; E. Mancke, 'Empire and state', in Armitage and Braddick, *The British Atlantic world*, p. 183.

[96] A. J. O'Shaughnessy, *An empire divided: The American Revolution and the British Caribbean* (Philadelphia: University of Pennsylvania Press, 2000), p. 86.

Barbadians were the 'most faithful Subjects' of an 'ancient and loyal Colony' was an important aspect of the Barbados-as-Little-England discourse. As one early nineteenth-century commentator put it:

Many of the Colonies have been . . . colonized by the best blood of England, flyers from the invaders and usurpers of the church and state. In the Colonies last of all the King's dominions [was] . . . Barbados . . . [F]rom this honourable circumstance, and from priority of settlement, [it is] justly styled most ancient and most loyal.[97]

In the early nineteenth century, defenders of Barbadian slavery used the island's reputation for ancient loyalty and the rights their ancestors had won to forestall what they considered to be metropolitan 'interference'.[98] Moreover, parallels were drawn between the 'Puritan' abolition of the monarchy and the agenda pursued by the antislavery campaign, which drew much of its support from Nonconformists, to portray a contemporary threat of 'Usurpation'. Both were characterised as anti-Establishment forces, opposed to the Anglican Church and a state that respected liberty.[99] According to Nathaniel Lucas, a Barbadian planter and commentator on local affairs, this could be seen in the 'malign influence' of 'puritanism' over the British Cabinet that had been demonstrated in the adoption of the ameliorative policy in 1823.[100] Accounts of the strength of anti-Methodism in Barbados also evoked the period of 'Usurpation':

The Antipathy towards the Methodist was rooted, the seed . . . was sown in the days of the Usurpation and has at various Seasons ever since produced fruit. The Sufferings of the Episcopalians of former days had only increased in their descendants their fixed Attachment to the Church, which they had so laudably evinced, and their destation [sic] of the Dissenters which, they had so distinctly declared; foreseeing, that if they acquired that, which no man can be so blind, as not to perceive is their object, Ascendancy, the Church and State would, as in former time, fall under their control and persecution. These were the existing feeling [sic] of the Barbadians.[101]

---

[97] G. W. Jordan, *An examination of the principles of the Slave Registry Bill, and of the means of emancipation, proposed by the authors of the Bill* (London: T. Cadell and W. Davies, 1816), pp. 13–14.

[98] Andrew O'Shaughnessy argues that the rhetoric of the 'seventeenth-century Parliamentarians' continued to be deployed in the colonies because of the 'similarity of the colonists' political circumstances with those of seventeenth-century English citizens'. See O'Shaughnessy, *Empire divided*, pp. 117–119.

[99] M'Queen, *The West India colonies*.

[100] BPL, Lucas Manuscripts, Miscellaneous Items, Volume 1, N. Lucas, 'Methodists', c. 1823, p. 417. Lucas was a planter, judge, surgeon and Council member. See W. Marshall and B. Brereton, 'Historiography of Barbados, the Windward Islands, Trinidad and Tobago, and Guyana', in B. W. Higman (ed.), *Methodology and historiography of the Caribbean* (London: UNESCO Publishing, 1999), p. 550.

[101] *John Bull*, 9 May 1824, quoted in Lucas Manuscripts, Miscellaneous Items, Volume 1, Reel 15, p. 388, BPL. See also Snape, 'Anti-Methodism in eighteenth-century England', 258.

In this way, the strength of colonial loyalty and 'zeal for Episcopacy', both rooted in events of the middle of the seventeenth century, explained and justified the form that anti-Methodism had taken in early nineteenth-century Barbados.

Drawing in the 1820s, then, upon earlier opposition to Cromwell, white Barbadians claimed that it was possible to be loyal to British values whilst being opposed to the British state. The notion of 'loyal' resistance to renewed 'Usurpation' was a discursive strategy of negotiation. It paralleled those arguments that the opposition of the colonial legislatures to antislavery measures was a sign of the cultural sameness of white West Indian and white metropolitan, whilst a lack of resistance would have been 'unworthy to the name of Britons'.[102] Both the anti-Methodists' representation of themselves as defenders of 'Church and State', *and* the enforcement of the Conventicles Act by the island's authorities to suppress contemporary Dissenters, served to locate Barbados in a post-Cromwellian, pre-Toleration era, in which 'Puritan enthusiasticks' – and therefore contemporary antislavery campaigning – could be forthrightly resisted by loyal, British Anglicans. Indeed, opposition to the imperial state became a marker of colonial adherence to essential English values.

Nevertheless, the evocation of ancient loyalty during the 'Usurpation' was problematic because it was also an acknowledgement that the interests of Barbados's white colonists might not always coincide with those of the metropole. Evoking the 'Usurpation' left open the possibility of future colonial estrangement and was indicative of the anxiety-ridden nature of the negotiation process in that it expressed an uncertainty about the Britishness of West Indian identity. Similar forms of anxiety can be seen in other texts that sought to define a stable moment of origin to defend slavery. For example, Lucas was concerned to show that West Indian slavery was almost as old as the colonisation of the region and was therefore a fully British institution:

England has given every encouragement to the Slave Trade . . . By such assurances, our Ancestors, relying on the faith of England, invested their Capitals here on as firm a basis, as if the Colonies had been the Fifty Third County of that Kingdom.[103]

By demonstrating that the imperial government had 'given every encouragement to the Slave Trade', Lucas claimed that it had to respect the *current* rights of slaveholders. He contested the free world/slave world demarcation asserted by antislavery campaigners and placed Barbados firmly at the heart of metropolitan culture ('as if the Colonies had been the Fifty Third County of that Kingdom').[104] Nevertheless, Lucas was forced to acknowledge the novelty of British West Indian plantation slavery in the seventeenth century and that it was Dutch capital and expertise that had transformed Barbados into the 'original and quintessential' sugar

---

[102] M'Queen, *The West India colonies*, p. xviii.
[103] BPL, Lucas Manuscripts, Miscellaneous Items, Volume 1, N. Lucas, 'The introduction of the Negro and other slaves in Barbados', c. 1823, p. 46.
[104] Compare C. Hall, *Civilising subjects*, p. 102.

colony. Moreover, that this occurred in the context of the English Civil War and its aftermath – when 'The Mother Country forgot she had Colonies' – seemed to show that slavery was a foreign-financed, 'New World' innovation, rather than the trans-Atlantic transference of something essentially English. Although Lucas was at pains to demonstrate that slavery had been 'anglicised' after the Restoration, his recognition that 'Negro Slavery was established here during the Anxiety and Confusion of the Civil Wars, without any authority whatsoever from the Parent State' was a fundamental weakness in his arguments.[105] In this way, he had to acknowledge that slavery could be seen as a prime marker of creole difference.

The British backlash

The anxiety apparent in the discourse of anti-Methodism seemed justified in the light of the opprobrium expressed in Britain. The antislavery campaign condemned the 1825 Consolidated Slave Bill as further evidence of planter intransigence.[106] Nevertheless, '[t]he issue that undercut the West Indians' propaganda, discredited the very concept of amelioration, and evoked a massive and irrepressible outcry in Britain was not slavery per se but religious persecution'.[107] The treatment of John Smith in Demerara had already excited great interest and become a subject of parliamentary debate in June 1824.[108] Highlighting anti-missionary hostility in the West Indies and resistance to amelioration, Smith's death was instrumental in focussing antislavery public opinion. The events in Barbados also attracted considerable public interest and became a *cause célèbre* for the antislavery movement.[109] The wider significance of anti-Methodism was apparent immediately after the chapel's demolition, when the Methodist Missionary Society sought to establish Shrewsbury's innocence by sending Rayner from St Vincent to Barbados to collect testimonials from landowners who had allowed Shrewsbury to visit their estates. All found him blameless of any guilt and complimented him on the spirit of duty he inculcated in enslaved people.[110] Such opinions were published in the *Methodist Magazine* as part of the propaganda war over missionary activity and formed moral capital for the antislavery campaign. Other sources were sermons that Shrewsbury had given in Barbados, letters from Gill detailing her persecution, as well as the

---

[105] N. Lucas, 'The introduction of the Negro and other slaves in Barbados', pp. 46, 44, 47. See also Craton, *Testing the chains*, p. 105; N. Zahedih, 'Economy', in Armitage and Braddick, *The British Atlantic world*, pp. 56–57. Larry Gragg has recently questioned the prominence of Dutch investment in the development of Barbados's sugar economy. See Gragg, *Englishmen transplanted*.

[106] Society for the Mitigation and Gradual Abolition of Slavery, *The slave colonies of Great Britain; or a picture of Negro slavery drawn by the colonists themselves; being an abstract of the various papers recently laid before Parliament on that subject* (London, 1825).

[107] D. B. Davis, *Slavery and human progress*, p. 195. For an account of the importance of martyrdom for the antislavery campaign – and the troubling implications of this – see M. Wood, *Slavery, empathy, and pornography* (Oxford: Oxford University Press, 2002), pp. 399–427.

[108] House of Commons, *Hansard Parliamentary Debates*, 1 June 1824, 2nd Series, vol. XI, 961–1076.

[109] J. Walvin, *Black ivory: A history of British slavery* (London: Harper Collins, 1992).

[110] Testimonials for Shrewsbury, 10–11 November 1823, MMS, Box 5, No. 206.

full text of Shrewsbury's 1820 letter, which had attracted such early hostility in the island.[111] Copies of the anti-Methodist proclamations were also published in pamphlet form '*for the greater convenience of circulation*'. These humanitarian accounts sought to place the suffering, innocence and godliness of the Methodists before the British public and confirm the religious bigotry of the Barbadians.[112] Their publication and dissemination through the networks of Methodism were part of the intense 'war of representation' over missionary activity in the West Indies that was a crucial part of the slavery controversy. The Methodists sought to establish the 'proper contrast between the spirit of the persecuted and his persecutors' not only to exonerate Shrewsbury from any wrongdoing, but also to establish the aberrance of Barbadian anti-Methodism.[113]

The wider significance of the Methodist persecution was clear in June 1825, two months after Rayner's decision not to land, when Buxton, leader of the British anti-slavery campaign, introduced a Commons' motion calling for the condemnation of the chapel's demolition, its reconstruction at local expense and the protection of religious freedom.[114] Drawing on the publications of the Methodist Missionary Society, he described the events of the previous two years as 'an insurrection', a 'stark-staring rebellion' and the 'most daring riot and mutiny that ever was heard of'. In portraying them as 'a triumph not merely over Methodism . . . but a triumph over the Governor there, over the Parliament here, and over the feeling of the people of England', Buxton linked anti-Methodism, anti-abolitionism, anti-imperialism and even anti-Britishness.[115] The assertion of the rebellious nature of Barbados recurred and articulated a difference between Britons and West Indians. For example, in describing the actions of two British men who had attempted to prevent an attack on Shrewsbury's chapel before its final destruction, Buxton distinguished their actions from those of the Barbadian agitators:

These men, having none of the feelings of true Barbadians, but feeling as every Englishman would feel under such circumstances, – and as I trust we shall shew by our vote to-night that we feel – thinking that the authors of such an outrage ought not to be unpunished, pursued them and put them to flight.[116]

By linking these actions to the votes of fellow MPs, Buxton sought to mobilise a morally outraged metropolitan identity that would tolerate neither religious

---

[111] W. J. Shrewsbury, *Sermons preached on several occasions in the island of Barbados* (London, 1825); Gill to WMMS, 16 May 1825, MMS, Box 5, No. 228.
[112] Methodist Missionary Society, *Late insurrection*. Compare C. Hall, *Civilising subjects*, pp. 107–115. See also A. Lester, 'Obtaining the "due observance of justice": The geographies of colonial humanitarianism', *Environment and Planning D: Society and Space* 20 (2002).
[113] Methodist Missionary Society, *Late insurrection*.
[114] House of Commons, *Hansard Parliamentary Debates*, 23 June 1825, 2nd Series, vol. XIII, 1285–1347. The debate also appears in Methodist Missionary Society, *Authentic Report*. All references are to this latter source.
[115] Speech of Thomas Buxton, in Methodist Missionary Society, *Authentic Report*, pp. 40–42.
[116] Methodist Missionary Society, *Authentic Report*, p. 16.

persecution nor colonial defiance.[117] This was also the first of several occasions in the debate when speakers mocked aspects of the Barbados-as-Little-England discourse. The deliberate use of 'true Barbadians' derided this rhetoric by linking it to immoral violence. Buxton concluded his speech with a comparison of the consequences that would have followed if the rioters had been *black*:

[W]hat a massacre, what lashings, what gibbeting, would have followed! – how would the Mac Turks have rioted in the blood of the slaves! – But, being white men, and not blacks; civilized men, and not savages – 'gentlemen', forsooth, 'of respectability', which aggravates their guilt a thousand fold – their riot is patriotic – their proclamation is loyal.[118]

As Catherine Hall notes, events such as the destruction of the chapel were read by abolitionists and others as a sign that the 'order of civilisation had been turned upside down: Englishmen were savages, and the enslaved and missionaries were their victims'.[119] In the light of such events, how could white West Indians claim to be 'English' at all? As well as deriding Little Englandist claims, Buxton also evoked the suppression of the 1816 revolt as another marker of Barbadian otherness. Such antislavery attacks drew on a tradition within British humanitarian discourse in which Barbados was represented as a particular site of planter intransigence.[120]

As well as condemning the actual persecution and relating it to a broader context of West Indian opposition to amelioration, supporters of Buxton's motion challenged those representations that sought to portray anti-Methodism as proof of Englishness or an act of colonial loyalty. This was exemplified by the speech of William Smith, a vehement opponent of slavery who also argued that a strong response to the anti-Methodists was necessary if 'the honour of this country' was to be restored.[121] Smith ridiculed the Barbados-as-Little-England rhetoric deployed by Barbadian planters in their defence of slavery:

There has always existed, on the part of the inhabitants of that Island, the most inordinate and ridiculous ideas of their own importance. They seemed, in this instance to be nearly on the same level with the poor simple Welchman [sic], who exclaimed, when he was about to leave the city of Bristol, "Alas! What will become of thee, poor Bristol, when I am gone!"[122]

This deliberate, mocking reference to the white Barbadian aphorism 'What would poor old England do, were Barbados to forsake her?' – a central trope within the discourse of Barbados-as-Little-England – encapsulated the antislavery reaction to West Indian opposition. Echoing Buxton's reference to the 'Irish extraction' of anti-Methodism, Smith compared Barbadian identity with a non-English form of white identity and marginalised white Barbadians to the peripheries of Britain.

---

[117] C. Hall, *Civilising subjects*, p. 114.
[118] Speech of Thomas Buxton, in Methodist Missionary Society, *Authentic Report*, p. 48.
[119] C. Hall, *Civilising subjects*, p. 112.
[120] C. Levy, 'Slavery and the emancipation movement in Barbados, 1650–1833', *Journal of Negro History* 55 (1970).
[121] Speech of William Smith, in Methodist Missionary Society, *Authentic Report*, p. 62.
[122] Methodist Missionary Society, *Authentic Report*, p. 66.

Like Clarkson's questioning of the importance of the West Indies, this represented a rejection of the notion that Barbados had a special relationship with Britain or deserved exceptional treatment with regard to amelioration. Smith went further:

They should be taught, that, however valuable to a few individuals may be the Estates they possess there, to the empire of Great Britain, as a national possession, their Island is but as a toy, which, if destroyed, would, in a very short time, be scarcely missed, and ere long be quite forgotten: and that, instead of being one of the props of this country, as had been sillily boasted, her conduct tended only to embarrass and to tease the too-forbearing Government of the Mother Country, and to bring the Colonies into contempt.[123]

Through the language of schooling, Barbados was portrayed as a disobedient offspring requiring instruction. Yet, Britain should not be an indulgent parent, but one that must teach its child to be seen and not heard. Instead of being either one of the 'props' of the 'Mother Country' or the linchpin of empire, Barbados was an ungovernable embarrassment whose politicians' dark allusions to the American Revolution were 'justly a subject of ridicule'. Other supporters of the bill combined such dismissals of Barbados's imperial status with a reassertion of the need to enforce ameliorative measures.[124]

At the end of the debate, although Buxton's motion was amended, the tone of censure remained: the demolition was condemned and religious freedom was to be protected. Parliament had been united in its denunciation of anti-Methodism. Canning, the foreign secretary, received cheers from across the House when he described the events as 'unjustifiable, indefensible – a violation of law and justice – a defiance of all legal authority – a flying in the face of Parliament, and of the country'.[125] The debate was published outside Parliament because it had 'excited much interest throughout this country' and was given particular coverage in the antislavery and missionary press. Davis accounts for the strength of such metropolitan condemnation in stark terms:

The West Indian planters, who were still living in an eighteenth-century world, had little comprehension of the changes taking place in English society. When they harassed and persecuted Nonconformist missionaries, expecting that wild 'enthusiasticks' would receive little support from home, they sealed their fate. The social transformations of the first two decades of the nineteenth century made it certain that any attempt to keep the Gospel from the slaves would succeed in turning the vast indignation of English Dissent into channels of protest that won official sanction.[126]

Alongside this 'temporal' mismatch between white Barbadian and British values, which stemmed in large part from the impact of the metropolitan Evangelical

---

[123] Ibid.
[124] Speech of William Smith, ibid.; speech of Henry Brougham, in Methodist Missionary Society, *Authentic Report*, p. 90.
[125] Speech of George Canning, in Methodist Missionary Society, *Authentic Report*, p. 76.
[126] D. B. Davis, *Problem of slavery in the age of revolution*, p. 451.

Revival, there was a changing imperial cartography in which the West Indies was an increasingly marginalised slave world.[127]

The metropolitan reaction was also manifest in imperial demands for the Barbadian legislature to bring about substantive reforms of slavery. In his response to the Consolidated Slave Act, Bathurst expressed his 'surprise and mortification' that it was all that was forthcoming in two years, and that the will of Parliament and the people remained unsatisfied. As a result, he advised against the granting of Royal Assent and sought assurances that a revised act would be produced immediately.[128] Nevertheless, whilst conflict between the Barbadian legislature and Colonial Office continued over the adoption of ameliorative reforms, it was religious persecution that had focussed anti-Barbadian feelings. The resultant backlash involved the strong inscription of Barbados's aberrant status, the articulation of a morally outraged British identity and the rejection of Little Englandist claims.

Repairing Little England's reputation

The anger expressed in Parliament, as well as antislavery threats to step up campaigning, stung many white Barbadians. Some elite planters sought to distance themselves from the incident, believing that other colonists had gone too far in their opposition to antislavery – in their expressions of West Indian difference – and had only succeeded in alienating metropolitan opinion. Instead they sought to articulate a more accommodationist line. Such elite white responses were not a wholly new phenomenon. In 1823, plantocrats such as Sir Reynold Alleyne had proposed using the positive growth of Barbados's enslaved population to make an argument in favour of *local* amelioration and '[b]y linking "growth" to "good treatment", they sought to promote themselves as "ideal" administrators and business managers in command of a paternalistic social order'.[129] Such moves evoked the planter ideal expressed in late eighteenth-century plantership literature and were augmented in the 1820s by arguments in favour of the *Anglican* Christianisation of enslaved people. Symptomatic of this was the formation of the Association for the Purpose of Affording Religious Instruction to the Slave Population in Barbados in September 1823, only months after the receipt of Bathurst's ameliorative instructions. It was elite planters, such as Alleyne, who supported these efforts. Nevertheless, they were at odds with broader white supremacist attitudes to the religious instruction of enslaved people, which saw them as threats to the socio-racial order.[130] That Alleyne acted as a manager for absentee planters suggests that he was closer

---

[127] For an account of the influence of evangelicalism on British society, see D. Hempton, *Religion and political culture in Britain and Ireland* (Cambridge: Cambridge University Press, 1996).

[128] Bathurst to the Officer Administering the Government of Barbados, 25 August 1825, CO 29/31, fos. 57–62; 12 December 1825, CO 29/31, fos. 75–95, TNA.

[129] Beckles, *History of Barbados*, p. 86.

[130] *Barbados Mercury and Bridgetown Gazette*, 20 September 1823, Reel 26, BPL; R. Alleyne to H. Fitzherbert, 4 December 1823, Fitzherbert Collection, Reel 1, E20579, BDA.

to the accommodationist strategies of the metropolitan West India Interest. Nevertheless, in the aftermath of the chapel's destruction and especially after the arrival of Bishop Coleridge in 1825, there was a general effort by defenders of slaveholding interests in Barbados to show that it was not the Christianisation of enslaved people that was opposed *per se*, just the wrong sort of missionary activity.[131]

Differences between white elite and non-elite responses to antislavery were particularly marked after Buxton's motion. For example, the Assembly and Council reacted very differently to Bathurst's attacks on the Consolidated Slave Act in 1825. The Council disavowed responsibility for the inadequacy of the act, arguing that the Assembly's opposition had left it caught between delaying the implementation of amelioration by returning the bill to the Assembly and settling for something 'utterly inadequate to its object'.[132] The Council's reply was conciliatory in tone, full of familial metaphors and celebrations of the relationship between Barbados and Britain. The dominant theme was accommodation, seeking to explain tensions between centre and colony rather than to excuse them. In contrast, the Assembly was far more strident. Characterising Bathurst's comments as 'repulsive clouds of censure and menace' aimed almost entirely at the Lower House, Assembly members argued that, as representatives of local interests and knowledge, they were best placed to determine which measures were most applicable for Barbados. For the Assembly, Bathurst's ameliorative proposals amounted to 'a mere catalogue of indulgences to the blacks' that would endanger white lives and property.[133]

Such different responses must be related to developments within intra-white politics from the late eighteenth century. By 1810, a two-party system had emerged in Barbados. The 'Pumpkins' derived their support from the plantocracy and represented a 'patrician class, with vested interests to protect, powerful, conservative, and with a deep-seated feeling of class superiority'. Their opponents were the 'Salmagundis' – a term 'used to denote a general mixture/miscellaneous collection'.[134] They were made up of Barbados's enfranchised middle class (white men with 10–50 acres of land), and often receiving popular support from poorer whites unable to vote. The Salmagundis identified themselves as the island's yeomanry, expressed strong support for the Church and state and, although firmly tied to the system of slavery, resisted plantocratic socio-economic dominance. The Assembly elections of 1819 were a bitterly fought contest. Campaigning on an anti-humanitarian, white supremacist platform, the Salmagundis won a landslide victory and took control of the Lower House. This was the basis for the conflict

---

[131] Carrington to CCHA, 5 July 1825, ALB, Reel Bs. 9, BDA; *Barbados Mercury and Bridgetown Gazette*, 28 October 1823, Reel 26, BPL.

[132] Address of the Council to President Skeete, 15 November 1825, CO 31/50, fo. 1, TNA. See also Anonymous, *Some remarks in reference to recent proceedings of the legislature of Barbadoes, etc. etc. etc.* (London, 1826).

[133] Address of the Assembly to President Skeete, 15 November 1825, CO 31/49, fos. 240–242, TNA.

[134] K. Watson, 'Salmagundis vs Pumpkins: White politics and creole consciousness in Barbadian slave society, 1800–1834', in H. Johnson and K. Watson (eds.), *The white minority in the Caribbean* (Kingston: Ian Randle, 1998), pp. 24, 30 n. 30.

of the 1820s between the Salmagundi-controlled Assembly, led by the middle-class speaker, Cheesman Moe, and the planter-dominated Council, as well as the intense opposition that Governor Warde faced from the Lower House. Much of this antagonism related to conflicting visions of how best to respond to antislavery, for whilst Pumpkins and Salmagundis agreed on the need to defend slavery, the former tended to be more accommodationist, whilst the latter saw any concessions as undermining the white-dominated colonial order.

The political rivalry institutionalised in the two-party system represented the most formalised manifestation of white class-based tensions between racialised and propertied visions of Barbadian society, as previously evident in John Poyer's attacks on elite corruption, and the popular, anti-ameliorative sentiments margina-lised in the Assembly report into the 1816 revolt.[135] Yet, this cannot be reduced to class divisions and must also be seen as a sign of the uncertain place in which the slavery controversy left the white inhabitants of a colonial society, in which groups and individuals could, and did, react in different ways – by virtue of wealth, status and power – to 'external metropolitan pressures and at the same time to internal adjustments made necessary by the juxtaposition of master and labour, white and non-white'. In other words, the development and formalisation of discordant white identities and visions were part of the creolisation of Barbadian society.[136]

The post-demolition humanitarian attack on white Barbados had not acknowl-edged these divisions. Rather, anti-Methodism had been used to vilify white society as a whole – much to the chagrin of elite Barbadians:

I much fear this catastrophe will tend to increase the prejudice so industriously (and so unjustly) excited against the West India proprietors, though be persuaded every man in this community is filled with disgust at the proceedings of the lawless rabble. I need not describe to you what ingredients they are composed of; and it would be hard indeed if the inhabitants of this island generally were to be branded for their misdeeds.[137]

In similar terms, Alleyne described the anti-Methodists as a 'Rabble' and the destruction of the chapel as a 'disgraceful outrage on private property'.[138] This portrayal of the anti-Methodists was a clear attempt to exonerate the planter elite from blame and a concerted effort to provide such an elitist representation of the Shrewsbury incident came in late 1825. Although it is not possible to attribute the Methodist persecution solely to Salmagundi supporters, or even to the mid-dling or lower classes, this was precisely what some members of the white elite attempted. At a public meeting in Bridgetown in December 1825, a declaration

---

[135] See chapter 3 and chapter 4, pp. 123–124.

[136] E. K. Brathwaite, *Contradictory omens: Cultural diversity and integration in the Caribbean* (Mona: Savacou, 1974), p. 11.

[137] Letter from Barbados, *The Times*, 12 December 1823, printed in Methodist Missionary Society, *Late insurrection*, p. 2. See also Anonymous to Rayner, 11 November 1823, MMS, Box 5, No. 206.

[138] Alleyne to Fitzherbert, 4 December 1823, Fitzherbert Collection, Reel 1, E20579, BDA.

was signed by over a hundred elite whites and later published.[139] It expressed great disapproval for the chapel's destruction and accepted Parliament's censure, but the most striking aspect of the declaration was the internal division posited *within* the white population of the island. There was no talk of 'Barbadians', rather, as with other references to the 'rabble', a distinction was drawn between the 'respectable part of the community', which had not been involved in the demolition and had always condemned it, and the rest. As part of the effort to resist the uncompromising spatial othering of antislavery attacks and assert a more nuanced account of Barbadian society, the declaration was sent to Britain and set before Parliament by the colonial agent.[140]

The public meeting and declaration articulated an elitist and more accommodationist response to antislavery in the 1820s. Some acknowledgement of this was apparent in the steadfastly anti-Methodist *Barbadian*. Referring to the December meeting, its editor, Abel Klinkett, stated that he supported the intention of repairing Barbados's relationship with Britain, but objected to the idea that it was a response to the threats made by antislavery campaigners that they would intensify their efforts. Indeed, the editorial set forth its hopes that the evangelical elements of the antislavery campaign were detested as much in Britain as they were in Barbados. Nevertheless, the normally strident Klinkett admitted that he could be wrong in this hope. Alongside the unopposed arrival of Rayner in 1826,[141] this momentary acknowledgement of the influence of Christian evangelism on metropolitan British society indicated that outright opposition to antislavery was recognised as an increasingly untenable and counter-productive position by the mid- to late 1820s. This was also manifest in other realms. For example, although Rayner faced difficulties in re-establishing an official Methodist missionary presence, there was nothing like the opposition of 1823–5 and, by 1832, two new Methodist chapels had been officially registered. Meanwhile, a revised Barbadian Consolidated Slave Act was accepted by Parliament. With the lessening of anti-Methodism in Barbados, Jamaica would become the site of missionary persecution in the 1830s. Meanwhile, in Barbados and its absentee diaspora, whites would do their utmost to ensure that the approaching 'freedom' of the enslaved majority did not threaten the white-dominated order.

Henry Nelson Coleridge was a metropolitan witness to the varied white colonial responses to the ameliorative turn in imperial policy, of which anti-Methodism was merely the most striking manifestation. He also commented on the anxious and ambivalent nature of this response. For instance, his statement that, although Barbadians were 'the most genuine Creole of the West Indies', the island society nevertheless went 'a great way in justifying the appellation of Little England'

---

[139] J. Barrow, *A declaration of inhabitants of Barbados, respecting the demolition of the Methodists Chapel. With an appendix* (Barbados, 1826).

[140] Carrington to CCHA, 10 April 1826, ALB, Reel Bs. 9, BDA.

[141] Rayner to WMMS, 25 March 1826, MMS, Box 6, No. 272.

encapsulated the ambiguity around loyalty and opposition in the period 1823–5.[142] This was the same uncertainty evident in claims that resistance to the 'Usurpation' was an act of loyal rebellion and could be a model for colonial reaction to anti-slavery. As this suggests, anti-Methodism was a locus of creole complexities. It was an articulation of a strident colonial project of identification that engendered metropolitan assertions of the otherness of white Barbadians *and* was characterised by attempts to resolve West Indian difference through what Keith Sandiford terms 'negotiation'. In the context of the latter, the evocation of the Conventicles Act was significant. This act and its contemporary mobilisation in Barbados connected a mythologised past to a contested present in the 1820s. Aware of the ambiguous nature of their position and fearing the implications of opposition to antislavery, white Barbadians sought to pre-empt metropolitan criticisms. Attempting to win 'tenuous legitimacy', particularly through the foundational and mythologised moment of the Usurpation, those involved in anti-Methodism and the broader defence of slavery sought to negotiate between the poles of loyalty and opposition to the imperial centre. This goal could never be achieved, however, and the very process of negotiation was beset by anxiety. The origin of this uncertainty was not only class tensions between elite and non-elite, Pumpkins and Salmagundis, but the creolising consequences of slavery – and the *controversy* over slavery – on white Barbadian society. As Coleridge wrote:

> The old remark that the masters of slaves, if free themselves, are always the freest of the free, is as eminently true of them as it was of the citizens of Athens or Sparta; submission from those below them is so natural to them that submission to any one above them seems unnatural, and that which would be considered as advice or remonstrance in England is resented in the West Indies as interference or tyranny.[143]

Barbadian slaveholders were so attached to freedom and liberty in part because they were aware of the consequences of unfreedom and made a fundamental distinction between those who did or did not deserve liberty. At the heart of the latter, of course, was race. Indeed, both the oppositional and accommodationist responses to antislavery – and their associated assertions of loyalty and opposition, white difference and sameness – were not antithetical, but rather different intensities of colonial resistance. Both challenged the free world/slave world divide with a different definition of freedom – the freedom to (dis)possess others. This was based on the articulation of English liberties in a racialised colonial setting. In this way, it was a marker of the creolisation of white Barbadian society. Such ideas, though perhaps contradictory from a metropolitan perspective, were crucial to the world the slaveholders had made and that they sought to defend as emancipation approached.[144]

---

[142] Coleridge, *Six months*, p. 130.   [143] Coleridge, *Six months*, p. 291.
[144] E. D. Genovese, *The world the slaveholders made: Two essays in interpretation* (New York: Random House, 1969); E. S. Morgan, *American slavery, American freedom: The ordeal of colonial Virginia* (New York: Norton, 1975).

6

'Days of misery and nights of fear': white ideas of freedom at the end of slavery

In a published 'letter' of 1834 to Earl Grey, First Lord of the Treasury, Henry Peter Simmons expressed grave concerns about what freedom would mean for the West Indies:

[U]nless you have the active assistance of the planter in this new arrangement, (and that you cannot expect but by dealing justly with him,) commerce will lose her energies, the hum of active enterprise will cease, and in lieu of the exuberance, richness, and fertility of the Caribbean isles, all will be silence, and desolation, days of misery and nights of fear.[1]

Simmons was an absentee planter with property in Barbados, and this was his third published letter to Grey.[2] In these, Simmons articulated West Indian colonial concerns about the effects of immediate emancipation ('this new arrangement'). His dystopian vision of freedom was encapsulated by the reference to 'days of misery and nights of fear', which pointed to the twin white West Indian concerns about the economic costs of uncompensated emancipation and the social dangers posed by the unfettered black body. Both were recurrent themes in white West Indian articulations of freedom as the end of slavery approached.

Simmons's letters were written in the context of social and political developments in Britain in the 1830s, combined with economic weakness and large-scale enslaved resistance in the West Indies, that brought the ending of slavery in the empire closer. These years were also characterised by intensive proslavery efforts, which shifted from the defence of slavery to attempts to shape the emancipation process and the societies it would produce. White Barbadians were involved in not only formal lobbying and petitions, but also more diffuse performances that centred on the subjugation of non-whites and white self-assurance. They wrote pastoral verse, directed and attended plays, and engaged in public demonstrations. These

---

[1] H. P. Simmons, *A letter to the Right Hon. Earl Grey, First Lord of the Treasury, etc. on the question of negro emancipation* (London, 1834), p. 8.

[2] The other letters are H. P. Simmons, *A letter to the Right Honourable Earl Grey, First Lord of the Treasury, etc. on the subject of West Indian property* (London, 1832), and H. P. Simmons, *A letter to the Right Hon. Earl Grey, on the West India question* (Liverpool, 1833).

various cultural productions and acts show that emancipation could never be an abstract project for white West Indians. Instead, it seemed to augur, paraphrasing Eugene Genovese, the 'end of the world' the slaveholders had made. Anthony Giddens defines 'ontological security' as 'a sense of confidence or trust in the world as it appears to be' and slavery was central to the white sense of security in Barbados. As Seymour Drescher and Frank McGlynn put it: '[t]he planters saw everything that was once theirs about to be taken from them – manpower, money, power, prosperity and history'.[3]

This chapter examines how such white anxieties about the 'end of the world' were framed by earlier discourses of white colonial identity and considers how these articulations shaped the efforts that were made to prevent the 'end of the world'. In so doing, it explores the negative meanings that white slaveholders attributed to black freedom and the efforts they made to control freedom in the 1830s. To examine this, I focus on the signifying practices associated with the 1831 'Great Hurricane' and a rape case in 1832. These events were *premonitions* of freedom, *echoes* of past events – including the trial of Joseph Denny and the 1816 rebellion – and *tests* of black people's capacity for freedom that confirmed white notions about black disorder. They were also used to *demonstrate* the perils of freedom to the metropolitan authorities and, hence, strengthen West Indian lobbying efforts.

Although 'freedom' is of key concern here, it was a complex and contested term in the 1830s, conceived of in different ways by the competing interests within the slavery controversy.[4] For British policymakers, freedom was understood within a developing liberal context as the ability to work in a capitalist wage system. Humanitarians understood it in terms of the full realisation of Christian subjecthood under missionary tutelage. In contrast, many slaveholders argued that enslaved black people were 'freer' from need than wage labourers, but that formalised freedom would engender licence and licentiousness.[5] For enslaved people themselves, freedom meant escape from the plantations, the end of violence and lives

---

[3] E. D. Genovese, *The world the slaveholders made: Two essays in interpretation* (New York: Random House, 1969); A. Giddens quoted in G. Valentine, '"Sticks and stones may break my bones": A personal geography of harassment', *Antipode* 30 (1998), 321; S. Drescher and F. McGlynn, 'Introduction', in F. McGlynn and S. Drescher (eds.), *The meaning of freedom: Economics, politics, and culture after slavery* (London: University of Pittsburgh Press, 1992), p. 19.

[4] O. N. Bolland, 'The politics of freedom in the British Caribbean', in McGlynn and Drescher, *The meaning of freedom*; D. B. Davis, *Slavery and human progress* (Oxford: Oxford University Press, 1984); T. C. Holt, *The problem of freedom: Race, labor, and politics in Jamaica and Britain, 1832–1938* (London: Johns Hopkins University Press, 1992), pp. 33–34; D. Roediger, *The wages of whiteness: Race and the making of the American working class* (London: Verso, 1991), p. 49. For more on post-emancipation freedom in idea and practice, see F. Cooper, T. C. Holt and R. J. Scott, *Beyond slavery: Explorations of race, labor, and citizenship in post-emancipation societies* (London: University of North Carolina Press, 2000); S. R. Frey and B. Wood (eds.), *From slavery to emancipation in the Atlantic world* (London: Frank Cass, 1999); H. Temperley (ed.), *After slavery: Emancipation and its discontents* (London: Frank Cass, 2000).

[5] Genovese, *The world the slaveholders made*, pp. 124–125; A. O. Thompson, '"Happy – happy slaves!": Slavery as a superior state to freedom', *Journal of Caribbean History* 29 (1995).

of their own. In the midst of this was the question of 'white freedom'. Slaveholders saw their freedom as based on, and entitling, the (dis)possession of others. As in the American South, this was manifested in Barbados by the seemingly paradoxical emphasis on 'liberty' in white culture and in complaints that the imposition of emancipation would 'enslave' the slaveholders.[6] Conflicting ideas about freedom impacted upon the societies that emerged after formal emancipation on 1 August 1834, and the struggle would continue for decades afterwards.

Towards emancipation

Amelioration had been codified as official imperial policy in 1823. Nevertheless, by 1830 the West Indian plantocracies had succeeded in evading most reforms and had become relatively complacent about the permanence of slavery.[7] Yet, a series of developments in Britain and the West Indies brought emancipation closer. Firstly, there was a renewed attack by the antislavery campaign in Parliament and Britain at large, with Thomas Fowell Buxton announcing his intention to introduce a parliamentary motion for complete emancipation in March 1831. Such efforts fell on fertile ground because the reform-minded Whigs had come to power in 1830 after the Tories had been split by the Catholic Emancipation Act. This heralded a new era in British politics and, whilst the Reform Act of 1832 produced a Parliament that was far from democratic, it was more open to the voice of urban and industrial Britain. Slavery was a major issue in the 1833 election campaign and many candidates pledged themselves for emancipation.[8]

Whilst the antislavery campaign grew stronger, proslavery forces grew weaker. The parliamentary West India Interest was almost completely wiped out after 1833, but even prior to that the plantation colonies were experiencing economic distress, owing to the long-term decline in sugar prices, falling access to metropolitan credit, increased competition, attacks on the home-market monopoly from Indian producers in the wider context of free tradism and increasingly exhausted soils.[9] Planters blamed this 'sugar crisis' on the antislavery campaign and demanded compensation.

The actions of enslaved people also hastened emancipation. The outbreak and violent suppression of the Jamaican Emancipation Rebellion of 1831–2 confirmed the belief amongst the imperial authorities that slavery was a system beyond

[6] P. Parish, *Slavery: History and historians* (New York, 1989), pp. 132–145.
[7] W. Marshall, 'Amelioration and emancipation (with special reference to Barbados)', in A. O. Thompson (ed.), *Emancipation I: A series of lectures to commemorate the 150th anniversary of emancipation* (Bridgetown: Cedar Press, 1984).
[8] J. Walvin, *Black ivory: A history of British slavery* (London: Harper Collins, 1992), pp. 263–264.
[9] K. M. Butler, *The economics of emancipation: Jamaica and Barbados, 1823–1843* (London: University of North Carolina Press, 1995); W. A. Green, *British slave emancipation: The sugar colonies and the great experiment, 1830–1865* (Oxford: Clarendon Press, 1976); R. B. Sheridan, 'The West India sugar crisis and British slave emancipation, 1830–1833', *Journal of Economic History* 21 (1961).

repair.[10] Under antislavery pressure, facing enslaved unrest and with the proslavery lobby weakened, the gradualist focus of amelioration that had been pursued since the 1820s was abandoned. In May 1832, Parliament appointed a select committee to report on how slavery could be ended as quickly and safely as possible. By this point, the formal ending of slavery had become almost inevitable.[11]

Despite this, the final phase of the slavery controversy was characterised by intense West Indian lobbying to postpone emancipation, obtain compensation and secure local control of the emancipation process. The colonial agents of the West Indian colonies in Britain played an important role in this. In the 1830s, the colonial agent for Barbados was John Pollard Mayers, one of the most active of all the West Indian agents. He was a source of information for Barbados's slaveholders and their first line of defence.[12] Moreover, as a Barbadian planter himself, he shared white fears about the ending of one 'world' and hopes about shaping a 'new' one. As well as Mayers, individual planters, such as Simmons, were also involved in the lobbying efforts.

West Indian responses to the emancipationist shift in metropolitan politics were also manifest in the 'Colonial Congress' held in Barbados in March 1831 and attended by delegates from most of the West Indian colonies.[13] The resolutions passed emphasised the sanctity of private property, claimed that the West Indian legislatures had a good record on amelioration and argued that emancipation would produce 'confusion and ruin to all'. The press coverage and the language used by the delegates echoed the revolutionary rhetoric of the Continental Congress in the North American colonies in 1774 and Woodville Marshall suggests that the Colonial Congress 'could have been (and was probably in some people's minds) ... the first step to secession and independence'.[14] Yet, the meeting represented the last vestiges of the proto-regionalism or embryonic nationalism in Barbados discussed in chapter 5 because, whilst such sentiments would remain strong in Jamaica, secessionist fantasies were ended on Barbados when it was struck by a severe hurricane.

'Days of misery': freedom as economic desolation

The 'Great Hurricane' of 11 August 1831 exacerbated the 'sugar crisis' of the early 1830s, causing damage worth £1,602,798 in lost property and killing 1,165

---

[10] C. Hall, *Civilising subjects: Metropole and colony in the English imagination, 1830–1867* (Oxford: Polity, 2002), p. 106.

[11] M. Craton, *Testing the chains: Resistance to slavery in the British West Indies* (London: Cornell University Press, 1982).

[12] B. M. Taylor, 'Our man in London: John Pollard Mayers, agent for Barbados, and the British Abolition Act, 1832–1834', *Caribbean Studies* 16 (1977).

[13] B. W. Higman, 'The Colonial Congress of 1831', in B. Moore and S. Wilmot (eds.), *Before and after 1865: Education, politics and regionalism in the Caribbean* (Kingston: Ian Randle, 1998).

[14] W. Marshall, 'Amelioration and emancipation', p. 82.

enslaved people.[15] The Colonial Office was flooded with letters, petitions and appeals from individual proprietors and the legislature. Although a British grant of £50,000 and the temporary suspension of the 4.5 per cent export duty did help alleviate the situation, this reliance on imperial aid undermined Barbadian proto-nationalism by making it necessary for the West Indian colonies 'to look more to Britain for relief than to each other for solidarity against Britain'.[16] The hurricane was also significant for what it represented. For Mayers, it highlighted the connections between planter distress and the slavery controversy, and was a reminder of the duties that Britain had to its colonies.[17] Moreover, whites saw the unwillingness of many enslaved people to work in the hurricane's aftermath as a portent of the idleness that might accompany black freedom. Thus, the hurricane was a premonition for the possible destruction of the plantation system, its workforce standing idle and its landholders' prosperity lost.

The plantation pastoral

The post-hurricane landscape represented the desolation that freedom might bring. Such fears can be understood in terms of the dominant mode through which the plantation system was represented: the pastoral. This mode of representation was often used in proslavery accounts of the West Indies and it worked by 'naturalizing slaves to the conditions of colonial acquisition . . . while obfuscating the rigours of pain and loss that are inherent to their experience in those contexts'. In this way, it was closely associated with paternalistic claims about the nature of slaveholding that were part of the planter ideal.[18] The pastoral was also particularly associated with descriptions of Barbados, as the island had long been represented as a cultivated garden (see figure 6.1).[19] The most developed form of Barbadian pastoral in the 1830s was Matthew James Chapman's poem *Barbadoes*. Written by a Barbadian and published in 1833, *Barbadoes* was 'an indisputable heir' to

---

[15] 'Report of a committee of the General Assembly appointed to ascertain the Deaths and Losses occasioned by the hurricane of the 11th August, 1831', CO 28/110, fos. 13a–18a, The National Archive (henceforth TNA). For examples of the appeals for relief, see CO 28/108, fos. 253a–304a, TNA.

[16] W. Marshall, 'Amelioration and emancipation', p. 82.

[17] J. P. Mayers to Committee of Correspondence of House of Assembly (henceforth CCHA), 20 October 1831, Agents' Letter Books (henceforth ALB), Reel Bs. 9, Barbados Department of Archives (henceforth BDA).

[18] S. V. Hartman, *Scenes of subjection: Terror, slavery, and self-making in nineteenth-century America* (Oxford: Oxford University Press, 1997), p. 52; K. A. Sandiford, *The cultural politics of sugar: Caribbean slavery and narratives of colonialism* (Cambridge: Cambridge University Press, 2000), pp. 79–80; S. Seymour, S. Daniels and C. Watkins, 'Estate and empire: Sir George Cornewall's management of Moccas, Herefordshire and La Taste, Grenada, 1771–1819', *Journal of Historical Geography* 24 (1998).

[19] See J. P. Greene, 'Changing identity in the British Caribbean: Barbados as a case study', in N. Canny and A. Pagden (eds.), *Colonial identity in the Atlantic world, 1500–1800* (Princeton: Princeton University Press, 1987); M. Sheller, *Consuming the Caribbean: From Arawaks to zombies* (London: Routledge, 2003), pp. 46–53.

Figure 6.1 'Plantation scene and slave houses, Barbados, 1807–8', from J. A. Waller, *A voyage in the West Indies* (London, 1820), PP.3904.i.1. By permission of the British Library.

James Grainger's *The sugar cane* (1764) – an early example of the West Indian georgic tradition.[20] Although artistically inferior, *Barbadoes* is similar in its scenes of pastoral escapism:

> From their embowered huts come forth in throngs
> The sable race, and wake their joyful songs:
> They come to labour, but they come with joy,
> While themes of happiness their minds employ.
>
>   . . .
>
>   All to their different tasks with speed repair,
> Where guide their steps the planter's ruling care.
> Each trim plantation like a garden shines –
> Here waves the cane, there creep the nurturing vines.[21]

Idyllic scenes of mutual dependency, agrarian prosperity and paternalism litter the poem. Descriptions of frolicking nymphs and singing birds parallel those of happy enslaved workers, fixing slavery in the pastoral landscape, like the rushing streams and well-ordered fields. By articulating the connections between the 'natural' landscape and its cultivated 'constructedness' in and through the bodies of enslaved people, arguments about slaveholders' property rights were reinforced and enslaved labour was represented as integral to the plantation system.[22] Moreover, the pastoral mode augmented claims that enslaved people were better off than metropolitan labourers (and that paternalistic slavery was superior to 'free wage' capitalism) by contrasting the picturesque plantation with the 'unwholesome factories' of industrialising Britain.[23]

Barbadoes was an explicit representation of an idealised landscape of home by a white Barbadian. Chapman's deployment of the pastoral was not only a late attempt to defend slavery, but also a deliberate effort to represent a *functioning plantation system* that emancipation – without compensation – threatened to desolate. The pastoral landscape was the marker of a prosperous plantation system, controlled by improving and ameliorating 'good masters'. This aesthetic echoed the late eighteenth-century literature on plantership and could also be found in

---

[20] L. Brown, *West Indian poetry*, 2nd edn (London: Heinemann, 1984), p. 4; M. J. Chapman, *Barbadoes, and other poems* (London, 1833). For more on the Grainger and the West Indian georgic, see M. Ellis, '"The cane-land isles": Commerce and empire in late eighteenth-century georgic and pastoral poetry', in R. Edmond and V. Smith (eds.), *Islands in history and representation* (London: Routledge, 2003); J. Gilmore, *The poetics of empire: A study of James Grainger's* The Sugar Cane *(1764)* (London: Athlone Press, 2000); Sandiford, *Cultural politics of sugar*, pp. 67–87. For information on Chapman, see F. Hoyos, 'Dr. M. J. Chapman', *Journal of the Barbados Museum and Historical Society* 16 (1948–9).

[21] Chapman, *Barbadoes*, p. 10.

[22] L. Brown, *West Indian poetry*, p. 20. For other accounts of the proslavery work performed by pastoral and georgic forms, see R. McCrea, 'The Caribbean in the metropolitan imagination', paper presented at the Society for Caribbean Studies, Bristol University, 2003; Sandiford, *Cultural politics of sugar*; L. Stewart, 'Louisiana subjects: Power, space and the slave body', *Ecumene* 2 (1995).

[23] Simmons, *Letter on the subject of West Indian property*, p. 4.

contemporary West Indian accounts of the conditions in which enslaved people supposedly lived:

[They] are all well clothed, their houses are comfortable, and form a very pretty village, which is surrounded by a neat fence, and their own pieces of ground, around each of their cottages, are cultivated in the highest manner, and afford them so many provisions, etc., in addition to their other allowances.[24]

Whilst *Barbadoes* was, in part, propaganda, such a view of slavery 'was not uncommon among Barbadian whites of the period'.[25] The pastoral was one of the ways in which slaveholders understood their 'world' and was especially associated with the articulation of white Barbadian identity through the planter ideal.

The anti-pastoral

If the pastoral mode was used to represent an idealised plantation system, then its inverse – ruin and desolation – informed descriptions of the aftermath of the 'Great Hurricane':

On the evening of the 10th the sun set on a landscape of the greatest beauty and fertility, and rose on the following morning over such utter desolation and waste.[26]

The hurricane had transformed the pastoral landscape of the improved 'garden' into one of waste. As Chapman wrote:

> Thrice has the scourge laid bare the bearded isle,
> Marred her sweet face, nor left a single smile,
> Stripped her of man's adornment, nature's dress,
> And for a garden left a wilderness.[27]

Other accounts that the 1831 hurricane had 'laid waste this fertile Colony and plunged its Inhabitants into an abject state of Misery and Distress' echoed planter claims that they 'were all but ruined due to oppressive fiscal legislation and the competition of East India sugar' and that 'Emancipation would complete their bankruptcy'.[28] The desolation of post-hurricane Barbados served as a portent for

---

[24] Anonymous, *Brief observations on the West India question in the Quarterly Review for April 1831; with remarks on the continuation of the slave trade; by a West India proprietor* (London, 1831). See also T. Rolph, *A brief account, together with observations, made during a visit in the West Indies, and a tour through the United States of America, in parts of the years 1832–3* (Dundas, 1835), pp. 13–58.

[25] J. S. Handler, *A guide to source materials for the study of Barbados history, 1627–1834* (Carbondale: Southern Illinois University Press, 1971), p. 87.

[26] J. Lyon to Goderich, 13 August 1831, CO 28/107, fos. 206a–209b, TNA.

[27] Chapman, *Barbadoes*, p. 71.

[28] 'Report of a committee of the General Assembly', CO 28/110, fos. 13a–18a, TNA; *The present state of the British sugar colonies [by] a gentleman of Barbados to his friend in London* (London, 1831), cited in L. J. Ragatz, *A guide for the study of British Caribbean history, 1763–1834* (Washington, DC, 1932), p. 263.

the post-slavery misery that would exist if the 'planter interest' was not safeguarded. For white Barbadians, the main cause of this misery lay with the 'idleness' of the black population that would be unleashed by freedom, for while 'free' signified self-control when applied to whites, it meant uncontrolled and uncontrollable when applied to non-whites. Only through the institution of slavery could black people 'achieve the limited freedom which they were [deemed] capable of enjoying'.[29] For this reason, the vast majority of planters and their supporters remained opposed to the general emancipation of the enslaved people as late as 1833.

The hurricane was a testing ground for the black capacity for freedom. Accounts asserted that in its aftermath 'the negroes refused to work, or to do any thing but plunder their Masters' Properties' and that if they had not been promptly checked in these actions they 'would have involved this wretched country in all the miseries of famine'.[30] Reflecting and heightening such concerns, the post-hurricane period saw militia detachments deployed to guard against looting, return enslaved people to work and retrieve stolen property, whilst newspapers printed lists of captured runaways.[31] Of course, such descriptions of enslaved people's unwillingness to work point to their resistance to slavery. Nevertheless, for white slaveholders they were proof that '*the negro is not yet fitted for his freedom*' and were used to articulate similar arguments to a metropolitan audience.[32] As Keith Sandiford notes:

A social order rearranged by violent cataclysmic events, of slaves seizing the initiative to right long-suffered wrongs . . . of civil peace dissolved in an orgy of looting and plunder – all these are images that had wide currency in slavery propaganda.[33]

For example, Simmons supplemented descriptions of the unwillingness of even favoured enslaved people to help their owners escape from demolished buildings or bury the dead with arguments about 'natural' black inferiority – which drew on craniology, zoological comparisons and environmental determinism – to demonstrate the supposed unreadiness of enslaved people for freedom:

[I]n nearly every instance they plundered without remorse; nor was the island restored to quiet until the soldiers from St Ann's were turned out, and one of the misguided wretches shot, and then, after much trouble, they were brought round to their usual occupations. Now, my Lord, ask yourself seriously . . . do you think that it would be either safe, politic, or humane, to emancipate these beings, who have shown what a miserable perversion they would make of freedom?[34]

---

[29] J. Pope Melish, *Disowning slavery: Gradual emancipation and 'race' in New England, 1780–1860* (London: Cornell University Press, 1998), p. 77; Thompson, '"Happy – happy slaves!"', 93.

[30] R. Alleyne to H. Fitzherbert, 31 August 1831, Fitzherbert Collection, Reel 1, E20591, BDA; S. Hyde, *Account of the fatal hurricane, by which Barbados suffered in August 1831* (Bridgetown, 1831); Lyon to Goderich, 16 August 1831, CO 28/107, fos. 210a–b, TNA.

[31] Proclamation, 15 August 1831, CO 28/107, fo. 212a, TNA; *Barbadian*, 7 September 1831, Reel UF15, Bridgetown Public Library (henceforth BPL).

[32] Simmons, *Letter on the West India question*, p. 4.

[33] Sandiford, *Cultural politics of sugar*, pp. 148–149.

[34] Simmons, *Letter on the West India question*, pp. 16–17.

Dystopian economic visions of freedom in the 1830s were not only expressed with reference to the post-hurricane desolation, but also in terms of the failure of other colonial projects based on free black labour – such as Sierra Leone[35] – and other places where emancipation had occurred. These failures could be read in the landscape: with emancipation 'the West Indian islands [will] be rendered, like St Domingo, a prey to indolence, the fairest, loveliest, and most productive garden under heaven, will be transformed into a black and sterile wilderness; and the negroes will become either bandits or beggars'.[36] In these post-slavery spaces the economic consequences of freedom were apparent.

The pastoral, which symbolised the natural and prosperous functioning of the plantation system, contrasted with the desolate landscapes of Haiti, Sierra Leone and post-hurricane Barbados. Their 'waste' was the inverse of the 'improved' estate of the ideal planter. Such accounts confirmed and reflected white fears about emancipation and especially the unreliability of free black labour. These idle or criminal black people contrasted with the contented figures of the plantation pastoral. Indeed, descriptions of post-hurricane Barbados articulated an *anti-pastoral* discourse, the island's landscape ruined and its fractious enslaved population no longer working to nature's rhythms. They were used to argue against immediate emancipation:

[T]hose who are best acquainted with the present state of the negroes of Barbados were of [the] opinion that much the larger proportion of them would, in a state of freedom, give themselves up to the habits of indolence and licentiousness, and would prefer starvation to labour.[37]

As 'good masters' with 'local expertise' of the 'negro character', white Barbadian slaveholders 'knew' that rational self-interest did not apply to black people and that some way of retaining agricultural labour, or some sort of compensation, was needed.[38] In fact, Barbadian proprietors were extremely successful at controlling labour after emancipation: the lack of employment opportunities outside the estates and the high population density provided the basis for the maintenance of the plantation system. This was operationalised in new laws and disciplinary institutions. Although some white Barbadians may have foreseen this situation, accounts of the hurricane expressed white fears about the unreliability of black labour outside the system of slavery and point to the concerns that informed the need to bring in social and political instruments that would support the retention of the plantation system.[39] Such concerns were informed by the certainties of the planter ideal and white supremacist fears. It must be reiterated, of course, that accounts

---

[35] Simmons, *Letter on the West India question*, pp. 10–11.
[36] Simmons, *Letter on the subject of West Indian property*, p. 7.
[37] Mayers to CCHA, 21 February 1833, ALB, Reel Bs. 10, BDA.
[38] Simmons, *Letter on the question of negro emancipation*, p. 5.
[39] Drescher and McGlynn, 'Introduction'.

of the hurricane's aftermath were more than just a product of white fears and also represented the resistance of enslaved people to their (dis)possession.

Winning 'just' compensation

The aftereffects of the hurricane served as a portent for the post-slavery collapse of prosperity. Efforts at obtaining 'just' compensation for the abolition of slavery – paralleling that for the hurricane – were an attempt to defend the plantation system, for it was claimed that, without white capital and civilisation, Barbados would 'speedily sink into a state of anarchy and moral debasement'.[40] The promise of some form of compensation for the 'loss' of labour was part of the imperial authorities' attempt to retain control over the amelioration and emancipation processes. It had been added to the government's amendment of Buxton's 1823 ameliorative proposals and had ensured the support of the West India Interest at the time. In the 1830s, planters attempted to shore up the plantation system by extracting 'as high a level of monetary compensation as possible by emphasizing what a great hardship to the planter would result from the loss of the controllable labor of the slaves'.[41] Given the economic difficulties they faced, this was an imperative.

In their demands for compensation, planters used arguments about the sanctity of private property. For example, Simmons argued that laws protecting inanimate property also applied to enslaved people and that emancipation without compensation was an unconstitutional and dangerous precedent.[42] He also linked colonial property rights to those in the metropole and portrayed antislavery as an attack on propertied interests in general. Such claims carried some weight amongst Britain's landed classes, especially in the context of the British social upheavals of the early 1830s. These arguments were augmented by the insistence that as Britain had encouraged slavery it 'had a full share of guilt and ought to bear its proportion of the indemnity'.[43] This evocation of national guilt points to the importance of 'duty' in the campaign for compensation. Indeed, Barbadian slaveholders insisted that they *deserved* special treatment. For example, *Barbadoes* concludes with an appeal that sought to contest the slave world/free world division on which calls for immediate, uncompensated emancipation rested:

> England! our country! which we call our own,
> In our homes belted by the torrid zone;
> Land of our fathers! wilt thou scorn us now,
> And wear disdain on thy majestic brow?[44]

---

[40] Minutes of the Committee of West India Planters and Merchants, in Mayers to CCHA, 5 April 1832, ALB, Reel Bs. 9, BDA.

[41] Butler, *Economics of emancipation*; Taylor, 'Our man in London', 72.

[42] Simmons, *Letter on the subject of West Indian property*, p. 8.

[43] Mayers to CCHA, 18 November 1830, ALB, Reel Bs. 9, BDA; Minutes of the Committee of West India Planters and Merchants, in Mayers to CCHA, 1 March 1833, ALB, Reel Bs. 10, BDA. See also Butler, *Economics of emancipation*.

[44] Chapman, *Barbadoes*, p. 81.

Such appeals for British support can be thought of as a particular mobilisation of the discourse of Barbados-as-Little-England in order to defend the plantation system. This mobilisation rested on positive articulations of white Barbadian identity and claims that were specific to Barbados. It drew on, and reinforced, the 'self-image of the planter class as enlightened managers who did not deserve all the abuse that had been heaped on them'.[45]

Such concern with the image of Barbados was particularly evident in Mayers's lobbying efforts.[46] In autumn 1832, the House of Lords launched an investigation into the state of slavery in each colony, starting with Jamaica. Mayers was confident that the Barbadian record on amelioration would set the island in good stead in the investigation. He also sought to mobilise the planter ideal by gathering evidence of paternalism, good treatment and enslaved contentment. This was not to oppose emancipation *per se*, but an attempt to gain 'justice' for the reforms that – supposedly – had already been made by Barbadian slaveholders. Simmons, for example, asserted that it had been 'the object of my whole life, so to treat my negroes . . . as to render them but slaves in name' and, as a result, had been welcomed by his enslaved workforce during his last visit to Barbados.[47] It was such 'evidence' of paternalism that Mayers sought to deploy in his representation of a white slaveholding culture that deserved compensation. Despite his confidence in the Barbadian record, however, Mayers was less certain about the other islands, noting in an aside that negative accounts of Jamaica were 'probably truthful as I have heard'. Such concerns seemed warranted when the report from the House of Lords on Jamaica was so damning that Mayers feared it threatened to undermine the paternalistic claims of Barbadian slaveholders.[48] In response, he sought to establish exceptionalist arguments about the *local* condition of slavery in Barbados.

The spoils of freedom

In seeking to represent Barbados in as favourable a light as possible, other parts of the West Indies were denigrated. This was another attempt to contest the slave world/free world division by stressing Barbados's differences from other West Indian colonies and emphasising its similarity to Britain. Whilst the Colonial Congress of 1831 had hinted at the possibilities of a pan-West Indian opposition to the imperial authorities, the colonies *were* divided, particularly between the 'old' colonies of Barbados, Antigua and St Kitts, and 'new' colonies such as British Guiana, Trinidad and St Lucia.[49] Meanwhile, Jamaica stood geographically and economically alone, and its increasing domination of imperial policy formulation further exacerbated intra-colonial tensions.[50] There were also divisions between

---

[45] Taylor, 'Our man in London', 76.   [46] Taylor, 'Our man in London', 75.

[47] Simmons, *Letter on the subject of West Indian property*, pp. 3–4.

[48] Mayers to CCHA, 3 October 1832, ALB, Reel Bs. 10, BDA; Taylor, 'Our man in London'.

[49] Higman, 'Colonial Congress'. As noted previously, the colony of British Guiana was created in 1831 from the unification of Demerara, Essequibo and Berbice.

[50] Green, *British slave emancipation*.

residents and absentees, planters and merchants, all of which coloured Mayers's lobbying efforts:

Mayers began to see himself in competition not only with the West Indian Body whom he felt was dominated by merchants' interests who would want to get their share first, but also with the younger colonies, particularly British Guiana and Jamaica, with which Barbados was often being compared.[51]

Reflecting these divisions were Mayers's concerns that deputations from the Committee of West India Planters and Merchants appointed to lobby the Colonial Office did not properly represent Barbadian interests, something he sought to counter with vigorous personal efforts:

I have never allowed myself to be absent for the shortest interval, under an apprehension that the interest of Barbados might suffer from the cupidity of those who advocate the interests of some of the neighbouring colonies.[52]

Tensions between the different colonies and within the West India Interest became pronounced over the issue of how compensation should be allocated. The emancipation bill of 1833 set the indemnity at £15 million in loans. This was increased to a £20 million cash payment after heavy lobbying by the West India Interest. The sum each colony was to receive was determined by multiplying the average local price for enslaved people in the period 1822–30 by their number. This figure was then calculated as a percentage of the total value of all enslaved people in the British empire, which was put at just over £45 million. Each colony was to receive this percentage of the £20 million. On this basis, Barbados was allocated £3,897,276 in compensation (8.6 per cent of the total), whilst Jamaica and British Guiana were to receive £13,951,139 (30 per cent) and £9,729,047 (21 per cent) respectively.[53]

The decision to distribute the compensation on such an *ad valorem* basis raised protests from slaveowners in more densely populated colonies, such as Barbados, where the average price of enslaved labour was low (£47 in Barbados, compared with £115 for the 'new' colony of British Guiana). Instead, slaveholders in the 'old' colonies pressed for a *per capita* distribution, which they argued was fairer, simpler and cheaper to administer. The most sustained criticism came from Mayers, who lobbied the Colonial Office by using arguments about Barbadian specificity to maximise the island's indemnity.[54] For example, he argued that the *ad valorem* system penalised the ameliorative efforts that Barbadian proprietors had been engaged in even before 1823. Thus, whereas Barbados's enslaved population had been rising since 1800, British Guiana had a declining enslaved population and higher prices, and yet would be rewarded with over twice the compensation:

---

[51] Taylor, 'Our man in London', 73.
[52] Mayers to CCHA, 6 June 1833, ALB, Reel Bs. 10, BDA; Mayers to Goderich, 2 March 1833, ALB, Reel Bs. 10, BDA.
[53] Butler, *Economics of emancipation*, pp. 25–43.
[54] Mayers to CCHA, 11 February 1833, ALB, Reel Bs. 10, BDA.

[This] plan was less equitable and would operate as a bonus to those proprietors whose over production, the consequence of the severe working of the slaves had been justly reprobated, that on the contrary, they, who from kind and humane treatment had increased the number of their slaves and lessened their imports, ought to be benefited instead of infined [sic] by such conduct.[55]

For Mayers, it was unjust that Barbados would be 'penalised' for the ameliorative reforms its proprietors had undertaken, particularly as these 'reforms' were portrayed as a sign of colonial loyalty. Although this was a disingenuous account of amelioration, the idea that the loyalty of Little England, as evident in its planters' commitment to reform, was being penalised recurred in efforts to maximise compensation.

Barbadian arguments about the justice of a *per capita* distribution of the compensation were predicated on a distinction between 'old' and 'new' West Indian colonies, and an emphasis on the planter ideal versus short-termist frontier 'speculation'. This division was articulated particularly in relation to British Guiana. For Mayers, the uncivilised nature of this colony's system of slavery was evident in a declining enslaved population and the illegal importation of enslaved people that he claimed occurred. In contrast, the 'improved' nature of Barbados was apparent in the large amount of fixed capital (as also portrayed in the cultivated pastoral imagery of *Barbadoes*) and the fact that the colony was self-sufficient in providing food for its enslaved population. Mayers argued that this 'improved' condition should be accounted for in the distribution of compensation through a bounty paid by the 'new' colonies to Barbados.[56] Such geographical arguments were also made by a group of absentee Barbadian proprietors, who insisted that the distribution of compensation required 'an accurate knowledge of the laws, wages and customs of each colony'.[57] According to them, the *ad valorem* distribution was not based on such knowledge. Similar arguments were made by Simmons who contrasted the settlers of British Guiana – a colony of 'merchants' and 'a few Irish and Scotch adventurers' – with the paternalistic behaviour of Barbados's implicitly English 'good masters'. He insisted that the inhumanity (and un-Englishness) of the former should not be rewarded.[58]

Despite the vehemence with which the *per capita* case was made by those associated with Barbados, the *ad valorem* system was retained. Indeed, the Colonial Office asserted that the island's high population density gave it an advantage because 'freed' workers would have little choice but to work on the estates.[59] For Lionel Smith, the governor at the time, Barbadian complaints were a function of

---

[55] Mayers to CCHA, 12 June 1833, ALB, Reel Bs. 10, BDA.
[56] To the Right Honourable The Secretary of State for the Colonial Department, in Mayers to CCHA, 25 June 1833, ALB, Reel Bs. 10, BDA.
[57] Memorial to E. Stanley, in Mayers to Lefevre, 1 July 1833, ALB, Reel Bs. 10, BDA.
[58] Simmons, *Letter on the question of negro emancipation*, p. 12.
[59] Mayers to CCHA, 11 February 1833, ALB, Reel Bs. 10, BDA.

local insular pride, which had been offended by an allocation of compensation to Barbados less than that for other colonies:

A Barbadian can never be brought to understand that there is any other Colony of half the Value and Consequence to the Mother Country than this is.[60]

This dismissal was reminiscent of the mocking attacks on Barbados-as-Little-England that had accompanied the 1825 motion on anti-Methodism and pointed to the marginalisation of Barbados within the slavery controversy, particularly given Jamaica's centrality to policymaking.[61] From 1832, the efforts of the imperial authorities to achieve emancipation focussed on the absentees (who it was presumed would welcome any compensation), whilst resident West Indians were treated with increasing condescension and dismissed as politically insignificant attorneys and overseers.[62] Given the high level of resident ownership in Barbados, this amounted to a virtual disregard for the colony's importance and pointed to its marginalisation in the imperial imagination. The importance of resisting this marginalisation and representing Barbados in as favourable light as possible was clear from Mayers's swift response to an attack on the island in Parliament by the Secretary of State for the Colonies, Edward George Stanley. Stanley had described the local opposition to amelioration in the 1820s as exemplifying a 'contumacious indifference to the wishes of Parliament'.[63] In response, Mayers attempted to use Barbados's (unexceptional) record on legal reform to defend the colony's reputation. Although he won an apology, the 'reforms' that Mayers evoked did not amount to much. For Bruce Taylor, this is symptomatic of the 'total lack of moral capital' that was at Mayers's disposal.[64] Nevertheless, in seeking to contrast Barbados favourably with the 'new' colonies, such as British Guiana, defenders of Barbadian 'interests' sought to mobilise what they saw as the *relative* cultural and moral capital of Little England.

In their calls for the *per capita* distribution of compensation, white Barbadians drew on the planter ideal, as demonstrated by the rising enslaved population and the 'improved' landscape, and the loyalty they had supposedly demonstrated in the local reform of slavery. This articulation of the white colonial identity contrasted Barbados with the ruthless 'speculation' that supposedly occurred in the 'new' colonies. In mobilising such discourses, the specificity of Barbadian society was evoked to defend the plantation system. Barbadian slaveholders attempted to transform the cultural and moral capital of the planter ideal and colonial loyalty into a maximised financial compensation. Yet, the difficulties that Mayers had in establishing this image of Barbados, particularly after the parliamentary censure of 1825, and the failure to shift the compensation policy suggest that Barbadian cultural 'stock' had declined in value. Nevertheless, Mayers and some of the more

---

[60] L. Smith to Stanley, 28 September 1833, CO 28/111, TNA.
[61] See chapter 5, pp. 167–168.   [62] Holt, *Problem of freedom*, p. 29.
[63] Taylor, 'Our man in London', 75.   [64] Ibid.

pragmatic proprietors realised that with virtually all of the island's land divided into estates, and little opportunity for 'freed' people to work elsewhere, the outlook for planters was not too bad.[65] For these reasons, it was perhaps the potential *social* consequences of freedom – the danger of the unfettered black body rather than its idleness – which was of greater concern.

'Nights of fear': freedom as black peril

Within white Barbadian society, freedom was understood not only as a threat to plantation prosperity, but to the socio-racial order. This was 'freedom' as 'black peril' and was largely informed by a white supremacist understanding of Afro-Caribbean people.[66] Accounts of the 1831 hurricane betrayed such anxieties by focussing on evidence of disorderly black behaviour. For example, in his 'Refractory account of the Slaves on some Estates in the Leeward Parishes', Samuel Hyde concentrated on events such as the discovery of gunpowder, an enslaved man who was shot after attacking a soldier and another who had sought to ferment unrest by claiming that Christ had told him that the hurricane was a means of emancipation and that others would follow. In his attempt to quell insubordination, one militia commander, Reynold Alleyne, had ordered fifty lashes for the 'unbecoming and insolent language, and the menaces of the ringleaders'.[67] Such accounts pointed not only to resistance amongst the enslaved population, but also to white fears of the vengeance that might be unleashed with emancipation. There was a concern that 'in the calamitous confusion of the moment the evil [sic] disposed might take possible advantage'; the parallels between this and claims that antislavery campaigning had incited unrest are clear.[68] If the traumatic, though temporary, disruption caused by the hurricane had revealed such a disposition, how could white authority survive externally imposed emancipation? Accounts of religious visions and the belief of some enslaved people that the hurricane was 'to be the instrument of their liberation' evoked an almost apocalyptic understanding of emancipation, suggesting perhaps that, for white and black people alike, the 'end of the world' the slaveholders had made might be coming.[69]

Such white concerns were given weight by events elsewhere in the Caribbean. The violent freedom won in St Domingue had haunted slaveholders throughout the early nineteenth century.[70] Furthermore, on 27 December 1831, the largest ever enslaved revolt in the British West Indies broke out in Jamaica. The Emancipation Rebellion – labelled the 'Baptist War' by slaveholders who blamed missionary

---

[65] M. Sheller, *Democracy after slavery: Black publics and peasant radicalism in Haiti and Jamaica* (London: Macmillan Education, 2000), p. 52; Taylor, 'Our man in London', 69.

[66] Thompson, '"Happy – happy slaves!"', 110.

[67] Hyde, *Account of the fatal hurricane*, p. 120. See also Alleyne to Fitzherbert, 31 August 1831, Fitzherbert Collection, Reel 1, E20591, BDA.

[68] Minutes of Assembly, 18 August 1833, CO 31/51, TNA.

[69] Simmons, *Letter on the West India question*, p. 16.   [70] See chapter 4, pp. 136–139.

activity – involved 20,000 enslaved people and was led by Christian converts. It was eventually and brutally suppressed in April 1832.[71] The rebellion was a significant event because it made the imperial authorities realise the necessity of immediate abolition. Moreover, whilst Barbados was spared this bloodshed, the revolt heightened local white supremacist fears that post-slavery society would be violent and black-dominated, either by virtue of a pre-emancipation rebellion or having resulted from a collapse in white authority with the demise of slavery.[72]

White fears were deepened by a set of local events that came to be regarded as a premonition for the dangers of the end of the slavery. In October 1832, an enslaved man, Robert James, was imprisoned for the rape of a poor white woman, Margaret Higginbotham, in the parish of St Philip. He was convicted and sentenced to death. After the trial, John Brathwaite Skeete, a white Barbadian plantocrat who was acting as president in the governor's absence, sought information about the case from the chief justice and solicitor general.[73] Concerned about the lack of interrogation of Higginbotham's character and suspecting that she and James might have been sexually involved in the past, Skeete suspended the execution and sought the Crown's judgement.[74] In April 1833, the colonial secretary wrote back to Governor Lionel Smith – who by then had replaced Skeete as the executive – with the opinion that the prosecution had been improperly undertaken and that punishment should be commuted to transportation.[75] As with the case of Joseph Denny nearly four decades earlier, the affair provoked great anger amongst Barbados's white population. As one contemporary writer put it:

I saw the negro, Robert James, in confinement, whose outrage on a white female had excited such an intense feeling. Nothing could exceed the excitement introduced by the President's remission of the extreme penalty of the law.[76]

Such feelings were evident in legislative investigations into the affair, public meetings held across the island and petitions that called for the removal of Skeete. Before discussing these, however, the significance of the case deserves consideration. Although the (alleged) rape was only a single incident, it came to symbolise the potential danger posed by the black (male) body that might be released and realised by emancipation.

---

[71] M. Turner, *Slaves and missionaries: The disintegration of Jamaican slave society, 1787–1834* (London: University of Illinois Press, 1982), pp. 148–178.

[72] *Barbadian*, 26 January 1833, Reel UF15, BPL.

[73] J. Skeete to J. W. Jordan, 17 December 1832, fos. 20a–b; Jordan to Skeete, 24 December 1832, fos. 21a–23a; W. Gibbons to R. Clarke, 27 December 1832, fos. 24a–25a; Clarke to Gibbons, 28 December 1832, fos. 26a–29a: all CO 28/111, TNA. For another treatment of the case, see M. Newton, 'The King v. Robert James, a slave, for rape: Inequality, gender and British slave amelioration, 1823–1834', unpublished paper. Like Newton, I do not attempt to conclude whether James was actually guilty of the rape of Higginbotham or not.

[74] Gibbons to B. Walrond, 2 January 1833, CO 28/111, fo. 31a; Skeete to Goderich, 4 January 1833, CO 28/111, fos. 10a–12a, TNA.

[75] Stanley to Smith, 3 April 1833, CO 29/33, pp. 122–123, TNA.

[76] Rolph, *Brief account . . . made during a visit in the West Indies*, p. 45.

Violation and defilement

In her discussion of accounts of the Indian 'Mutiny', Alison Blunt demonstrates how 'the severity of conflict came to be embodied by the fate of British women and the defilement of their bodies and their homes'. She shows how the feminisation of victimhood, especially through the figure of 'mother', served to legitimise masculine retaliation.[77] In accounts of the James case, Higginbotham's status as a 'poor widow' drew repeated comment, emphasising her vulnerability (there was no male 'protector') and the enormity of the offence. In similar terms, the *Globe* published a 'letter' from 'A Widow Woman' warning that 'The poor violated woman's case may, tomorrow, be that of a mother, a sister, a daughter or a wife of any man's' and calling for the white masculine defence of white Barbadian femininity.[78] Elsewhere, the attack on Higginbotham was described as 'one of the flagitious offences in the black catalogue of crime' and of the 'blackest' nature. This 'colouring' was far from coincidental and pointed to the crime's metaphorical elevation in relation to questions of 'freedom' and racialised notions of (sexual) violence. This, in turn, reflected the linkage between white womanhood and the reproduction of freedom in the West Indies, and the fact that 'the entire ideological fabric of the slave-based civilization was conceived in terms of sex, gender and race'.[79]

The importance of the alleged rape in the early 1830s was unsurprising and Dane Kennedy notes that 'most outbreaks of black peril hysteria occurred when the white settler communities were under considerable social and/or economic stress'. This was clearly the case after the outbreak of the 1816 rebellion, even though there was no evidence of any black sexual attacks.[80] This white supremacist terror recurred in the 1830s and echoes of the 1816 revolt were evident in Chapman's poem, *Barbadoes*, which was published soon after James's conviction. In an idyllic scene, the 'embrace' between two young white Barbadian lovers is disturbed by the revolt of a 'ruthless race':

> The heavens are red with wild-devouring fire;
> Fierce shouts come onward – nigher still and nigher!
> As though mad Uproar, disenchained from hell,
> Had burst on earth, and shrieked his horrid yell.
> Too well they knew what meant those fearful sounds;
> For him fierce conflict, agony and wounds;
> For her the rude insulter's heated breath,

---

[77] A. Blunt, 'Embodying war: British women and domestic defilement in the Indian "Mutiny", 1857– 8', *Journal of Historical Geography* 26 (2000), 403. See also V. Ware, *Beyond the pale: White women, racism and history* (London: Verso, 1992), p. 40.

[78] CO 28/111, fo. 45a, TNA. Although Skeete's decision was met with incomprehension, his attitude to Higginbotham was, to some extent, consistent with white elite attitudes to poor whites. See Newton, 'The King v. Robert James'.

[79] *Barbadian*, 12 January 1833, Reel UF15, BPL. See H. McD. Beckles, 'White women and slavery in the Caribbean', *History Workshop Journal* 36 (1993), 69.

[80] D. Kennedy, *Islands of white: Settler society and culture in Kenya and Southern Rhodesia, 1890– 1939* (Durham, NC: Duke University Press, 1987), p. 146. See chapter 4, pp. 131–133.

And outraged modesty, and brutal death;
The wildered virgin thousand horrors sees, –
In one short hour ten thousand agonies.[81]

Contrasting sharply with the dancing, laughing and play of the 'happy negro-throng' described elsewhere, the rebels portrayed here sought to 'rule their rulers, and embrace/The blooming daughters of a fairer race'.[82] Along with contemporary events in Jamaica, the 1816 revolt was clearly the inspiration for this anti-pastoral passage. Nevertheless, it is worth reiterating that there was no evidence of any sexual attacks by black people on whites during the revolt, even if the rebels had made play of this threat. Indeed, Chapman's account is as much a white supremacist warning about what post-slavery society might entail as a description of previous examples of black behaviour. Although the Barbadian plantocracy may not have been as 'negrophobic' as that of Jamaica,[83] which experienced many revolts and large-scale marronage, there were still concerns about black violence. Thus, Simmons warned about the dangers of a 'servile war in a tropical climate', or as Chapman put it, if immediate emancipation were to occur 'rapine, murder, anarchy defile/The peaceful glories of the bearded Isle!'[84] James's conviction for rape focussed white supremacist fear and anger in 1833.

Blunt also shows how the violation of white femininity in imperial accounts of colonial insurgency was linked to domestic defilement. Similarly, the case of James was significant because it was a violation of domestic space and evoked white fears about whether Barbados would continue to be 'home' with the end of slavery. During the trial, Higginbotham described being woken at night by a knock at her bedroom door, which was then thrown open by a naked James. After he had fled following the alleged attack, Higginbotham left the house and called for help. Higginbotham's description of the invasion of her house and her subsequent unwillingness to return became immensely significant in the controversy that followed.[85] Indeed, given the difficulty with representing rape,[86] Higginbotham's domestic estrangement served to symbolise the horror of the crime amongst the white public:

Let it be remembered . . . that the insulted, the injured, the violated female, as soon as she escaped from the grasp of the ruffian flew from her humble dwelling – let it be remembered that she has never since returned to her habitation – it is polluted! she cannot return to a spot which has been the scene of her dishonour – the scene of her ruin.[87]

[81] Chapman, *Barbadoes*, p. 77.   [82] Chapman, *Barbadoes*, p. 78.

[83] M. Steel, 'A philosophy of fear: The world view of Jamaican plantocracy in comparative perspective', *Journal of Caribbean History* 27 (1993).

[84] Chapman, *Barbadoes*, p. 84; Simmons, *Letter on the question of negro emancipation*, p. 9.

[85] Jordan to Skeete, 24 December 1832, CO 28/111, fos. 21a–23a, TNA; Report of the Protector of Slaves, Appended to Council Minutes, 18 January 1833, CO 28/111, fos. 40a–42b, TNA.

[86] J. Sharpe, 'The unspeakable limits of rape: Colonial violence and counter-insurgency', *Genders* 10 (1991).

[87] Speech of W. Griffith, *Barbadian*, 12 January 1833, Reel UF15, BPL; *Barbados Mercury*, 12 January 1833, CO 28/111, fo. 45, TNA.

Useful for elucidating the significance of domestic space in the James case is Peter Somerville's discussion of seven dimensions of the meaning of 'home'.[88] As well as invading the physical space of Higginbotham's house (what Somerville terms home as 'shelter') and place of sleep ('abode'), James's attack violated the domesticity of home as 'hearth' and 'heart'. Higginbotham described being in bed with her two young children, when James forced his way into her room, one of whom said 'What Robert James are you going to kill my mother?'[89] The violent disturbance of this scene of familial intimacy and dependency reinforced the domestic violation of the act. The attack also shattered Higginbotham's 'privacy' – home as a place of control – and doubly so because it transgressed those laws and norms codified in James's black and enslaved status. Moreover, Somerville's discussion of home as 'roots', as source of identity and ontological security, links domestic defilement to Kennedy's observation that interracial rape or 'black peril' was held to threaten the proper reproduction of the white race.[90] Finally, that home is also 'paradise' – 'an idealisation of all the positive features of home fused together'[91] – suggests how Higginbotham's house could come to stand for Barbados within a white supremacist imagination and how its violation was a key aspect of the metaphorical elevation of the James case to a harbinger for the 'end of the world'. In the final years of slavery, the defilement of Higginbotham's house was portentous of freedom and raised the question of whether post-slavery Barbados could ever be safe for whites.

'Reward instead of punishment'

It was not only the alleged offence that made the case significant but also Skeete's intervention. Eight days after his decision to suspend James's execution, the first of a series of public meetings was held in which the president was condemned as a traitor to his Barbadian home and demands were made for his removal from office. Skeete's actions were related to the humanitarian turn in imperial policy and the intensity of antislavery campaigning in the 1830s. Paralleling the formal investigations into the state of slavery was a close imperial scrutiny into the workings of the West Indian legal systems. In 1830, the execution of an enslaved man, Edward, for burglary had been criticised by Secretary of State for the Colonies George Murray. He called for the Barbadian executive to be more careful in examining capital evidence. Skeete was acting as president at the time, and the criticism clearly affected him, as he later used it to explain his decision to suspend James's execution.[92] At the same time that Mayers was seeking to maximise Barbados's share of imperial

---

[88] P. Somerville, 'Homelessness and the meaning of home: Rooflessness or rootlessness?', *International Journal of Urban and Regional Research* 16 (1992).

[89] Jordan to Skeete, 24 December 1832, CO 28/111, fos. 21a–23a, TNA.

[90] Kennedy, *Islands of white*.   [91] Somerville, 'Homelessness and the meaning of home', 533.

[92] G. Murray to J. Lyon, 31 August 1830, CO 29/31, pp. 421–427, TNA; Minutes of Privy Council, 18 January 1833, CO 28/111, fos. 37a–39a, TNA.

compensation, Skeete was under pressure from the Colonial Office to demonstrate that there had been legal reform of slavery in Barbados. For Barbados's whites, the pressure on Skeete to tend towards leniency was another symptom of metropolitan interference in local affairs.

Compounding white fears was the belief that the pardon of James would result in his freedom. The legal precedent for this had been set in 1830 when three enslaved men – Will Thomas, George Smith and Italy – were granted a Crown pardon and freed after being sentenced to death for plotting to murder their owner. The decision generated local anger as it was seen as rewarding crime with freedom.[93] Skeete's actions in 1832–3 provoked even greater ire and, for white Barbadians, they seemed to be a metaphor for the insanity of emancipation: '*reward* instead of *punishment* may now be secured by the commission of crime'.[94] There were also concerns that this would act as an example to other enslaved people, as Mayers wrote to the colonial secretary:

> It is impossible for your Lordship to form any conception of the horror and alarm excited in the community of Barbados . . . at the bare apprehension of the direful consequences to society if from any defective administration of the law, an act of such atrocity should pass unpunished and more so in consideration of the impunity with which offences of a similar magnitude have been perpetrated and the apprehension lest the boon of emancipation should become the concomitant of the Royal Pardon.[95]

In the aftermath of the James case, white Barbadians would link his treatment to that of other enslaved people who had committed crimes and apparently escaped justice. These included George Hackett and Joseph Denny (*not* the free man of colour discussed in chapter 3) who received royal pardons, were freed and remained at large on the island.[96] In the context of the entrenched white supremacism roused by the James case, the lenient treatment of these men was seen as evidence of the dangerous precedent set when a local system of law was disrupted by misinformed and distant interference. It undermined the idea that freedom had to be learnt and earned *gradually*. These formerly enslaved criminals were an omen for emancipation, their collective haunting presence 'at large' in Barbados a premonition of post-slavery society.

For many white Barbadians, the treatment of James seemed to make freedom a reward for black sexual violence. Such a perversion and reversal of norms was also evident in Skeete's actions, for whilst it was incumbent on him, as chief magistrate, 'to insure to society the full benefit of that protection which it derives from the consigned punishment of the guilty . . . [especially] considering the nature of the offence, the circumstance and situation of the parties and the horribly dangerous

---

[93] Lyon to Murray, 12 January 1830, CO 28/105, fo. 52a; Lyon to Murray, 8 February 1830, CO 28/105, fos. 80a–b, TNA. See also Newton, 'The King v. Robert James'.
[94] *Barbados Mercury*, CO 28/111, fo. 45b, TNA.
[95] Mayers to Goderich, 6 March 1833, ALB, Reel Bs. 10, BDA.
[96] Minutes of Assembly, 19 March 1833, CO 31/51, TNA.

tendency of impunity for such a crime . . . in a society composed as this is', instead the president seemed more concerned with protecting the rights of an enslaved rapist.[97] This idea of the perversion and reversal of norms was articulated in the public meeting held to condemn Skeete:

> Gentlemen, she [Mary Higginbotham] is a poor woman, it is true, and her skin is white, which, gentlemen, is perhaps the reason why, in the opinion of the *President*, SHE is not entitled to the protection of the law.[98]

Such complaints point to another way in which the case of James was significant, in that it seemed to herald the reversal of 'common-sense' white supremacism and portend the chaotic confusion that might accompany freedom.[99] Echoing that incident in 1831 in which an enslaved man had claimed Christ as liberator, these reversals seemed almost apocalyptic for white Barbadians.

The spectacle of white authority

In response to Skeete's intervention, the Assembly demanded copies of the letters he had sent to the Colonial Office about the James case – which he refused to do – and eventually petitioned the Crown to remove him from office.[100] These actions reflected the strength of white public opinion, as demonstrated by a series of meetings held across the island. At the first in Bridgetown on 10 January 1833, the crowd was addressed by speakers, including William Griffith, the barrister who had represented James at his trial. The speeches not only attacked Skeete himself, but also the antislavery campaign, which provided a humanitarian backdrop to the events. Setting the model for subsequent meetings, resolutions were passed that asserted the horrific nature of the crime, condemned Skeete's disregard for the opinions of the jury, solicitor general and protector of slaves, and expressed grave concern at the example set to the rest of the enslaved population. These resolutions were codified in a petition submitted to the Assembly. Other meetings were held across the island and by the time the Assembly requested the removal of Skeete on 25 January, petitions had arrived from eight of the eleven parishes.

As well as seeking to influence the imperial authorities, these petitions were part of the re-articulation of white Barbadian identities along white supremacist lines. This was occasioned by concerns over the possible future state of Barbadian society and the loss of white authority that the case seemed to augur. As *The Barbados Mercury* put it:

> [W]hen a public offender escapes the punishment of his crime, it is not merely the victim of his atrocity that enlists our sympathies . . . but a community of interest, a sense of common

---

[97] Minutes of Privy Council, 18 January 1833, CO 28/111, fos. 37a–39a, TNA.
[98] Speech of Griffith, *Barbadian*, 12 January 1833, BPL.   [99] Newton, 'The King v. Robert James'.
[100] Minutes of Assembly, 25 January 1833, CO 31/51, TNA. See also Minutes of Privy Council, 18 January 1833, CO 28/111, fos. 37a–39a, TNA.

danger, impels each individual to cooperate with his neighbour in the general cause, or the midnight assassin would soon become the noon-day destroyer of his species, and cease to lurk in the darkness to commit outrage.[101]

Along with the representation of the alleged rape as 'black' and concerns that freedom would be seen as reward for criminality, this emphasis on the public wrong of the crime ('a community of interest, a sense of common danger') served to expand the significance of the rape, making it a metaphor for the dangers of freedom and emphasising the need for a unified response. The public meetings performed – they brought forth and made manifest[102] – a white supremacist identity that became articulated as 'THE PEOPLE'.[103] Echoing the identity articulated through anti-Methodism in the 1820s, this involved acts of public gathering, as well as the speeches, cheers and threats; the resolutions passed unanimously; the petitions submitted and the communication sent to the colonial agent. Joseph Roach's emphasis on transmission within the performance of subjectivity also highlights the role of the media in constituting 'THE PEOPLE'.[104] The press coverage of these meetings was more than a description of this project of identity-formation and was itself part of the effort. The local press were crucial in mobilising public opinion by printing free advertisements for the meetings and the minutes of those held. In press reports and in the actions of those people who read the reports, a collective white colonial identity was imagined and performed.

This imagined and performed community was highly racialised, gendered and spatialised. 'THE PEOPLE' may have been the term used in the press, but it was clearly white upper- and middle-class men who claimed to speak for the whole, and speeches addressed the crowds as 'Gentlemen'. Higginbotham's status and the nature of the crime were used to emphasise that the offence had been against 'the female sex, which man is bound by Divine and humane laws to cherish, defend and protect against all insult and injury'.[105] An outraged white masculinity was evoked, ready to act now – and in a post-slavery future – to defend the white-dominated socio-racial order:

Are the slaves to be told in this country . . . that the arm of our King will be extended to protect them in the commission of crime? It is true that a Despatch has gone to the Colonial Office, and with that, without question, has gone the expression of the President's doubt, which would lead to the pardon and emancipation of the felon – which would teach him and others to commit any crime to which their depraved inclinations may lead them, crimes, gentlemen, like those they threatened to commit in 1816.[106]

[101] *Barbados Mercury*, 12 January 1833, CO 28/111, fos. 45a–47b, TNA.
[102] J. Roach, *Cities of the dead: Circum-Atlantic performance* (New York: Columbia University Press, 1996), p. xi.
[103] *Globe*, 14 January 1833, CO 28/111, TNA.   [104] Roach, *Cities of the dead*, pp. 11–13.
[105] *Barbadian*, 12 January 1833, Reel UF15, BPL.
[106] Speech of Griffith, *Barbadian*, 12 January 1833, BPL.

Similarly, an active and violent white masculinity was performed through the crowds' cheers, the signing of the petitions with 'heart and hand' as if in 'blood', and in the threats made to Skeete and James:

[W]ill you permit such monstrous perversion of justice? – (Cries of No! No! No!) . . . What, then, is to be done? Gentlemen, here is a tree; the traitor to his country merits the fate of the felon, Robert James, and if justice were done he would be suspended from that tree between Heaven and Earth, as unworthy of either. (Tremendous cheering.)[107]

Whilst calls to lynch James and Skeete were rejected, not least because of concerns that this would only add weight to antislavery attacks on Barbados's aberrant slave world status, the meetings remained a demonstration of the willingness of white Barbadians to defend their social dominance, as symbolised by the white female body.[108]

'THE PEOPLE' was also a spatial subjectivity and, for those at the forefront of organising and orchestrating a response to Skeete, the physical act of holding meetings across the island served to demonstrate white Barbadian strength and unity:

Is there *one* of the eleven parishes which, on an occasion like the present, would shrink from the public expression of the honest indignation that fills the breast of every member of this injured and insulted community, who is not a slave to power or a foe to virtue?[109]

The 'flame of patriotism' had been lit by the first meeting in Bridgetown and then spread throughout the island to encompass 'a WHOLE PEOPLE' – whole as 'all' and as 'unified'. The importance of organising geographically was also evident in newspaper attacks on those parishes that had not produced petitions – St Peter, St James and St John – and in the desire of their political representatives to justify their apparent silence.[110]

Demonstrating authority

According to James Scott, a significant aspect of the maintenance of relations of (dis)possession 'consists of the symbolization of domination by demonstrations and enactments of power', or as Saidiya Hartman puts it: 'representing power was essential to reproducing domination'.[111] The 'lynching ritual' was the ultimate form of the power of white spectacle in slave societies and whilst such threats were not carried out in Barbados, the discourse of white supremacism enacted in the

---

[107] Ibid.   [108] See N. Yuval-Davis, *Gender and nation* (London, 1997), esp. chapter 3.

[109] *Globe*, 14 January 1833, CO 28/111, TNA.

[110] *Barbados Mercury*, 15 January 1833, CO 28/111, TNA; *Barbadian*, 23, 26 January 1833, CO 28/111, fos. 50a, 63b, TNA.

[111] Hartman, *Scenes of subjection*, p. 7; J. Scott, *Domination and the arts of resistance* (New Haven: Yale University Press, 1991), p. 45.

public meetings was also a demonstration of power.[112] The public response to the James case was ritualistic.[113] Although the size of the meetings varied, the format was similar in each case. Meticulous reporting in the press and the presentation of each petition to the Assembly established a reiterative impact that formulated an imagined white community that was strong and unified. The meetings were also an example to the free coloured and enslaved populations. They echoed the drills and mustering of the militia, and were even reminiscent of the geographical terror that had been evident in the display of executed rebels across the island after the 1816 revolt. In short, the meetings carried a threat. They were immanent with white supremacist violence, itself based on white supremacist fear of black freedom. This performance of the white Barbadian identity was part of an attempt to maintain the world the slaveholders made.

Symptomatic of the power at play in these demonstrations of white strength and unity was the opposition and anger directed at a meeting that some free people of colour attempted to hold on 18 January 1833 to articulate support for Skeete. When the purpose of this meeting became public, it was disrupted with 'Ridicule, insults, civil commotion, threats' and 'many were deterred from showing their opposition to the predominant class'.[114] Although the meeting was broken up, an address was still produced expressing 'unshaken loyalty to the British Government' and support for Skeete amidst the white 'clamour of prejudice'.[115] From 1832, British opponents of slavery came to see the free coloured populations of the West Indies as potential counterweights to the white plantocracies. The free people of colour themselves also sought to exploit white colonial/metropolitan tensions in an anti-racial struggle that increasingly encompassed all non-whites, free and (formerly) enslaved. This portent for post-slavery racial mobilisation in Barbados was resisted by whites who sought to ensure that only they could occupy the public space, that only the 'voice' of 'THE PEOPLE' – the master's voice – would be heard from Barbados.[116]

---

[112] T. Harris, 'White men as performers in the lynching ritual', in D. R. Roediger (ed.), *Black on white: Black writers on what it means to be white* (New York: Shocken Books, 1998).

[113] The numbers attending each meeting ranged widely, from 72 in St Thomas to 413 in Bridgetown, St Michael. Yet, all followed the same basic pattern and the resolutions passed at each were very much alike.

[114] Address of the Free Coloured and Black Deputation to Skeete, Addendum, 8 March 1833, CO 28/111, fos. 86a–87b, TNA.

[115] Address of the Free Coloured and Black Deputation to Skeete, 8 March 1833, CO 28/111, fos. 82a–85a, TNA.

[116] For a discussion of the James case and its relation to free coloured politics, see M. Newton, '"The Children of Africa in the Colonies": Free people of colour in Barbados during the emancipation era', unpublished DPhil. thesis, Oxford University (2001). Newton argues that the free people of colour's support for Skeete was both the articulation of an 'embryonic "race consciousness"', based on a shared history of racial oppression', and an expression of 'tacit support for an imperial emancipation measures': Newton, '"The Children of Africa in the Colonies"', p. 142. Such post-slavery racial mobilisation was epitomised by the anti-planter politics of the free coloured liberal, Samuel Jackman Prescod, in the 1830s and 1840s. See A. Johnson, 'The abolition of chattel slavery in Barbados, 1833–1876', unpublished Ph.D thesis, Cambridge University (1995).

Kennedy notes that episodes of 'black peril' served, and were used, to promote settler unity by clarifying and enforcing certain notions of what it meant to be 'white'.[117] In the disruption of the free coloured counter-meeting and the threat of lynching, as well as in the meetings, cheers, votes, petitions and press coverage, a unified and determined white community was performed. These responses were a white supremacist articulation of white Barbadian identity that foreshadowed, and contributed to, the rise of even more explicitly racialised conceptions of the socio-racial order after emancipation.

'Duties to perform'

The public response to the James case was a demonstration of dominance. A contemporary but very different form of performance, which drew more on the paternalism of the planter ideal, was Isaac Williamson Orderson's play, *The fair Barbadian and faithful black; or a, cure for the gout* (figure 6.2).[118] In considering this cultural articulation, I not only want to explore what the play's textual form reveals about the articulation of white identity at the end of slavery, but also suggest that its performance prefigured the attempt to maintain white authority through self-assurance and the (dis)possession of black subjectivities.

Orderson was a white Barbadian whose writing reflected, and was written to support, his proslavery position.[119] The play, ostensibly a comedy, was set just before emancipation. It has eight main characters, including a white planter, Judge Errington, and his 'confidential black servant', Hampshire – the 'faithful black' of the title. The plot revolves around Errington's daughter, Emily, the 'fair Barbadian', who is betrothed to her cousin, Tom Applebury. Tom only wants to marry Emily for her estate and is pursuing illicit sexual relations with enslaved people. Emily herself is more attracted by Captain Carlove, a British officer whom she met as she sailed home from Britain. A series of problems beset Errington's family, usually solved by Hampshire's quick-wittedness, and farce is used to generate much of the humour. The play concludes with Tom discredited as a libertine and a gold-digger, and Emily free to marry Carlove – a union that clearly symbolised Orderson's hopes for reconciliation between Britain and its West Indian colonies. For his efforts, Hampshire is rewarded with his freedom.

The play was first performed in Barbados in 1832. Although later published in Britain in 1835 to demonstrate the supposedly good relationship that had existed between enslaver and enslaved, and to suggest a bright post-emancipation future,

---

[117] Kennedy, *Islands of white*.

[118] J. W. Orderson, *The fair Barbadian and faithful black; or, a cure for the gout. A comedy in three acts* (Liverpool, 1835). Although he was named Isaac, Orderson's work was often printed with the initial 'J'. See E. Shilstone, 'Orderson family records', *Journal of the Barbados Museum and Historical Society* 25 (1957–8).

[119] E. Shilstone, 'Some notes on early printing presses and newspapers in Barbados', *Journal of the Barbados Museum and Historical Society* 26 (1958–9).

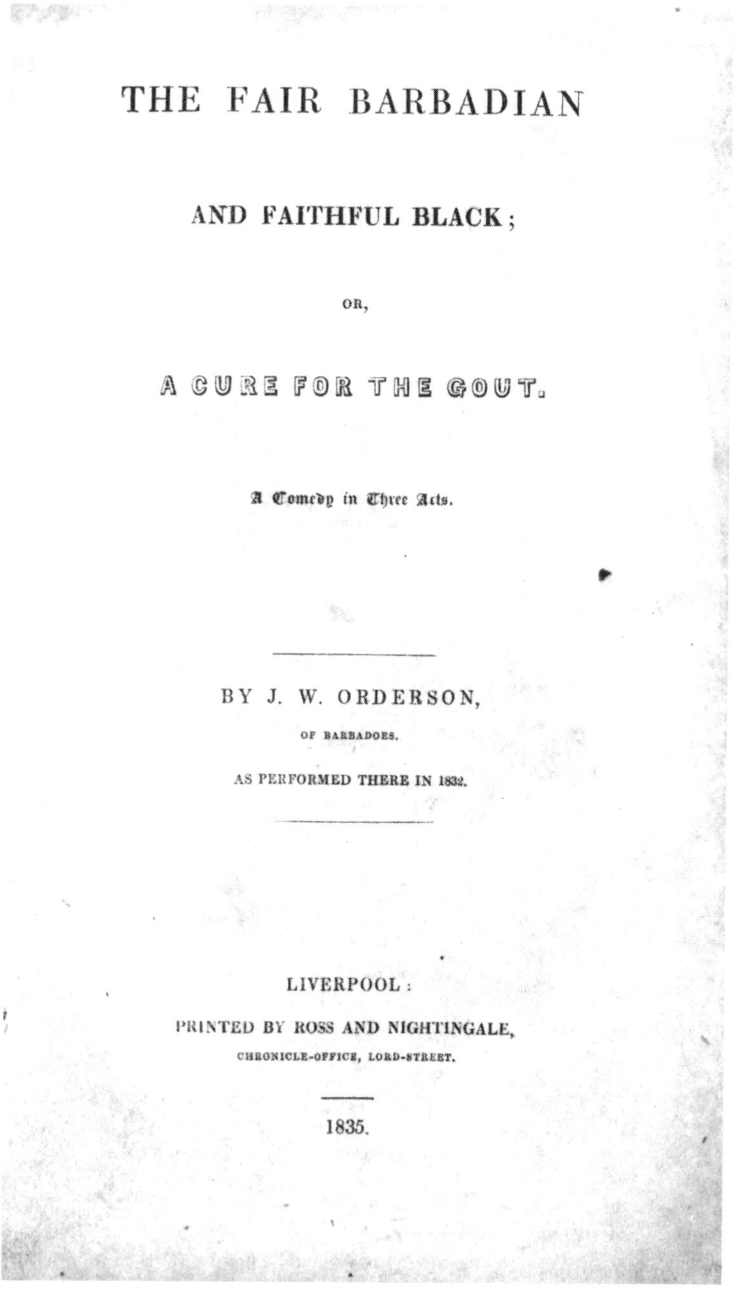

THE FAIR BARBADIAN

AND FAITHFUL BLACK;

OR,

A CURE FOR THE GOUT.

A Comedy in Three Acts.

BY J. W. ORDERSON,

OF BARBADOES.

AS PERFORMED THERE IN 1832.

LIVERPOOL:

PRINTED BY ROSS AND NIGHTINGALE,

CHRONICLE-OFFICE, LORD-STREET.

1835.

Figure 6.2 Title page of J. W. Orderson, *The fair Barbadian and faithful black; or, a cure for the gout. A comedy in three acts* (Liverpool, 1835), 1344.k.7. By permission of the British Library.

my interest is to read the play in the context of the James case in terms of 'how many upper stratum whites chose to present themselves and their society *to themselves*'.[120] Whilst we have no information as to where, when and how often it was performed, and are left to wonder 'what sort of effect it had when the play was actually produced on a Barbados stage', it is clear that a central theme was white self-assurance.[121] Slavery is portrayed in a favourable light, echoing the plantation management literature to which Orderson also contributed.[122] Errington emphasises his paternalistic credentials and is constantly praised by Hampshire as an ideal planter. This is confirmed by the festival of enslaved people on Errington's estate during which 'Negro music' is sung:

God bless Massa! *Huzza!* God bless nyung Misse. *Huzza!*
Good crops and good prices, that Massa may live as well as his Negroes. *Huzza!*[123]

Like American minstrelsy, such scenes 'dramatically resolved the tensions between domination and intimacy by recourse to sentimental tropes of reciprocity, domesticity, and kinship'. This scene echoes the kind of paternalism that Mayers had sought to mobilise in his lobbying, as well as the pastoralism of Chapman's *Barbadoes*. Other than the favoured domestic, Hampshire, enslaved people are 'virtually part of the scenery'.[124]

Aside from the favourable staging of slavery, the representation of the central relationship between 'the fair Barbadian and faithful black' deserves particular attention in the light of the James case. This link is suggested by Errington's discussion of the importance of Christian inculcation to prepare enslaved people for emancipation and of the dangers of other paths to freedom:

JUDGE: Yes, but progressive amendment is all that we can at present aim at; therefore, the first lesson that should be given them is – that disgrace is not in the *punishment* but in the *commission* of crime. This, however, I fear will now become more difficult to teach, since they have lately seen successful crime and daring profligacy favoured and flattered by the undue exercise of a false philanthropy![125]

Although probably a reference to the free pardons received by Will Thomas, George Smith, Italy, Joseph Denny and George Hackett between 1830 and 1832, the James

---

[120] J. S. Handler, *Supplement to a guide to source materials for the study of Barbados history, 1627–1834* (Providence, RI: John Carter Brown Library and Barbados Museum and Historical Society, 1991), p. 41, emphasis added.

[121] J. Gilmore, *'Creoleana: or, social and domestic scenes and incidents in Barbados in days of yore' and 'The fair Barbadian and faithful black; or, a cure for the gout', by J. W. Orderson: Edited and with a new introduction* (Oxford: Macmillan, 2002), p. 15.

[122] J. W. Orderson, *Directions to young planters for their care and management of a sugar plantation in Barbadoes* (London, 1800). See chapter 2, pp. 66–68.

[123] Orderson, *The fair Barbadian*, Act ii, Scene 2, p. 180. All page references are to the reprint of the play in the Gilmore edition.

[124] Gilmore, *'Creoleana'*, p. 11; Hartman, *Scenes of subjection*, p. 30.

[125] Orderson, *The fair Barbadian*, Act i, Scene 2, p. 174.

case would have dominated white concerns after the suspension of his execution. Orderson's play also evokes the James case through its portrayal of a relationship between a black enslaved man and white woman, though in *The Fair Barbadian* this is idealised. Rather than the 'violation' of Higginbotham or the 'hot breath' of the rebels in Chapman's *Barbadoes*, Hampshire is the completely trustworthy servant and Emily's protector, holding her hand tenderly and, by acting as her go-between with Carlove, facilitating the proper reproduction of the white race. His initial unwillingness to accept his manumission ('No gee he free!'[126]) contrasts with an attempt made by James to escape from prison.[127] The justice of the former's reward for loyalty contrasts with the injustice of James's free pardon. As an 'anti-James', Hampshire is the dramatic antidote to the rebels of 1816, the unruly enslaved people after the hurricane and the disorderly free blacks that whites feared would be the product of emancipation.

At the end of the play, when Hampshire is persuaded to accept his manumission, an exchange occurs between him and Errington over the nature of freedom:

JUDGE: Hampshire . . . will then be a hired servant – no longer a slave! And now, Hampshire, that you are free, by the liberal spirit of our laws you are possessed of all the rights and privileges of a British subject, equalling with myself.

HAMPSHIRE: *(With amazement, examining his hands and opening his bosom.)* Hey! – I like you? Massa, you making you fun! – I tan like you? Ha, ha! *(With surprise and half-gratified feelings.)*

JUDGE: No, Hampshire! – no human laws can counteract nature! – your condition in society is changed, but not your complexion, and though free and having rights and privileges conferred on you, you yet have *duties* to perform![128]

This passage is significant in the period just prior to emancipation because it represents a white slaveholding manifesto for freedom. Hampshire is an idealised enslaved subject, reluctant to accept his freedom, partly because of his own sense of inferiority ('I like you? Massa, you making you fun!'), which he expresses with reference to his own racialised corporeality. Errington's reassurances evoke a racially differentiated notion of freedom ('no human laws can counteract nature!') through which post-slavery white domination and black subjugation is naturalised. Hampshire's initial unwillingness to accept his freedom and Errington's reassurance that he will still serve was an idealised portrayal of what freedom should be. It was Orderson's attempt to dramatically portray a 'world' in which emancipation was neither a social nor economic danger. The central message of *The Fair Barbadian* was paternalistic self-assurance: slavery was a system of mutual dependency and therefore there was no reason to fear the vengeance of black people.

---

126 Orderson, *The fair Barbadian*, Act iii, Scene 4, p. 206.
127 Minutes of Assembly, 31 December 1833, CO 31/51, TNA; Rolph, *Brief account . . . made during a visit in the West Indies*, p. 45.
128 Orderson, *The fair Barbadian*, Act iii, Scene 4, p. 207.

Whilst *The Fair Barbadian* was a dramatic form of white self-assurance, there is no mistaking its (dis)possessive qualities, and to this extent – like the public meetings of protest held in the aftermath of the James trial – the play was a demonstration of white domination and a form of black subjugation. For example, at the end of the discourse on freedom, Hampshire seeks to clarify the boundaries of his new condition:

HAMPSHIRE: But, Massa, you no say I hab right and privilege fau do waugh I
please?

JUDGE: No, my good man! – They who do what they *please*, seldom do what they ought, and those who may do evil with impunity generally do it with licentiousness; for men are least likely to offend, when they *dare not!*[129]

Errington's insistence on the prescribed and policed limits of freedom was a reassertion of white domination even after slavery. The menacing flourish ('they *dare not!*') and the 'farcical' blows that Hampshire's body is subjected to by all the white Barbadian characters throughout the play (apart from Emily) are just the most obvious forms of black subjugation. Indeed, the play *itself* was a form of slavery. When discussing the coerced black performances of happiness at auctions where enslaved people were bought and sold, Hartman notes that 'what was being staged . . . was nothing less than slavery itself'.[130] Hampshire's 'acts' of loyalty and the 'Negro festival' of Orderson's play were more removed from such brute forms of (dis)possession, but they were similar manifestations of the 'theatricality' of slavery. Whether the enslaved characters were played by black people or white actors in 'blackface', as tended to be the custom on the British stage at the time,[131] this was a form of (dis)possession that involved taking over the black body. The staged nature of the play portrayed an idealised system of slavery, not simply in terms of black contentment and loyalty, but *as complete white authority*.

Hartman notes that 'minstrelsy reached its zenith' in the American South during the Civil War because Southern identity depended on the performance of black-ness.[132] The 1830s was a similar time for Barbadian slaveholders when their own sense of self – their 'world' – was in something of a crisis. In response to fears of loss of authority, white Barbadians reacted in a variety of expressive ways. Whilst the self-directed and staged contentment of *The fair Barbadian* enacted a pater-nalistic form of (dis)possession that would become increasingly uncommon after emancipation, both it and the demonstrations of strength by 'THE PEOPLE' were spectacles of black subjugation and articulations of the 'master subject'.

The imperial Emancipation Act of 1 August 1833 set emancipation for one year later. Although the self-legislating colonies were left to draft their own legisla-tion, the British government attempted to direct emancipation by loosely joining

---

[129] Ibid.   [130] Hartman, *Scenes of subjection*, p. 41.
[131] Gilmore, *'Creoleana'*, pp. 255–256.   [132] Hartman, *Scenes of subjection*, p. 46.

Barbados and the other Windward Islands under a common governor-general in 1833 – an ironic reversal of the regional manifesto of the 1831 Colonial Congress. Nevertheless, the Barbadian legislature was slow in passing the Emancipation Bill, which was only finally enacted in April 1834, and it was not until August 1835 that Barbadian proprietors qualified for their share of the compensation by amending the local act to the satisfaction of the Colonial Office. When emancipation did occur, it did not produce a 'free' society, but one characterised by new forms of dominance in the context of pre-emancipation patterns of wealth, property and institutional control. The apprenticeship system that replaced slavery, supposedly to allow 'master' and 'slave' to adjust to the new situation, continued to tie workers to the estates. Moreover, new systems of public education, focussing on 'obedience to teacher, parent, minister; respectfulness to one's betters; industriousness, neatness, cleanliness' were instigated and seen by whites as 'invaluable for inculcating the ex-slaves with moral attitudes which in turn encouraged the acceptance of the existing social and economic system'.[133]

From the political lobbying and cultural expressions of the early 1830s it is apparent that the white slaveholders' view of the 'world' that emancipation threatened was framed by discourses of white supremacism and the planter ideal. The 'world the slaveholders made' consisted of a prosperous plantation system and a framework of white domination and black subjugation. Through these, the proper reproduction of the white race, capital and authority could occur. With the ending of slavery seemingly inevitable, white imaginings of freedom as desolation and idleness, peril and defilement, suggested that emancipation had the *potential* to bring about the 'end of the world'. Such apocalyptic imaginings of freedom echoed, and were predicated upon, earlier discourses of white identity. These framed, and gave weight to, the portentous status of the 'Great Hurricane' and the (alleged) rape of Mary Higginbotham.

Such articulations also informed the efforts that were made to prevent the 'end of the world'. For example, to avoid the negative economic realisation of freedom, discourses of loyalty and the planter ideal were mobilised to maximise compensation. This defence of the prosperity of the plantation system was a struggle over the slave world/free world division and, in seeking to establish that Barbados was not an aberrant space, its planters and agents emphasised the differences between the island and the 'new' West Indian colonies. Although they failed to win a *per capita* allocation of the indemnity, the nearly £4 million in compensation that Barbados did receive – 90 per cent of which remained in the hands of the island's proprietors – served to shore up the plantation system by improving proprietors' liquidity, allowing debts to be settled and enabling access to fresh metropolitan

---

[133] O. M. Blouet, 'Education and emancipation in Barbados, 1833–1846: A study of cultural transference', *Ethnic and Racial Studies* 4 (1981), 223, 228–229. For more on post-emancipation forms of education, see C. Campbell, 'Towards an imperial policy for the education of negroes in the West Indies after emancipation', *Jamaican Historical Review* 7 (1967); T. G. Marshall, 'Post-emancipation adjustments in Barbados, 1838 to 1876', in Thompson, *Emancipation I.*

credit. Unlike most of the West Indian colonies, compensation served to maintain, or even raise, the value of Barbadian estates in the late 1830s.[134] With whites able to retain control of viable plantations, the newly emancipated workers were unable to purchase even small freeholds for many years. Few free villages were founded until the 1850s – in contrast with Jamaica – and most black people lived as tenants on the estates.[135]

White supremacism, on which fears of 'black peril' were predicated, fuelled the determination of the plantocracy to perpetuate a submissive and disciplined labour force after emancipation:

By combining franchise restrictions, legislative fraud, collusion and the fear of the masses, the planter class strove to keep the newly freed subservient. Where the plantation survived, the state's fear of revolt and the plantocracy's [fear of] confusion and labor disorganization were codified in the new canons of law and order.[136]

Even when the apprenticeship system was brought to a premature end on 1 August 1838, the position of Barbados's formerly enslaved population was the 'bleakest of all'.[137] The linchpin of plantocratic dominance was the Masters and Servants Act of 1840, which tied agricultural labourers to the plantations. Moreover, the constitution of the 'THE PEOPLE' in early 1833 was part of the re-articulation of the white colonial identity, which foreshadowed the more overt white supremacism of the post-slavery period. This was evident in the expansion of the list of capital offences and the criminalisation of acts that had previously been ignored, which contributed to a steady rise in the conviction of black people. There is also evidence that the paternalism manifested in the planter ideal was abandoned. For example, proprietors refused to supply customary allowances of food to the 14,000 freed children in the apprenticeship period.[138] In such post-slavery developments, whites translated their pre-emancipation determination to dominate into new forms of black subjugation.

White supremacist discourses and practices came to the fore in Barbados in the 1830s, particularly in terms of how interracial relations were conceived. Whilst loyalty and the planter ideal were deployed in the effort to maximise compensation, this was mainly directed at the imperial government. Similarly, the paternalistic response to the James case represented by *The fair Barbadian and faithful black* was a form of white *self*-assurance, not black inculcation, and it is significant that Orderson's next piece of paternalistic escapism in the 1840s was a nostalgic novel

---

[134] Butler, *Economics of emancipation*, pp. 74–91.

[135] J. Besson, 'Freedom and community: The British West Indies', in McGlynn and Drescher, *The meaning of freedom*.

[136] Drescher and McGlynn, 'Introduction', p. 19; Holt, *Problem of freedom*.

[137] M. Craton, 'Continuity not change: The incidence of unrest among ex-slaves in the British West Indies, 1838–1876', in H. McD. Beckles and V. Shepherd (eds.), *Caribbean freedom: Society and economy from emancipation to the present* (London: James Currey, 1993), p. 199.

[138] Green, *British slave emancipation*; C. Levy, *Emancipation, sugar and federalism: Barbados and the West Indies, 1833–1876* (Gainesville: University of Florida, 1980), p. 49.

set in the late eighteenth century, *not* the highly politicised contemporary context of the post-apprenticeship period.[139] Yet, post-slavery Barbados was not simply the site for new forms of white supremacist dominance. Despite the apparent 'success' of the Barbadian plantocracy in defending their 'world', the newly freed population continued to strive to improve its living standards:

While the former masters sought new forms of coercion, the former slaves sought new forms of freedom. The change in legal status changed the terms of, but did not abolish, their struggle.[140]

The fight for freedom would continue.

[139] Gilmore, *'Creoleana'*, p. 10; J. W. Orderson, *Creoleana: or, social and domestic scenes and incidents in Barbados in days of yore* (London, 2002).
[140] O. N. Bolland, 'Systems of domination after slavery: The control of land and labour in the British West Indies after 1838', in Beckles and Shepherd, *Caribbean freedom*, pp. 107–108.

Epilogue

Theodore Easel was an English traveller who spent a few weeks in Barbados shortly after the end of apprenticeship in 1838. In his *Desultory sketches and tales of Barbados* (1840), he recorded an incident that occurred whilst out walking with two white Barbadian planter friends:

A field negro without shoes or stockings, and in his ordinary working dress, was going along with a basket of yams on his head. "You gentleman with the yams!" bawled a slip-shod dirty cook wench from a street-door, "are yer yams for sale?"

"Yes, my lady," replied the vender [sic] of vegetables.

Seagrave and myself burst into an immoderate and uncontrollable fit of laughter, while X's face actually glowed with passion; which was by no means appeased, when the cook wench, divining the cause of our mirth, sung out with the most contemptuous emphasis: – 'Kigh, what them *white people* laugh at – we no ladies and gentlemen, eh?'[1]

Throughout his travel account, Easel sought to assert that emancipation had not produced the sort of 'free' society in Barbados that many in Britain had hoped.[2] He used this particular episode to argue that the pedagogical instruments directed towards free black people after the end of slavery, primarily through religious instruction, had not inculcated a proper sense of their supposedly 'natural' inferiority:

[T]he over-estimate of himself, which self-importance is apt to engender in his present comparatively unenlightened condition, is attended with many evils . . . it causes him to be indifferent to the part of his duty toward his neighbour as taught by the catechism, 'to order himself lowly and reverently to his betters'.[3]

---

[1] T. Easel, *Desultory sketches and tales of Barbados* (London, 1840), p. 255.
[2] See also C. Hall, *Civilising subjects: Metropole and colony in the English imagination, 1830–1867* (Oxford: Polity, 2002); A. Lester, *Imperial networks: Creating identities in nineteenth-century South Africa and Britain* (London: Routledge, 2001), pp. 139–142.
[3] Easel, *Desultory sketches*, p. 256.

The contrast that Easel attempted to draw between the two black people's opinion of themselves, as manifested in their mutual terms of address, and their appearance, which was supposedly indicative of their 'naturally' degraded status, was intended to portray the pair as ludicrous. Yet, the black cook's response contested this by challenging the white men's objectivisation and debasement of her and the vendor, and reversing their surveying gaze ('what them *white people* laugh at . . .?'), which consequently enraged X.

This incident encapsulates central themes in this book. The black cook's saucy question and the passion of X's angry reaction – so much so that his complexion changed from white to red – can be seen to stand for the intense relationship between the articulation of white identities and the exercise of (dis)possessive power over black bodies, *and* the role of non-white and non-elites in interfering with this relationship. In this incident, Easel was sympathetic to the white West Indians, joining in with Seagrave's laughter at supposed black conceit but, through much of the age of abolition, metropolitan disquiet and antipathy had been a common response to white creole cultures. Indeed, this book has addressed an encounter between the white metropole and its white creole self/other in a West Indian colony, the institutions, practices and ideologies of which were increasingly seen as a 'problem' ('of slavery'). Prior to the abolition of the Atlantic trade in enslaved people in 1807, Barbados's planters were relatively unconcerned about the controversy over slavery and the emergent 'anti-Caribbean animus' in the metropole,[4] although there were debates about the colony's socio-racial order. With the shift, from the mid-1810s, in the focus of antislavery campaigning to the internal state of Barbados, however, the possibility of imperial intervention brought to the fore questions about Barbados's relationship with Britain. These two dimensions to the slavery controversy came together in the 1830s as Barbadian planters sought to maintain white dominance as emancipation approached.

For some five decades during the age of abolition, white creole culture, politics and identity had been articulated through four main sets of discourses and practices in Barbados: white supremacism, the planter ideal, colonial loyalty and colonial opposition. The first pair of discourses related to the relationship between enslaver and enslaved. *White supremacism* had developed with the entrenchment of plantation slavery in Barbados and was predicated upon the assertion of absolute racial otherness between a white, free, Christian 'master subject' and subhuman 'other' of African origin, which included both enslaved people and the free people of colour. The dominant attitude towards the 'other' combined terror, hatred and loathing, as expressed in the dread of interracial sex, sexual violence and 'black peril', the brutal counter-insurgency after the 1816 revolt, the public reaction to the Robert James case and the new measures of social control introduced at emancipation. Although such attitudes were particularly articulated by non-elite whites,

---

[4] G. K. Lewis, *Main currents in Caribbean thought: The historical evolution of Caribbean society in its ideological aspects, 1492–1900* (Baltimore: Johns Hopkins University Press, 1983), p. 25.

such as plantation overseers, militiamen and middling commentators like John Poyer, the planters also rationalised slavery in these terms. In contrast, the *planter ideal* was a less overtly racialised discourse that was evident by the late eighteenth century. Racial difference was articulated as white duty and responsibility, and not cast in antagonistic terms. The planter was represented as a paternalistic father figure, tied to 'his' enslaved workforce by bonds of mutual dependency. Enslaved people were undoubtedly inferior but, with good treatment and care, their loyalty could be guaranteed. The extent to which Barbadian planters *were* paternalistic is not at issue. Rather, the ameliorative sentiments of plantation management literature, the exteriorisation of blame on to the 'insurgent' after the revolt and the arguments for 'fair' compensation in the 1830s indicate that one of the ways in which Barbadian planters understood their world was through the idea and ideal of the 'good master'. Pastoralism was a dominant trope within this discourse, serving to naturalise slavery within the colonial landscape.

The second pair of discourses was connected to Barbados's relationship with Britain. *Colonial loyalty* was based on an assertion of identity that evoked the political, social and cultural sameness of metropole and colony. Through the geographical imaginary of Little England, Barbados was represented as Britain's oldest and most loyal colony, and one that deserved protection and special treatment. The dominant theme within this discourse was the evocation of strong familial symbolism, as well as a more equal assertion of a shared trans-Atlantic identity. It is no coincidence that such rhetoric was deployed during the slavery controversy when white Barbadian identity was under assault from antislavery campaigners. It was part of the attempt to challenge humanitarian claims that Barbados was an aberrant slave world or that its slaveholders were 'un-English'. Barbadian loyalty was manifest in calls for 'just' compensation and worries about metropolitan abandonment, as well as in the evocation of Barbados's contribution to British imperial military success. It was also evident in the strident response to various attacks on the Englishness of white Barbadian identity: in opposition to Joshua Steele's 'improvement', in anti-registration texts that sought to blame the antislavery campaign for the 1816 revolt and in John Mayers's concern with the colony's image. In contrast, *colonial opposition* reflected a more hostile reaction to the increasing influence of abolitionism on metropolitan policy. It was often expressed through allusion to the American Revolution or in terms of the inviolable rights of the Assembly. White Barbadians represented themselves as oppressed colonists who suffered from the interference of an imperial government that was spatially distant and, to some extent, culturally different. In this way, it could take on an embryonic nationalist form. Colonial opposition was evident in the legislative obstacles placed before amelioration in the 1820s, in the violence of anti-Methodism and in the hopes for the West India Congress of 1831. Whilst this was a reaction to antislavery renderings of Barbados as a slave world, its articulation often merely served to *confirm* metropolitan perceptions about Barbados's ungovernable, reactionary and aberrant status, such as in the 1825 parliamentary censure of Barbados's colonists. This resulted in attempts to re-articulate the white colonial identity in terms of the discourse of loyal Little England.

These four discourses should be seen as ideal types, not discrete systems of signification. In reality, they were overlapping and vacillating. For example, the (dis)possessive acts and representations of enslavement, through which the white creole identities were constituted, were characterised by both paternalistic and supremacist elements.[5] In this way, enslaved people were both objects to possess and subjects who *needed* to be dispossessed. Similarly, the dominant form of white Barbadian self-identity combined a sense of English sameness and West Indian difference, with resistance to imperial 'tyranny' represented as indicative of a strong commitment to English liberty on the part of the colonists – as loyal opposition. For this reason, the discursive difficulties of separating 'English identity' from 'English values' – and therefore the ambivalence of 'Anglo-Saxon and anti-English'[6] – must be recognised. The mythology of the 'Usurpation' was used in an attempt to manage this uneasy combination of colonial loyalty and opposition by positing resistance to the imperial authorities as a marker of Englishness. As well as overlapping 'horizontally' (white supremacism/planter ideal; colonial loyalty/colonial opposition), these discourses also combined 'vertically' (white supremacism/colonial opposition; planter ideal/colonial loyalty) in terms of general white Barbadian responses to the slavery controversy. For example, white supremacism and colonial opposition came together in fears about the impact of antislavery campaigning on the enslaved population. These were articulated in a hard-line defence of local white interests, the refusal to compromise on reform and an emphasis on protecting the racial order. The political agenda of the Salmagundis encapsulated this. Such a response to antislavery produced some ironic rhetorical forms, as when slavery was used as a metaphor for the tyranny of the imperial authorities, whilst arguments were also made for the maintenances of black (dis)possession at home. On the other hand, a more accommodationist approach combined the planter ideal and colonial loyalty to defend the institution of slavery through better treatment of enslaved people, forging alliances with non-white slaveholders and concessions to the imperial government to stave off more radical reform. This accommodationism tended to find expression in the Council, and amongst the Pumpkins and absentees.

These four discourses do not represent the only articulations of white creole culture, politics and identity apparent in Barbados during the age of abolition. For example, the planter description of poor whites as 'redlegs' was linked to the practices of abandonment and debasement of this marginalised white group.

---

[5] This relates to Homi Bhabha's idea of 'ambivalence' within colonial discourse, which stems largely from tensions between its othering and universalising tendencies. See H. K. Bhabha, 'The other question', *The location of culture* (London: Routledge, 1994). See also D. Spurr, *The rhetoric of empire: Colonial discourse in journalism, travel writing, and imperial administration* (London: Duke University Press, 1993), p. 7.

[6] G. K. Lewis, *Main currents*, p. 75.

The 'redleg' discourse was a manifestation of an elite white supremacism that denied whiteness to subaltern whites. Such elite representations were linked to the four main discourses. For instance, the representation of the anti-Methodists as a 'rabble', which was very similar to the 'redleg' discourse, was part of an elite white attempt to reassert their colonial loyalty. The articulation of white colonial identities was also contested. The fragmentary evidence available from the 1816 rebellion shows that enslaved people's resistance and signifying practices served to challenge the planter ideal and the discourse of colonial loyalty. By mocking and provoking white supremacist practices, and playing on tensions between colony and metropole, the rebels forced Barbados's whites into more extreme reactions to antislavery. The electoral success of the Salmagundis from 1819 suggests that they were somewhat successful in this and, thus, the conflict between the British authorities and the Assembly in the 1820s might be related, in part, to rebel resistance. Elite free people of colour also engaged in the constitution of white Barbadian identity by supporting the planter ideal and challenging the white supremacism of Poyer and others. By the 1830s, non-elite free people of colour sought to contest white colonial loyalty and provoke Barbadian colonial opposition by proclaiming themselves to be the section of Barbadian society with the strongest allegiance to the imperial authorities. Their support for President Skeete, when most whites were attacking him, was an example of this. Such a political agenda would become increasingly important in the period just after emancipation.

The scornful amusement and fury expressed by Seagrave and X towards formerly enslaved Afro-Barbadians with supposedly too high an opinion of themselves was an expression of centuries of the white physical, psychic and sexual (dis)possession of black people in a plantation society. Yet this relationship between white practices, white identities and white power in the West Indies had become a 'problem' during the age of abolition. Theodore Easel might have joined in with the laughter of the locals but, between the late eighteenth and early nineteenth centuries, many Britons saw the claims and actions of white creoles as something to be spurned. Moreover, as the cook's disrespectful rejoinder shows, it was not just metropolitan whites who contested the articulation of white creole culture, politics and identity. By refusing to order themselves 'lowly' and questioning the whites' status as 'betters' in their practices and imaginations, people of African descent creolised the identities and spaces of the Caribbean.

Bibliography

Main archives and libraries consulted (with abbreviations)

Barbados Department of Archives, Black Rock, Barbados (BDA).
Barbados Museum and Historical Society Library, St. Ann's Garrison, Barbados.
Bridgetown Public Library, Barbados (BPL).
British Library, London, UK.
Duke University, Durham, NC, USA.
Foreign and Commonwealth Office Library, London, UK.
Institute of Commonwealth Studies Library, Russell Square, London, UK (ICS).
Lambeth Palace Library, London, UK.
Methodist Missionary Society Archives, 28 March 1820–25 March 1826, Special Reading
    Collection, School of Oriental and African Studies Library, London, UK.
The National Archives (formerly the Public Record Office), Kew, UK (TNA).
National Archives of Scotland (formerly Scottish Record Office), Edinburgh, UK (NAS).
New York Public Library, New York City NY, USA (NYPL).
Royal Commonwealth Society Library, Cambridge, UK.
Royal Society of Arts Library, 8 John Adams Street, London, UK (RSA).
Senate House Library, University of London, UK.
University Library, Cambridge, UK.
University of the West Indies Library, Cave Hill Campus, Barbados.

Primary sources

Note: Where possible, folio references have been given for Colonial Office references.
When a number is followed by the letter 'a', it indicates the right-hand side sheet bearing
that folio number. The letter 'b' signifies the *following* page (the left-hand side sheet on the
reverse).

Alleyne, J. F., Letters, 10 September 1801–1 February 1802, Alleyne Letters, West India
    Committee Collection, ICS.
Alleyne, R., Letters to H. Fitzherbert, 4 December 1823–31 August 1831, Fitzherbert Col-
    lection, reproduced in microfilms, BDA.

Anonymous, *Brief observations on the West India question in the Quarterly Review for April 1831; with remarks on the continuation of the slave trade; by a West India proprietor* (London, 1831).

Anonymous, *Instructions for the management of a plantation in Barbados. And for the treatment of Negroes, etc. etc. etc.* (London, 1786).

Anonymous, *A narrative of facts relative to the tryal of Joe Denny, a free coloured man for the murder of John Stroud, a white-man* (Barbados, 1797).

Anonymous, *Remarks on the insurrection in Barbados, and the bill for the registration of slaves* (London, 1816).

Anonymous, *Sketches and recollections of the West Indies by a resident* (London: Smith, Elder, and Co., 1828).

Anonymous, *Some remarks in reference to recent proceedings of the legislature of Barbadoes, etc. etc. etc.* (London, 1826).

Anonymous, 'Spirit of West Indian society – outrage at Barbadoes', *Edinburgh Review*, August 1825, 479–499.

The Barbadian, 1830–4, reproduced in University of Florida microfilms, BPL.

Barbados Advocate, 2 August 2000.

Barbados Council, Minutes, 1781–1801, 1803–1827, Lucas Manuscripts, Volumes 30–35, reproduced in UNESCO microfilms, BPL.

   Report of a debate in Council on a despatch from Lord Bathurst to His Excellency Sir Henry Warde, Governor of Barbados (Bridgetown, 1823).

Barbados Gazette or General Intelligencer, 1787–1789, reproduced in UNESCO microfilms, BPL.

Barbados House of Assembly, Minutes, 1781–1815, reproduced in University (College) of the West Indies microfilms, BDA.

   Minutes, 1816–1818, reproduced in University (College) of the West Indies microfilms, BPL.

   The report from a select committee of the House of Assembly, appointed to inquire into the origin, causes, and progresses, of the late insurrection (Barbados, 1818).

Barbados Mercury, 1783–1789, reproduced in UNESCO microfilms, BPL [became the *Barbados Mercury and Bridgetown Gazette* from 1 January 1805].

Barbados Mercury and Bridgetown Gazette, 1805–1825, reproduced in UNESCO microfilms, BPL.

Barrow, J., *A declaration of inhabitants of Barbados, respecting the demolition of the Methodists Chapel. With an appendix* (Barbados, 1826).

Bayley, F., *Four years' residence in the West Indies, during the years 1826, 7, 8 and 9* (London: William Kidd, 1830).

Best, J. R., Letters to A. Dottin, 27 April and 28 September 1816, Barbados Manuscripts, NYPL [bound in the library's copy of J. Poyer, *The history of Barbados*].

Brathwaite, J., 'Evidence to the Lords of the Privy Council, 21 February 1788', reproduced in *Journal of the Barbados Museum and Historical Society* 18 (1950–1), 24–38.

Canning, G., 'The speech of the Rt. Hon. George Canning, in the House of Commons, on the 16th day of March, 1824, on laying before the House the Papers in explanation of the measures adopted by His Majesty's Government, for the amelioration of the condition of the Slave Population in His Majesty's Dominions in the West Indies', in Lee, *Slavery, abolition and emancipation*, vol. III, pp. 219–262.

Carrington, G., Correspondence with Committee of Correspondence of House of Assembly, 18 October 1823–10 April 1826, Agents' Letter Books, reproduced in microfilms, BDA.

Chapman, M. J., *Barbadoes, and other poems* (London, 1833).

Clarke, F., 'Plan of treatment of the negroes on the estates in Barbados, 1823', reproduced in *Journal of the Barbados Museum and Historical Society* 2 (1934–5), 29–31.

Clarkson, T., 'Encomium' on Joshua Steele, c. 1815, Additional Manuscripts, 41267A, British Library.

   Thoughts on the necessity of improving the condition of the slaves in the British colonies, with a view to their ultimate emancipation (London: Richard Taylor, 1823).

Coleridge, H. N., *Six months in the West Indies in 1825* (London, 1826).

Colonial Office, Acts: Barbados, 1782–1834, CO 30/16–CO 30/21, TNA.

   Entry Books: Barbados, 1782–15 August 1836, CO 29/20–CO 29/33, TNA.

   Original Correspondence: Barbados, 1780–1833, CO 28/58–CO 28/112, TNA.

   Sessional Papers: Barbados, 1779–1834, CO 31/39–CO 31/51, TNA.

Colthurst, J. B., 'Journal as a special magistrate in the islands of Barbados and St. Vincent, July 1835–August 1838', no date.

Committee of West India Merchants and Planters, Minutes, 1778, West India Committee Collection, ICS.

Cracknell, E. M. W. (ed.), *The Barbadian diary of Gen. Robert Haynes, 1787–1836* (Medstead, Hampshire, 1934).

Daily Nation, 5–15 April 2001.

Davy, J., *The West Indies, before and since slave emancipation* (London, 1854).

Dickson, W., *Letters on slavery, to which are added addresses to the whites and to the free negroes of Barbados; and accounts of some negroes eminent for their virtues and abilities* (London, 1789).

   Mitigation of slavery in two parts. Part 1: letters and papers of the late Hon. Joshua Steele . . . Part 2: letters to Thomas Clarkson (London, 1814).

Easel, T., *Desultory sketches and tales of Barbados* (London, 1840).

Edwards, B., *History, civil and commercial, of the British colonies in the West Indies* (London, 1793).

Fitzherbert, W., Letters to, 9 June 1788–14 July 1788, Fitzherbert Collection, reproduced in microfilms, BDA.

[Flannigan, Mrs.], *Antigua and the Antiguan: A full account of the colony and its inhabitants*, vol. II (London, 1844).

Francklyn, G., *Observations, occasioned by the attempts made in England to effect the abolition of the slave trade; shewing, the manner in which Negroes are treated in the British colonies in the West Indies* (Kingston, 1789 reprint).

Gibbes, P., *Instructions for the treatment of Negroes, etc. etc. etc.* (London, 1786, 1797 reprint).

Gibbes, S. P., *Letter to John Beckles, Esq., Attorney General at Barbados, and correspondence between them on the subject of the conveyance of the Kendal plantation being unfairly obtained* (London, 1802).

The Globe, 1833, CO 28/111, TNA.

Hampden, R. J., 'A commentary on Mr. Clarkson's pamphlet, entitled "Thoughts on the necessity of improving the condition of the slaves in the British colonies, with a view to their ultimate emancipation"', in Lee, *Slavery, abolition and emancipation*, vol. III, pp. 147–215.

Hay, S. A. L., *Memoirs of the late Lieutenant General Sir James Leith, GCB, with a precis of some of the most remarkable events of the peninsular war, by a British officer* (Bridgetown, 1817).

Haynes, R., Letters to T. Lane, 16 September 1806–23 September 1816, Newton Manuscripts, Senate House Library.

Holder, H. E., *Fragments of a poem, intended to have been written in consequence of reading Major Majoribank's slavery* (Bath, 1792).

  A short essay on the subject of Negro slavery, with particular reference to the island of Barbados (London, 1788).

House of Commons, *Hansard Parliamentary Debates*, 19 June 1816, 1st Series, vol. XXXIV, 1151–1168.

  Hansard Parliamentary Debates, 15 May 1823, 2nd Series, vol. IX, 255–360.

  Hansard Parliamentary Debates, 1 June 1824, 2nd Series, vol. XI, 961–1076.

  Parliamentary Debates, 23 June 1825, 2nd Series, vol. XIII, 1285–1347.

Hughes, G., *The natural history of Barbados* (London, 1750).

Hyde, S., *Account of the fatal hurricane, by which Barbados suffered in August 1831* (Bridgetown, 1831).

Jeffery, R. W. (ed.), *Dyott's diary, 1781–1845, a selection from the journal of William Dyott, sometime general in the British Army and Aide-de-Camp to his Majesty King George III*, vol. I (London: Archibald Constable and Co., 1907).

Jordan, G. W., *An examination of the principles of the Slave Registry Bill, and of the means of emancipation, proposed by the authors of the Bill* (London: T. Cadell & W. Davies, 1816).

  Papers on subjects relating to the British colonies in the West Indies, by the late G. W. Jordan, Esq., . . . colonial agent for Barbados (London, c. 1820).

Kelly, J., *Jamaica in 1831: Being a narrative of seventeen years' residence in that island* (Belfast, 1838).

Long, E., *The history of Jamaica* (London: T. Lowndes, 1774).

Lords of the Committee of Council Appointed for the Consideration of All Matters Relating to Trade and Foreign Plantations, Report . . . presented by Hon. William Pitt, 25 April 1789, Part 3, Barbados [facsimile], reproduced in S. Lambert (ed.), *House of Commons Sessional Papers of the Eighteenth Century*, vol. LXIX (Wilmington, 1975), pp. 286–318.

Lucas Manuscripts, Miscellaneous items, Vols. 1, 2, 5, 6, 8, 9, reproduced in UNESCO microfilms, BPL.

M'Callum, P., *Travels in Trinidad during the months of February, March and April 1803* (Liverpool, 1805).

M'Queen, J., *The West India colonies: The calumnies and misrepresentations circulated against them by the Edinburgh Review, Mr. Clarkson, Mr. Crupper, etc. etc.* (London: Baldwin, Cradock and Joy, 1824).

Marryat, J., *More thoughts still on the state of the West India colonies, and the proceedings of the African institution* (London, 1818).

Mayers, J. P., Correspondence with Committee of Correspondence of House of Assembly, 16 September 1829–5 August 1834, Agents' Letter Books, reproduced in microfilms, BDA.

McKinnen, D., *A tour through the British West Indies, in the years 1802 and 1803* (London: J. White, 1804).

Methodist Missionary Society, *An authentic report of the debate in the House of Commons, June the 23rd, 1825, on Mr. Buxton's motion relative to the demolition of the Methodist chapel and mission house in Barbadoes, and the expulsion of Mr. Shrewsbury, a Wesleyan missionary, from that Island* (London: J. Hatchard and Son, 1825).

The late insurrection in Demerara, and riot in Barbados (London, 1823).

Riot in Barbadoes, and destruction of the Wesleyan chapel and mission house (London, c. 1824).

Nation, 4 August 2000.

Nicholls, R. R. B., *A letter to the treasurer of the society instituted for the purpose of effecting the abolition of the slave trade* (London, 1787).

Orderson, J. W., *Creoleana: or, social and domestic scenes and incidents in Barbados in days of yore* (London, 2002).

Cursory remarks and plain facts connected with the question produced by the proposed Slave Registry Bill. By J. W. Orderson, late of Barbadoes (London, 1816).

Directions to young planters for their care and management of a sugar plantation in Barbadoes (London, 1800).

The fair Barbadian and faithful black; or, a cure for the gout. A comedy in three acts (Liverpool, 1835).

Peirce, W., *The ecclesiastical principles and polity of the Wesleyan Methodists*, 3rd edn (London: Wesleyan Conference Office, 1873).

Philo-Xylon [J. Steele], *Letters of Philo-Xylon, first published in the Barbados Gazettes, during the years 1787 and 1788. Containing the substance of several conversations, at sundry times, for seven years past, on the subject of Negro laws and Negro government on plantations in Barbados* (London, 1789).

Pinckard, G., *Notes on the West Indies: Written during the expedition under the command of the late General Sir Ralph Abercromby; including observations on the island of Barbadoes, and the settlements captured by the British troops upon the coast of Guiana*, 3 vols. (London, 1806).

Poyer, J., *The history of Barbados from the first discovery of the island, 1605, till the accession of Lord Seaforth, 1801* (London: J. Mawman, 1808).

History of the administration of the Rt. Hon. Lord Seaforth late governor etc. etc. etc. (Bridgetown, 1808), reproduced in H. Vaughan, 'Poyer's last work', *Journal of the Barbados Museum and Historical Society* 21 (1954), 155–174.

Letter to Lord Seaforth, reproduced in *Journal of the Barbados Museum and Historical Society* 8 (1941), 150–165.

Ramsay, R. J., *An essay on the treatment and conversion of African slaves in the British sugar colonies* (London, 1784).

Rolph, T., *A brief account, together with observations, made during a visit in the West Indies, and a tour through the United States of America, in parts of the years 1832–3* (Dundas, 1835).

Schomburgk, R., *The history of Barbados* (London, 1848).

Seaforth, Letters and miscellaneous items, Seaforth Muniments, 27 June 1801–1809, NAS.

Sealy, H., Letter, 26 February 1824, printed in *Gentleman's Magazine* 94 (1824), 420–421.

Senhouse, J., Memoirs, 1779, Senhouse Papers, BDA.

Sharp, G., *A representation of the injustice and dangerous tendency of tolerating slavery* (London, 1769).

A short sketch of temporary regulations (until better shall be proposed) for the intended settlement on the Grain Coast of Africa, near Sierra Leona, 3rd edn (London: Printed by H. Baldwin, 1788).

Shrewsbury, J. V. B., *Memorials of the Rev. William J. Shrewsbury* (London, 1868).

Shrewsbury, W. J., *Sermons preached on several occasions in the island of Barbados* (London, 1825).

Simmons, H. P., *A letter to the Right Hon. Earl Grey, First Lord of the Treasury, etc. on the question of negro emancipation* (London, 1834).

A letter to the Right Hon. Earl Grey, on the West India question (Liverpool, 1833).

A letter to the Right Honourable Earl Grey, First Lord of the Treasury, etc. on the subject of West Indian property (London, 1832).

Society for the Encouragement of Arts, Manufactures and Commerce in Barbados, *Institution and first proceedings*, 5 July 1781–30 August 1784 (Barbados, 1784).

Society for the Mitigation and Gradual Abolition of Slavery, *The slave colonies of Great Britain; or a picture of Negro slavery drawn by the colonists themselves; being an abstract of the various papers recently laid before Parliament on that subject* (London, 1825).

Steele, J., 'Account of a musical instrument, which was brought by Captain Fourneaux from the Isle of Amsterdam in the South Seas to London in the year 1774, and given to the Royal Society', *Philosophical Transactions* 65 (1775), 67–71.

An Essay towards establishing the melody and measure of speech to be expressed and perpetuated by certain symbols (London, 1775).

Letters to J. Banks, 3 June 1779–27 May 1793, Additional Manuscripts, British Library.

Letters to the London Society for the Encouragement of Arts, Manufactures and Commerce, Letters, 14 July 1781–10 September 1786, RSA.

'Remarks on a larger system of reed pipes from the Isle of Amsterdam, with some observations on the nose flute of Otaheite', *Philosophical Transactions* 65 (1775), 72–78.

To the equity and policy of a great nation (Bridgetown, 1789).

Stephen, J., *Reasons for establishing a registry of slaves in the British colonies* (London: Ellerton & Henderson, 1815).

Sunday Advocate, 26 March–30 April 2001.

Sunday Sun, 6 August 2000.

Waller, J. A., *A Voyage in the West Indies* (London, 1820).

Warde, H., Letters to W. H. Clinton, 1823, Warde Papers, BDA.

Watson, R., *A defence of the Wesleyan Methodist missions in the West Indies* (London, 1817).

Wedd, A. F. (ed.), *The fate of the Fenwicks: Letters to Mary Hays (1796–1828)* (London, 1927).

Wesley, J., *Thoughts on slavery* (London, 1774).

Wilberforce, W., 'An appeal to the religion, justice and humanity of the inhabitants of the British Empire, on behalf of the Negro Slaves in the West Indies', in Lee, *Slavery, abolition and emancipation*, vol. III, pp. 3–79.

Williamson, J. W., *Medical and miscellaneous observations relative to the West India islands* (Edinburgh, 1817).

Yearwood, S., Letters, March 1796–2 August 1810, reproduced in *Journal of Barbados Museum and Historical Society* 16 (1948–9), 113–117.

Secondary sources

Abrahams, R. G. and J. F. Szwed (eds.), *After Africa* (New York: Yale University Press, 1983).

Allan, D. G. C., 'Joshua Steele and the Royal Society of Arts', *Journal of the Barbados Museum and Historical Society* 22 (1954–5), 84–104.

William Shipley, founder of the Royal Society of Arts: A biography with documents (London, 1979).

Allen, C., 'Creole: the problem of definition', in V. A. Shepherd and G. L. Richards (eds.), *Questioning creole: Creolisation discourses in Caribbean culture* (Kingston: Ian Randle, 2002), pp. 47–63.

Allen, J., D. Massey and A. Cochrane, *Rethinking the region* (London, 1998).

Allen, R. B., *Slaves, freedmen, and indentured laborers in colonial Mauritius* (Cambridge: Cambridge University Press, 1999).

Allen, T., *The invention of the white race: Racial oppression and social control*, vol. I (London: Verso, 1994).

The invention of the white race: The origin of racial oppression in Anglo-America, vol. II (London: Verso, 1997).

Altink, H., '"The agonies of a negress on the loss of her children": Representations of Jamaican slave motherhood in the 1780–1838 discourse on child-death', *Women's History Notebook* 6 (1999), 8–15.

Anderson, B., *Imagined communities: Reflections on the origin and spread of nationalism* (London: Verso, 1991).

Anderson, W., *The cultivation of whiteness: Science, health and racial destiny in Australia* (New York: Basic Books, 2003).

Anonymous, 'Some Nelson statues', *Journal of the Barbados Museum and Historical Society Library* 18 (1950–1), 4–17.

Armitage, D., 'Three concepts of Atlantic history', in Armitage and Braddick, *The British Atlantic world*, pp. 11–27.

Armitage, D. and M. J. Braddick (eds.), *The British Atlantic world, 1500–1800* (Basingstoke: Palgrave Macmillan, 2002).

'Introduction', in Armitage and Braddick, *The British Atlantic world*, pp. 1–7.

Arnold, D., *The problem of nature: Environment, culture and European expansion* (Oxford: Blackwell, 1996).

Baker, A. R. H., *Geography and history: Bridging the divide* (Cambridge: Cambridge University Press, 2003).

Ballantyne, T., *Orientalism and race: Aryanism in the British empire* (New York: Palgrave, 2002).

Balutansky, K. and M. Sourieau (eds.), *Caribbean creolization: Reflections on the cultural dynamics of language, literature, and identity* (Gainesville: University Press of Florida, 1998).

Barker, A. J., *Slavery and antislavery in Mauritius, 1810–1833: The conflict between economic expansion and humanitarian reform under British rule* (London: Macmillan, 1996).

Barnes, T. J. and J. S. Duncan (eds.), *Writing worlds: Discourse, text and metaphor in the representation of landscape* (London: Routledge, 1992).

Barnett, C., 'Impure and worldly geography: The Africanist discourse of the Royal Geographical Society', *Transactions of the Institute of British Geographers* 23 (1998), 239–251.

Barton, G. A., *Empire forestry and the origins of environmentalism* (Cambridge: Cambridge University Press, 2002).

Baucom, I., *Out of place: Englishness, empire, and the locations of identity* (Princeton, NJ: Princeton University Press, 1999).

Bayly, C. A., 'The British and indigenous peoples, 1760–1860: Power, perception and identity', in M. Daunton and R. Halpern (eds.), *Empire and others: British encounters with indigenous peoples, 1600–1850* (London: UCL Press, 1999), pp. 19–41.

Beahrs, A., '"Ours alone must need be Christians": The production of enslaved souls on the Codrington estates', *Plantation Society in the Americas* 4 (1997), 279–310.

Beckles, H. McD., *Afro-Caribbean women and resistance* (London: Karnak House, 1988).
'Black over white: The "poor-white" problem in Barbados slave society', *Immigrants and Minorities* 7 (1988), 1–15.
'Black people in the colonial historiography of Barbados', in W. Marshall (ed.), *Emancipation II: A series of lectures to commemorate the 150th anniversary of emancipation* (Bridgetown: Cedar Press, 1987), pp. 131–143.
Black rebellion in Barbados: The struggle against slavery, 1627–1838 (Bridgetown: Antilles Publications, 1984).
Bussa: The 1816 revolution in Barbados (Barbados: Department of History, UWI, and Barbados Museum and Historical Society, 1998).
Centering woman: Gender discourses in Caribbean slave society (Oxford: James Currey, 1999).
'Creolisation in action: The slave labour elite and anti-slavery in Barbados', *Caribbean Quarterly* 44 (1998), 108–128.
A history of Barbados: From Amerindian settlement to nation-state (Cambridge: Cambridge University Press, 1990).
'The "hub of empire": The Caribbean and Britain in the seventeenth century', in N. Canny (ed.), *The Oxford history of the British Empire*, vol. I, *The origins of empire* (Oxford: Oxford University Press, 1998), pp. 218–240.
'Inside Bussa's rebellion: Letters of Colonel John Rycroft Best', *Journal of the Barbados Museum and Historical Society* 37 (1984), 101–111.
Natural rebels: A social history of enslaved black women in Barbados (New Brunswick, NJ: Rutgers University Press, 1989).
'On the backs of blacks: The Barbados free-coloureds' pursuit of civil rights and the 1816 slave rebellion', *Immigrants and Minorities* 3 (1984), 167–188.
'Rebels and reactionaries: The political responses of white labourers to planter class hegemony in the seventeenth-century Barbados', *Journal of Caribbean History* 15 (1981), 1–19.
'Social and political control in slave society', in F. W. Knight, *The slave societies of the Caribbean*, vol. III, pp. 194–221.
'To buy or to breed: The changing nature of labour Supply policy in Barbados during the 18th century', unpublished paper, University of the West Indies (1987).

'White women and slavery in the Caribbean', *History Workshop Journal* 36 (1993), 66–82.

Benítez-Rojo, A., *The repeating island: The Caribbean and the postmodern perspective*, translated by J. Maraniss (London: Duke University Press, 1992).

Bennett, J. H., *Bondsmen and bishops: Slavery and apprenticeship on the Codrington plantations of Barbados, 1710–1838* (Berkeley: University of California Press, 1958).

Besson, J., 'Freedom and community: The British West Indies', in McGlynn and Drescher, *The meaning of freedom*, pp. 183–219.

Bhabha, H. K., *The location of culture* (London: Routledge, 1994).

Blackburn, R., *The overthrow of colonial slavery, 1776–1848* (London: Verso, 1988).

Blackman, F. W., *Methodism: 200 years in Barbados* (Bridgetown: Caribbean Contact, 1988).

National heroine of Barbados: Sarah Ann Gill (Barbados: Methodist Church in Barbados, 1998).

Blomley, N., D. Delaney and R. T. Ford (eds.), *Legal geographies reader: Law, power and space* (Oxford: Blackwell, 2001).

Blouet, O. M., 'Education and emancipation in Barbados, 1833–1846: A study of cultural transference', *Ethnic and Racial Studies* 4 (1981), 222–235.

Blunt, A., 'Embodying war: British women and domestic defilement in the Indian "Mutiny", 1857–8', *Journal of Historical Geography* 26 (2000), 403–428.

Blunt, A. and C. McEwan (eds.), *Postcolonial geographies* (London: Continuum, 2002).

Boehmer, E., *Empire, the national, and the postcolonial, 1890–1920: Resistance in interaction* (Oxford: Oxford University Press, 2002).

Bolland, O. N., 'The politics of freedom in the British Caribbean', in McGlynn and Drescher, *The meaning of freedom*, pp. 113–146.

'Systems of domination after slavery: The control of land and labour in the British West Indies after 1838', in H. McD. Beckles and V. Shepherd (eds.), *Caribbean freedom: Society and economy from emancipation to the present* (London: James Currey, 1993), pp. 107–123.

Bolton, C. C., *Poor whites of the antebellum South: Tenants and labourers in central North Carolina and northeast Mississippi* (London: Duke University Press, 1994).

Bonnett, A., 'Geography, "race" and Whiteness: Invisible traditions and current challenges', *Area* 29 (1997), 193–199.

White identities: Historical and international perspectives (London: Prentice Hall, 2000).

'White studies: The problems and projects of a new research agenda', *Theory, Culture and Society* 13 (1996), 145–155.

'Who was white? The disappearance of non-European white identities and the formation of European racial whiteness', *Ethnic and Racial Studies* 21 (1998), 1029–1055.

Bowen, H. V., 'British conceptions of global empire, 1756–1783', *Journal of Imperial and Commonwealth History* 26 (1998), 1–27.

Braddick, M. J., 'Civility and authority', in Armitage and Braddick, *The British Atlantic world*, pp. 93–112.

'The English government, war, trade, settlement, 1625–1688', in N. Canny (ed.), *The Oxford history of the British Empire*, vol. I, *The origins of empire* (Oxford: Oxford University Press, 1998), pp. 286–308.

Brathwaite, E. K., *Contradictory omens: Cultural diversity and integration in the Caribbean* (Mona: Savacou, 1974).

The development of creole society in Jamaica, 1770–1820 (Oxford: Clarendon Press, 1971).

Roots (Ann Arbor: University of Michigan Press, 1993).

Brathwaite, J. A., *Methodism in the Caribbean* (Bridgetown, 1998).

Brereton, B., 'Text, testimony and gender: An examination of some texts by women on the English-speaking Caribbean from the 1770s to the 1920s', in V. Shepherd, B. Brereton and B. Bailey (eds.), *Engendering history: Caribbean women in historical perspective* (London: James Currey, 1995), pp. 63–93.

Bridge, C. and K. Fedorowich, 'Mapping the British world', in C. Bridge and K. Fedorowich (eds.), *The British world: Diaspora, culture and identity* (London: Frank Cass, 2003), pp. 1–15.

Brown, C. L., 'Empire without slaves: British concepts of emancipation in the age of the American Revolution', *William and Mary Quarterly* 3rd Series 56 (1999), 273–306.

'The politics of slavery', in Armitage and Braddick, *The British Atlantic world*, pp. 214–232.

Brown, L., *West Indian poetry*, 2nd edn (London: Heinemann, 1984).

Buckley, R. N., *Slaves in red coats: The British West India Regiments, 1795–1815* (New Haven: Yale University Press, 1979).

Burnard, T., '"The countrie continues sicklie": White mortality in Jamaica, 1655–1780', *Social History of Medicine* 12 (1999), 45–72.

Bush, B., *Slave women in the Caribbean society, 1650–1838* (London: James Currey, 1990).

Butler, K. M., *The economics of emancipation: Jamaica and Barbados, 1823–1843* (London: University of North Carolina Press, 1995).

Campbell, C., 'Towards an imperial policy for the education of negroes in the West Indies after emancipation', *Jamaican Historical Review* 7 (1967).

'Trinidad's free coloreds in comparative Caribbean perspectives', in H. McD. Beckles and V. Shepherd (eds.), *Caribbean slavery in the Atlantic world* (Kingston: Ian Randle, 2000), pp. 597–612.

Campbell, M. C., *The dynamics of change in a slave society: A sociopolitical history of the free coloureds of Jamaica, 1800–1865* (London: Associated University Press, 1976).

Canny, N. and A. Pagden (eds.), *Colonial identity in the Atlantic world, 1500–1800* (Princeton, NJ: Princeton University Press, 1987).

Carrington, S. H., 'West Indian opposition to British policy: Barbadian politics, 1774–1782', *Journal of Caribbean History* 17 (1982), 26–49.

Cateau, H., 'Conservatism and change implementation in the British West Indian sugar industry, 1750–1810', *Journal of Caribbean History* 29 (1995), 1–36.

'The new "negro" business: Hiring in the British West Indies 1750–1810', in A. O. Thompson (ed.), *In the shadow of the plantation: Caribbean history and legacy* (Kingston: Ian Randle, 2002), pp. 100–120.

Cell, J., 'The imperial conscience', in P. Marsh (ed.), *The conscience of the Victorian state* (Hassocks: Harvester Press, 1979), pp. 173–213.

Chandler, M., *A guide to records in Barbados* (Oxford, 1965).

Chaplin, J. E., 'Race', in Armitage and Braddick, *The British Atlantic world*, pp. 154–172.

Clarke, A., *Growing up stupid under the Union Jack* (Havana: Casa de las Americas, 1980).

Clarke, R. L. W., 'The literary nature of the historical text: Some implications of the post-modernist critique of "realism" for Caribbean historiography', *Journal of Caribbean History* 32 (1998), 46–81.

Clayton, D. W., *Islands of truth: The imperial fashioning of Vancouver Island* (Vancouver: UBC Press, 2000).

Coetzee, J. M., *White writing: On the culture of letters in South Africa* (New Haven: Yale University Press, 1988).

Cohen, D. W. and J. P. Greene, *Neither slave nor free* (London: Johns Hopkins University Press, 1972).

Coleman, D., 'Bulama and Sierra Leone: Utopian islands and visionary interiors', in Edmond and Smith, *Islands in history and representation*, pp. 63–80.

'Janet Schaw and the complexions of empire', *Eighteenth-Century Studies* 36 (2003), 169–193.

Colley, L., *Britons: Forging the nation, 1707–1837* (London: Yale University Press, 1992).

Comaroff, J. and J. Comaroff, *Of revelation and revolution: Christianity, colonialism and consciousness in South Africa*, 2 vols., vol. I (London: University of Chicago Press, 1991).

Comaroff, J. L., 'Images of empire, contests of conscience: Models of colonial domination in South Africa', in Cooper and Stoler, *Tensions of empire*, pp. 163–197.

Cooper, F., T. C. Holt and R. J. Scott, *Beyond slavery: Explorations of race, labor, and citizenship in post-emancipation societies* (London: University of North Carolina Press, 2000).

Cooper, F. and A. L. Stoler (eds.), *Tensions of empire: Colonial cultures in a bourgeois world* (Berkeley: University of California Press, 1997).

Cox, E., *Free coloreds in the slave societies of St. Kitts and Grenada* (Knoxville: University of Tennessee Press, 1984).

Craton, M., 'Continuity not change: The incidence of unrest among ex-slaves in the British West Indies, 1838–1876', in H. McD. Beckles and V. Shepherd (eds.), *Caribbean freedom: Society and economy from emancipation to the present* (London: James Currey, 1993), pp. 192–206.

'Forms of resistance to slavery', in F. W. Knight, *The slave societies of the Caribbean*, vol. III, pp. 222–270.

'The rope and the cutlass: Slave resistance in plantation America', in M. Craton (ed.), *Empire, enslavement and freedom in the Caribbean* (Oxford: James Currey, 1997), pp. 185–202.

Sinews of empire: A short history of British slavery (London: Temple Smith, 1974).

'Slave culture, resistance and emancipation in the British West Indies', in M. Craton (ed.), *Empire, enslavement and freedom in the Caribbean* (Oxford: James Currey, 1997), pp. 263–281.

'Slave culture, resistance and the advancement of emancipation in the British West Indies, 1783–1838', in Walvin, *Slavery and British society, 1776–1846*, pp. 100–122.

Testing the chains: Resistance to slavery in the British West Indies (London: Cornell University Press, 1982).

Curtin, P., *The Atlantic slave trade: A census* (Madison, 1969).

Daniels, S., S. Seymour and C. Watkins, 'Enlightenment, improvement, and the geographies of horticulture in later Georgian England', in Livingstone and Withers, *Geography and enlightenment*, pp. 345–371.

Davis, D. B., *The problem of slavery in the age of revolution, 1770–1823* (London: Cornell University Press, 1975).

The problem of slavery in Western culture (Ithaca: Cornell University Press, 1966).

Slavery and human progress (Oxford: Oxford University Press, 1984).

Davis, K., *Crown and cross in Barbados: Caribbean political religion in the late nineteenth century* (Frankfurt: Peter Lang, 1983).

Dayan, J., *Haiti, history, and the gods* (Berkeley: University of California Press, 1995).

de Groot, S. W., C. A. Christen and F. W. Knight, 'Maroon communities in the circum-Caribbean', in F. W. Knight, *The slave societies of the Caribbean*, vol. III, pp. 169–193.

Dirks, N. B., *Colonialism and culture* (Ann Arbor: University of Michigan Press, 1992).

Drayton, R., *Nature's government: Science, imperial Britain, and the 'improvement' of the world* (London: Yale University Press, 2000).

Drescher, S., 'Public opinion and the destruction of British colonial slavery', in Walvin, *Slavery and British society, 1776–1846*, pp. 22–48.

Drescher, S. and F. McGlynn, 'Introduction', in McGlynn and Drescher, *The meaning of freedom*, pp. 3–23.

Driver, F., *Geography militant: Cultures of exploration and empire* (Oxford: Blackwell, 2000).

'Geography's empire: Histories of geographical knowledge', *Environment and Planning D: Society and Space* 10 (1992), 23–40.

Duncan, J. S., 'Complicity and resistance in the colonial archive: Some issues of method and theory in historical geography', *Historical Geography* 27 (1999), 119–128.

'Embodying colonialism? Domination and resistance in nineteenth-century Ceylonese coffee plantations', *Journal of Historical Geography* 28 (2002), 317–338.

'The struggle to be temperate: climate and "moral masculinity" in mid-nineteenth century Ceylon', *Singapore Journal of Tropical Geography* 21 (2000), 34–47.

Dunn, R. S., *Sugar and slaves: The rise of the planter class in the English West Indies, 1624–1713* (Chapel Hill: University of North Carolina Press, 1973).

Dyer, R., *White* (London: Routledge, 1997).

Edmond, R., 'Abject bodies/abject sites: Leper islands in the high imperial era', in Edmond and Smith, *Islands in history and representation*, pp. 133–145.

Edmond, R. and V. Smith (eds.), *Islands in history and representation* (London: Routledge, 2003).

Elliott, J. H., 'Introduction: Colonial identity in the Atlantic world', in Canny and Pagden, *Colonial identity in the Atlantic world*, pp. 3–13.

Ellis, A., *The history of the First West India Regiment* (London, 1885).

Ellis, M., '"The cane-land isles": Commerce and empire in late eighteenth-century georgic and pastoral poetry', in Edmond and Smith, *Islands in history and representation*, pp. 43–62.

Eltis, D., 'Abolitionist perspectives of society after slavery', in Walvin, *Slavery and British society, 1776–1846*, pp. 195–213.

'New estimates of exports from Barbados and Jamaica, 1665–1701', *William and Mary Quarterly* 3rd Series 52 (1995), 631–648.

Farmer, P., *AIDS and accusation: Haiti and the geography of blame* (Berkeley: University of California Press, 1992).

Fick, C. E., *The making of Haiti: The Saint Domingue revolution from below* (Knoxville: University of Tennessee Press, 1990).

Fine, M., L. Weis, L. Powell and L. Wong (eds.), *Off white: Readings on race, power and society* (London: Routledge, 1997).

Foucault, M., *Discipline and punish: The birth of the prison* (London: Penguin, 1979).

Frankenberg, R., *White women, race matters: The social construction of whiteness* (London: Routledge, 1993).

Frey, S. R. and B. Wood (eds.), *From slavery to emancipation in the Atlantic world* (London: Frank Cass, 1999).

Galloway, J. H., *The sugar cane industry: An historical geography from its origins to 1914* (Cambridge: Cambridge University Press, 1989).

'Tradition and innovation in the American sugar industry, c. 1500–1800: An explanation', *Annals of the Association of American Geographers* 75 (1985), 334–351.

Games, A., 'Migration', in Armitage and Braddick, *The British Atlantic world*, pp. 31–50.

Gascoigne, J., *The Enlightenment and the origins of European Australia* (Cambridge: Cambridge University Press, 2002).

Joseph Banks and the English Enlightenment: Useful knowledge and polite culture (Cambridge: Cambridge University Press, 1994).

Gaspar, D. B. and D. P. Geggus, *A turbulent time: The French Revolution and the Greater Caribbean* (Bloomington and Indianapolis: Indiana University Press, 1997).

Geggus, D., 'British opinion and the emergence of Haiti, 1791–1805', in Walvin, *Slavery and British society, 1776–1846*, pp. 123–149.

'The enigma of Jamaica in the 1790s: New light on the causes of slave rebellions', *William and Mary Quarterly* 3rd Series 44 (1987), 274–299.

Haitian revolutionary studies (Bloomington: Indiana University Press, 2002).

Genovese, E. D., *Roll, Jordan, roll: The world the slaves made* (New York: Pantheon Books, 1972).

The world the slaveholders made: Two essays in interpretation (New York: Random House, 1969).

Gibbons, L., 'Between Captain Rock and a hard place: Art and agrarian insurgency', in T. Foley and S. Ryder (eds.), *Ideology and Ireland in the nineteenth century* (Dublin: Four Courts Press, 1998), pp. 23–44.

Gilmore, J., 'Church and society in Barbados, 1824–1881', in W. Marshall (ed.), *Emancipation II: A series of lectures to commemorate the 150th anniversary of emancipation* (Bridgetown: Cedar Press, 1987), pp. 1–22.

'Creoleana: or, social and domestic scenes and incidents in Barbados in days of yore' and 'The fair Barbadian and faithful black; or, a cure for the gout', by J. W. Orderson: Edited and with a new introduction (Oxford: Macmillan, 2002).

The poetics of empire: A study of James Grainger's The Sugar Cane *(1764)* (London: Athlone Press, 2000).

Gilroy, P., *The black Atlantic: Modernity and double consciousness* (London: Verso, 1993).

Gott, R., 'Little Englanders', in R. Samuel (ed.), *Patriotism: The making and unmaking of British national identity* (London: Routledge, 1989), pp. 90–102.

Gould, E. H., 'Revolution and counter-revolution', in Armitage and Braddick, *The British Atlantic world*, pp. 196–213.

Goveia, E. V., *Slave society in the British Leeward Islands at the end of the eighteenth century* (London: Yale University Press, 1965).

A study of the historiography of the British West Indies to the end of the nineteenth century (Mexico City: Instituto Panamerico de Geografia e Historia, 1956).

Gragg, L., *Englishmen transplanted: The English colonization of Barbados, 1627–1660* (Oxford: Oxford University Press, 2003).

Green, W. A., *British slave emancipation: The sugar colonies and the great experiment, 1830–1865* (Oxford: Clarendon Press, 1976).

Greene, J. P., 'Changing identity in the British Caribbean: Barbados as a case study', in Canny and Pagden, *Colonial identity in the Atlantic world*, pp. 213–266.

'Empire and identity from the Glorious Revolution to the American Revolution', in P. J. Marshall, *The Oxford history of the British Empire*, vol. II, pp. 208–230.

'Liberty, slavery, and the transformation of British identity in the eighteenth-century West Indies', *Slavery and Abolition* 21 (2000), 1–31.

Peripheries and center: Constitutional development in the extended policies of the British Empire and the United States, 1607–1788 (Athens, GA and London: University of Georgia Press, 1986).

Gregory, D., 'Between the book and the lamp: Imaginative geographies of Egypt, 1849–1850', *Transactions of the Institute of British Geographers* 20 (1995), 29–57.

Grove, R. H., *Green imperialism: Colonial expansion, tropical island Edens and the origins of environmentalism, 1600–1860* (Cambridge: Cambridge University Press, 1995).

Guha, R. and G. C. Spivak (eds.), *Selected subaltern studies* (Oxford: Oxford University Press, 1988).

Haggis, J., 'White women and colonialism: Towards a non-recuperative history', in C. Midgley (ed.), *Gender and imperialism* (Manchester: Manchester University Press, 1998), pp. 45–75.

Hall, C., *Civilising subjects: Metropole and colony in the English imagination, 1830–1867* (Oxford: Polity, 2002).

'What is a West Indian?' in B. Schwarz (ed.), *West Indian intellectuals in Britain* (Manchester: Manchester University Press, 2003), pp. 31–50.

White, male and middle class: Explorations in feminism and history (New York: Routledge, 1988).

Hall, D., 'Absentee-proprietorship in the British West Indies, to about 1850', *Jamaican Historical Review* 4 (1964), 15–35.

A brief history of the West India Committee (Bridgetown: Caribbean Universities Press, 1971).

Hall, N., 'Governors and generals: The relationship of civil and military commands in Barbados, 1783–1815', *Caribbean Studies* 10 (1971), 93–112.

'Law and society in Barbados at the turn of the nineteenth century', *Journal of Caribbean History* 5 (1972), 20–45.

Handler, J. S., 'Freedmen and slaves in the Barbados militia', *Journal of Caribbean History* 19 (1984), 1–25.

A guide to source materials for the study of Barbados history, 1627–1834 (Carbondale: Southern Illinois University Press, 1971).

'Memoirs of an old army officer', *Journal of the Barbados Museum and Historical Society* 35 (1975), 21–30.

'Plantation slave settlements in Barbados, 1650s to 1834', in A. O. Thompson (ed.), *In the shadow of the plantation: Caribbean history and legacy. In honour of Professor Emeritus Woodville K. Marshall* (Kingston: Ian Randle, 2002), pp. 121–161.

Supplement to a guide to source materials for the study of Barbados history, 1627–1834 (Providence, RI: John Carter Brown Library and Barbados Museum and Historical Society, 1991).

The unappropriated people: Freedmen in the slave society of Barbados (Baltimore: Johns Hopkins University Press, 1974).

Hanger, K. S., *Bounded lives, bounded places: Free black society in colonial New Orleans, 1769–1803* (Durham, NC: Duke University Press, 1997).

Haraway, D. J., 'Situated knowledges: The science question in feminism and the privilege of partial perspective', in D. J. Haraway (ed.), *Simians, cyborgs and women: The reinvention of nature* (London: Free Association, 1991), pp. 183–201.

Harris, T., 'White men as performers in the lynching ritual', in Roediger, *Black on white*, pp. 299–304.

Hartman, S. V., *Scenes of subjection: Terror, slavery, and self-making in nineteenth-century America* (Oxford: Oxford University Press, 1997).

Haskell, T. L., 'Capitalism and the origins of the humanitarian sensibility, part 1', *American Historical Review* 90 (1985), 339–361.

'Capitalism and the origins of the humanitarian sensibility, part 2', *American Historical Review* 90 (1985), 547–566.

Hempton, D., *Methodism and politics in British society, 1750–1850* (London: Hutchinson, 1984).

Religion and political culture in Britain and Ireland (Cambridge: Cambridge University Press, 1996).

Heuman, G. J., *Between black and white: Race, politics, and the free coloreds in Jamaica, 1792–1865* (Westport, CT: Greenwood Press, 1981).

'The British West Indies', in A. Porter, *The Oxford history of the British Empire*, vol. III, pp. 470–493.

'The social structure of the slave societies in the Caribbean', in F. W. Knight, *The slave societies of the Caribbean*, vol. III, pp. 138–168.

Higman, B. W., 'The Colonial Congress of 1831', in B. Moore and S. Wilmot (eds.), *Before and after 1865: Education, politics and regionalism in the Caribbean* (Kingston: Ian Randle, 1998), pp. 239–248.

Writing West Indian histories (London: Macmillan Education, 1999).

Hill, C., 'The Norman Yoke', in J. Saville (ed.), *Democracy and the labour movement: Essays in honour of Dona Torr* (London: Lawrence & Wishart, 1954), pp. 11–66.

Hilton, B., *The age of atonement: The influence of evangelicalism on social and economic thought, 1785–1865* (Oxford: Clarendon Press, 1988).

Hobsbawm, E. J., *Primitive rebels: Studies in archaic forms of social movement in the nineteenth and twentieth centuries* (New York: Norton, 1965).

Holt, T. C., *The problem of freedom: Race, labor, and politics in Jamaica and Britain, 1832–1938* (London: Johns Hopkins University Press, 1992).

hooks, b., 'Representations of whiteness in the black imagination', in b. hooks (ed.), *Black looks: Race and representation* (Boston: South End Press, 1992), pp. 165–178.

'Travelling theories, travelling theorists', *Inscriptions* 5 (1989), 159–164.

Hoyos, F., 'Dr. M. J. Chapman', *Journal of the Barbados Museum and Historical Society* 16 (1948–9), 14–20.

Hughes, R., 'The origin of Barbadian sugar plantations and the role of the white population in sugar plantation society', in Thompson, *Emancipation I*, pp. 26–32.

Ignatiev, N., *How the Irish became white* (London: Routledge, 1995).

James, C. L. R., *The black Jacobins: Toussaint L'Ouverture and the San Domingo revolution*, revised edn (London: Allison and Busby, 1980).

Jansson, D. R., 'Internal orientalism in America: W. J. Cash's *The Mind of the South* and the spatial construction of American national identity', *Political Geography* 22 (2003), 293–316.

Jennings, J., *The business of abolishing the British slave trade, 1783–1807* (London: Frank Cass, 1997).

Jennings, L. C., *French anti-slavery: The movement for the abolition of slavery in France, 1802–1848* (Cambridge: Cambridge University Press, 2000).

Johnson, A. 'The abolition of chattel slavery in Barbados, 1833–1876', unpublished Ph.D thesis, Cambridge University (1995).

Johnson, H. and K. Watson (eds.), *The white minority in the Caribbean* (Kingston: Ian Randle, 1998).

Jones, C., 'A darker shade of white? Gender, social class, and the reproduction of white identity in Barbadian plantation society', in H. Brown, M. Gilkes and A. Kaloski-Naylor (eds.), *White?women: Critical perspectives on race and gender* (York: Raw Nerve Books, 1999), pp. 159–180.

'Mapping racial boundaries: Gender, race, and poor relief in Barbadian plantation society', *Journal of Women's History* 10 (1998), 9–31.

Jones, R., 'The Bourbon Regiment and the Barbados slave revolt of 1816', *Journal of the Society for Army Historical Research* 78 (2000), 3–10.

Jordan, W., *White over black* (Chapel Hill, 1968).

Kennedy, D., *Islands of white: Settler society and culture in Kenya and Southern Rhodesia, 1890–1939* (Durham, NC: Duke University Press, 1987).

Kitson, P. J. (ed.), *Slavery, abolition and emancipation: Writings in the British Romantic period – the slavery debate*, 8 vols. vol. II (London: Pickering and Chatto, 1999).

Knight, D., *Gentlemen of fortune: The men who made their fortunes in Britain's slave colonies* (London: Frederick Muller, 1978).

Knight, F. W., 'Pluralism, creolization and culture', in F. W. Knight, *The slave societies of the Caribbean*, pp. 271–286.

(ed.), *The slave societies of the Caribbean*, vol. III of *General history of the Caribbean* (London: UNESCO Publishing, 1997).

Kossek, B., 'Representing self/otherness and "white women" slaveowners in the English-speaking Caribbean, 1790–1830', paper presented at the Caribbean Studies Seminar Series, Institute of Commonwealth Studies, London, 13 March 2000.

Lacey, B. E., 'Visual images of blacks in early American prints', *William and Mary Quarterly* 3rd Series 53 (1996), 137–180.

Lambert, D., 'Deadening, voyeuristic and reiterative? Problems of representation in Caribbean research', in S. Courtman (ed.), *Beyond the beach, the blood and the banana: New directions in Caribbean research* (Kingston: Ian Randle, 2004), pp. 3–14.

Lamming, G., *In the castle of my skin* (Harlow: Longman, 1953).

Laqueur, T., 'Bodies, details, and the humanitarian narrative', in L. Hunt (ed.), *The new cultural history* (London: University of California Press, 1989), pp. 176–204.

Lee, D. (ed.), *Slavery, abolition and emancipation: Writings in the British Romantic period – the emancipation debate*, 8 vols., vol. III (London: Pickering and Chatto, 1999).

Lester, A., *Imperial networks: Creating identities in nineteenth-century South Africa and Britain* (London: Routledge, 2001).

'Obtaining the "due observance of justice"': The geographies of colonial humanitarianism', *Environment and Planning D: Society and Space* 20 (2002), 277–293.

Levy, C., *Emancipation, sugar and federalism: Barbados and the West Indies, 1833–1876* (Gainesville: University of Florida, 1980).

'Slavery and the emancipation movement in Barbados, 1650–1833', *Journal of Negro History* 55 (1970), 1–14.

Lewis, G. K., *Main currents in Caribbean thought: The historical evolution of Caribbean society in its ideological aspects, 1492–1900* (Baltimore: Johns Hopkins University Press, 1983).

Lewis, K., *The Moravian mission in Barbados, 1816–1886* (Frankfurt: Peter Lang, 1985).

Linebaugh, P. and M. Rediker, *The many-headed hydra: Sailors, slaves, commoners, and the hidden history of the revolutionary Atlantic* (London: Verso, 2000).

Livingstone, D. N., 'The moral discourse of climate: Historical considerations on race, place and virtue', *Journal of Historical Geography* 17 (1991), 413–434.

Livingstone, D. N. and C. W. J. Withers (eds.), *Geography and enlightenment* (London: University of Chicago Press, 1999).

Lorimer, D. A., *Colour, class and the Victorians* (Leicester: Leicester University Press, 1978).

Malchow, H. L., *Gothic images of race in nineteenth-century Britain* (Stanford: Stanford University Press, 1996).

Mancke, E., 'Empire and state', in Armitage and Braddick, *The British Atlantic world*, pp. 175–195.

Mani, L., 'Cultural theory, colonial texts: Reading eyewitness accounts of widow burning', in L. Grossberg, C. Nelson and P. Treichler (eds.), *Cultural studies* (London: Routledge, 1992), pp. 392–405.

Marshall, P. J., 'Britain without America – a second empire?' in P. J. Marshall, *The Oxford history of the British Empire*, vol. II, pp. 576–595.

(ed.), *The Oxford history of the British Empire*, vol. II, *The eighteenth century* (Oxford: Oxford University Press, 1998).

Marshall, T. G., 'Post-emancipation adjustments in Barbados, 1838 to 1876', in Thompson, *Emancipation I*, pp. 88–107.

Marshall, W., 'Amelioration and emancipation (with special reference to Barbados)', in Thompson, *Emancipation I*, pp. 72–87.

Marshall, W. and B. Brereton, 'Historiography of Barbados, the Windward Islands, Trinidad and Tobago, and Guyana', in B. W. Higman (ed.), *Methodology and historiography of the Caribbean* (London: UNESCO Publishing, 1999), pp. 544–603.

Martin, M., 'Joshua Steele', *Journal of the Royal Society of Arts* 117 (1968), 41–45, 132–136, 225–229.

Matthews, G., 'The other side of slave revolts', *The Society for Caribbean Studies Annual Conference Papers*, 1 (2000), available from http://www.scsonline.freeserve.co.uk/olvol1.htlm.

'The rumour syndrome, sectarian missionaries and nineteenth-century slave rebels of the British West Indies', *The Society for Caribbean Studies Annual Conference Papers*, 2 (2001), available from http://www.scsonline.freeserve.co.uk/olvol2.html.

McCrea, R. 'The Caribbean in the metropolitan imagination', paper presented at the Society for Caribbean Studies annual conference, Bristol University, 2003.

McCulloch, J., *Black peril, white virtue: Sexual crime in Southern Rhodesia, 1902–1935* (Bloomington: Indiana University Press, 1999).

McEwan, C., 'Cutting power lines within the palace? Countering paternity and eurocentrism in the "geographical tradition"', *Transactions of the Institute of British Geographers* 23 (1998), 371–384.

McGary, H., 'Paternalism and slavery', in T. L. Lott (ed.), *Subjugation and bondage: critical essays on slavery and social philosophy* (Lanham, MD: Rowman & Littlefield, 1998), pp. 187–208.

McGlynn, F. and S. Drescher (eds.), *The meaning of freedom: Economics, politics, and culture after slavery* (London: University of Pittsburgh Press, 1992).

Meinig, D. W., *Atlantic America, 1492–1800* (New Haven: Yale University Press, 1986).

Midgley, C., 'Slave sugar boycotts, female activism and the domestic base of British anti-slavery culture', *Slavery and Abolition* 17 (1996), 137–62.

Mills, S., *Discourse* (London: Routledge, 1997).

Mintz, S., *Sweetness and power: The place of sugar in modern history* (New York: Viking, 1985).

Mohammed, P., '"But most of all mi love me browning": The emergence in eighteenth- and nineteenth-century Jamaica of the mulatto woman as the desired', *Feminist Review* 65 (2000), 22–48.

'The emergence of a Caribbean iconography in the evolution of identity', in B. Meeks and F. Lindahl (eds.), *New Caribbean thought: A reader* (Kingston: University of the West Indies Press, 2001), pp. 232–264.

Morgan, E. S., *American slavery, American freedom: The ordeal of colonial Virginia* (New York: Norton, 1975).

Morin, K. M., 'British women travellers and constructions of racial difference across the nineteenth-century American West', *Transactions of the Institute of British Geographers* 23 (1998), 311–330.

Morris, R., '"The 1816 uprising – a hell-broth"', *Journal of the Barbados Museum and Historical Society* 46 (2000), 1–39.

Mullin, M., *Africa in America: Slave acculturation and resistance in the American South and the British Caribbean, 1736–1831* (Urbana and Chicago: University of Illinois Press, 1992).

Murray, D. J., *The West Indies and the development of colonial government, 1801–1834* (Oxford, 1965).

Newman, G., *The rise of English nationalism: A cultural history, 1740–1830* (New York, 1987).

Newman, J., 'The enigma of Joshua Steele', *Journal of Barbados Museum and Historical Society* 19 (1951), 6–20.

Newton, M. '"The Children of Africa in the Colonies": Free people of colour in Barbados during the emancipation era', unpublished DPhil. thesis, Oxford University (2001).

'The King v. Robert James, a slave, for rape: Inequality, gender and British slave amelioration, 1823–1834', unpublished paper.

O'Callaghan, E., *The earliest patriots* (London: Karia Press, 1986).

O'Shaughnessy, A. J., *An empire divided: The American Revolution and the British Caribbean* (Philadelphia: University of Pennsylvania Press, 2000).

'The formation of a commercial lobby: The West India Interest, British colonial policy and the American Revolution', *Historical Journal* 40 (1997), 71–95.

Ogborn, M., 'Historical geographies of globalisation, c. 1500–1800', in B. Graham and C. Nash (eds.), *Modern historical geographies* (Harlow: Prentice Hall, 2000), pp. 43–69.

Olson, A. G., *Making the empire work: London and American interest groups, 1690–1790* (Cambridge, MA: Harvard University Press, 1992).

Olwig, K. F. (ed.), *Small islands, large questions: Society, culture and resistance in the post-emancipation Caribbean* (London: Frank Cass, 1995).

Palmer, C. A., 'The slave trade, African slavers and the demography of the Caribbean to 1750', in F. W. Knight, *The slave societies of the Caribbean*, pp. 9–44.

Parish, P., *Slavery: History and historians* (New York, 1989).

Penson, L. M., *The colonial agents of the West Indies: A study in colonial administration, mainly in the eighteenth century* (London: University of London Press, 1924).

Pestana, C. G., 'Religion', in Armitage and Braddick, *The British Atlantic world*, pp. 69–89.

Philo, C., 'Edinburgh, enlightenment, and the geographies of unreason', in Livingstone and Withers, *Geography and enlightenment*, pp. 372–398.

Pope Melish, J., *Disowning slavery: Gradual emancipation and 'race' in New England, 1780–1860* (London: Cornell University Press, 1998).

Porter, A. (ed.), *The Oxford history of the British Empire*, vol. III, *The nineteenth century* (Oxford: Oxford University Press, 1999).

'Religion, missionary enthusiasm, and empire', in A. Porter, *The Oxford history of the British Empire*, vol. III, pp. 222–246.

'Trusteeship, anti-slavery, and humanitarianism', in A. Porter, *The Oxford history of the British Empire*, vol. III, pp. 198–221.

Porter, R., *Enlightenment: Britain and the creation of the modern world* (London: Penguin, 2000).

Pratt, M. L., *Imperial eyes: Travel writing and transculturation* (London: Routledge, 1992).

Puckrein, G. A., *Little England: Plantation society and Anglo-Barbadian politics, 1627–1700* (New York: New York University Press, 1984).

Quilley, G., 'Pastoral plantations: the slave trade and the representation of British colonial landscape in the late eighteenth century', in Quilley and Kriz, *An economy of colour*, pp. 106–128.

Quilley, G. and K. D. Kriz (eds.), *An economy of colour: Visual culture and the Atlantic world, 1660–1830* (Manchester: Manchester University Press, 2003).

Ragatz, L. J., *A guide for the study of British Caribbean history, 1763–1834* (Washington, DC, 1932).

Richardson, B. C., *The Caribbean in the wider world, 1492–1992: A regional geography* (Cambridge: Cambridge University Press, 1992).

'Detrimental determinists: Applied environmentalism as bureaucratic self-interest in the fin-de-siècle British Caribbean', *Annals of the Association of American Geographers* 86 (1996), 213–234.

Richardson, R. K., *Moral imperium: Afro-Caribbeans and the transformation of British rule, 1776–1838* (London: Greenwood Press, 1987).

Roach, J., *Cities of the dead: Circum-Atlantic performance* (New York: Columbia University Press, 1996).

Roediger, D. R. (ed.), *Black on white: Black writers on what it means to be white* (New York: Shocken Books, 1998).

  Towards the abolition of whiteness: Essays on race, politics, and working-class history (London: Verso, 1994).

  The wages of whiteness: Race and the making of the American working class (London: Verso, 1991).

Rose, G., *Feminism and geography: The limits of geographical knowledge* (Cambridge: Polity Press, 1993).

Said, E. W., *Orientalism: Western conceptions of the Orient* (London: Penguin, 1978).

Sandiford, K. A., *The cultural politics of sugar: Caribbean slavery and narratives of colonialism* (Cambridge: Cambridge University Press, 2000).

Schwarz, B., 'Introduction: The expansion and contraction of England', in B. Schwarz (ed.), *The expansion of England: Race, ethnicity and cultural history* (London: Routledge, 1996), pp. 1–8.

Scott, J., *Domination and the arts of resistance* (New Haven: Yale University Press, 1991).

Segal, R., *The black diaspora* (London: Faber and Faber, 1995).

Seymour, S., 'Historical geographies of landscape', in B. Graham and C. Nash (eds.), *Modern historical geographies* (Harlow: Prentice Hall, 2000), pp. 193–217.

Seymour, S., S. Daniels and C. Watkins, 'Estate and empire: Sir George Cornewall's management of Moccas, Herefordshire and La Taste, Grenada, 1771–1819', *Journal of Historical Geography* 24 (1998), 313–351.

Sharpe, J., 'The unspeakable limits of rape: Colonial violence and counter-insurgency', *Genders* 10 (1991), 25–46.

Shaw, C. M., *Colonial inscriptions: Race, sex, and class in Kenya* (London: University of Minnesota Press, 1995).

Sheller, M., *Consuming the Caribbean: From Arawaks to zombies* (London: Routledge, 2003).

  Democracy after slavery: Black publics and peasant radicalism in Haiti and Jamaica (London: Macmillan Education, 2000).

Sheppard, J., *The 'redlegs' of Barbados: Their origins and history* (Millwood, NY: KTO Press, 1977).

Sheridan, R., *Doctors and slaves: A medical and demographic history of slavery in the British West Indies, 1680–1834* (Cambridge: Cambridge University Press, 1985).

  Sugar and slavery: An economic history of the British West Indies, 1623–1775 (Baltimore: Johns Hopkins University Press, 1973).

  'The West India sugar crisis and British slave emancipation, 1830–1833', *Journal of Economic History* 21 (1961), 539–551.

  'Why the condition of the slaves was "less intolerable in Barbados than in the other sugar colonies"', in H. McD. Beckles (ed.), *Inside slavery: Process and legacy in the Caribbean experience* (Bridgetown: Canoe Press, 1987), pp. 32–50.

Shilstone, E., 'Orderson family records', *Journal of the Barbados Museum and Historical Society* 25 (1957–8), 152–157.

'Some notes on early printing presses and newspapers in Barbados', *Journal of the Barbados Museum and Historical Society* 26 (1958–9), 19–33.

Sinha, M., *Colonial masculinity: The 'manly Englishman' and the 'effeminate Bengali' in the late nineteenth century* (Manchester: Manchester University Press, 1995).

Sio, A., 'Marginality and free coloured identity in Caribbean slave society', *Slavery and Abolition* 8 (1987), 166–186.

Smith, F., *Creole recitations: John Jacob Thomas and colonial formation in the late nineteenth-century Caribbean* (Charlottesville and London: University of Virginia Press, 2002).

Snape, M. F., 'Anti-Methodism in eighteenth-century England: The Pendle Forest riots of 1748', *Journal of Ecclesiastical History* 49 (1998), 257–281.

Somerville, P., 'Homelessness and the meaning of home: Rooflessness or rootlessness?', *International Journal of Urban and Regional Research* 16 (1992), 528–539.

Sontag, S., *Illness as metaphor/AIDS and its metaphors* (London: Allen Lane, 1991).

Southall, H., 'Agitate! Agitate! Organize! Political travellers and the construction of a national politics, 1839–1880', *Transactions of the Institute of British Geographers* 21 (1996), 177–193.

Spivak, G. C., 'Can the subaltern speak?' in C. Nelson and L. Grossberg (eds.), *Marxism and the interpretation of culture* (London: Macmillan, 1988), pp. 271–313.

'Subaltern studies: Deconstructing historiographies', in D. Landry and G. MacLean (eds.), *The Spivak reader* (London: Routledge, 1996), pp. 203–235.

Spurr, D., *The rhetoric of empire: Colonial discourse in journalism, travel writing, and imperial administration* (London: Duke University Press, 1993).

St Pierre, M., *Anatomy of resistance: Anti-colonialism in Guyana, 1823–1966* (London: Macmillan Education, 1999).

Steel, M., 'A philosophy of fear: The world view of Jamaican plantocracy in comparative perspective', *Journal of Caribbean History* 27 (1993), 1–20.

Steele, I. K., *The English Atlantic, 1675–1740: An exploration of communication and community* (Oxford: Oxford University Press, 1986).

Stewart, L., 'Louisiana subjects: Power, space and the slave body', *Ecumene* 2 (1995), 227–245.

Stinchcombe, A. L., *Sugar island slavery in the age of Enlightenment: The political economy of the Caribbean world* (Princeton, NJ: Princeton University Press, 1995).

Stoler, A. L., 'Carnal knowledge and imperial power: Gender, race, and morality in colonial Asia', in G. Quilley (ed.), *Feminism and history* (Oxford: Oxford University Press, 1996), pp. 209–266.

Race and the education of desire: Foucault's History of sexuality *and the colonial order of things* (London: Duke University Press, 1995).

'Sexual affronts and racial frontiers: European identities and the cultural politics of exclusion in colonial southeast Asia', in Cooper and Stoler, *Tensions of empire*, pp. 198–237.

Stoler, A. L. and F. Cooper, 'Between metropole and colony: Rethinking a research agenda', in Cooper and Stoler, *Tensions of empire*, pp. 1–56.

Sussman, C., *Consuming anxieties: Consumer protest, gender and British slavery, 1713–1833* (Stanford: Stanford University Press, 2000).

Taylor, B. M., 'Our man in London: John Pollard Mayers, agent for Barbados, and the British Abolition Act, 1832–1834', *Caribbean Studies* 16 (1977), 60–74.

Temperley, H. (ed.), *After slavery: Emancipation and its discontents* (London: Frank Cass, 2000).

British antislavery, 1833–1870 (London, 1972).

Thomas, N., *Colonialism's culture: Anthropology, travel and government* (Oxford: Polity, 1994).

Thompson, A. O. (ed.), *Emancipation I: A series of lectures to commemorate the 150th anniversary of emancipation* (Bridgetown: Cedar Press, 1984).

'"Happy – happy slaves!": Slavery as a superior state to freedom', *Journal of Caribbean History* 29 (1995), 93–119.

Thorne, S., '"The conversion of Englishmen and the conversion of the world inseparable": Missionary imperialism and the language of class in early industrial Britain', in Cooper and Stoler, *Tensions of empire*, pp. 238–262.

Titus, N. F., *The development of Methodism in Barbados, 1823–1883* (Berne: Peter Lang, 1994).

Turley, D., *The culture of English antislavery, 1780–1860* (London: Routledge, 1991).

Turner, M., 'Religious beliefs', in F. W. Knight, *The slave societies of the Caribbean*, pp. 287–321.

Slaves and missionaries: The disintegration of Jamaican slave society, 1787–1834 (London: University of Illinois Press, 1982).

Valentine, G., '"Sticks and stones may break my bones": A personal geography of harassment', *Antipode* 30 (1998), 305–332.

Wallerstein, I., *The modern world-system I: Capitalist agriculture and the origins of the European world-economy in the sixteenth century* (London: Academic Press, 1974).

The modern world-system II: Mercantilism and the consolidation of the European world-economy, 1600–1750 (London: Academic Press, 1980).

Walvin, J., *Black ivory: A history of British slavery* (London: Harper Collins, 1992).

'The propaganda of anti-slavery', in Walvin, *Slavery and British society, 1776–1846*, pp. 49–68.

'The public campaign in England against slavery, 1787–1834', in D. Eltis and J. Walvin (eds.), *The abolition of the Atlantic slave trade: Origins and effects in Europe, Africa, and the Americas* (London: University of Wisconsin Press, 1981), pp. 63–79.

Questioning slavery (London: Routledge, 1996).

(ed.), *Slavery and British society, 1776–1846* (London: Macmillan Press, 1982).

Ward, J. R., *British West Indian slavery, 1750–1834: The process of amelioration* (Oxford: Clarendon Press, 1988).

'The British West Indies in the age of abolition, 1748–1815', in P. J. Marshall, *The Oxford history of the British Empire*, vol. II, pp. 415–439.

Ware, V., *Beyond the pale: White women, racism and history* (London: Verso, 1992).

Watson, K., *The civilised island, Barbados: A social history, 1750–1816* (Bridgetown: Graphic Printers, 1979).

'The iconography of the 1816 slave revolt: Some brief comments', *Journal of the Barbados Museum and Historical Society* 46 (2000), 40–46.

'Salmagundis vs Pumpkins: White politics and creole consciousness in Barbadian slave society, 1800–1834', in H. Johnson and Watson, *The white minority in the Caribbean*, pp. 17–31.

Watts, D., *The West Indies: Patterns of development, culture and environmental change since 1492* (Cambridge: Cambridge University Press, 1987).

Welch, P. L. V., *Slave society in the city: Bridgetown, Barbados, 1680–1834* (Kingston: Ian Randle, 2003).

Welch, P. L. V. and R. A. Goodridge, *'Red' and black over white: Free coloured women in pre-emancipation Barbados* (Bridgetown: Carib Research and Publications, 2000).

Werbner, P., 'The limits of cultural hybridity: On ritual monsters, poetic licence and contested postcolonial purifications', *Journal of the Royal Anthropological Institute* 7 (2001), 133–152.

Wetherell, M. and J. Potter, *Mapping the language of racism: Discourse and the legitimation of exploitation* (Hemel Hempstead: Harvester Wheatsheaf, 1992).

Williams, E., *Capitalism and slavery* (London: André Deutsch, 1964).

Wilmot, S., *'The business of improvement': Agriculture and scientific culture in Britain, c. 1700–c. 1870*, Historical Geography Research Series, vol. 24 (1990).

Wilson, K., *The island race: Englishness, empire and gender in the eighteenth century* (London: Routledge, 2003).

Withers, C. W. J. and D. N. Livingstone, 'Introduction: On geography and enlightenment', in Livingstone and Withers, *Geography and enlightenment*, pp. 1–28.

Wolf, E., *Europe and the people without history* (Berkeley: University of California Press, 1982).

Wood, H. T., *A history of the Royal Society of Arts* (London: John Murray, 1913).

Wood, M., *Blind memory: Visual representations of slavery in England and America, 1780–1865* (Manchester: Manchester University Press, 2000).

Slavery, empathy, and pornography (Oxford: Oxford University Press, 2002).

Yelvington, K. A., 'The anthropology of Afro-Latin America and the Caribbean: Diasporic dimensions', *Annual Review of Anthropology* 30 (2001), 227–260.

Yuval-Davis, N., *Gender and nation* (London, 1997).

Zahedih, N., 'Economy', in Armitage and Braddick, *The British Atlantic world*, pp. 51–68.

Index

Cambridge Studies in Historical Geography

*Titles marked with an asterisk * are available in paperback.*